Black and Catholic in Savannah, Georgia

Graduating Class 1932. St. Benedict's Junior High. Savh. Ga.

Black and Catholic in Savannah, Georgia

Gary Wray McDonogh

THE UNIVERSITY OF TENNESSEE PRESS / KNOXVILLE

Frontispiece. Saint Benedict's graduation, 1932. Photograph courtesy of Mrs. Mildred Chisholm.

Library of Congress Cataloging-in-Publication Data

McDonogh, Gary Wray, 1952–
    Black and Catholic in Savannah, Georgia / Gary Wray McDonogh. —
1st ed.
        p.   cm.
    Includes bibliographical references and index.
    ISBN 0-87049-810-X (cloth : alk. paper).
    ISBN 0-87049-811-8 (pbk. : alk. paper)
    1. Afro-American Catholics—Georgia—Savannah—History.
2. Catholic Church—Georgia—Savannah—History. 3. Savannah (Ga.)—
Church history. I. Title.
BX1418.S38M33 1993
282'.758724'08996073—dc20   93-15389
                                                                          CIP

To my godchildren—
Meghan, Nicholas, Julian, Jimmie, Joe Bob, and Samantha—
who are the future; to Cindy, of course;
to Pie, a miraculous mother;
and to Larissa Jiit-Wai McDonogh-Wong,
with all our love

Contents

Figures

Maps

Tables

Acknowledgments

It seems fitting that a text revindicating creative human community in the face of contradictions should begin by acknowledging three disparate communities within which this work has taken shape. These communities, each defined by social networks bonded to a strong sense of place, have been my source of data, my arena for criticism, and my life-worlds over the past decade, and all three—Savannah, New College, and Barcelona—have left their mark on this work as they have on me.

Savannah's role transcends its meaning as a field site or ethnographic case study. In 1982 I began research for this work under the aegis of a grant from the University of South Florida Creative Research Fellowships. At that time, I knew the city only as a casual tourist with a secondhand introduction to friends of family friends. By the end of the summer, the people of Savannah had made me feel at home by their generous cooperation in interviews, observation, research, and teaching, a process that has intensified in the subsequent years. The convenience of Savannah as a field site, seven hours from my university, allowed frequent weekend visits in addition to two semesters of sabbatical research supported in part by New College. My acknowledgments there begin in Saint Benedict's with my adopted mother, Mildred "Pie" Chisholm, and her household and breakfast club; Jimmie Reynolds, my godson; Geraldine Abernathy; Annie and David Polite; Devon Mayo; Otis and Lillie Mae Charlton; Willowdean and Herbert Brown and the Scurdy family; Franklin Jenkins; Deacon Prince Jackson; Bobby McCallister; Mary Lockwood; Delores Howard; Carlos and Tamika Washington; and many others. Outside this immediate family, the late Veronica Arnold provided a unique historical link to both Matilda Beasley, her step-grandmother, and W. E. B. Du Bois, her teacher. Others from the parish who have helped me during the years include Boston and Geraldine Williams, Ann Bell, Ronnie Bell,· Jackie Rainey, Father Robert Chaney and his family, Dorothy Campbell, and Oscar Daub. In Saint Anthony's, my headquarters was the home and family of Gloria and Evelyn Daniels, but generous cooperation also came from Georgia Mae Tanxley Lucas, Mr. and Mrs. Lotson, Mr. and Mrs. Williams, Ann Bower, Gwen Goodman, Rick Moore, and others with whom I worked on the parish history project. In Saint Mary's, the late Rosalie Williams and her sister Marie Williams, the late Clarabelle Moore, Donna Myers, Lucy West, Joe Turner, and Deacon Frank Mathis have been among those who have helped me immeasurably. I have tried to be faithful to their voices and insights.

I also learned from many others in Savannah outside these parishes. The late Hugh Grady, Mr. and Mrs. Patrick Buttimer and their family, Catherine Lingenfelser, William Canty, Aline Saunders, and others participated in an oral history project and general interviews from which background for this project has come. The late Patricia Bravo, diocesan archivist, was a guide and friend, as have been the subsequent archivists there. Similarly, the staff of the Georgia Historical Society, especially Bobbi Bennett, Ann Smith, Tony Dees, T. Bearden and K. Osvald, went far beyond their administrative roles to provide family records and useful critiques during my visits there. W. W. Law has also guided me in the appreciation of African-American history and action in a way that I can only hope this book begins to repay.

Father Liam Collins in Saint Mary's, Father Michael Smith in Saint Anthony's, and Father James Mayo in Saint Benedict's welcomed me both into their parishes and their friendships, for which I am eternally in their debt. From these men and from other priests and religious in Savannah, including Father Patrick Shinnuck, Father Frank Higgins, Sister Mary Laurent, Sister Virginia Ross, Sister Nancy Ross, and Bishop Raymond Lessard, I have grown in my knowledge of anthropology, of faith, and of myself. Father Daniel Bourke deserves extra thanks as well for being one of the best teachers of Irish history I have encountered. Also generous in sharing rich historical knowledge, were the retired priests of the Society of African Missions and the sisters of the Franciscan Sisters of the Immaculate Conception, including Father Adolf Gall, Father Feeley, Father Burke, Sister Robert, Sister Vergilius, Sister Ursula, Sister Clare, and Sister Emily. The archival assistance of the diocese, now under the direction of Sister Felicitas Powers, has provided able assistance in many areas.

ACKNOWLEDGMENTS

Savannah, over the years, has been a home to New College students who have shared the drive and the experience, as well as the research that inform the present work. This in part defines the way my teaching at the college has been linked to this project, which began in my first year here. Donald Moore spent a summer—and a busy Thanksgiving weekend—in Savannah and has read the drafts of all my work with intellectual acumen and human care. Chuck Rutheiser has also shared his critical insight and indeed opened up a world of educational anthropology to me that underlies all of chapter 4. Other visitors and critics over the years include Michael Russell, Dale Nelson, Chris Pallm, Marsha Pool, David Dewey, Geoff Mohlman, Carolyn Miller, Will and Susan Snedden, Jerry Felz, and the late Jay Feight. Not all my critics have yet shared the experience of Savannah, although their readings have also been essential to this text. Dan Bosch has kept me keenly aware of voice, while Andy Workman has kept me posted on southern history. In this group I also include my Linguistics Reading Group—Jonathan Loftin, Wendy Hoon, Amy Waller, Robin Reed, Buffy Weathington, Karina Mertzman, and Will Snedden—who carefully worked through chapter 2, and my Culture and Education Tutorial—Jonathan, Wendy, and Geoff—who worked through chapter 4 with equal force. Mary Andrews as well as Amy and Jonathan devoted extensive effort to critiquing most of the manuscript. Will Snedden devoted hours to drafting tables, which were later completed by Charlene Saeman and Donald Hayward. Christian Perez worked on maps. Ethel Caddell and Charlene Saeman have coordinated typing and other assistance throughout the project.

More than individual debts, this project has involved the whole experience of teaching at the college, of having to think through a program in anthropology from scratch with my compadre Tony Andrews, and of facing the challenges of bright students through the years in all areas of theory and practice. In this educational project, many colleagues who have taught me and talked with me, especially Gene Lewis, Cathy Elliott, and Justus Doenecke, deserve credit for my development of a coherent perspective on teaching and research. The college, too, has been a home where students and friends have kept me sane at various stages and crises in this research. A special debt of that nature is due to a set of remarkably tolerant housemates, Dale Nelson, Jerry Felz, and Jay Feight, and to an even more tolerant colleague and wife, Cindy Hing-Yuk Wong.

Finally, it is impossible to separate this work from my ongoing commitment to urban anthropology in Barcelona. What I have gained from seventeen years of fieldwork there, in approaching the complexities of urban life and generalizing from Savannah to a more theoretical vision of the city, permeates these pages. My ideas on Savannah have often been the subject of discussion with colleagues there, while their studies have inspired new looks at American society. Among those who must be acknowledged as colleagues and friends are Jim Amelang and Elena López, Susan DiGiacomo and Oriol Pi-Sunyer, Carlos Carreras and Mercedes Marín, Kit Woolard, Josefina Roma and Joan Santomá, Pep Fradera, Xavier Gil, Gaspar Maza, Josep Maria Gallart, Florentino and Cristina de Retana (on whose balcony I edited the final drafts), Juanjo Pujadas and M. Dolores Comas d'Argemir, and Jesús Contreras.

Even as I try to focus on these three central communities, there are others whose contributions become more apparent. Sidney Mintz and Richard Price introduced me to African-American studies at Yale and continued this training, along with my other teachers at Johns Hopkins. Randall Miller, Sam Hill, George Pozzetta, and James Peacock have encouraged me in earlier publication of sections of this work, and Carol Orr patiently encouraged its completion. Greer Gordon and other guest speakers of the 1985 meetings of the National Office of Black Catholics in Atlanta oriented me toward many questions of ethnographic interest. Jon Anderson of Catholic University has asked interesting new questions and given me a new vision of being informant as well as analyst.

These communities have become extensions of an older family that has been with me for decades: my brother Allen McDonogh, my former sister-in-law Karen O'Connor, and my niece Meghan O'Connor McDonogh, the Henson family in Louisville, Tom Szydlowsi and Didi Coyle (and Nicholas and Emily), Ed Hansen, Tom O'Connor, and Bob and Cathi Cunningham and my newest godchildren, Joe Bob and Samantha, as well as others I have inadvertently failed to recognize here. And of course, my wife, Cindy, who has also become very much a part of my life in Savannah and everywhere else. The kind of involvement and study that I have undertaken in Savannah have called upon my humanity as well as my scholarship; and all of these friends, among others, deserve credit for whatever good has resulted.

Introduction

The controversial nomination of Clarence Thomas to the United States Supreme Court in the summer of 1991 and the subsequent publicity and hearings that explored his past focused national attention on those who are African American and Catholic in his hometown of Savannah. Thomas's story, in the hands of local and national media, became an American myth to be believed or attacked: a "black Horatio Alger," to be understood through examination of his race, his region, his era, and his religion. While his former teacher, Sister Mary Vergilius Reidy, appeared on television, testifying in a Senate chamber, journalists called on my friends in St. Benedict the Moor Parish for their memories of the nominee, of Savannah life and ambiance, and of the meaning of a Catholic education in black success.

I do not know Judge Thomas; he left Savannah years before I began my work there in 1982 and no longer practices as a Catholic. Yet the "Thomas story," as I interpreted it within my work among African Americans and Catholics in Savannah as well as conversations with members of Saint Benedict's who became excited by his nomination, highlights many anomalies of race, religion, and individual choice that have shaped southern life and belief. Remarks about his sister being on welfare, for example, have pointed out the divisions of opportunity as well as religion that have torn apart black families in Savannah. Thomas recalled racism within both integrated seminaries and the all-black parochial school where students paid attention to skin shades as marks of class. These echo the memories of southern racial divisions and Christian ideals in Savannah Catholicism that friends have shared over the years as they themselves have sought to make sense of racism within their lives. Even his differences from the positions of other black activists suggest the ambivalent heritage of Roman Catholicism within the civil rights era as well as the agonies of many contemporary Catholics facing issues such as abortion or war (Lancaster and Lafraniere 1991).

Nor is Thomas the only African-American Catholic to claim national attention in recent years. The separatist church of Reverend George Stallings in Washington, whose appeal to Afrocentric worship has included African-American followers in Georgia, has decried conflicts of values within black and Catholic traditions. Meanwhile, the consecration of Archbishop Eugene Marino of Atlanta as the first black archbishop in the United States, his stepping down, and his replacement by fellow black prelate Joseph Lykes underscored the ambiguous spotlight on blacks within the Catholic church.

This book, however, does not focus on the famous or powerful, whether Clarence Thomas, George Stallings, Eugene Marino, Joseph Lykes, or such past actors as Bishop James Healy, Reverend Andrew Marshall, Mother Matilda Beasley, James Cardinal Gibbons, or Father Divine. Nor does it attempt to trace the complex national and institutional panorama of black Catholicism in the United States, which has recently attracted the increasing attention of authors such as Stephen Ochs (1990) and Cyprian Davis (1991). Instead, it focuses on many lives, relationships, institutions, and beliefs that have constituted key facets of Catholicism in a city divided by conflicts over culture, class, and ethnic or racial differences. Those who have been black and Catholic in Savannah over the past two centuries have formed their lives, families, parishes, and city among conflictive identities and interpretations of the world. Ambiguities pervade belief and rite as much as they shape meanings of education and economic opportunities. Questions arise before the altar in the relations of authority between blacks and whites while they permeate the meanings of such everyday acts as sharing food. In this study, religion provides an important cultural medium through which to understand both the general situation of black and Catholic life and the meaning of divided cultures in the modern city. At the same time, religion remains a theme of study in itself within the social and cultural contexts in which it has evolved.

This study is constructed out of voices, memories, acts, and observations constituting the basis of both ethnology and practice. As such, its local knowledge provides the basis for comparative insights and theoretical generalization. The construction of community through ritual, school, and society can be framed by insights into other Catholic communities, black and white, as well as ethnohistorical approaches to the South. This book also moves further afield into social studies of symbolism, gender, class, authority, and power. The imagery of mass media evoked by Thomas, Stallings, and Marino makes us focus on how "we"—Americans, anthropologists, or readers of many heritages and interests—think and talk about religion and race in contemporary society and deal with the many conflicts that arise among social identities in urban life. The violent divisions that flared up in many American cities in 1992, from Los Angeles to Atlanta and Savannah, underscore the ongoing need to understand these issues and to act on them.

This dialectic of local experience and wide generalizations, so central to the anthropological imagination, can be evoked through two events that I attended on Sunday, September 15, 1985, after several years of fieldwork. The first, from 12:30 to 3:00 p.m., was the solemn reopening of Savannah's Saint John the Baptist Cathedral and the dedication of its new altar. The second, from 5:00 to 8:00 P.M. of the same day, was the twelfth anniversary concert of the Saint Benedict the Moor Gospel Choir, held at the mother church of black and Catholic Savannah.

CATHOLICISM AS SYMBOL AND PRACTICE

Savannah's eighty-five-year-old cathedral, the center for worship in South Georgia, was closed in 1982 when structural damage became evident. A diocesan campaign raised $2 million for repairs, interior restoration, and a new main altar. The liturgy celebrating the reopening of the building evoked the splendor, order, and unity of the Roman Catholic church of decades past. Catholics from the entire diocese crowded the cathedral. Urban dignitaries, Catholic and non-Catholic, also joined the assembly. Blacks were present throughout the church as representatives of the traditionally black parishes of the diocese as well as of parishes that had become mixed through consolidation and recruitment; African Americans were also prominent in the procession and ceremonial. Yet, to me, the black presence took on meanings with regard to other groups—including women, youth, and the laity—whose positions reflect the distribution of power within the church and the city.

The entrance procession, for example, sanctioned classic Roman Catholic hierarchy. Young male acolytes led the double files that moved

3

between the central pews. Their dress and roles were analogous to those of priests, whom they assist during the mass. Senior males from Catholic military orders followed. They represented European institutions such as the Knights of Saint Gregory and better-known American groups like the Knights of Columbus. A member of the traditionally black Knights of Saint Peter Claver proved the only black in the honor salute through which others in the procession passed.

Priests and deacons of the diocese followed the knights. This order enforced a distinction between deacons—who may be either men training for the priesthood or laymen acting as ordained associates in the parish—and the ritual leaders set apart by further training, ordination, and vows of celibacy. Black and white clerics joined the procession. Another black deacon later helped bring gifts to the altar while a third worked with the ushers. Finally, the bishops of Savannah and neighboring dioceses entered the cathedral sanctuary with local abbots and the apostolic nuncio, Pio Laghi, who represented the pope.

The mass itself emphasized interlocking differences of space and rank. The bishops and abbots, colorfully vested, sat behind and around the altar, with other clerics, robed in white, on either side. An altar rail separated them from the laity in their crowded pews. Musicians sang from a back choir loft above the participants. This geography of power was underscored by the boundaries of participation. No women—religious or lay—participated in the procession, although women later read and brought forward gifts to the sanctuary. Apart from the knights, nonordained males took even more limited roles in the ceremony as ushers, gift bearers, and musicians. Almost everyone who took on a public role was a mature adult; youth and children were not nearly as well represented as they are in normal parish life.

Actions inside the sanctuary affirmed the imagery of political, social, and religious power. After two women, including the chancellor of the diocese, proclaimed the first readings, a black deacon read the Gospel (which can only be delivered by a consecrated specialist). Later, bishops and priests concelebrated the Eucharist, the central act of belief and worship in the Catholic church. Although most parishes nationwide rely on the laity to distribute communion to the congregation, only priests and deacons performed the task in the cathedral. Thus, the laity physically moved toward the priests to participate in full union with the church and with God. This ceremony identified the cathedral with the clergy, the episcopacy, and the papacy, whose representatives held the central

4

ceremonial space even while lay members came forward to affirm belief by their participation in communion.

Ironically, despite the intense stratification of ritual leadership and space that I have highlighted, this ceremony clearly differed from many standards of the Catholic church and the American South of earlier decades. When this cathedral building was first dedicated in 1900, the United States had only two black priests.[1] In the 1980s, blacks in Savannah still recalled earlier eras when they were relegated to the back or the balcony of the cathedral, apart from the white congregation, or told "you have a church of your own down the street." Women as well had emerged from subordination to scattered leadership roles such as chancellor, although some women whom I knew well complained bitterly of the hierarchical message of the ceremony. Finally, most Catholics present received the Eucharist, which, prior to the 1960s reforms of the Second Vatican Council, had become a ritual act dominated by the priest and some faithful followers, usually watched by many in their pews. In the cathedral, social values and belief were enacted and made concrete by sharing in this culturally defined sign of God's presence.

These historical changes, however, did not belie contradictions and compromises within the ceremony. Despite the presence of a black in the honor guard, the diocese had not encouraged the Knights of Saint Peter Claver for various reasons, including a historic conflict among the white religious orders responsible for black evangelization in the United States. Savannah's Knights of Columbus, by contrast, had remained resolutely segregated until the civil rights era, when determined white priests and the bishop intervened.

Moreover, the black priests who participated in the procession were not strictly diocesan. One had served as a replacement pastor in Saint Benedict's in 1975. The only regular black priest in the diocese came from the Society of the Divine Word, a missionary order, and later was reported to associate with schismatic black Catholics in Washington, D.C. Savannah, the heartland of the cathedral and cradle of Catholicism for the diocese, would not ordain a local black diocesan priest until 1988.

Indeed, one might explore this ceremony from other perspectives of diversity and compromise. Its music, for example, evoked a Western ecclesiastical tradition ranging from Gregorian chant to modern compositions without ethnic references to European immigrant communities or to African Americans, much less to newer minority presences of Vietnamese and Hispanics within the church. As a Roman Catholic layman

5

as well as an anthropologist, I myself was disturbed by the extreme regalism of the ceremony, which challenged my own democratic models of Catholicism. Yet this should not imply that the ceremony was intrinsically racist, sexist, or offensive to those who planned it or participated in it. Rather, the ceremony represented a classic multivalent key symbol of both social and cultural meanings, performed within a shared religious act.

The gospel concert at nearby Saint Benedict's that evening evoked other ambiguities of black and Catholic communities within traditions of black religious expression. The Gospel Choir developed in 1973 out of liturgical innovations and the ethnic self-realization encouraged by the Second Vatican Council. Gospel music is strongly identified with many contemporary black Protestant denominations, although it has been accepted in mainline churches only since the 1940s (Southern 1971). Thus, gospel music postdates the origins of black and Catholic Savannah but has been popularized as a black symbol within the Catholic church by converts, workshops, and white leaders as well as traditional families.

The setting of this concert contrasted sharply with the architectural and decorative richness of the cathedral. Saint Benedict's simple, sweeping brick church replaced a nineteenth-century wooden mission church in 1949.[2] It lies in a historically black neighborhood on the fringe of urban revitalization, surrounded by other black congregations and institutions. The four hundred people who filled the church were almost exclusively black, with perhaps a dozen whites—including the priest and white parishioners. Many non-Catholics joined in; the pianist and invited master of ceremonies were Baptist. Guests arrived from other black parishes but almost none from white congregations.

The rhythmic marching entrance of the choir in their blue and gold robes drew the audience together; the entire ceremony focused on shared participation rather than the division of roles. The choir moved from the back of the church to the sanctuary, whose religious significance had been reduced by removal of the reserved Eucharist. Their chosen theme was "We're Just About to Make It Over to the Promised Land," which again stressed movement, unity, and fulfillment. Turning to face their audience, the choir shared songs emphasizing general Christian themes of personal struggle and divine salvation. They avoided potentially divisive Roman Catholic elements such as the Eucharist, the Virgin Mary, the saints, or the nature of authority. As a series of guest choirs from other black churches came forth from the pews to sing, the spatial boundaries of power observed in weekly masses dissolved.

Figure 1. Saint Benedict the Moor Church, showing bell tower, 1991. Photograph by the author.

Men and women shared in all aspects of this service. The choir was predominantly female, although it had a male leader and pianist. Although the 1985 master of ceremonies was a male Baptist minister, women have served in this role in other concerts. Singers representing a wide range of ages and social backgrounds also appeared among the invited choirs.

This celebration also encouraged continual rather than punctuated response, sharply contrasting the ritualized speech, the limited formal movement, and the tepid singing of the cathedral. People joined in freely with the songs, singing, clapping, swaying, and responding "Thank you, Jesus," "Amen," or "Yesss" within the songs. As the service closed, the white priest led everyone, with linked hands, in an enthusiastic recitation of the Lord's Prayer. This hand-holding characterizes all black and Catholic parishes but is not central to other local churches, Protestant or Catholic.

The varied responses of Saint Benedict's parishioners set them apart from the rest of the audience. Many joined their choir enthusiastically.

Others sat silently and respectfully as they might when attending a more traditional Roman Catholic liturgy, formal rather than expressive in their participation. Another large segment suggested their attitude by their absence. Gospel music predominates at one of the three Sunday liturgies in the parish, but members may also choose choral or folk masses according to their tastes and schedule. My role was self-consciously divided between observer and participant, adopted member of the congregation and white outsider.

In this celebration, Saint Benedict's congregation chose to emphasize its common heritage with other black churches. Nonetheless, some of the very same parishioners had earlier shared in the representation of Catholic unity at the cathedral. Elements of denominational distinctiveness were suppressed in Saint Benedict's as they had been emphasized in the cathedral; dialogue and scenarios of conversions were stressed over central symbols. The silence of some who are both black and Catholic, however, set them apart from other blacks in attendance. Moreover, the paucity of whites at Saint Benedict's, whether Catholic or not, repeated general patterns of segregation of the Christian community of Savannah. Blacks may be brought into previously white and dominant institutions, but whites will rarely venture into black neighborhoods, churches, or associations. The priest as ritual leader and representative of church hierarchy was white, but he has also adapted—and been tested—and has become a central pillar of the Saint Benedict's community.

These two events vividly embody the problems analyzed in the pages that follow, as well as my own responses and participation in them. This book traces the divisions, dominations, and contradictions of race and religion in Savannah that have shaped the black and Catholic experience; it also traces the impact of these forces on many aspects of everyday life. Such an analysis is a construct that has not been in the forefront of consciousness of those who have participated in this experience and shared it with me, but my analysis tries to make sense of words and actions with which I have lived for nearly a decade. I wish to build from a complex yet caring community, within both its analytic and its personal dimensions, to more general themes of religion, race, and identity.

FROM PRACTICE TO THEORY

This project began from the basic question of cultural anthropology: the relationship between beliefs, expression, and interpretation—culture—and human social behavior. My prior work as an urbanist, as well as my experience growing up in a lapsed but sociologically Catholic family in Kentucky, had introduced me to the clash of identities and ideologies that have focused my work. My development as a Europeanist in fifteen years of work in Barcelona has also insisted on the historical dimensions of culture and the power relations contested in urban society. From my earliest plans, then, this project has sought to link these themes through an understanding of the voices and actions of individuals and the long-term formation of social groups. As my ethnographic focus narrowed from broader questions of urban southern Catholicism to the formation of black and Catholic relations in Savannah, my theoretical questions became more precise approaches to community and contradiction.

Contradiction as a theme pervades the scant but growing materials on black Catholics. In her popular history of black Catholics in South Georgia, for example, the late black nun M. Julian Griffin reflected on her research: "It is a story of great love and sacrifice amid apathy, neglect and indifference. It is a story of belief emerging against all odds. It describes some idealistic efforts which failed because of lack of money or lack of cultural understanding. And it includes the record of other initiatives which succeeded surprisingly, receiving an overwhelming response to an invitation offered without much hope of results" (Griffin and Brown 1979, 7). The pervasive narrative motifs of Sister Julian's text do not bespeak growth or mission so much as an image of churches emergent despite continual problems. Her book, though patronized by the local church, conveys the paradoxes of shifting attitudes and policies that have shaped black and Catholic history.

Other sources reinforce this message in their very titles, ranging from Rev. Albert Foley's *Bishop Healy: Beloved Outcaste* (1954) and William Osborne's *The Segregated Covenant* (1967) to the contemporary *Desegregating the Altar* (Ochs 1990). Contradictions have imbued works from Father John Gillard's pioneering *The Catholic Church and the American Negro* (1929) to the essays collected by the United States Catholic Conference in *Families: Black and Catholic, Catholic and Black* (1985). The few local studies I have found on black communities also mark distinctiveness and even unease—*A Special Pilgrimage* in Richmond (N. T. B.

9

Johnson 1978) or the telling *Silent Believers*, which revealed a facet of my own Louisville heritage that I had not really known (Green 1972). A sense of separation demanding a responsive witness is particularly clear in works where black Catholic religious address the church, ranging from Sister Sandra Smithson's *To Be a Bridge* (1984) to Father Lawrence Lucas's *Black Priest, White Church* ([1970] 1989) and encompassing the Black Bishops' Pastoral Letter of 1984, *What We Have Seen and Heard* (Howze et al.). All these sociological, historical, and theological studies repeatedly focus on questions such as "What makes blacks Catholic?" or "How are black Catholics different from other blacks?"—underscoring perceptions of a historical anomaly (see Feagin 1968; Collins 1971; Hunt and Hunt 1975, 1976, 1977; Copeland 1989). They have provided suggestions for my research in Savannah and questions for future investigations. Nevertheless, Catholics still receive only minor references in some overviews of black faith (Lincoln and Mamiya 1990).

The recognition and analysis of contradictions cannot be limited, however, to a structural depiction of a historic community. Instead, these open up wider ethnographic and theoretical issues. The simple presence of the white priest at the front altar, for example, highlights relationships of power and race that imbued missionary Catholicism in Savannah. Yet this presence also raises questions about relations of race and gender transcending the historical experience of any parishes, such as how the social roles of black women in many parishes come to balance this white priest while the black male feels denied the altar. And it begs comparisons with the feelings and power relations of parishes defined as white, ethnic, middle-class, or Hispanic in order to understand more general contexts of representation and response. Finally, one must ask, however tentatively, how social historical processes impinge upon belief. At what point do features of *race* challenge rather than merely contradict responses of *faith?*

My approach to such problems has been refined by perspectives from a number of disciplines, centered in anthropology. My approach involves not only reading texts but looking at everyday experience and structural paradox, and it listens to the voices of those who participate. Thus, I seek power, belief, and community in formal expression as well as apparently offhand remarks. I integrate other perspectives through concrete human lives while looking to general processes of historical change, contested actions, and urban division.

Yet this approach has been refined by the same factors that have shaped Savannah Catholicism itself. Working with the Catholic church and with black theology, for example, has introduced diverse models arising from contemporary ecclesiology, liberation theology, and feminist approaches to religion (Cone 1969, 1975; Dulles 1974, 1982, 1988; West 1982, 1988; Keightley 1988; Kennedy 1988). Similarly, my reading of social historians of European Catholicism, especially John Bossy (1985), Natalie Davis (1975), and Carlo Ginzburg (1980, 1984), has suggested approaches to ethnographic investigation of contemporary Catholicism glimpsed in recent movements toward parish studies (McNally 1987) as well as classic work by Fichter (1951). Training in African-American studies by Richard Price and Sidney Mintz (Mintz and Price 1976; Price 1984) provided background and a sense of historical process tempered by day-to-day contact.

The primary theoretical influence of this decade has been neo-Marxist scholarship, especially as it can be developed in relation to the framework of cultural studies in Britain (Willis 1977; Hebdige 1979; R. Johnson 1987) and in reflections on ideology and society in French and Italian Marxist thought (Gramsci 1971; Mouffe 1979) and the work of Pierre Bourdieu (1972, 1975, 1979). Contradiction as a fundamental problem emerges from these debates without my holding specifically to any single figure or discourse. Yet the analysis of contradictions provides powerful insights into the problematic processes that underlie Savannah's religious beliefs and urban social interactions.

Similarly, my interest in the actions and language of the situation as well as its history reflects a confluence of many speakers including theorists who emphasize categorization, oppression, and resistance (Thompson 1966; Genovese 1974; Said 1978; Williams 1983; Okihiro 1986). These themes come together in a basic concern with how people respond to their dominated and contradictory status, whether explored through neo-Gramscian discussions of hegemony, through Christian models of empowerment or through the ideas of habitus, as a shared and yet inchoate set of dispositions to act, and clashing systems of cultural capital developed by Pierre Bourdieu (1972, 1975). Another significant guide to understanding this response in an urban context has been work by Abner Cohen on small and informal groups (1969, 1976, 1980, 1981), which has helped me to deal with the meanings and identities that Savannah's black Catholics have constructed in their social historical context.

In a study that has for so long been part of my teaching and thought, it is frustrating to try to identify specific ancestors or opponents. The communities constituted by those who are black and Catholic in Savannah will appear here as models of a church, as responses to contradiction, as foci of resistance, and as small groups constituted by diverse individuals and choices. Although the study transcends its ethnographic limits to engage in wider debates in anthropology, nonetheless it must remain true to Savannah itself.

SETTING AND CONTEXT

Despite a disciplinary mythology encompassing magical islands, classic kin-ridden tribes, and unique villages, the choice of a site for anthropological research represents a set of compromises among practical, theoretical, and personal choices. My selection of Savannah as a field site emerged from preliminary research on conflicts between southern and Roman Catholic identity in which I sought a setting that combined a "classic" southern urban history with a long-term Catholic presence. An urban setting was preferable due to my general theoretical interests and comparative background; southern Catholicism, as well, has been profoundly linked to urban and immigrant life. New Orleans, Baltimore, St. Louis, and even Miami have strong Roman Catholic presences but complex southern identities (Baudier 1939; Fichter 1951; Faherty and Oliver 1977; McNally 1982). Capitals such as Atlanta, Tampa, and perhaps Richmond have modern Catholic presences as well as rapidly changing relationships to any traditional South (N. Johnson 1978; Pozzetta and Mormino 1987). Louisville, Kentucky, seemed an ideal possibility, as my home, but it, too, had a regional identity caught between northern industrialism and southern culture (Green 1972; Crews 1973 and 1987; Wright 1985). All of these provide general comparisons, although few have detailed studies that would provide sufficient information on blacks and whites.

Among potential dioceses, then—including Charleston, Mobile, and Natchez—Savannah offered strong historical resources, intriguing design as a city, and the accessibility of its inhabitants during a preliminary field season in 1982 that led to my concentrated work there. The setting of the city, as well as its classic beauty, remains as striking as its racial and cultural complexity. Savannah's location on a bluff overlooking the Savannah River, surrounded by rivers and tidal marshes yet with access to the sea, contributed to its career; although Georgia's population shifted inland to the north, Savannah has remained the state's primary seaport. Nonetheless, its very geography isolates it; residents jokingly refer to the "free and independent state of Chatham," while civic publicity emphasizes its centrality as capital of the "Coastal Empire." Historian Richard Haunton, analyzing the nineteenth-century city, concurred: "In 1898, Savannahian Richard Clark recalled in his memoirs that the Georgia port 'was much better acquainted with Boston, New York and Philadelphia than with our interior towns and counties' in the antebellum era, and in 1929 historian Richard Shryock claimed that Savannah was possessed of a sort of 'coast-line' sectionalism" (1968, 324).

Savannah today is a center for tourism, retirement, and sunbelt development. Its metropolitan area has grown to over 250,000, served by major highways, airports, and the continuing river port (see map 1); roughly half the city's population is black. Within this growth, however, there remains a culture and society of biracialism that every day tempers opportunities and actions in the city. Its twelve parishes embody the tradition of many black and Catholic experiences amid other communities, including the most recent Vietnamese parish of Saints Peter and Paul.

My work with those who are black *and* Catholic developed further within my increasing familiarity with Savannah, its history, and its myths, as well as the power relations that shape them (McDonogh 1984, 1988a, and 1988b). At the same time, I have learned that Savannah, like any other city, is idiosyncratically rather than "classically" southern, although its inhabitants have shared many general social and cultural patterns of the South. Nor would I want its history of Roman Catholicism or black life to *typify* the South as a whole: Savannah represents an important and suggestive case but one that should be read carefully and comparatively.

Savannah has a long, rich history of Baptist, Jewish, Episcopalian, and Lutheran life, for example, that has influenced black and white. It has been a center for charismatic leaders such as Father Divine and "Daddy" Grace. Within Catholicism, the diocese is the birthplace of America's first black priest bishop, James Healy. The city also merits interest as the site of the foundation of one of only three black religious orders founded in the United States and a unique site of interest by the Society for African Missions in America.

Overall, Savannah is also a city of tremendous charm and tremendous ugliness as closely interwoven as the elegant Victorian façades of

13

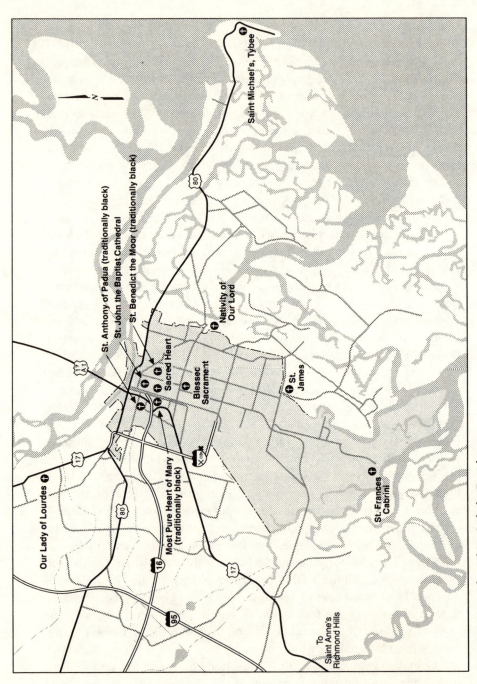

Map 1. *Savannah and Its Catholic Parishes*

an azalea-laden square that clash with collapsing shanties in the lanes behind them. It is a city in which arguments about the past and its ownership
can override debates about the present and future, and one in which complex problems are often masked within shifting metaphors of race. As in
any modern city, complaints and problems abound. Unlike many cities,
Savannah also inspires tremendous pride for residents, black and white:

> The national press has been good to Savannah, giving it mostly rave
> notices, calling it the "most restored city in America" and a "city of Eu-
> ropean atmosphere, with charming manners." The old town has been
> sucked into the twentieth century by the tornadoes of change. Despite
> conservatism, tradition, and a reluctance to completely let go of the old
> ways, a city which lay sleeping and almost unconcerned with national
> and world affairs now finds itself affected by such matters as Japanese
> import quotas. . . . Savannah is leaving behind its old reputation for
> insularity and xenophobia, abandoning at last the hollow smugness of
> its "State of Chatham" image. (Sieg 1985, 147)

At present, however, the individuality of these experiences can only
suggest more general comparisons to be built on the basis of detailed
local knowledge and interpretation. Nativism and immigration, black repression and opportunity, and the city's interaction with regional, national, and international affairs have all contributed to black and Catholic community and demand detailed and open future studies of the many
communities that have constituted black, southern, and American Catholicism. Unfortunately, the bibliography of social studies of actual
Catholic day-to-day life in its historical context remains scant, limiting
comparisons and generalizations. I have tried, nonetheless, to suggest
parallels and differences in white ethnic Catholicism as well as black
Protestant traditions. Other social and cultural factors will be adduced
where relevant to the ethnological questions of the chapters that follow,
beyond the bounds of American religious life and history.

This study is unique as an ethnographic examination of the formation,
contradictions, and voices of a single black and Catholic urban tradition
from which we might, in the future, draw more important conclusions. As
race and racial tension scar American life in political debates and urban
violence, Savannah also becomes emblematic of wider concerns. The formation and participation of black and Catholic communities within Savannah life illuminate wider urban prospects of contemporary America.

RESOURCES AND METHODS:
THE PERSONAL CONSTITUTION OF FIELDWORK

My own contradictions have been constitutive, although not distorting, throughout parts of this entire analysis, from the choice of the original topic to the development of final arguments. I am a southern, white, middle-class, male, Irish-French, Roman Catholic anthropologist. Yet I hold strong emotional and intellectual feelings of love and hate for almost all these categorizations and perhaps the process of categorization itself. I am a third-generation Kentuckian, but I always attended at least officially integrated schools and went on to the North—Yale and Toronto—before returning southward to Johns Hopkins to complete my anthropological training. Though my parents were Catholic and I was baptized as an infant, I grew up in the Protestant milieu of Louisville public schools with little religious commitment until college, which has shaped my sense of Roman Catholicism as an adult community. Even my ethnic identity while growing up in Louisville was much weaker in that divided society of the 1950s and 1960s than my racial one; I feel incongruous as an "Irish-American" in contrast to ethnic communities of the North. I am, of course, always white.

I have also been forced to relearn these identities through the meanings they have to those with whom I work in Savannah, where Irish is used as a shorthand for "all" Catholics, and whites live in southern worlds I had never before defined or shared. I had to seek acceptance in a black community whose experience of these categories long preceded my arrival. The words that follow are the measure of how we have dealt with these distances.

Religious practice has obviously been a crucible of contradiction throughout this work. I have attended mass in Savannah and elsewhere as both a Roman Catholic and a participant observer. While I separate these roles, they overlapped continually in both my experience and my comparative vantage from attending three to five masses each weekend in the field. This experience differed from the parochial identity of most Savannah Catholics. Yet as my interests became focused, my life also became increasingly bound to black and Catholic parishes as social worlds. I have shared both my beliefs and my analyses in discussions in Savannah over the years, which has also given me an appreciation of the range and privacy of devotions practiced by individuals within Catholicism. In the end, I have been forced to embrace this conflict and

16

contradictions, working with Catholics as spiritual advisors, informants, and friends. A subsequent project, in which I have consulted for the Bible Belt Catholic project under Jon Anderson at Catholic University has allowed me to interrogate these stances anew as both analyst and informant. Therefore, I have tried to show both public action and the structures of a Catholic vision of the world as I see them in Savannah and can relate them to my own experience and readings.

Yet the story of Savannah black Catholicism cannot simply be a story of religion, nor can my involvement with it ignore other social questions that my own presence could raise. Being white, middle-class, and male, for example, are hardly extraordinary traits, especially within the framework of the dominant cultural categories of Savannah and southern society. Indeed, being identified with such hegemonic and unmarked categories generally made it easier for me to deal with the power structures of the city. While I might self-consciously try to reject race or class as primary factors of my identity, these characteristics were immediately and complicitously marked by others, black and white.

Cross-cutting categories proved vital to my participation in the black and Catholic community. As a practicing white Catholic resident in a black household during much of this work, my situation was anomalous enough to permit close communication with those from whom race would normally divide me in Savannah. My sponsorship (adoption) by Mrs. Mildred Chisholm and other friends over a decade has been critical to my access to the entire black community, including internal conflicts and divisions. At the same time, her experiences and those shared with me by other blacks have tended to alienate me from the white Savannah community and perhaps from other white communities in which I live and work.

Other personal elements of academic reflexivity underpin this study as well. My Savannah fieldwork has always existed in counterpoint to my prior and continuing study in Barcelona. This project, in fact, became a bridge from a more academic and historical analysis of Barcelona elites to a more activist stance, working with social service colleagues to examine the ideology of marginality that has set aside one neighborhood as evil, and the social and cultural responses of its inhabitants to this moral geography. Ultimately, Savannah has led me to look at comparative ideologies and implications of racism in Europe and the United States (McDonogh 1986, 1987, 1991; McDonogh and Maza, in press). Savannah work has also been deeply linked to my teaching and student fieldwork. Finally, as I have researched and written, I have continually been able to discuss and debate my analyses with Savannahians. As drafts were completed, whether at the dining room table in Savannah or in a study in Sarasota, they became new pieces to take back to friends for criticism. They have been shared in public forums, critiqued in close readings, and explored in family discussions over meals. Although the responsibility for analysis and writing is ultimately mine, I have tried to incorporate a decade of listening to and learning from many people in Savannah, to present their voices as well as my own. This is not simply a methodological commitment, but also a personal one, meaningful in situating the life of black Savannah in a culture that has denigrated black history.

Within this general framework of values and commitments, my methods and resources follow those of ethnographic social history and participant observation, conditioned by my focus on a literate but subordinate community. Thus, while I have had generous access to the archives of the Diocese of Savannah, the collection of the Georgia Historical Society, and the files and texts of the Chatham County Public Library, the silences of such collections can be as meaningful as their riches for the analysis of black life. Diocesan archives, whose organization began shortly before my arrival, are dominated by records of bishops and clergy, leaving aside the history of the black laity who are the major actors in this text. Public archives, part of the very definition of public life, have overlooked blacks for decades. Efforts have been made since integration to expand resources, but holdings remain biased. Moreover, blacks remain marked as a category (e.g., "Savannah-schools" will be complemented by a category "Savannah-schools—Negro"). In one library, at least, this was changed after discussion of the implications of such categories.

White-controlled mass media also have been biased in historical accounts. It is often possible only to tease out the early history of black Catholics by isolated reports of their contacts with white figures like the bishop. This problem reappears in scrapbooks of the civil rights movement of the 1960s assembled by Louella Hawkins and others and now in the archives of Savannah State College, the local historically black college. Clippings in these scrapbooks depict a local mass movement giving way over time to a nationally dominated campaign charged with erratic violence. Those active in the movement, however, have pointed out that this vision is a reflection of news management even more than historical change. After they realized that their coverage revealed information and success to local blacks, white news media replaced their organizational analyses with charges of criminality, outside agitation, and violence. The local black newspaper was silenced by white pressure; a local black leader told me "You just cannot expect a newspaper always supporting the status quo to report these things."

Despite integration and modernization, the major local media in Savannah during my stay tended to be slow, distorted, or silenced in comparison to black weeklies and the lively oral exchange of black community news. Newspaper sources also reflect historical divisions within the black communities. The local black newspaper has given little coverage to Catholic activities apart from an aggressive campaign by the Society of African Mission fathers between 1910 and 1914. Meanwhile, Roman Catholic journalism paid scant attention to black affairs in the early years of the century either, although this has improved over time.

Other sources for the study of black life can prove frustrating. Traditionally black parishes, unfortunately, have kept minimal archives apart from baptismal, marital, and funeral records—a trait they share with most parishes of the diocese. Saint Benedict's has been more sensitive than most to history and has sponsored both publications and historical commemorations since its centennial anniversary in 1975. It also has a regular historian who has assembled archives. Most Pure Heart of Mary assembled information and photos for its rededication in 1978, but the files needed to be reorganized and completed, a project that I undertook in 1985. Similarly, Saint Anthony's had maintained little documentation of its origins, which proved a challenge when I was asked to write a parish history for its seventy-fifth anniversary in 1985. This document became the touchstone for renewed research in the parish as well as commentary in the public historical ceremony. It also provided a basis for its eightieth anniversary commemorative volume (Saint Anthony's 1990).

Yet the major resource for the present study, in its historical dimensions as well as contemporary analysis, has been the people of the Savannah black and Catholic community. More than a hundred of the twenty-three hundred black Catholics in the city have participated in interviews, some stretching into multiple discussions as well as frequent informal contacts. Among those in my residential circle, the project was the focus of almost daily discussions and questions. Friends and strangers have responded to a wide range of questions, whether set in the context of formal research or shared after mass or over meals. Discus-

sions have also included ex-Catholics and non-Catholics, both those specifically contacted for information and others connected by neighborhood and household ties. Ministers in other congregations, neighborhood
leaders, educators, and historical activists have all contributed. Priests
and religious, current and retired, have also participated in the study
through recollections, discussions, and readings of the work in progress.
Retired priests of the Society of African Missions (SMA) fathers and
Franciscan Missionary Sisters were generous with their time and memories during my visits to their New Jersey retirement homes, as well as
during their trips south.

In the course of the study, I have also talked with whites outside the
predominantly black parishes. My original focus on the contradictions of
southern and Catholic identities brought me into contact with members
from a wide range of ethnic and class backgrounds (McDonogh 1988a).
Between 1982 and 1993, any white network has withered: black and
white social networks do not intersect well in Savannah. By the end of
my work, the whites with whom I associated were, with rare exceptions,
priests, religious, or white laity in black parishes.

All of these people have been informed of my project and interests;
indeed, I am regularly questioned about my progress. In most cases,
unless working from public documents, taped interviews, or with specific permission, I have not cited anyone by name. While I believe that it
is necessary to ground anthropology in concrete settings of history rather
than adopting an uncomfortable pseudonym for the city, I also recognize my responsibility to guard the privacy of those with whom I have
worked. In one or two isolated cases, this has limited what I can say
about a theme; in general, I hope to provide sufficient information by
which to situate an informant without specifically identifying him or her
and to draw general conclusions while protecting particulars.

Nonetheless, the voices of Savannahians and others are present in
the text, while respecting personal wishes and privacy. They are part of
the polyphony that constitutes black and Catholic Savannah. Some
friends participate actively in the text as they have in my research; others have preferred to remain anonymous. The interplay of public voice
and private conversations is also present in my use of public texts produced by those with whom I have worked.

At the same time, this is a community of many voices that must be
recognized beyond the informant/collaborator relationship that has characterized much of anthropological research and writing. Voices of his-

tory and historical narration, of mass media and public speeches also constitute primary sources in this urbane community. Most significantly, I believe that even as I have worked with individual members and groups within the Catholic church, the "voices" of that institution must be recognized as primary sources. These include texts from clerics, homilies, formal statements of belief and theology, and commentaries. To treat these as primary to the experience of those who are Catholic as well as to the constitution of the Catholic church as institution sheds critical light on the levels of constitution of community and identity central to the black and Catholic experience.

Oral history and interviews have consistently meshed with participant observation in church and city. I observed the celebration of masses in all the parishes regularly, while visiting predominantly white parishes and, when possible, attending services at black Protestant churches. This established both a comparative perspective on liturgy and a wide exchange of information during the coffee and conversation that often followed worship. Even going to the store in my racially integrated and gentrifying neighborhood becomes an occasion of interaction and observation, as have libraries, schools, parks, and historical tours, which have divided the history of the city along racial lines.

The heart of my experience—indeed, of this book—has been Mildred "Pie" Chisholm's house on East Gordon Street, where I have lived in Savannah over the past eight years. Pie's house has been a place of meeting, discussion, pain—in times of illness or death—and celebration of friendship, marriage, and life. Without Pie, and without her gift of a home where people enjoy coming and being, this book would have been impossible.

In a sense, then, methods and resources have been set by the basic conditions of opposition and domination that have divided white and black in Savannah. Yet I have struggled to go beyond them, to deal with both local ideology and its history as keys to a more general understanding. While I am white, these conditions often forced me to respond as a black and Catholic would and taught me to ask new questions, including the nature of categorization itself. Building my own community has been a fundamental part of this book, which I can now return to Savannah.

Although my research was concentrated in the summers of 1982, 1983, 1984, and 1987, and longer field stays in the autumn of 1985 and 1988, my proximity allowed me to normalize participant observation through monthly and holiday visits, often accompanied by students, family, or friends. I also returned to Saint Benedict's for my wedding in 1990 and now return frequently with my wife. While I continue to incorporate these visits as insights into problems and processes, in general the ethnographic present for the study, unless noted, represents the late 1980s, and first years of the 1990s.

ORDER AND DEVELOPMENT

The chapters that follow, then, try to bring together a great number of perspectives and ideas on black Catholic life and belief in Savannah. The first two chapters trace the ethnohistorical context of the formation of black and Catholic community. Chapter 1 presents facets of the ethnohistory of black religion in Savannah as an area of creative response to white racism. It traces the divergences among predominantly black congregations as well as their members' changing consciousness. The chapter also explores in more detail the themes of black history intrinsic to later analyses. Chapter 2 situates this community within the evolving cultural meanings of white and black within Savannah, with an emphasis on the ambiguous relations of Catholicism to both categories. White and black, as symbols, obscure other relations of class, gender, and power within the meaning of domination and resistance in black and Catholic life.

Chapters 3 and 4 concentrate on the formation of the black and Catholic community itself and on the tensions of institutional policy and community actions. Chapter 3 traces education as a primary process through which a white church and its episcopal hierarchy established itself in black Savannah. The top-down quality of the analysis echoes the history of the missions themselves, imposed upon blacks rather than sought by them, yet it includes commentary from those educated which casts important light on policy failures. Chapter 4 turns to black response as evidenced in the development of three distinct parish communities, as well as in a range of participation in the wider church by both blacks and whites. Here, historical sources provide groundwork for later discussion of grass-roots action and leadership in contemporary parishes.

Chapters 5 and 6 develop a similar balance with the consideration of processes of social structure and leadership in both official and informal roles. Chapter 5 faces the central contradictions of the black and

Catholic tradition: the insistent presence of white leadership, priests and nuns, over time in black parishes. Chapter 6 balances this historical discussion with an analysis of a continuum of formal and informal leadership through which the laity have constituted their own transgenerational structure of parish and society, outside of ritual affairs, as well as making demands within that clerical domain.

Finally, chapters 7 and 8 link the liturgical and institutional meanings of community to urban life. In chapter 7 the juxtaposition of life cycles, domestic and gender-specific roles, and public opportunities are linked to a universalist ritual-moral code, embodied in the seven sacraments of the Roman Catholic church, and to black social and cultural norms. Chapter 8 returns from houses and streets to ritual space and action to explore the Eucharist as the central sign of the church amidst questions of unity, belief, and differentiation. All these lead to more general considerations and suggestions for future work in the conclusion.

1. The Evolution of Black Religion in Savannah: Choice and Constraint

God of our weary years, God of our silent tears
Thou who has brought us thus far on the way;
Thou who hast by thy might, Led us into the light
Keep us forever in the path, we pray.
Lest our feet stray from the places, our God, where we met thee,
Lest our hearts, drunk with the wine of the world, we forget thee;
Shadowed beneath thy hand, May we forever stand,
True to our God, true to our native land.

—*James Weldon Johnson and Rosamund Johnson,*
"Lift Ev'ry Voice and Sing"

The contradictions and responses of those who are black and Catholic in Savannah have been enacted in a history of inequality, of white dominance over blacks as a fundamental feature of American life. Nowhere has black resistance to the enforced domination of whites in southern culture been more evident than in the evolution and consciousness of black churches. Religion in early African-American communities synthesized the African spiritualities of those kidnapped to the New World with Christian dogmas and rituals. Beliefs, practices, and congregations emerged within the oppression of blacks in their new environment, while providing a commentary upon that environment. Creolized systems of expression and belief came forth from bondage within a divided society in which race and power remained symbolically equated. With changing opportunities, however, African-American religion has ranged from individualistic possession to the liturgical solemnity of a conscious "high church" elite, from charisma to philosophical theology. Moreover, it has contested its place as a narrative of black life with other, secular ways of seeing the black world. Nonetheless, in Savannah, black religious expressions have comprised a source of hope, strength, and understanding while providing a template for individual and group difference.

This chapter situates Savannah black and Catholic practice within the historical development of urban black religious life and identity. It emphasizes religious beliefs and organizations as a range of responses to enduring political, economic, social, and cultural contradictions as well as evoking symbolic means of incorporating strategic actions into the reproduction of social roles. Moreover, it recognizes religion as a key symbolic model through which to talk about many other aspects of urban life. The segregation of Christian congregations itself has been a powerful statement on American society; as one black civil rights leader commented, recalling an observation of Martin Luther King, "11 A.M. Sunday is the most segregated hour in Savannah." Meanwhile, black religions have confronted the evolving conditions of a marked and dominated group in a variety of ways, reflecting the ranges of choice available in an urban context, a spectrum of individual needs and beliefs, and the shifting imposition of constraints on black life.

This chapter follows the evolution of hundreds of black churches and varied religious actions in Savannah within a framework of choices and constraints as a key to understanding urban history and culture. While highlighting the minority who have chosen to be Roman Catholic, I have been selective in other areas without distorting the overall panorama. Thus Baptists and Methodists, who have long and tangled histories involving scores of churches, are represented only by leading congregations. Similarly, while many smaller churches have emerged around sanctified beliefs or charismatic leaders, I use only Father Divine and Bishop C. R. "Daddy" Grace to exemplify such congregations. At the same time, this overview also pays attention to the unfolding awareness of self and of community identity within the churches themselves. The historiography of the august First African Baptist Church, for example, includes not only the growth of the congregation over two hundred years but also its changing self-consciousness. These recognitions provide insight into how black Savannahians have formulated religious identity and community over time.

SLAVERY DAYS: CHARISMA AND INSTITUTION

Savannah was settled in 1733 by Col. James Oglethorpe as the capital of the Georgia colony, a buffer zone between the English Carolinas and Spanish Florida. Oglethorpe envisioned a colony of yeoman farmers, without slaves, and recruited diverse settlers ranging from prisoners to Jews and Lutherans escaping religious persecution. The colony, however, discouraged Roman Catholics because of their suspected affinity to the enemy Spanish.

Slavery soon brought a dominated black population who disrupted ideal equality. The ambivalent situation of slaves became apparent during the Revolutionary War, when the citizens of Savannah had divided loyalties. The British took the city in 1778 and held it until 1782 despite attacks by American, French, and Haitian forces. In this period of tumult, black Savannahians found a foretaste of freedom exemplified by the independent First African Baptist congregation, which the British permitted in order to counter any black allegiance to white revolutionary activity.

After independence, state government moved inland to Augusta in 1786, while Savannah incorporated as a city in 1789. In the closing decades of the eighteenth century, West Indian immigration formed the nucleus of Georgia Roman Catholicism while bringing a new population of slaves and free men of color. The city allocated the first church lot to Catholics in 1799 (Ruskowski 1940, 33, 42).

Despite periodic fires and the War of 1812, the city grew on the basis of regional (slave) agriculture and trade with the North and Europe. In 1819 the SS *Savannah* made the first transatlantic crossing by a steamship, from Savannah to London. Canals and railroads channeled the wealth of inland plantations into this commerce (Haunton 1968; Chalker 1970; Bartley 1983). While trade and growth attracted new immigrants (Weaver 1953; Sieg 1985), slaves and free blacks constituted a separate yet interlocking society within the city (Blassingame 1973a). Savannah was a haven for escaped slaves, but all blacks were bound by a segregated society in which "Negroes exercised and socialized at the sufferance of the white community, never knowing when the capricious arm of the law might intervene in their activities" (Haunton 1968, 365).

By 1850 the city's population had reached 13,573, including 7,270 whites; 5,686 black slaves; and 637 free blacks (Sholes 1900, 74). As local institutions matured, schools were established—the Sisters of Mercy opened a Catholic girls' academy in the 1840s—although none were available for blacks (Powers 1956; Haunton 1968, 335-40). Meanwhile, residential ostentation and religious power increased. The city already had become a center for evangelicals, black and white. In addition, it was the home of the Episcopal diocese of Georgia, and separated from Charleston as a Catholic see in 1850. The Savannah, Albany, and Gulf Railroad reorganized, and trade in cotton grew. Nonetheless, the yellow fever epidemic of 1854, which caused over a thousand deaths, was a setback to this period of growth.

Thus, black religion in antebellum Savannah took shape amidst social divisions aggravated by intermittent growth and decline. Those taken into slavery in the New World had brought with them diverse traditions of religious belief and practice. For some, enslavement destroyed institutions and disrupted the transmission of culture while mingling many groups and traditions. The new urban environment posed questions about existence while traditional answers were challenged by the domination of the white population. Owners, furthermore, preached a religion that came to defend slavery as part of the natural order and to reify it in ritual segregation. Meanwhile, whites suspected independent black religious gatherings for their promotion of cultural separateness as well as potential rebellion. Within these struggles, slave religion emerged along a creolized continuum, combining African elements with American creeds and experience (Woodson 1945; Frazier 1963; Blassingame 1972; Genovese 1974; Cone 1975; Mintz and Price 1976; Levine 1977; Raboteau 1978; Sobel 1979; Hoskins 1980; Mills 1983; Giddings 1984; Andrews 1986a; Stuckey 1987; Lincoln and Mamiya 1990; Davis 1991; Mohlman 1991). Questions of faith and world were accompanied by adaptations of style in continuity and change: "Even as the gods of Africa gave way to the god of Christianity, the African heritage of singing, dancing, spirit possession, and magic continued to influence Afro-American spirituals, ring shouts, and folk belief. That this was so is evidence of the slaves' ability to adapt to new contexts but also to do so creatively" (Raboteau 1978, 92).

Creolization went hand-in-hand with ambiguity, concealment, and manipulation. The covert collective meanings of overt religious acts, for example, evoked the public-versus-private contrasts of white and black discussed in the next chapter. Even the public religion observed by the masters carried other meanings for blacks antagonistic to the dominant system. Religious songs like "Steal Away" or "I'm-a Gonna Tell God How

27

You Treat Me," for example, used a public Christian idiom to protest mistreatment by the master or to communicate an escape (Genovese 1974, 251-70; Levine 1977). Susie King Taylor, raised a slave in Savannah, recalled this dual signification in her grandmother's meeting's use of "Yes, we shall all be free / When the Lord shall appear." She wrote "the police came and arrested all who were there, saying they were planning freedom and sang 'the Lord' in place of 'Yankee,' to blind anyone who might be listening" (1902, 8).

Similarly, leadership in black religious life might be taken on by those who would not be so easily recognized by masters in public forums. Although assimilated and free males might achieve more prominence in public, women and African-born slaves were valued for traditional knowledge in the slave community (Levine 1977; Giddings 1984; White 1985, 135-41; Andrews 1986b).

Yet, religion in antebellum black Savannah offered an adaptive range of ways of talking about the world and making sense of it, of looking beyond slavery to a better world while consoling the sorrows of the present. To see religion as a creolization process, in which a new language of experience formed from contact and disruption in separate systems, also highlights the differences among antebellum black religions. Slave religious expression ranged from the quarters' "folk" traditions to the public attendance of slave and master in the same, if divided, church. Also prominent in this range were the early autonomous churches, especially the evangelical congregations in which blacks assembled in public with minimal white supervision, and other areas where free blacks participated. Secret, dominated, and autonomous responses all became foundations for later development.

Conjure, for example, might be characterized as domestic belief and folk actions where African ideas or practices were maintained or reconstructed. Spells, tales, ethics, and occult medicinal knowledge of the plantation, in fact, have survived into modern times. Fragments of tribal traditions also represent a more general pattern of imposing personal relationships upon the world and its misfortunes as well as the recognition of special figures who manipulate these relationships (Mintz and Price 1976; Levine 1977; Raboteau 1978).

Works Progress Administration (WPA) researchers in Savannah in the 1930s, for example, documented root workers, spells, and other magical beliefs that long had coexisted with black churches. The local root worker and fortune teller James Washington then proclaimed "I hab a deep knowledge uh magic. Deah's magic wut gahd yu from hahm and deah's ebil magic wut kin put yuh down sick and eben kill you. Wen yuh bin fix yuh caahn get well wid regluh medicine . . ." (Georgia Writers' Project 1940, 38-39). While this example involves a male practitioner, general evidence on slave society suggests that other experts in charms, healing, and manipulation of the world were women whose secret power might reach beyond the quarters as well into the world of white women (Hurston [1935] 1963; White 1985; Fox-Genovese 1988; Roggow 1988). Historiography probably reflects the public domestication of women more than the social experience of the slave world, an insight present in modern black females' exploration of slavery and its heritage (Giddings 1984; Morrison 1987; Hooks 1990).

Root workers continue to practice in the community today, often mingling gypsy, Christian, and neo-pagan beliefs. They are also successful in nearby rural and island communities (Jones-Jackson 1987, 24-31). My Catholic friends in the present labeled these practitioners and those who use them "primitive Negroes" or country people. Nonetheless, contemporary urban practitioners were readily identifiable by name, and some customs, especially those related to health and to the dead, linger in orthodox Catholic homes.

Conjure and folk traditions balanced Christianity in the way witchcraft has balanced socially established cults in both Africa and Europe. As Albert Raboteau notes, "not only was conjure a theory for explaining the mystery of evil, but it was also a practice for doing something about it." Moreover, "the world of conjure answered deeply felt needs within the slaves' own community, where white control inhibited the outward expression of social conflict" (Raboteau 1978, 276; see Levine 1977). Eugene Genovese summarizes this pervasive and subversive form of religious expression:

> The social significance of voodoo and conjure among the slaves lay less in some direct threat to the whites, much less in their alleged use by whites to control blacks, than in the degree of autonomy they provided the quarters. The slaves saw other slaves with great power and by that belief alone they offered resistance to that doctrine of black impotence which the slaveholders worked incessantly to fasten on them. (1974, 221)

Conjure generally did not become a public challenge to the discourse of white Christianity, although its doctors advised in some slave rebellions.

In the slave-owning community, magic could be perceived as disruptive and dangerous, above all when directed against the masters, when it became tantamount to rebellion. After Emancipation, conjure continued in secrecy, although generally without this political antihegemonic component.

The creole spectrum also included the white slave-owners' churches who received blacks into mixed congregations even while physically and culturally affirming their subordinate position. The Episcopalians who dominated Savannah's early white population pioneered this subordinating incorporation. Christ Church baptized its first black member in 1750, just as slavery became legal in the fledgling colony. Later, it sent missions to blacks in urban and rural areas, through which the Episcopalian white elite incorporated a black elite, slave and free, into urban churches (Hoskins 1980, 1983). Yet according to a scholar of Episcopalian history, later freedmen "remembered the Church more as a master than as a mother" (Lines 1960, 298).

Roman Catholics held a different position due to their general exclusion from colonial society and minority status throughout the plantation South (Miller and Wakelyn 1983). Although black Catholics participated in the origins of Savannah Catholicism in the eighteenth century, any black congregation was swamped thereafter by the demands of nineteenth-century European immigrants (Weaver 1953; Chalker 1970). Religious schools, the other Catholic linchpin in the antebellum city, made only covert and unsystematic attempts to serve blacks in a climate that formally forbade such education.[1]

Hence, white and "public" churches provided ambivalent instruments of integration, especially from the vantage of the slaves. These institutions ritualized the boundary of marked and unmarked categories so that blacks often had tenuous loyalties to those who asked them to sit silently in the back, to climb up to separate galleries, or even to stand outside during the shared services while preachers praised the Biblical order of servitude (see Joyner 1984; Johnson and Roark 1984a, 1984b on South Carolina). The beliefs and practice of these churches imposed, rather than discussed, a European cultural tradition. A pedagogy of subordination and physical separation in the church itself must have reinforced the impression that blacks were not perceived as sisters and brothers so much as children to be watched.

Thus, many slaves departed when freedom permitted, including black Catholics. Indeed, this pattern recurred throughout the South, with some exceptions among large, rooted Catholic populations such as Louisiana (Miller 1983a, 1983b; Mills 1983; see Baudier 1939; Green 1972; Woods 1972; Dominguez 1986). The Lutheran church, which had arrived in Savannah in 1734, almost at the foundation of the colony, by 1859 included 655 whites and 61 blacks (Ahrendt 1979, 33). By 1868, however, all these black members seem to have disappeared (1979, 39).[2] Nonetheless, some blacks in white churches, especially in the loosely independent congregation of Saint Stephen's Episcopal church, also emerged as a wealthy, powerful and often mulatto group, whose roles of caste and color would continue after the war (see Johnson and Roark 1984b on Charleston; Hoskins 1980, 1983; Williamson 1980, 1984 on mulattos).

Blacks also developed creative, autonomous alternatives between private conjure and public "white" churches, which are epitomized in the history of black evangelicals. Baptists and Methodists—as scholars have argued since Herskovits (1958) and Frazier (1963)—held a special attraction for slaves because of their message of reform, their loose congregational structure, and the range of expression permitted within worship. Moreover, both "had retained some interest in ameliorating plantation conditions; their congregations long had been racially mixed and had never wholly accepted the white pressure to segregate; and above all, their preachers spoke plainly. . . ." This confrontation with the divisions of slavery clearly permeated actions as well as preaching: "they worked hard to reach the blacks and understood the need to enlist black preachers and 'assistants' to work with them. Emotional appeal and organizational flexibility gave the Baptists the edge, but they might have thrown it away had they not undertaken the task of conversion with the vigor they did" (Genovese 1974, 234). Baptist communities permitted more equality and recognized blacks as preachers rather than treating them merely as a passive flock. Flexibility and autonomy allowed Baptist congregations also to address their emotional and social experiences as slaves.

Theology and belief were also important to the success of evangelical denominations. The Baptists' emphasis on individual salvation responded to the bondage of the blacks, whether as a call for rebellion (Genovese 1974, 158-59) or as a personal cosmology:

Blacks began joining black congregations as they spread through the South and soon formed their own black congregations as well. . . .

> They were welcomed into almost equal fellowship with the whites.
> They were not judged on their ability to memorize a simple catechism
> such as the Anglicans required, they had *to be* something. . . . They
> had to be Christians reborn through the love of Jesus Christ. They had
> to retell their spirit travels and symbolize their death and rebirth in
> 'drowning' and yet live again. While many feared this act, they never-
> theless had ecstatic experiences during and as a result of baptism in
> the living waters. They were rewarded by knowing that God was with
> them. (Sobel 1979, 139)

The evangelical tradition, especially that of the Baptists, retains primacy
in the number of churches and church members in Savannah to this day.

One of the first independent black Baptist churches in the United
States was formed in Savannah in the eighteenth century. George Leile,
its founder, was a Virginia-born slave who came to Burke County, Georgia, before the Revolutionary War. Leile converted and was baptized by
his owner, a white deacon. Ordained in 1775, Leile preached in the city
and nearby plantations until he sought British protection during the war;
he later accompanied the British to Jamaica in 1783 as they relinquished
Savannah. Another slave, Andrew Bryan, was ordained on January 20,
1788, a date now taken as the foundation of the First African Baptist
Church (Thomas 1925, 11-21).

Bryan began to buy land for a new church even while he bought his
own freedom. He was joined by other slaves, male and female; Leile had
baptized Bryan's wife, while other women worked with the preparation
and baptism of female candidates (Simms 1888, 88-89). The congregation
joined the Georgia Baptist Association in 1790 and formed the Savannah
.Baptist Association, in conjunction with smaller white churches, in 1802.

As First African grew, other congregations split off from the mother
church. In 1802 Second African Baptist was formed on the east side of
the city, dominated, according to oral tradition, by light-skinned house-
servants and artisans in that area. Nonetheless, a subsequent pastor of
the mother church noted:

> many families of worth and intelligence are divided between the First
> African and the Second African Churches. To-day the wives of three of
> the deacons of the First Church belong to the Second Church. In many
> cases the wife and some of the children belong to one church and the
> father and some of the children belong to another. This interchange of
> families in the two churches form[s] almost a demand for the pastors
> of the two families to be on friendly terms. (Love 1888, 25)

Figure 2. First African Baptist Church, 1990. Photograph by Cindy Hing-Yuk Wong.

Divided congregational loyalties, even within the same denomination, remain striking in Savannah, as do mixed marriages among Protestants and Catholics in the black community.

Ogeechee Baptist Church split off in 1803. In that year, the mother church had 400 members, while the Second African Baptist church had 200 and Ogeechee, 250. Some 850 of the 1,289 Baptists in Savannah were black (Thomas 1925, 39-40). As these churches grew, whites attempted to limit their assembly and worship:

> Very seldom were night services held, unless some of the white ministers preached to them. Even then such meetings had to be early and of short duration, for by the rule the drum of the city's patrol guards must beat at eight o'clock in winter and nine in summer. . . . The statute laws of the State and ordinances of the city forbade the slaves to assemble for any purpose (except funerals) to the number of seven without the presence of a white person, under penalty of fine or whipping with stripes, yet under these regulations the church could find pleasure and comfort. . . . (Simms 1888, 63-64)

After Bryan's death in 1812, his nephew, Andrew Marshall, succeeded him as pastor; again, a free black male led the predominantly slave congregation. By 1821, the church had 1,916 members; by 1831, 2,795 (Thomas 1925, 46-47). It began a Sunday School with the white First Independent Presbyterian Church in 1826 and took full control in 1835 (Thomas 1925, 47-48; Williams and Williams 1977). Under Marshall, the congregation also acquired a new church, the first black-owned brick building in Georgia. A later pastor recalled with pride the composition and beliefs of this early congregation:

> Some among them had worked out their time, as was then the expression for those who had purchased their freedom, or had procured it by gift of their owners on account of blood relationship or faithful and independent services rendered. Some were allowed to hire their time, because their owners were among the middle or poorer classes of whites who invested their money in this species of property that paid the best interest upon the capital surer and sooner. Yet out of each and all of these conditions in which the members of the churches were situated, they were doing something for God's glory, as the only glory they had in the world, the advancing of the light and liberty of the gospel among their race. (Simms 1888, 87)

Marshall himself gained fame throughout Savannah, the state, and the nation as an able preacher who baptized nearly four thousand people and who could also manipulate the multiple forces of his environment. "His personal influence extended over the plantations through several counties around Savannah and the planters were generally satisfied with the beneficial effects of his labors. He was often sent for to preach and to perform funeral services at great distances, and such visits were urged by the planters and the white people at large, as well as by the blacks" (Love 1888, 51). Marshall transcended the urban and racial boundaries that constrained most Savannah blacks. "He occasionally preached in Augusta, Macon and Milledgeville, as well as in Charleston, and even as far off as New Orleans. On some occasions his audiences were composed, in large part, of the most respectable white people, and the Legislature of Georgia at one time gave him a hearing in an entire body" (Love 1888, 51).

Nonetheless, Marshall's success and renown also incited religious and racial tension that cast doubt on his very independence:

> Rev. Marshall, having accumulated considerable wealth, began the execution of a two-story brick residence, which caused considerable jealousy and persecution. He was charged with purchasing brick from slaves who had no power to sell, and was sentenced to a public whipping. Mr. Richard Richardson, who bought Rev. Marshall that he might set him free, came to his rescue, claiming that he was his property and, by the grace of God, had his punishment so modified that the whipping was merely a semblance. (Thomas 1925, 46; see Love 1888, 43, 53; Simms 1888, 81-83)

The presence and manipulation of white patronage remained crucial even in the most autonomous of black churches.

This was evident again as Marshall became involved in a widespread Baptist controversy by receiving the Rev. Alexander Campbell, founder of the Christian Church, in his congregation. Marshall was denied his seat in the Baptist Association and his church dissolved, a move that was possible since the white officers of the federation had to act legally for black congregations (Simms 1888, 96). The West-Indian born deacon Adam Johnson rallied forces against Marshall, and the church split in 1833. Both men called on the aid of powerful white supporters, while whites had variable interests in healing the rift or in destroying the institution. "The white church and the friends of the church were laboring to settle this strife that the great church might settle down and pursue its marvelous labors with peace and prosperity. Still some of the whites had never looked kindly upon this band of organized slaves and were bent on its destruction" (Thomas 1925, 50).[3]

Despite the split, Marshall and his congregation were readmitted into the Baptist Association in 1837. Marshall's funeral, some two decades later, showed the power that a black preacher could attain even in antebellum Savannah "An immense procession of about a mile long, with fifty-eight carriages—either loaned by families in the city to their servants or other colored friends or occupied (as in many instances) by respectable white people themselves—followed him from his church to his grave" (Love 1888, 56).

The array of religious expression of antebellum Savannah blacks, which has shaped contemporary black practice, encompassed strategy, assimilation, autonomy, and rejection by individuals and groups, although never reaching the violent messianic opposition exemplified by Denmark Vesey in nearby Charleston. Each community and pathway reflected different social opportunities, often shaped by white masters, and expressed nascent divisions in the black community on the basis of free status, occupation, and gender. Three recurrent points, however, deserve emphasis.

First, divisions were not ironclad. Deacons in one church might have children in another. Those who faithfully attended liturgies with their white master also might sneak away to "free" black gatherings later on the Sabbath. Others had no church but turned to an established group in times of trouble. Even the same songs, Biblical passages, or preaching imagery, as mentioned above, might evoke different responses within congregations divided by color and caste or within different contexts. Second, each of these religious responses would evolve through time. Humble missions and isolated plantation congregations in the eighteenth century became urban landmarks with respected preachers in the twentieth. Lutherans and Catholics, meanwhile, experimented with unsuccessful strategies of recruitment that would change in later decades; Episcopalians crystallized a social black elite in counterpoint to the evangelical leaders. Finally, despite the deep division of black and white that scarred Savannah life and mocked Christian brotherhood, no black religious option could be divorced from the public and dominant presence of whites as teachers, owners, or spectators. However blacks expressed themselves, whites provided both stimulus to resistance and constraints on public action within a divided world.

EMANCIPATION AND EDUCATION

In the Civil War, as in the American Revolution, Savannah held an ambiguous position. While its white leadership originally sided with the Confederacy, the city surrendered to Sherman as he concluded his devastating march to the sea (Lawrence 1961).[4] In Savannah, Sherman issued his Field Order No. 15, authorizing the newly freed blacks to occupy coastal islands abandoned by Confederate sympathizers. The freedom of black slaves in the South transformed religious organization and expression as it did so many other aspects of black life. If religion had previously emphasized deliverance yet to come, after the Civil War, many black churches became the primary institutions to foster citizenship in earth and heaven. Black Savannah churches became centers in the Reconstruction period for political action; their pastors and deacons became major public leaders. Reconstruction also forged a strong unification of church, class, and education.

Open conflicts between blacks and whites emerged in Reconstruction Savannah, as economic, social, and political boundaries were challenged. To a white historian of the city, this period was "more disastrous to the people and brought more uneasiness and heartburnings than the dreadful years of war. . ." (Harden 1908, 1:466). For black Savannah, however, this was a time of growth in power and institutions, including schools, political associations, churches, and active public voices (Love 1888; Perdue 1973).

The new tasks of religious institutions and groups were met both by existing groups and by missionaries from outside the region. In Savannah, members of First African Baptist Church, Bryan Baptist Church, and Saint Stephen's Episcopal Church continued their antebellum public leadership in new political, economic, and social roles. They were joined by African Methodist Episcopal and other Methodist congregations. New educational institutions under religious aegis (and later, supported by city or state funds) complemented religious initiatives. The Republican party also incorporated blacks within its newly important ranks, while social and fraternal organizations took more prominent public positions.

After the war, white and black missionaries came South to preach and teach to the newly freed slaves; both bemoaned excesses they perceived in traditions of plantation shouts (Levine 1977). Education was a solution in both religion and everyday life. Congregationalists, for example, formed the Oglethorpe school in 1865 in Savannah, which became the Alfred Beach Institute thereafter. This school, founded by white northern teachers as a challenge to urban cultural mores, became a nucleus for urban black higher education through the 1920s. Indeed,

> The city of Savannah was selected by the American Missionary Association as the place for beginning its work of preparing Negro people and their children for responsible citizenship in a situation hostile to them, due to its location in the Deep South, in one of the states that had been reluctant to give up the master-slave relationship that had served them for more than one hundred years. (Waring 1969, 4)

Clearly, this could also be interpreted by white southerners as a dangerous alliance of northern outsiders and disfranchised blacks.

The nucleus of a Congregational community began to meet in the school in 1869, acquiring its church in 1878. By the late 1870s, this group had accepted its first known black members, school teachers who had graduated from Atlanta University (Gadsden 1969, 4). Their first black minister, R. B. Maxwell, arrived in 1887, although white ministers served in temporary capacities as late as 1904. The church, like the school, devoted itself to charitable programs for the larger black community, including a kindergarten in Savannah's Old Fort area. For more educated blacks, the church sponsored afternoon cultural programs in conjunction with nearby Beth Eden Baptist and Saint Philip African Methodist Episcopal church. As the only Congregational church in the city, it seems to have remained integrated through the decades that followed, and it maintained links with support from inside and outside the South. In 1989, for example, such prominent figures as former mayor and congressman Andrew Young of Atlanta, a Congregationalist minister, attended the installation of a new pastor.

The postwar period also became a time of expansion in both black and immigrant urban Catholicism. Saint Patrick's opened in 1863, and a new cathedral building was consecrated in 1876. This period also saw extensive Catholic missionary and schooling efforts among blacks under the aegis of activist bishops like Augustine Verot (1861-72) and William Gross (1873-85). The once black but subsequently immigrant Sacred Heart parish followed in the 1880s. The Benedictine Military Academy later separated from Sacred Heart to become a central institution for white Irish Catholicism in Savannah.

Yet any implications of continuity in black Catholicism deserve scrutiny. In Savannah, despite new efforts, the church did not reach a coher-

Figure 3. Saint Patrick's Church: a white downtown church destroyed after the 1940 hurricane. Photograph courtesy of the Georgia Historical Society, Cordray-Foltz Collection.

ent institutional framework vis-à-vis blacks until the twentieth century. A later black Savannah commentator, Sister Julian Griffin, concluded:

> Why is the Catholic church less effective than others in its efforts to reach the Black population during these years of Reconstruction? Various answers have been put forward. Some were of the opinion, at the time, that Blacks would respond better if the liturgy of the Church were more exciting, with the use of brighter colors and tuneful hymns. Others felt that the Church, with its hierarchical structure, presented barriers to leadership—that the freedmen preferred to set up their own sects, with their own leaders. The prejudices of the time, which were shared by most White Catholics, did little to improve matters. (Griffin and Brown 1979, 28)

A nineteenth-century Benedictine missionary, Oswald Moosmuller, discussed in more detail in chapter 4, found his initiatives caught within sectarian struggles with established black churches:

I invited them to send their children, the School being free, no charge. One of them answered that they had to give their word to their preacher (a Baptist) not to send their children to any School except a Baptist school; afterwards I learned that there is one among them here (but who did not utter a word in this house) who is a Deacon and who told them at church that he would excommunicate anyone who would send his children to the 'Fathers" School; at the same time, he always flattered me; he is the foreman at our place, collects the rent, etc., etc., and has his own land free of rent from us. (Sept. 15, 1878, cited in Oetgen 1976a, 15; see Peterman 1982, 204)

This vignette stresses the naïveté of European models that the German Benedictines employed in dealing with a complex black religious system as well as their commitment to Catholic education. Yet Catholicism was marked by blacks as a white man's religion, to be rejected as a badge of slavery.

In contrast to the newly arrived Congregationalists and the struggling Catholic missions, the First African Baptist Church proudly grew during Reconstruction and early afterward to celebrate its centennial in 1888, already claiming to be the oldest independent black Baptist church in North America (Love 1888; Simms 1888). As a black congregation struggling under slavery, the church had become conscious of its leadership for the entire black population. Despite the powerful Episcopalian elite and new impetus from northern churchmen, no other congregations could claim the status that this congregation and its rival, Bryan Baptist, disputed. Its vision of leadership and destiny pervaded the centennial narratives, which reviewed the nature of church and community as well as the intervention of ministers and deacons in public life.

From its first pages, Reverend E. E. Love's centennial history focused on the power of the black presence in urban life and religion. Introductory comments by S. A. McNeal, secretary of the state Baptist convention, linked divine intervention with the struggle of blacks to break through into public written history (in Love 1888, 2). Another presenter elaborated:

The negro occupies a peculiar place in the drama of historical life. For the past three centuries, his story has been a record of trials, tribulations and disappointments, only flecked here and there by a few deeds of individual daring and heroism. Whether in the domain of story or song; whether in the arena of battle or the forum of eloquence, the writers of the past have not accorded to their black brother the dignity of an historical character. . . .

> The history of the past makes it reasonable to conclude that
> whether in general or specific history, an impartial record of the life
> and achievements of the negro will not be written until it is written by
> men of his own race. (Wright, in Love 1888, 12)

Speakers presented black historiography as a stark yet independent challenge to American society. Rather than silence, it must become a record of struggle to be told and retold by members of the race in contrast to the white suppression of black heroes, events, and memory. A dominated group recreated its identity out of their resistance to domination.

Rev. Love's narrative posed black pride against the white manipulation of the public historical record as circumstances of his era. In discussing the 1833 division of the congregation, for example, he noted, "Let us see, as we go along, if it was dissolved. Even in those terrible days of slavery, everything our white brethren considered as being so was not necessarily so" (10). At another point, Love highlighted visions of the slave congregation in relation to a white master by referring to them as "his slaves, but God's freedmen" (39). Throughout, Love created a narrative that explored the black experience in terms of historical pride and contemporary lessons. He extended this into his secular work as a prominent member of the Republican party and contributor to the new black newspaper, the *Savannah Tribune*. On Emancipation Day (January 1), 1888, Love stirred the black population of the city who had gathered for their major political holiday:

> Slavery was a system of inhuman hardships, wounds, bruises, cowhides, bullwhips and patrols, but finally the mighty God said to the raging billows of slavery, thus far and thou shalt go no further and there was a calm on this disturbed sea . . . yet those who opposed the birth of liberty, would continue to throw some hindrances. (Cited in Perdue 1973, 101-2)

Love's attitude was shared by his fellow Republican—yet rival historian—Rev. James Simms of First Bryan Baptist Church. Simms served as a state legislator as well as a delegate to the Republican national convention when this party became the patron of Reconstruction in Georgia. He had been a member of First African and seems to have collaborated in Love's history. In 1888, however, he published a counter-history to substantiate the primacy of Bryan Baptist as the true heir of Leile and Bryan. Simms's narrative, like Love's, relies on dramatic depictions of the sufferings of the church in slavery that underlie its historic and even political mission. He synthesized divine will with situational detail, as in this depiction of the whipping of Pastor Bryan:

> Frequent, then, became the whipping of individual members by the patrol on the plea of not having proper tickets-of-leave, which finally culminated in the arrest and punishment of a large part of the members; but Rev. Andrew Bryan, their pastor, and his brother, Sampson Bryan, one of their first deacons, were inhumanly cut, and their backs were so lacerated that their blood ran down to the earth, as they, with uplifted hands, cried unto the Lord; and this first negro Baptist pastor, while under this torture, declared to his persecutors "that he rejoiced not only to be whipped, but would freely suffer death for the cause of plotting insurrection." (21)

Simms teased out layers of significance, recalling the complex layering of antebellum religion. He depicted the incident through parallels to a New Testament church as a body of the saved persecuted by those around them. Simms made this reference explicit by a passage from the first epistle of Peter "their faith was put to a severe test . . . [that] though it be tried with fire it might be found unto praise and honour and glory at the appearing of Jesus Christ" (1 Pet. 1:7; Simms 1888, 21). He also reminded his audience of the suffering of blacks under the system that had been ended a quarter of a century before and how this was linked to faith in God. At a Republican political meeting, Simms declared that the "negro owed his deliverance to God and to no one else" (cited in Perdue 1973, 42). Yet his activist strain moved beyond faith, as he celebrated Bryan's defiance and spoke of plotting insurrection. For Simms, like Love, God was an active part of black history, yet God called upon blacks to act as well, through their strength of will, their votes, or their maintenance of historical consciousness.

A third major black leader passing through Savannah was Henry McNeal Turner, bishop of the African Methodist Episcopal Church and pastor of Saint Philip's. Turner became known for his promotion of a separatist black pride including African colonization, which achieved a limited impact in the city despite local opposition (Turner 1971; Perdue 1973).

In contrast to these black evangelicals, black Episcopalians remained attached to the white church and to white society. The congregation included active leaders of the Reconstruction-era black middle and upper

classes, who occupied positions as politicians, journalists, customs officers, merchants, and publishers. The color divisions of the slave community continued to mark class and network differences among free blacks,
raising a controversy around the Episcopal parishes. The Reverend
Charles Hoskins, historian and rector of Saint Matthew's Parish, records
such criticisms:

> The Reverend J. Robert Love's stay at St. Stephen's lasted eight
> months. Roi Ottley claims that this heavyset, jet black West Indian was
> simply too much for the 'high yellow' congregation to stomach. . . . It
> is true that apart from three exceptions, the majority of the clergy who
> ministered at St. Stephen's were decidedly not 'high yellow' and the
> three 'high yellow ones' served for relatively short periods. (1983, 20)

Hoskins dismisses these claims: "This myth of St. Stephen's being 'ob-
sessed by color' persists. What is true and can be demonstrated is that
St. Stephen's was a church of strivers, of people who put to good use all
the advantages available to them as Black Episcopalians well nigh the
leaders of Savannah during the Reconstruction period" (20). Robert Perdue, in his history of black life in postbellum Savannah, disagrees. "Mulattoes attended St. Stephen's Episcopal church where J. S. Atwell, Negro, and William Morris were the rectors. Negroes of a darker hue went
to St. Augustine, where Reverend Robert Love, a 'full-blooded African'
was the rector" (1973, 90). He adds that "open conflict came in 1872
when St. Stephen's near-white vestrymen sought to exclude all of the
black Negroes and convert the congregation to an all mulatto group"
(1973, 90).[6] To the present day, charges of favoring light-skinned blacks
may be used as a symbolic charge of class and caste against any black
upper-class group, whether Episcopalian, Congregationalist, or Catholic,
whatever the phenotypes of the congregation (Berzon 1978; Williamson
1980, 1984).

Besides missionaries and spokesmen, urban blacks also joined
smaller churches. Splinter groups from the Baptist churches and rural
meetings in simple wooden buildings served blacks who were less educated or less prominent than members of the major, downtown congregations. The church became a place of devotion, meeting and socializing, education, and the exchange of information. Some of these churches
have disappeared while others have grown into now-historic congregations, incorporated into the city's expansion over a century.

Moreover, other blacks lacked any religious affiliation. Yet even secular actions could carry a prophetic indictment, as the *Richmond Planet* noted in 1895 "All of the hog, sheep, cow and chicken stealing by the dishonest members of [our] race since the world began will not begin to equal one hundredth part of the amount of money which has been stolen by members of the white race, who lay claim to all of the intelligence, religion and learning" (cited in Ayers 1984, 228).

In general, however, the protagonism of churches in black life in this first period of freedom arose from those who constituted elite congregations, whether established and autonomous, whether linked to white churches or emergent denominations with access to education. Divisions of creed thus reflect divisions of relationship to white hegemony and may also have drawn on divisions of class and color within the free community. While ex-slaves were more free to choose, they were constrained by social values as well as belief. The power and assertions of all these churches, however, would be transformed by the resurgence of strong white control and the suppression of newly gained black political and economic rights. Here, older churches would once again adapt while black Savannahians would explore new religious options.

RELIGIONS OF PRIDE AND RELIGIONS OF DESPAIR

After Emancipation, Georgia had reentered the Union in 1868, only to be expelled in 1869 for failing to ratify the Fifteenth Amendment. It was finally readmitted in 1870, and power relations of black and white began to shift—despite the proud endurance of black institutions through the 1880s. Although blacks built new institutions and world views through their churches, white Democrats worked steadily to eliminate the gains of the black population. By the end of the century, as elsewhere in the South, blacks were disfranchised, denied rights, and increasingly segregated:

> To be sure, racism was a consistent feature of race relations in Savannah both before and after 1875, but the racism of the nineties was harsher, more rigid, and more degrading. . . . The Jim Crow laws of the 1890s and the disenfranchising legislation of that decade dimmed the bright hopes with which blacks had begun the last third of the nineteenth century. (Perdue 1973, 25)

44

By the late nineteenth century, white Savannah had reestablished its earlier hegemony, as Jim Crow restrictions eclipsed black political opportunities. Economic growth fueled urban expansion when "in the 1880s, the Cotton Exchange building made Savannah the Wall Street of the South, as a million bales were shipped all over the world, more than twice any pre-war level" (Sieg 1985, 75). Yet this growth encompassed active discrimination against nonestablished groups, including both blacks and non-natives.

In the early twentieth century, political and economic changes continued to shape black urban life. When cotton initially remained a strong trading base in the early 1900s, civic pride burst forth in a set of histories and celebrations for the white community and the physical expansion of the city southward, at the cost of the destruction of previously rural black settlements (Blassingame 1973a; Dittmer 1977). The collapse of cotton due to international competition, regional boll weevil infestation, and black rural emigration hit the city hard. This was followed by problems in naval stores—turpentine and other derivatives from local agriculture—which also had provided an important income for Savannah commerce. The city sought new industries that included the development of outlying areas such as Port Wentworth and the attraction of new groups like the Cajun Catholics who came to work and live at the Savannah Sugar Refinery. In the 1930s, Union Camp became a major, if controversial, employer (Fallows 1971). Meanwhile, Savannah lost ground to Atlanta as a commercial center.

The redevelopment of segregation as both practice and ideological strategy was at first slow, even piecemeal. Blacks resisted any loss of power in 1872 when a black strike kept city transportation integrated; as late as 1902, coalitions of blacks and whites maintained this arrangement. Yet by 1906, despite an arduous boycott, streetcars became segregated (Henri 1975, 15; Dittmer 1977, 17-18). Neighborhoods became increasingly divided as white immigrants gained status and forged concord with native whites, leaving behind marginal integrated zones (Work 1904). Still, blacks held onto some power in the Republican party until that foothold crumbled entirely in the 1920s. Savannah State continued to be an intellectual center, and various businesses served increasingly segregated clienteles. Yet the collapse of the local naval stores industries after World War I, the failure of the Wage-Earners Bank (the largest black-owned financial institution in the city), and the Depression under-

45

cut black action, decade by decade. Thus, "during the first few decades of the twentieth century, segregation in Georgia reached a new plateau [as] the color line gave way to a color wall, thick, high, almost impenetrable" (Dittmer 1977, 21).

In twentieth-century crises, racial and religious prejudice ran high. Ku Klux Klan activity increased in Atlanta and Savannah, and an agreement that had allowed Catholics in Savannah to use public schools dissolved. Black and white resistance to such impositions nonetheless continued. Savannah's Bishop Benjamin J. Keiley (1900-1922) at times spoke out against prejudice and lynching. By 1919, white Catholic laymen from around the state also had founded a newspaper and an association to combat prejudice (Cashin 1962). This group grew under Keiley's successors, Michael Keyes (1922-35) and Gerald O'Hara (1936-49).

As the twentieth century increased the economic, political, social, and cultural impact of segregation in Savannah, blacks sought new responses within the religious frameworks that interpreted the world as well as secular reactions that acted more directly on the society around them. Among religious groups, responses encompassed ideological shifts as well as programmatic developments. Migration also became an important black response to racism throughout the South in this period. Boll weevils in the cotton fields and the lack of opportunity in tenant farming and low-wage urban jobs, the threat of lynching, and the general degradation of the status of blacks by southern whites all forced blacks to leave the South and look for opportunity elsewhere "According to various contemporaneous estimates, between 1890 and 1910 around 200,000 black Southerners fled to the North; and between 1910 and 1920 another 300,000 to 1,000,000 followed . . ." (Henri 1975, 51; see Johnson and Campbell 1981; Harris 1982; Marks 1989; Trotter 1991). The baptismal records of black Catholic parishes in Savannah in this period, despite other factors that favored growth, include consistent notations of families "moved north." Ignatius Lissner, founder of the Society of African Missions (SMA) in Georgia, noted in an undated memo, probably from the 1930s, that missionaries faced problems with black migrants who "owing little or nothing, they move to larger and more industrial cities in search of more lucrative employment. This tendency has seriously effected ours, and in fact, all southern missions, which year after year lose several members to colored congregations in Chicago, New York, Detroit, etc., etc." (SMA File, Savannah Diocesan Archives). Louis B. Pastorelli, head of the Josephites who preached to blacks across the South, concurred in a 1918 letter to Keiley "Every year we lose members to the North. Last year over a hundred migrated, and these the best educated." (Keiley Files, Savannah Diocesan Archives).

Knowledge of opportunities for work and schools, family members who had established themselves in northern jobs, and the poverty of Savannah all figured in narratives of blacks whom I knew in the city who had chosen to sojourn in the North. Pie Chisholm, who worked as a domestic there in the 1930s, summed it up "They used to say you can go to New York and Harlem full of nothin' but Savannah people." Another woman, now deceased, who migrated to New York in 1927, recalled how family and church connections aided her:

All my sisters went up there and we had always been together so I
went up. I arrived May 23; Uncle Paul came up in September. He
asked if I had seen Mother Theodore [superior of the Handmaids of
the Most Pure Heart of Mary, a black order of nuns founded in Savan-
nah] I didn't know where she was but she was right around the corner
Lennox and 131. St. Benedict's nursery. I didn't believe it so I went to
church and asked for Mother Theodore, who was so excited she
threw her arms about me and kissed me. . . . I took a job with the
sisters and put the children in the nursery.

By 1917 black Savannah leaders complained of the drain of migration on churches, banks, insurance companies, and professional life (Dittmer 1977, 190-91). Some migrants moved permanently; others stayed on for decades, raising families in the North and maintaining only distant ties to Savannah. Still others found life less gratifying and returned home. Meanwhile, the black immigration from rural Georgia, South Carolina, and the nearby Sea Islands renewed the city's population. Reunions and funerals still link many Savannah blacks to Beaufort, Bamberg, Hilton Head, Hardeeville, and Daufuskie. In this demographic ferment in Savannah, as in the rest of the South, new religious dimensions took root, while changing power relations transformed the existing religious options of the city.

Rev. Charles Hoskins, for example, notes the shifts of the elite black Episcopalians over half a century:

During Reconstruction, black Episcopalians were well-nigh the leaders
of black Savannah. The rise of "Jim Crow" and the expulsion of blacks
from the political life of Georgia greatly diminished the influence of

black Episcopalians in Savannah. John H. Deveaux, the most distinguished black Episcopalian in Savannah's history, was the last of the
politically active black Episcopalians. The period of the 1920s was
perhaps the most progressive era for black Episcopalians. . . . Blacks
in Savannah never recovered from the crash of 1929. By that time
they had succeeded, to some extent, in creating a parallel city—black
Savannah. From the 1920s on blacks were unable to protect themselves from the debilitating effects of racism, inferior schools, and very
limited economic opportunity. They have had, as their fathers of old,
"to make bricks out of straw." (Hoskins 1983, 67-68).[7]

Economics, politics, social status, and religious congregation were all involved in the rise and decline of the Episcopalian church. The decrease
of political and economic power in this group coincided with a national
decline in the power and prestige of mulatto elites (Williamson 1980,
1984). Episcopalians, despite continuing social prestige, have been less
significant thereafter in black political revindications.

The venerable First African Baptist church weathered the storm more
successfully as a social unit while undergoing ideological adjustments.
The 1925 history of the church,[8] in contrast to the 1888 volume, was
permeated by biblical motifs centered on the life of Jesus and the apostolic church. A positive view of the cumulative development of a black
struggle disappeared, replaced by a reliance on otherworldly salvation.
This evangelistic frame was then structured chronologically according to
the succession of pastors, eclipsing shared public markers of secular history like the Civil War or World War I, with repeated emphasis on divine
intervention in the call of the ministry. Thus the story became true,
whole, structured, and meaningful: "The First African Baptist Church is
verily a child of divine providence. A simple narrative of its origin, preservation, and progress, devoid of any rhetoric to embellish it or fabrica-
tion to bolster it, is a story more marvelous than fiction and more grip-
ping than romance" (Thomas 1925, 9-10).

The narrative itself shows significant differences from the earlier ver-
sions by Love and Simms. Structure and meaning were interwoven in an
updating of biblical narrative. Providence replaced human action,
biblicism replaced history, mystery replaced science:

God is mysterious, and his providences unfathomable. In the ordinary
affairs of men and nations, we daily scan His handiwork and think His
great thoughts after Him, feeling that we easily follow their logical se-

quences and accurately interpret the reasons for various succeeding events. But now and then, as from out of depths, He chooses an Abraham, or calls a Moses, or prompts a Columbus, or inspires an Edison or a Marconi, or a Carver; and inaugurates new orders, displays new worlds, and reveals new forces that startle our reason and frustrate our logic. And for the whence or the wherefore of either the man or his works, we have no answer but God. (Thomas 1925, 9)

Thomas's attitude toward history also changed from that of his predecessors. He defended the historiography of black churches in its impoverishment of sources, coming near to comparing it with the incomplete histories of "cultured white churches." Yet Thomas transformed his narrative into a pageant of divine intervention, a mark of favor rather than a lesson, a miracle rather than the proud black actions that dominated the 1888 texts "Through them, we are blessed with the story of a movement which, considering its mysterious background and the peculiar circumstances in which it developed reveals a miracle so astounding as to excite our continued admiration and amazement. 'What wonders hath God wrought!'" (Thomas 1925, 12-13).

The cadences, allusions, repetition, and ideas of Thomas's text recall the Bible (see Job 38-41; Psalms 90, 91). The text also focused on the prophetic figure, the Messianic leader who will lead the people out of darkness, an adaptation of Christ and Moses already used in slave days and now revived for another time of oppression. George Leile first appeared as such a figure (10-12), to be followed in apostolic succession drawing on Luke and Acts (Thomas 1925, 33-35; see Luke 24; Acts 2:4 and 9:2-22). Later figures were ennobled as befits actors in such a pageant, in sharp contrast to the critical portraits by Love and Simms. Love had decried Rev. George Gibbons, who served the church from 1878 to 1884, as a leader isolated from his people by his affiliation to whites "He had been so confined at home with the affairs of the old white people who raised him that he knew next to nothing of what was going on about negroes in everyday life" (Love 1888, 83). Thomas, by contrast, lauded Gibbons's unification of the church while labeling him "a model Christian of high moral tone and fine intellect" (1925, 84). Leaders had to be inspired to structure the history of the church.

Thomas concentrated on the first century of the church, rather than bringing his history into contemporary lessons as his predecessors had done. His theological history was one of mission, inspired or guided. The New Testament, mediated by sermons or songs, provided constant examples. Thus history became texts into which the congregation might look toward divine intervention. Thomas's narrative embodied a clearly Baptist sense of the immediacy of God, of mission, of call, while spurning public circumstances such as war, politics, or social change. Amidst the losses of the early twentieth century, Thomas turned toward a transcendent explanation of the past, just as slaves had once turned to Heaven for meaning in this world. In doing so, however, Thomas took the moral leadership of First African Baptist into a weaker and more conciliatory stance.

Despite migration, Catholicism made important gains in this period as the Franciscan Sisters of the Immaculate Conception and the Society of African Missions of Lyons reinaugurated major development, building schools in black neighborhoods as the foundations for stable parishes. The *Savannah Tribune* lauded Catholic biracialism and even sympathetic views from a white priest at Saint Benedict's Choir banquet in 1907 "Rev. Father O'Sullivan responded to the toast 'Jim Crow' and in his very eloquent way denounced the action of the City Council, thereby compelling our people to stay off rather than be humiliated by riding on street cars" (Dec. 19, 1907). Yet if Catholics were recognized as an integrating and sympathetic presence, they were still a white one until black congregations became stable in the 1920s and 1930s. In the 1930s, in fact, the *Yearbook of Colored Savannah* noted that "for many years Savannah has been blessed in having schools for Negroes operated by the Great Catholic Church which includes in its curriculum that vital element— religious education" (Smalls 1933-34, 23). While black *parishes* outnumbered white in the 1880s and again in the 1910s, black membership did not, and white suburban parishes would again eclipse black growth in later decades.

Other religious responses to the problems of the early twentieth century spurned established congregations for otherworldly sanctification or such charismatic figures as Father Divine and Daddy Grace. Father Divine emerged from poor, rural southern origins; after wandering the East Coast, he began to build an interracial kingdom in the Northeast, promoting political, economic, and social reform through a new religion, of which he himself was divinity (Frazier 1963, 53-66; Weisbrot 1983). WPA researchers claimed that Divine was originally George Baker, who was born in Savannah and began his ministry there as "The Son of Righteousness" in the 1890s; Weisbrot, Divine's modern biographer, calls the documentation unclear.

Drums and Shadows recorded a meeting of fifty of Father Divine's followers in Savannah's Old Fort that began with doctrinal themes, including surrender of personal identity, in return for which one member stated that Father Divine had given him a new and sanctified life and the power to raise his wife from the dead. Later, the evening gave way to more enthusiastic ritual:

> More of the devotees join in chanting and in the spirited singing of hymns. Demonstrations become more and more violent. Several of the congregation, caught in the throes of a powerful religious intoxication, begin to dance and sway with abandonment. Others in the group encourage the dancers with a rhythmic clapping of the hands and stamping of feet.
>
> On and on the dancers whirl while the piano pounds out its accompaniment; above the din rises the wailed repetition version of an improvised hymn. The participants in the dance seem oblivious to everything except the series of contortions which they are indulging. (Georgia Writers' Project 1940, 9-11)

This vignette, like other parts of WPA discussion, suffers from an exotic dramatization of the *other* on the part of white observers. Yet the details are not out of character for modern sanctified services. Father Divine's local influence, however, was limited and transitory; "they been through tellin' about him years ago."

Bishop C. R. "Sweet Daddy" Grace was less well known as a national figure, although he left an enduring legacy in Savannah. Grace was an Azorean immigrant who led a rich public lifestyle in which his predominantly black followers in the United House of Prayer for All People vicariously shared. The unrestrained services of his meetings, the lavishness of the congregation's adoration of their leader, and the spectacular annual meetings and parade of Daddy Grace and his followers from around the nation are deeply ingrained in black Savannah folklore. Even among those Catholics who profess little interest in other churches, almost everyone has a "Daddy Grace" story.

Drums and Shadows described a sanctuary in middle-class Brownville, across town from Father Divine, where Grace's followers still have an elaborate church:

> Regular members and visitors from outlying districts crowd the lumber benches of the House of Prayer. The air is tense with excitement.
> Above the confusion can be heard the strident but rhythmic beating of

51

drums. Bright splashes of color are given by the crepe paper decorations and the vividly contrasting costumes of members of the church
organization. . . .

The procession continues to the front of the church itself where,
with much ceremony, the Bishop seats himself upon a lofty throne set
far back on the spacious platform. The Queen stands at the Bishop's
right, facing the congregation. The music blares forth with renewed
intensity and the entire multitude, led by the uniformed guards, passes
in single file before the throne. As members approach the Bishop,
they pledge themselves to him by removing their hats and bowing
low. In the midst of all this commotion "Daddy" sits, a remote, detached figure, his downcast eyes indicating that he is scarcely aware of
this carefully planned reception. (Georgia Writers' Project 1940,
46-51)[9]

At Bishop Grace's death in 1960, the *Savannah Morning News Magazine*
reminiscences about the congregation's parade again betray exuberant
exoticism. "With Daddy riding regally in one of his Cadillacs, preceded
by brass bands and surrounded by his handmaidens in long bright
gowns. Flowing robes, a mass of grey curly hair, long claw-like
fingernails and an oddly painted mustache gave Grace the appearance
of a potentate from a strange land" (Jan. 17, 1960, 4).

Sanctified churches like the House of Prayer differed from many
older churches in their enthusiastic worship and music as well as their
devotion to an immanent savior. These denominations also imposed difference in belief and everyday action. As one member recalled, "It was a
difference in the life living of it. Certain things you did in the Baptist
church, the Sanctified church didn't allow it. Smoking. Drinking. And
what not, they didn't call for that" (Haygood in Teller 1973, 148).

Historians and theologians have underlined the widespread appeal
of enthusiastic and reformist cults to the disfranchised, including a potential for integration of new migrants to the city (Synan 1971, 165-84).
Savannah observers also remember details that may reflect the continuing differentiation of classes among blacks and the use of religions as
emblems of class mobility. Thus the "Baptist church had floors and what
not, more costly benches." (Haygood in Teller 1973, 149). Yet financial
gain was also directly part of the philosophy of the House of Prayer, as
were the displays of wealth of its leader. Grace's United House of Prayer
continues in Savannah despite schisms over succession. The red, white,
and blue-bedecked house of Grace dazzles passersby on Victory Drive,

and the famous parade has been revived once again. Yet the House of Prayer lacks the commanding presence among Holiness churches that it once had, due to the proliferation and expansion of tiny street-front churches like that in which Daddy Grace had his beginnings.

The emergence of Father Divine and Daddy Grace, along with smaller Pentecostal, holiness, sanctified, or messianic congregations, vastly amplified the range of black religious responses in a time of troubles. Tradition, class, color, and education could guide blacks in their choice of religious responses, although no one was so inspired to cross the boundaries of law and custom that divided black and white churches. Even among established churches, by the 1920s, arguments that once had used the church as the basis for politics shifted again to spiritual deliverance. These ideas would be tested again in decades of renewal and the fight for civil rights, in which churches recovered their protagonism.

THE CIVIL RIGHTS ERA

The quest for human rights, individual and collective, had built upon the foundations of religious community and leadership since slavery days. The vitality of black Savannah leadership in the Reconstruction period, the strike against streetcar segregation, and continued resistance demonstrated the continuing role of religious leadership in this struggle even as black power declined. It was with considerable irony that the writer of a 1933 Savannah yearbook declared, "Last but not least, Savannah Negroes do not worry about 'social equality.' These Negroes are too busy trying to acquire those things that are so necessary in the building of a race" (Smalls 1933-34, 51). Yet when the civil rights movement gained new impetus with national changes after World War II amidst a wider black experience and communication of freedom and social change, religious organizations again constituted frameworks to confront the contradictions of civil society.

World War II also marked new opportunities for blacks who soon explored the opportunities of home-ownership in new, segregated suburbs such as Liberty City and Cloverdale. Yet black postwar development did not parallel white shifts in status, residence, or historical consciousness. In the 1950s, blacks were expelled from decayed but historic buildings undergoing gentrification, and blacks continue to lack access to the white downtown.

At the same time, signs of new coexistence among white ethnics and evangelical denominations had altered ethnic Catholic participation in Savannah life. This white ethnic success underscores the barriers against which blacks still struggled. The Blessed Sacrament parish, founded in 1920, signaled Catholic expansion into new and wealthier suburbs of the city, while the political machine run by John Bouhan had established a parity for the Irish Americans in city government. While the Depression added to Savannah's economic problems, World War II renewed the city with the construction of nearby Fort Stewart and the Army Air Corps base, as well as shipbuilding. According to a modern historian, "the war turned Savannah from a sleepy, traditional, backward-looking town on a muddy river into a full-fledged twentieth-century American city" (Sieg 1985, 107).

The movement of white Catholics mirrored general movement among whites in these decades, as suburban congregations replaced older, downtown foundations. Children and grandchildren moved away from the poor neighborhoods, made up of a mixture of immigrants and blacks, in which the Irish had first settled. Saint Michael's on Tybee Island, a nearby resort spot, emerged as a parish. Our Lady of Lourdes Parish, serving the Cajuns of Port Wentworth, was founded in 1940. Nativity of Our Lord Parish, serving the traditional fishing village of Thunderbolt and nearby suburban islands, was founded in 1943. Alongside Blessed Sacrament, these formed a ring of new parishes around the historic core. The Queen of Apostles Motor Chapel took Catholicism into rural areas, its very mobility indicating the lack of missionary roots in whites or blacks there. Meanwhile, Saint Patrick's, the second oldest parish in the city, was closed after hurricane damage in 1940. Its families already had drifted southward to other white and suburban parishes, while its neighborhood had shifted from Catholic immigrants to industrial uses and housing projects. The decay of the downtown residential areas was only stopped by massive efforts, begun in the 1950s, to preserve the historic core with an extensive preservation district.

In Savannah, as in other areas of the South, questions about the status quo were voiced by black leaders in the 1940s and 1950s, despite the "passiveness" experienced by many residents. Mass movements for civil rights erupted in Savannah in 1960, as blacks attempted to integrate local restaurants and downtown businesses that had long been closed to them. For the next three years, local leaders such as W. W. Law, president of the Savannah NAACP, and national figures, such as Rev. Hosea

Williams, led a multifaceted attack on segregation in businesses, schools, libraries, government, and churches (Raines 1977, 435-45; Baldwin 1983). Perhaps the most dramatic assertion of black rights in this period was the eighteen-month boycott of downtown businesses that finally forced white merchants into concessions in hiring and service (*SMN* June 10, 1961). Other initiatives integrated the library (*Atlanta Constitution* Oct. 2, 1959; *SMN* Jan. 7, 1961); the beaches (*SMN* Aug. 8 and 31, 1960, oral narrative accounts); movie houses, if only temporarily (*SMN* June 4, 5, 1963); and hospitals (*Savannah Herald* Feb. 20, 1965; *SMN* May 5, 1965). In all cases, parallel but unequal opportunities had existed for blacks, who now demanded access to all facilities. Schools became the arena of longest controversy, in action and suits that continued until the late 1960s, with functional integration a continuing concern today at all levels.

Figure 4. The marginal presence of Catholics in the rural South: Queen of Apostles Chapel, the mobile Catholic chapel for rural Georgia. Photograph courtesy of the Georgia Historical Society, Cordray-Foltz Collection.

Black churches took on many roles during this decade of change. Ministers such as the Reverend Scott Snell and Reverend Gilbert joined NAACP and civic leaders in peaceful initiatives while young people provided bodies and enthusiasm. Churches became centers for mobilization, information, and development of consciousness, as they had across the South. A wide variety of major black congregations hosted the mass meetings that sustained the boycott. First African Baptist Church, with its large hall, was a frequent site, joined by Saint James AME, Bethlehem Baptist, Second Baptist, Bryan Baptist, Connor's Temple Baptist, and Saint Philip's AME. As NAACP leader and historian W. W. Law recalled, these mass meetings "informed them what was needed and what was expected for the next seven days; mass meetings became the real focus for voter registration, better school conditions, and myriad other things."

The seventh mass meeting, on May 1, 1960, was held at Pius X High School, the black Catholic high school. This meeting's program illustrates the mixture of civil religion and activism that recurred in nearly all the meetings. News commentaries reflected the perceived ambivalence of Catholicism in black Savannah, even though Catholics were the only predominantly white denomination to sponsor such a meeting:

> As the more than 2500 persons poured into this Catholic high school auditorium, there was no concern about creed. Baptists, Presbyterians, Methodists, Episcopalians, Congregationalists, and Catholics gathered for the 7th consecutive Sunday evening to consider ways and means to help America to become the great Democracy that she professes to be by extending first class citizenship and equal rights to Negro citizens. . . .
>
> Mrs. Annie K. Jordan, chairman of the membership committee of the NAACP served as the presiding officer. The singing of the majestic "Lift Every Voice and Sing" set the tone of the meeting. As the Rev. Dennis J. Begley [SMA from Saint Anthony's] gave the invocation, one could not refrain from thinking about the sincerity of the Catholic church in race relations. In the remarks of Rev. Father Raymond Bane [SMA], he was compelled to recall the recent election of a Negro to the College of Cardinals and the Pope's dedicated act of washing the feet of a negro student studying for the priesthood last Easter. . . . (*ST* May 7, 1960)

The Saint Pius choir contributed hymns. The main speaker was Dr. Carl Jordan, a prominent black physician and member of Saint Mary's, while Rev. Martin of Townsley Chapel AME led the appeal for funds. The description holds real questions, though, about what is meant by "one cannot refrain from thinking about the sincerity" of Catholics. And why did Bane, an SMA missionary, insist on African symbols as well as symbols of Catholic exclusivity, like the pope, within a mass meeting?

Other denominations faced challenges by black students who tried to enter all-white congregations for Sunday worship. Reactions varied widely. In 1960, Christ Church Episcopal and Tabernacle Baptist received black students openly, while several churches, including Ascension Lutheran and Independent Presbyterian, invited them to sit in the balcony, a former badge of inequality in theaters or churches. Other churches turned blacks away, telling them in the case of Saint John's Episcopal church that "the congregation would not welcome them." This congregation and its pastor eventually rebelled against the diocese over the issue of integration and many left the church organization to become an independent church. At Wesley Monumental Methodist, blacks "were told by Judge Geo. E. Olivier that they would not enjoy the services and they were directed to an excellent Negro church three or four blocks down the street" (ST Aug. 27, 1960). As the citation from Wesley Methodist suggests, whites seemed to be oblivious to the religious and civil issues involved. Nearly three decades later, I interviewed a vestryman at Saint John's who had denied blacks entrance, and he recalled that he had quizzed them on their catechism and discovered that they were not Episcopalian. Thus, he felt justified in turning them away.

Savannah blacks turned Christianity as well as the Constitution against the practices of the white community. W. W. Law declared that "the Sabbath became a day of shame for the churches that closed their doors to the Negroes. . . . Christ's ministry never conveyed the impression that to worship Christ is to create a disturbance" (ST Aug. 27, 1960). Nonetheless, these activities sometimes led to a counter-polarization in churches that whites had previously attended either as regular members or visitors. The Congregationalist church, for example, faced dwindling white membership after the 1960s, becoming all black in the 1980s. Other churches are still identified as militant, likely "to pit blacks against whites."

Civil rights agitation was not the product of a unified community so much as one moving toward goals in inchoate coalitions. Local and national leadership debated goals and recognition. Hidden class issues also arose. A domestic, for example, recalled her bitterness about Rev. Williams's call for a strike against white employers, which she felt misunderstood both her relationship with them and her need to earn a living. Nor were Christian churches the only focus of action. Blacks also explored new religious and political options, such as the Nation of Islam. The conversion of one black Catholic emphasized the disappointments he felt that his church would not address questions ranging from sex to racism, even though it educated him to think. In Islam, he found an answer "Muslims are the epitome of optimism. If God wants us to get $1,000,000, we will." Yet he reflected as well, "If nothing had pushed me away from Catholicism, I'd still be there."

Finally, still other blacks looked for identity outside traditional ecclesiastical formats of black identity, whether white-imposed or black-created. Students from regional black colleges in particular recalled the 1960s and 1970s as an era of search that looked to Africa and other sources (Teller 1973, 227-30; R. Brown interviewed by Don Moore, Moore 1985). A minister, who was then in college, later summed up the challenges "Black folks were pro-African just like whites were anti-Vietnam. Blacks stopped going to church."

Catholic development presents an interesting counterpoint to the growth and convulsions of Savannah society, black and white, in the 1950s and 1960s. Atlanta separated as a diocese in 1956, later becoming an archdiocese and metropolitan see for the region as sunbelt growth overtook traditional seats of power. Increasing and successful participation in Savannah life was evident in both white and black parishes—both Saint Benedict's (1949) and Saint Anthony's (1952) constructed new churches in these decades. Saint Anne's parish began as a mission in the city of Richmond Hills, near Savannah, while Saint James's parish was founded in southern Chatham County in 1956. Saint Pius X High School, which served the black Catholic community, was opened in the 1950s. Bishop Thomas McDonough (1957-69) built a minor (high-school level) seminary in 1959 and embarked on intensive recruitment of Irish priests to expand diocesan evangelization in Savannah and rural Georgia.

Moreover, the deliberations and aftermath of the Second Vatican Council (1962-65) fundamentally altered the course of Catholic development worldwide. The council sponsored changes in attitudes toward other churches—in liturgy and authority and in participation—that will be explored in the chapters that follow. It also opened a window to questions and challenges that became increasingly stressful in the late 1960s as disagreements arose over birth control, celibacy, and issues of conscience, causing priests, nuns, and laity to leave or change their roles within the church. For white Catholics, the 1960s became a time of social turmoil, in which Vatican II, civil rights, and other issues expressing American reactions to Vietnam and social change converged. Blacks interpret these events differently, using other crucial landmarks, especially the closing of the black schools in the late 1960s and 1970s.

In summary, as blacks demanded more rights across the South in the 1950s and 1960s, powerful Savannah whites, like many elsewhere in the South, attempted to maintain the status quo. The very rediscovery of history invoked problems; "shocked, fearful and resistant, Savannah leaders held back the tide of change for another decade before learning that integration was more profitable than resistance" (Sieg 1985). Indeed, the "profitability" of integration was only taught painfully in the 1960s by a long-term black boycott of the downtown, by sit-ins, by arrests, and even by riots. In this process, the churches of the black community recreated their dynamic leadership of the first Reconstruction as the second arrived a century later, yet amid more diversity and a wider range of leaders and participants. Diversity seems to be less dependent on color or doctrine than on age, education, and the presence of leaders. Congregations like First African Baptist drew upon their own history for inspiration and identity, overcoming the eclipse of the beginning of the century. Yet they were no longer the sole organizational resource in the quest for rights and identity amid a diverse black population. The NAACP, college groups, social leaders, and political spokesmen from the local area and national organizations converged in this struggle while debating new issues. Racial confrontation thus incorporated a new challenge to define "black" in a complex world.

CONTEMPORARY SAVANNAH RELIGION

Since the 1970s, the continuing dialectic of race, class, religion, and urbanism has intensified amid the continuing transformation of the city. Despite historical revival and tourism in the downtown, for example, residence for whites is again shifting to suburbs while black areas near or in the historic district deteriorate with an influx of drugs and crime. Even with intense black action, social gains from civil rights still have come only slowly to the city, changing and yet tempered by more enduring, if implicit, cultural values. School integration remains an ongoing process, as in the rest of the South, where changing living patterns and white choice constantly threaten a new class-based segregation. Closure of the black Catholic schools between 1968 and 1977, to integrate the entire Catholic school system, also pointed to disparities in voice and power, which I will discuss in later chapters. Gains in mass-media recognition, in the maintenance of black history and tradition, and in economic development for neighborhoods that are both black and poor have come even more slowly.

Again the Catholic church epitomizes these patterns of development not only in a new parish, Saint Frances Cabrini, founded in 1968 near the interstate fringe of the county, but also through changes in the older inner ring of suburban parishes of the 1930s and 1940s. Now, Blessed Sacrament's membership is declining in numbers, although more blacks have entered the school; Nativity has moved its school from the fishing village in which it was formed to suburban islands. While consolidated Catholic schools downtown have predominantly black student bodies, the new schools on the outskirts are almost all white. In 1990, problems in Sacred Heart's physical plant forced the temporary removal of students to the suburban former seminary complex and posed questions for the entire Catholic education system that seem to distill the changing relations of core and periphery in the city.

Religious institutions and belief retain a tremendous impact in contemporary Savannah, where over 250 churches serve the inhabitants. These congregations range from storefront churches with a handful of members to centuries-old fellowships with thousands of participants. Newspapers, both the white-oriented daily and the black weeklies, carry extensive reports of church activities. The local black newspapers de-.vote pages to reports on anniversaries, special events, installations, and departures among ten to fifteen major Protestant churches. The daily newspaper tends to be dominated by white church news. Individual congregations provide shorthand markers of class, interests, and heritage among both blacks and whites, to the point that an individual's lack of affiliation evokes surprise, discomfort, and criticism: one must be *something* in order to have social identity as well as belief.

The largest number of Savannah churches are Baptist, with parallel congregations among blacks and whites united in a single Georgia Association. Episcopalians, Presbyterians, Lutherans, Methodists, and Catholics repeat racial dualism to varying degrees. Some denominations are more exclusively monoracial, including some sanctified and Pentecostal groups. Other divisions have entered this religious mapping of community by location, with its corollaries of historical eminence for downtown churches. Size, ministerial prestige, and the wealth and power of the congregation also distinguish churches and denominations.

Within this system of churches, black congregants make individual and collective choices. Older churches continue their adaptation, building upon tradition while reshaping it. The symbolic dimensions of history and the struggle for freedom are developed in the context of a new respect for such churches; the anniversary celebrations of First African and Bryan Baptist now receive citywide attention. E. E. Love's spirit is present in the former's 1977 tourist flyer, which describes the congregation as "a survivor of the Revolutionary war during the over-awing hand of the hostile British, a growing body of the Reconstruction period and a strong force during the Revolutionary changes of the 1960s for the Black community." The pamphlet concludes that "through the years, the First African Baptist church has rendered service for all people and is a standing monument for the role she has played." Oral traditions mentioned in tours of the church, although not in published material, identify patterns on the oldest pews as African tribal designations stained by slaves. Guides proudly acknowledge the labor of the slaves on their day of rest to build the edifice, linking the modern congregation to historical consciousness, struggle, and self-esteem.

Other churches face problems that stem from their history. An analyst of the Congregationalists saw the problems that emerge from its ambiguous position as a nearly all-black representative of a predominantly white national church (which nonetheless has strong ties to black leadership in the South): "We have not had a rapid rise in membership. Rumors. The rumor to the white people is, 'Are we welcome?' To Black folks, 'Are we welcome in a church which favors light-complected people?' We need to define ourselves." Shades as well as color continue to be problematic within black life.

Churches have been changed by their social context as well. Neighborhoods have shifted as older black and white families have seen their children move to suburbs. Black churches have moved with the destruction of poorer neighborhoods or the gentrification of downtown black zones. Some others, such as Saint John Baptist and Saint Mary's Catholic church, have launched neighborhood stabilization plans to preserve historical black neighborhoods.

Despite twenty years' effort in schools, government, and business, few Savannah churches surpass token integration. Some traditional black churches, including the Catholic parishes, have a handful of white members. Blacks have joined Saint John's Episcopal Church; the formerly white Catholic parishes, especially in the downtown; and other churches. New suburban congregations tend to be proud of their interfaith and interracial commitments. Most churches, however, retain a known racial identification.

Thus, churches ritualize continuing social divisions within black and white Savannah. Elite churches are clearly identifiable. Various informants named Saint Matthew's Episcopalian, Butler Presbyterian, First Congregational, First African and Bryan Baptist, Saint John Baptist, and Catholic parishes among the most prominent and active black churches of the city. These evaluations, however, may include consideration of status among the congregation as well as the force of the leader in urban life. At the other extreme, Savannah's poorer black neighborhoods are full of "these little Baptist churches and Holiness churches that rent a storefront . . . not able to buy churches but rent them." In the black fringe of the urban core, every block has one or more churches, often of this type. They are often ephemeral, built on the charisma of a leader and his family. A minister summed up their careers: "Perfect pastor, perfect church, perfect people become imperfect when that pastor dies."

There may be nevertheless an increased tolerance, especially from the standpoint of changes in Catholic separatism. Thus a highly educated black man, active in Saint Benedict's, observed "We came up thinking they were crazy. But a lot of them are happy. They got something there and some of ours are not so happy." Ecumenical projects are more common among Protestant and Catholic churches or among those which define areas such as the downtown.

The variety of Savannah churches diversifies messages beyond their views of this world and the next. Churches since slave days have been centers for information, contact, organization, and recreation, roles revitalized in Reconstruction and the civil rights era. Veterans of the civil rights movement lament the decay of a social gospel in favor of display and socializing apparent in the voluble groups and expensive, stylish clothes that mark those who assemble at the churches each Sunday. Many are concerned with the appeal of Christian belief to youth and the specters of secularism and materialism. An older male community organizer in Most Pure Heart of Mary, in fact, worried that "Black people really think they've arrived to the point that they are not concerned with history."

Despite this strong and varied palette of religious organization, and its permeation of Savannah life, not all blacks belong to a church. Among adults, someone who dies without any affiliation is still considered by most to be an anomaly. Among youths, however, outreach programs recognize that many adolescents prefer the street to the sanctuary. A leader in Saint Mary's was only one of many who worried that "We gotta do something to keep people from moving away from the Catholic church with problems we never had before, which the Catholic church is not addressing. More are crying out for help. More are consumed by materialism. The church needs to address problems, not put on a band-aid." Although a young preacher lauded the return of 1960s dissidents as they raise their own families, other middle-class blacks lead increasingly secular lives. Generally, blacks still seem to emphasize church more than whites, although Savannah weaves an intensely denominational urban fabric for both. As black social horizons have expanded, however, it is clear that "church," however dominant, is one among many forms of social and ideological networks in which black Savannahians find identity and belief.

For over two hundred years, churches have been central institutions not only of faith expression but also of the entire life of the black community in and around Savannah. Organized in reaction to the oppression of slavery, religion allowed blacks to constitute groups, to interpret the world, and to act on it. As blacks gained freedom, these processes, in contest against the public power of white hegemony, were complicated by increasing differentiations among blacks on the basis of inheritance, education, and wealth. Later cycles of oppression and renovation have tempered these alternatives in relation to each other. Doctrine, community tradition, and leadership constitute further elements in a kaleidoscope meaningful in its every turning.

To understand the range of black religious institutions and expression in the present, we must comprehend its evolution within a dialectic of choice and constraint. Slave religion faced blunt disparities between public and private worship, between accommodation to white institutions and autonomy from them. After Emancipation, blacks created new alternatives as well, which channeled new divergences of class, region, and identification. As older congregations evolved in their constituency, structure, and voice, rural and island migrants to the city and the urban poor turned to other small-scale groups, often emotive, Pentecostal, or personalistic. The city, however, also provided opportunities for secular pleasures as well as denominational choices.

With time, alternate churches have become established, again changing the meaning of religious sectarianism. All these black churches, finally, have developed with an awareness of other creeds and preachers in the city, a self-consciousness of choice that both unites and divides their worship.

Constraints have also evolved. Under slavery, masters could impose legal and physical restraints on religious practice, even though slaves found limited autonomy or responded in secrecy. Later, segregation remained a reality, both of denominations and individual churches, until broached—if not destroyed—in the last two decades. Segregation still might be ambiguous. If it were impossible to join a white congregation, blacks might still constitute a unit of a dominantly white group such as Episcopalians or Roman Catholics.

The religious heritage of early choices also became transgenerational constraints. Individual converts, then, may feel forced to reject old family ways to accept new beliefs. Catholicism, with its reliance on conversion in the black community and its elaborate preparations for membership, thus has challenged an established social fabric. Catholics also have exercised different restraints on membership from those of the evangelicals or holiness traditions, which will be discussed in chapter 7.

This overview of black religious ethnohistory situates those who are black and Catholic within the social and cultural history of the many urban communities that constitute Savannah. Their lives have inherited traditions of black religious expression while they have chosen another tradition, that of Catholicism as a white, immigrant religion in the South. The next chapter will rephrase this history of adaptation and change within a discussion of more enduring cultural categories that also continue to pattern Savannah history, life, and expectations for the future.

2. The Divided City: Black and White as Metaphors and Action

In Christ there is no east or west
In Him no south or north,
But one great family bound by love
Throughout the whole wide earth.

—*Lead Me, Guide Me: The African American Catholic Hymnal*

City life is characterized by a continuous tension among discourses that sustain stereotypes, delimit social groups, and shape the activities of citizens who participate in urban cultures. The complexities of southern urban cultures have taken shape within conflicts where ideological domination is linked to struggles over economic, social, and political power. To understand the formation of black and Catholic communities within the urban setting of Savannah, both as an arena of ideological contradiction and as a process of community creation, we must understand the world within which this formation has taken place over-time. Complementing the more social historical approach of the last chapter, this chapter explores the cultural framework within which categories such as black, white, Catholic, Protestant, male, and female are valued in Savannah, are taken up as identities, or are posed in complex negotiations between achieved and imposed identities.

As the historical review of the previous chapter showed, in Savannah, as in most of the South, the dichotomy of white and black long has provided a key generative metaphor of inequality for all of urban life. "Whites" dominate, even to the extent of establishing the "public" categories of the city, while "black," despite centuries of struggle, has been associated with a dominated group. W. E. B. Du Bois put the problem of race personally yet ironically, at the turn of the century.

> Between me and the other world, there is ever an unasked question; unasked by some through feelings of delicacy; by others through the difficulty of rightly framing it. All, nevertheless, flutter round it. They approach me in a half-hearted way, eye me curiously or compassionately, and then, instead of saying directly How does it feel to be a problem? They say, I know an excellent colored man in my town; or, I fought at Mechanicsville; or, Do not these Southern outrages make your blood boil? At these I smile or am interested, or reduce the boiling point to a simmer, as the occasion requires. To the real questions, How does it feel to be a problem? I seldom answer a word. (1965 [1903], 213)

Even as we examine the historical changes over which blacks and whites have fought, we must recognize the historical presence and cultural meaning of race in the modern South. Perhaps the most difficult intellectual and personal adjustment for me, as an anthropologist working with those who are black and Catholic within my own culture, has been living with the arbitrary yet pervasive nature of these divisions, even as I sought to analyze and to change them.

In order to discuss contradictions that already have been signaled in the history of Savannah's black and Catholic life, I have focused on the pervasive meanings of "black" by treating it among the *marked* categories of city life within the power relations of white-established classifications and black resistance. This is as apparent in the voices of Savannahians, in the way they talk about race, in texts or in institutions. My usage follows that of linguistics, where a marked term is limited or derivative in relation to a more general and more loosely defined major category. Hence, in an example relevant to Savannah, masculine generally remains unmarked in English, inclusive of all human beings, while feminine represents the delimitation of a particular group. To say "Each anthropologist has his own methodology" appears neutral while implying masculinity, while "each anthropologist has her own methodology" suggests to most readers that all anthropologists must be female, despite authors' increasing flexibility in using gendered terms (Silverstein 1985). To say "each anthropologist reflected on her own black experience" underscores the political implications and concealments implicit in the creation of highly marked categories. How, then does the reading "we" bring to what is apparently the "unmarked" or "neutral" phrase come about and what weight does it carry in our actions?

As linguists argue, such a pattern implies no intrinsic social or cultural values. Yet power becomes represented when marked categories are read as abnormal, subordinate or incomplete. Thus power relations are clearly present when the ideological patterning of ideas of race, gender, or class repeatedly contrasts the unmarked social category "white" in Savannah to an interlocking range of marked categories. "White" has been taken as the normal state against which other conditions or groups must be defined, the "Savannah Schools" versus "Savannah Schools, Black" or "Savannah Schools, Catholic" in local archives. In everyday life, classification has transcended the definition of blacks as a group to encompass divisions of rights that have become enshrouded in customs, behavior and common sense as well as statutory discrimination.

Ultimately, the ideology of race becomes a disturbing foundation for the urban social world, its second nature. Citizens may accept this division as the foundation for action, rather than critiquing its formation. Or they may be forced to reject categories to find themselves. Historically, blacks have faced their categorization by others in order to create a positive valuation to it whether through economics, voting, historical awareness or black pride. Thus, a century ago, the Methodist bishop and Georgia State Senator Henry M. Turner called for a new consciousness emergent from the opposition of black and white:

> White is God in this country and black is the devil. White is perfection, greatness, wisdom, industry and all that is high and holy.
> Black is ignorance, degradation, indolence and all that is lowly and vile, and three-fourths of the colored people of the land do nothing day and night but cry: Glory, honor, dominion and greatness to White.
> . . . Neither the Republican nor Democratic party can do for the colored race what they can do for themselves. Respect Black. (Turner [1885] 1971, 71-72)

This chapter focuses on categories, then, as reflections of both white domination and responses by others.[1]

A critical perspective on the racial divisions of urban culture demands analysis of the relations among many categories of southern symbolic thought as exemplified in Savannah life. The meaning of blackness also has been tempered by other marked social categories against which whiteness also can be defined. These include oppositions of whites and non-native whites (foreigners and northerners), and of white Protestant society against "foreign" religions (Catholics and Jews). The local white elites form an unmarked category against "crackers," blue-collar workers or rural whites, while males form an unmarked backdrop for designation of females. The individual provides the ultimate "marked category." Yet even here one notes the differences between someone identified merely by name in the local news and someone defined as "X, a 20-year-old black female from the projects."

The varied relationships among marked categories—between black and Catholic, between black and poor, or between black and female—complicate culture and action in Savannah. A black female, for example, belongs to two marked and historically disfranchised groups, a position that ironically also has contributed to an experience of individual empowerment (Giddings 1984; Hooks 1990). Black and poor constitute marked categories that often have coincided in Savannah's history, since race classifications have justified exploitation as well as enforcement of domination. A symbolic analysis that controls for slow historical change highlights the contradictions that emerge in the attitudes of whites to the black middle and upper classes of the city, and of these black elites toward the black and white poor. Central to this examination, finally, is a preliminary sketch of the intersection of black and Catholic, in which two marked groups have created an anomalous new community.

These questions still constitute only part of the social meaning of urban categories, since they refer to the discourse of the dominator. In each case, blacks and others have subversively delineated the otherwise unlimited category of whiteness, or have redefined their own marked categories through a proud and positive cultural content. Nineteenth-century Catholics, like early evangelicals, could thus reject Episcopalian elites as damned. The subsequent economic and political development of both Catholics and Evangelicals within Savannah life has altered the meaning of categories within cultural systems of representation. The black community has maintained both social and cultural continuities of resistance from slave days to freedom to civil rights. These traditions, too, have intersected with the voluntary formation of religious communities as well as the missionary efforts of European Catholicism.

My dialectic analysis of "white" and "black" begins with an appreciation of the multiple symbolic associations of "black" in Savannah, in contrast to a rather amorphous but powerful whiteness. On this basis, I turn to an analysis of alternate projections of discourse, beginning with those of blacks. The·chapter continues with those who belong to doubly marked categories, such as black and female, and the critical space such categories create. These categories reflect, finally, on the special situation of those who are black and Catholic.

BASIC BLACK: CONSTRUCTION AND DECONSTRUCTION
OF A MARKED CATEGORY

"Black," throughout most of southern history, has implied a simple definition by race and rights, based on descent, phenotype, and perception. Modern Georgia legally defined a person of color within a category of "all Negroes, mulattos and their descendants having any ascertainable trace of either Negro or African, West Indian or Asiatic Indian blood in his or her veins" (Georgia Statute 79-103, in effect in 1958, cited in Dominguez 1986, 270). Corollary practices of social separation established a way of life beyond legal strictures throughout the South. Even after slavery was abolished, a turn-of-the-century Mississippi black observed, "White supremacy . . . was based on oral or traditional discrimination without legal sanction. Negroes accepted these traditions as a way of life and as a method of survival" (McMillen 1989, 10). Classification and practice reinforced each other, while both blacks and whites learned the place of members of the marked category within the system in their childhood. Lillian Smith, an eloquent white critic of the South, reflected on her bittersweet education in the early twentieth century:

> Neither the Negro nor sex was often discussed at length in our home. We were given no formal instruction in these difficult matters but we learned our lessons well. We learned the intricate system of taboos, of renunciations and compensations, of manners, voice modulations, words, feelings, along with our prayers, our toilet habits and our games. I do not remember how or when, but by the time I had learned that God is love, that Jesus is His Son and came to give us abundant life, that all men are brothers, with a common Father, I also knew that I was better than a Negro, that all black folks have their place and must be kept in it, that sex has its place and must be kept in it, that a terrifying disaster would befall the South if I ever treated a Negro as my social equal and as terrifying a disaster would befall my

family if ever I were to have a baby out of marriage. . . . I had learned
that white southerners are hospitable, courteous, tactful people who
treat those of their own group with consideration and who as carefully
segregate from all the richness of life "for their own good and welfare"
thirteen million people whose skin is colored a little differently from
my own. (1961, 28)

Here, as in the experience of many Savannahians with whom I have
spoken, race permeates other considerations of religion, gender, virtue,
and etiquette. Thus it fades into the background while it continues to be
hauntingly present.

For blacks, the discovery of social categorization has differed.
Throughout African-American autobiography, blacks have spoken of
their moment of discovery of white hegemonic categories as limits on
self-realization, a spur to protest for many black leaders from slavery to
the present (Du Bois 1965 [1903], 43-45, 214; 1969 [1920], 11-13; J. W.
Johnson 1965 [1927], 400-402; W. White 1948; McMillen 1989; for modern experiences see David 1968). Such a discovery may come from outside, a rejection by playmates or elders, or it may be fostered within the
black family, as McMillen noted in postbellum Mississippi: "No doubt
black children quite unconsciously discovered the social utility of deference by observing their elders. Yet a substantial body of social science
literature—and the testimony of the people themselves—demonstrates
that the black community left little to chance, that the black child was
usually given "specific training . . . within his own family to enable him
to adjust to white demands." (1989, 26). This discovery may also lead to
an unconscious acceptance of difference and discrimination. A very fair-
skinned member of Saint Anthony's, in her sixties during my fieldwork,
recalled her own experience in junior high school. The family insurance
man, a white man, checked out a civics text from the (white) library that
shocked her with its definition of her status: "I began to read the book. I
read in the book that any person regardless of the complexion of their
skin if they had just one drop of black blood in their system, they were
regarded as a negro—negro was the word in those days. When I read
that and told my mother and sister [they] said he must have gotten it off
the dump. They were quite upset" (see L. Smith 1961, 34-39). This book
dramatically reshaped this woman's perception of herself—not as an individual or even between groups, but as a member of an inferior caste.
Yet she simultaneously rebelled against classification with darker and
uneducated blacks, despite the everyday realities of neighborhood and

schools. Categories, whether unconscious or learned, accepted or resisted, became vivid realities for blacks.

To put this cultural formation in even more general terms, I have
also related it to literary and social critic Edward Said's vision of the
nature and power of the Western creation of another similarly marked
category, the "Oriental":

> Many terms are used to express the relation. . . . The Oriental is irra-
> tional, depraved (fallen), childlike, "different"; thus the European is
> rational, virtuous, mature, "normal." But the way of enlivening the re-
> lationship was everywhere to stress the fact that the Oriental lived in a
> different but thoroughly organized world of his own, a world with its
> own national, cultural and epistemological boundaries and principles
> of internal coherence. Yet what gave the Oriental's world its intelligi-
> bility and identity was not the result of his own efforts but rather the
> whole complex series of knowledgeable manipulations by which the
> Orient was identified by the West. (1978, 40)

The same adjectives—"irrational, depraved . . . childlike, 'different'"—
recur in white southern depictions of blacks, whether literary portrayals
or everyday conversations. The white definition of the black "other" became as intimate and convoluted as the Orientalist interpretation of body
and soul. Over centuries, blacks could be depicted as lazy, even as they
were forced into the hard-labor positions of the urban economy. White
men abused black women while creating a cult around the fear that black
men would "soil the purity" of the white woman (Turner 1971; Giddings
1984). White women could accommodate to the myth while retaining
black servants as intimate inferiors (Tucker 1988). Blacks were idealized
as docile yet feared as a threat (Friedman 1970). In general terms, white
hegemonic southern culture has depicted the "typical" black as a collective inferior, although rationales for this inferiority have ranged from ignorance to biological inferiority to evil. Hence "black" as an imposed
category shares the impact of Said's conclusion that "Knowledge of the
Orient, because generated out of strength, in a sense *creates* the Orient,
the Oriental and his world. . . . The Oriental is *contained and represented* by dominating frameworks" (1978, 40).

Yet in Orientalism, distance as well as ideology separated those who
created the Orient from those identified as Orientals and who would
develop a response. In the South, distancing, categorization, and domination were not played out across cultures, nations, or worlds. Catego-

ries were projected across neighborhoods, churches, and streets, or even within the household, between the parlor and the kitchen, mistress and servant (L. Smith 1961; Friedman 1970; Williamson 1984; C. Miller 1985; McLaurin 1987; Fox-Genovese 1988; Painter 1988; Tucker 1988; McMillen 1989). While resistance emerged in both private and public, it took on different forms shaped by this very intimacy of knowledge and control.

Ultimately, "black" also could become peculiarly mysterious and powerful, as in a vivid memory shared by white historian Melton McLaurin from his youth in rural North Carolina. Taking a basketball pump needle from a black friend and wetting it to insert it in the ball led to a painful epiphany: "I was jolted by one of the most shattering emotional experiences of my young life. Instantaneously an awareness of the shared racial prejudices of generations of white society coursed through every nerve in my body. Bolts of prejudice, waves of prejudice that I could literally feel sent my head reeling and buckled my knees." He follows with archetypal images of defilement and purification:

> The realization that the needle I still held in my mouth had come directly from Bobo's mouth, that it carried on it Bobo's saliva, transformed my prejudices into a physically painful experience. I often had drunk from the same cup as black children, dined on food prepared by blacks. It never occurred to me that such actions would violate my racial purity. The needle in my mouth, however, had been purposely drenched with Negro spit, and that substance threatened to defile my entire being. . . . The tainted substance on the needle also threatened, in a less specific but equally disturbing manner, my white consciousness, my concept of what being white meant. . . . It placed in jeopardy my racial purity, my existence as a superior being, the true soul of all southern whites. (1987, 37-38)[2]

McLaurin here becomes the victim of unconscious and enduring cultural categories that undercut his social interaction and throw him into self-contradiction. Yet this realization took place nearly a century after Emancipation, on the eve of renewed civil rights activism.

Indeed, the continuity of cultural systems, entailing both domination and resistance as chronicled in the last chapter, permeates Savannah life even as that life changes over time. At Emancipation, according to one historian of black Savannah, one saw many precursors of the later feelings of McLaurin and even the underlying rationale of actions and implicit feelings of recent decades:

> What Whites feared most, however, was that the abolition of slavery would lead to social equality of blacks and whites. The fact that some Union officers mixed freely with the Negroes made the thought of social inequality even more intolerable to Whites. They vowed never to accept blacks as their social equals. One man asserted that he would leave the country before he would "live in a country where I have got to mix with niggers." One woman declared: "My old mama who nursed me is just like a mother to me; but there is one thing I will not submit to . . . that the Negro is our equal. He belongs to an inferior race." (Perdue 1973, 5)

The incongruity of accepting a black woman as a mother but denying the Negro as a full human being is only one of the many contradictions that racial dichotomy produces in everyday life. From the fall of Reconstruction through the 1950s, whites who would prefer to have blacks cook for them at home would not eat with them—or allow them into most restaurants. In the 1960s, whites left the ocean when blacks integrated Savannah beach—a visceral response to contamination.[3] Today, blacks and whites brought together, whether in civic rallies or in a liturgy focused on love, still may refuse to recognize each other, despite the evidence of ongoing progress and integration.

The category of black as it has been perceived by whites for centuries in the South assembles multiple attributes: inferiority, savagery, evil, mystery, necessity, antagonism or, perhaps today, simply difference. Personal contacts may confuse the division, whether among whites who "adopt" a black servant as "one of the family" (Childress 1957; Hamburger 1978; Fox-Genovese 1988; Tucker 1988) or among blacks who accept white friends as "just like one of us." While isolated examples seem to undercut racist ideology, they also suggest the continuing presence of a process of *marking* blacks as "other" within the South. Similarly, while the social and individual impact of the civil rights era, as of abolition, should not be underestimated, neither can continuities be disregarded. The exploration of racial discourse, however, must be framed by comparison of blackness with the unmarked and itself hybrid category of whiteness.

WHITENESS AND DISCOURSE

Most white friends of mine have reacted with astonishment to the question, "What does it mean to be white in Savannah?" They sputter that they have not actually given it much thought and, after some struggle, they may reach the conclusion of a white priest: "It's a question that is as obvious as it is difficult." One is left with little content beyond Lillian Smith's sense of "hospitable, courteous and tactful." "White" does not need to be defined except to specify who is excluded. By contrast, a black woman in her fifties to whom I directed the question snapped back: "It means you own everything. . . . And you are racist."

Whiteness in hegemonic discourse remains undefined; it fact, its power is represented by this lack of definition. Yet it can be examined through the primary areas of contrast or exclusion by which white as an unmarked category is constituted. As I have suggested, these include the opposition of white to those who are dominated, and the association of white with public as opposed to private life. This network of associations also suggests related discourses in which white *becomes* unmarked in contrast to foreign immigration and the association of white in all these capacities with male as an empowered gender role in opposition to female. All form interlocking rather than isolated connotations, a network by which "white" has taken on and sustained implicit, even vaguely shifting meanings for centuries. In fact, "white" need not be unified or consistent; its identity and meaning, too, is defined by difference (Morrison 1992).

The establishment of "white" as a dominating term implies both the power of the category and the power of categorization as an ongoing process. Whites have held and *reproduced* political, economic, and social power for centuries, including the codification of public categories and their imposition on others. Blacks were introduced into Savannah society as property, commodities denied rights that were therefore left with the undefined group of "citizens" or "humans." After the Civil War, when constitutional amendments destroyed the principles of denial on the basis of race and caste, blacks fought for power while whites generally sought to manipulate or deny them (Perdue 1973; Painter 1988). By the late nineteenth century, white leadership clearly controlled the city and state again and imposed new restrictions upon those who could be defined as different. This situation has been slowly, formally altered in the twentieth century, in most cases, only since the 1960s.

"White" in Savannah has not represented a simple class domination over blacks so much as the imposition of a caste framework that also poses two class systems in unequal relationship to each other. That is, both blacks and whites as categories are internally divided by unequal access to production and by a related distribution of social rights and cultural values. Poor whites—immigrant or native—are marked in relation to a middle-class norm, to the extent that one scholar has proposed poor whites as a southern ethnic group (Flynt 1979, xv-xvii; see Dollard 1937). Yet even "poor white trash" were legally and publicly superior to any blacks, convoluting class and caste.

By contrast, black upper classes—proprietors, professionals, and leaders of major institutions—generally could not openly compete with white economic power or public presence until the 1960s. Wealthy, free blacks in the antebellum South owned slaves, but they could not be witnesses in a court, political officers, or social equals (Mills 1983; Johnson and Roark 1984a, 1984b). Black scholars, preachers, teachers, and bankers achieved international success at the turn of the century, but lines of caste denied them access to certain clubs, housing, and relations. Similarly, the black middle class tends to include other individuals who might be considered members of a stable working class among whites: municipal employees, seamstresses, long-term factory workers. Different discourses also represent class within each community: religion, residence, school or ethnicity among whites or discussions of color or congregation among blacks. Meanwhile, racial antagonisms further have divided white and black members of the working class (Woodward 1973; Morris 1990).

The power of cultural categories has its roots in political, economic, and legal controls but extends beyond them to everyday thought. Even after the changes of the civil rights era, for example, whites retain dominant exclusionary roles in Savannah. An elected black official is still identified as "spokesman for the black community." Longtime Mayor John Rousakis might be referred to by his Greek heritage in specific contexts, but it is unlikely that he would be labeled by his racial phenotype. Savannah usage also participates in a larger American society in which whites are numerically yet individually dominant while blacks are identified as a collective group:

> I don't think, for good or bad, that in any other ethnic group the fate
> of the individual is so inextricably bound to that of the group, and
> vice versa. To use the symbol of Willie Horton in another way, I do

75

not think that the lives of young white males are impacted by the existence of neo-Nazi skinheads, murdering Klansmen, or the ordinary thugs of Howard Beach. . . . It is not my intention to place value considerations on *any* of these events; I want to point out that in this society it seems legitimate, from the loftiest power to the streets of New York, to imply that one black man is them all. (Walton 1989, 77; see Clarke 1991)

This *New York Times* protest challenges the right of others to define a category in which blacks will be confined regardless of individual action. The author insists that marking combined with domination destroys individual identity for blacks in the urban setting, where even poorer whites have more rights to the public recognition of individual distinctiveness. Such patterns were more emphasized in the traditional South but have not disappeared in the "new South" (Clarke 1991).

The history of white classification also reveals a power over history, over learned values and alternative memories. Such power converted a 1982 celebration of black liberation in the Revolutionary War, for example, into a newspaper report that reduced blacks to minor actors: "Negroes who had sought shelter here throughout the British occupation watched in horror as a chance for an extension of their short-lived freedom disappeared along with the smoke of the battle" (Merkel 1982, 1; see McDonogh 1984). A black female historian of the South extended the critique of this control:

> Obviously those who are black or female and who write about Southerners who were black and female do not mean for Southern voices to be limited to the likes of Odum, Tate and Donaldson. We like to think that we are shaping a new way of listening to Southerners in the past that is more plural. We are convinced that our subjects are saying something about the South as a whole. So far, we have not been heard. Blacks may speak for blacks now, and women speak for women, but to judge from the books I have read, in 1984 as in 1967, elite white men still speak for the South. (Painter 1984, 93)

Indeed, southernness retains strong white male associations whether talking of academic historiography (Painter 1991) or popular media (Kirby 1978, xviii).

Struggles for history also imbue the gentrification of eighteenth- and nineteenth-century housing that has fueled Savannah tourism. In the reevaluation of postbellum mansions, whites have displaced blacks in both individual homes and downtown neighborhoods. Urban renewal threatened monuments such as Bryan Baptist Church, scion of the first free black Baptist church in the United States (Luster 1975, 1976a, 1976b). Even the history of black subordination embodied in shacks on the lanes behind white houses has been erased by conversion to carriage-house apartments (see Borchert 1980, 54-56, on a similar pattern in Washington). As a black critic, W. W. Law, has noted, "Everybody in Georgia wasn't born in a mansion. . . . There are other kinds of properties that ought to be placed on the register. The simple houses are important, too, because these people did much to make America great . . ." (Hepburn 1987, 326). Nonetheless, the structures of power, and the power to define, to exclude, and to denigrate have been a long-term process by which whites have limited blacks.[4]

A second opposition of white and other relates to the distinction of public and private life.[5] To be white has meant access to anywhere in the city, including a public privacy, a staged exclusion. One of Savannah's most exclusive older societies, for example, does not mention race in its founding statutes, defining only age (over twenty-one) and gender (male) as criteria for nomination by a member. Yet it is known throughout the city that the club does not accept blacks, however many blacks it hires as waiters and cooks. Nor does it accept Jews, while Catholics who have been permitted to join in recent decades have explained their presence as part of a quota. Whiteness is *presumed*; tacit exclusion defines others.

Since slavery and segregation days, white power over public life also has been spatial. Whites freely entered stores, theaters, and churches while blacks would either establish their everyday life outside these realms or fight to enter each. Geraldine Abernathy, a Saint Benedict's parishioner retired from teaching at Savannah State, described life behind the veil in the 1950s: "You knew what stores you could go into, where you could buy clothes, where you could try on clothes, where you would have to put something over your head to try on a hat. . . . It was kind of passive; no one made waves."

The public life of whites reappeared in neighborhoods and households. White neighborhoods, from the mid-nineteenth century onwards, were central; blacks and immigrants were confined to peripheral districts like the Old Fort or Yamacraw (Fogarty 1966; Ayers 1984, 81). In contrast to the urban heights, with their elegant row houses and oak-

77

shaded squares, marginal areas were lower, even swamplike, plagued by fires, disease, and the smells of the gas plant in the Old Fort (Blassingame 1973a). Within mixed housing areas, whites lived in the larger houses on the streets while blacks lived in shacks on the alleys behind. Within households, whites were owners and mistresses while blacks handled domestic tasks of cooking, child care, and cleaning. Finally, whites came in through front doors, even when they entered black households. Blacks, when they could enter white homes, generally came in the back.[6]

This approach to whiteness and blackness within the general context of southern and Savannah life focuses on the structuring of race as well as its content and the actions with which individuals manipulate it. It thus underscores the dialectic of symbolic action and power within which black and Catholic community has emerged. Two more content-oriented analyses of whiteness as a category raise further problems for the study: whiteness as opposed to Catholic immigrant, and whiteness as opposed to female.

ALTERNATE MARKINGS: WHITES, CATHOLICS, AND WOMEN

White domination of black has encompassed political hierarchy, economic control, and public prestige. Other discourses about whiteness, however, situate an elite which dominates and creates "white community" in contrast to others who are "not quite white" as signaled by the limitations on club membership noted above. The multiple referents that oppose an unmarked whiteness may be unrelated, but they also yield doubly marked categories that become foundations for social tension and help to explain social and cultural change.

Despite the mythology of Scarlett O'Hara, for example, Catholics were rarely incorporated into antebellum elites: Catholicism in Georgia, as in most of the South, has been shaped by exclusion (M. Mitchell 1936; Miller 1983a and 1983b; McNally 1987).[7] Georgia was founded as an Episcopalian colony where Catholics could not hold office, and their very presence proved suspect. After independence, Irish Catholic migrants swelled the southern urban working class, competing with blacks, slave and free. (Levine 1977, 301-4; Johnson and Roark 1984a, 177-80; 1984b). The rise of evangelical Protestantism, while it divided the native population, reinforced prejudice against Catholic ways. Elites coalesced images of race, ethnicity, and class in opposition to *proper* behavior. A New

England visitor commented on the antebellum riverfront, for example, that "The street is always so thronged by sailors, slaves and rowdies of all grades and colors that it is not safe for ladies to walk alone" (Ayers 1984, 79).

As Catholics struggled to establish community and identity in a southern context, their institutional separations became important. Savannah Catholics gained not only a church and a bishop but also separate schools and cemeteries prior to the Civil War. The Hibernian Society, now a bastion of an Irish Catholic elite, began in 1812 as a Protestant and Jewish charitable society for these immigrants (O'Hara 1912). The immigrant construction of separate communities, however, continued to face anti-Catholic strains in Savannah and the South. In 1895, for example, the self-proclaimed former priest Joseph Slattery sparked a riot by his attacks on the Catholic church, which ranged from their manipulation of mystery to the hierarchy's restraint on free speech (*SMN* Feb. 25 to Mar. 1, 1895; *Defamers of the Church* n.d.). Those who protested Slattery's appearance at the Masonic Hall nonetheless already belonged to a divided Catholic community. Priests and prominent citizens condemned the rioters whom they identified with the poor zone of Old Fort, insisting Savannahians know "the difference between the class that created the disorder and the true Catholics of Savannah" (*SMN* Feb. 27, 1895). Catholic assimilation coexisted with class differentiation as more and more white Catholics have gained higher status in the city.

Tom Watson and other turn-of-the-century Georgia politicians maintained this public antagonism against Catholicism via nativist rhetoric. Watson, United States Senator and former Populist vice-presidential candidate, launched vivid anti-Catholic, anti-Semitic, and racist drives through his newspapers in the early twentieth century. He pilloried the Catholic church for repression, while conjuring the specter of the "growing power and intolerance of popery, in this country" (1917; see Cashin 1962; Woodward 1973). Spurning his populist heritage, Watson manipulated stereotypes to divide Catholics, blacks, Jews, and rural whites against any shared reformist interests.

In the Watson era, religious institutions such as convents came under public suspicion with evocations of lechery and exploitation. Act 548 of the Georgia General Assembly of 1916, popularly known as the Veasey bill, asked grand jury committees to make regular inspections "into every such private sanitarium, hospital, asylum, House of the Good Shepherd, convent and monastery for the purpose of ascertaining what

79

persons are confined within said institutions, and by what authority such persons are held within the same" (Georgia Statutes 1916, 126-27; amended 1918, 165-67). The specificity of the list betrays the bill's attack on Catholicism, even though the religion itself is not mentioned, just as the lurid sexual implications of this attack throughout the South was made through elaboration of this bill as a challenge to white slavery in convents.

Anti-Catholicism diminished after the Depression, although the separation of schools and worship continued. Even in the 1980s, anti-Catholic posters still appeared in Savannah, although no visible anti-Catholic organization seems to exist. Chick Comics, fundamentalist tracts with virulent anti-Catholic messages linking the Pope with the Antichrist, communists, and Nazis, are published in California but sold in Savannah as in many other southern cities. In the area, they have been left on the cars of local priests. Most Savannahians, however, dismiss such incidents as aberrations within a more relaxed and tolerant religious world.

The domination of "cultural Protestantism" has also shaped southern Catholicism in fundamental ways. Georgia author Flannery O'Connor emphasized her duality: "To my way of thinking, the only thing that keeps me from being a regional writer is being Catholic and the only thing that keeps me from being a Catholic writer (in the narrow sense) is being a Southerner" 1979, 104, cited in McNally 1987, 125; see Coles 1980). Southern Catholicism has both accommodated to and rejected various forms of Protestant organization and thought (McDonogh 1991, 1992; Anderson 1992; Neville 1992).

These cultural evaluations of the correct religious categories of the evangelical South have provided foundations for the reproduction of divisions of consciousness and participation in urban life, as the previous chapter noted for black religious ethnohistory. In life narratives from my first general fieldwork in Savannah, structural differences between Catholic and non-Catholic memories were as salient as racial divisions (McDonogh 1988b). Most white Catholics, for example, arranged their memories around two traumatic periods. The first, roughly between 1915 and 1928, was a time of troubles in which Klan activity was perceived as particularly high. In 1982, an eighty-year old Irish Catholic male still excoriated Tom Watson: "He'll burn in Hell. If he isn't in Hell, I'll never go. He had them pass the act to go and inspect the convents because he said there was a tunnel so nuns could go and sleep with priests. And yet he sent his granddaughters to Catholic schools!"

Yet ethnic and class experiences also shaped memory. Anti-German prejudice in the World War I and anti-Italianism in World War II added periods of trouble not found in the dominant Irish picture. Cajuns who settled in a more rural section around the sugar refinery offered even more tightly woven recollections that did not share such early urban experiences. Class differences were particularly evident in access to bishops and clergy and the evaluations that flowed from this involvement with Catholic power.

Nonetheless, overall, a shared experience of prejudice became part of the memory and identity of the entire white Catholic community. Protestants, by contrast, not only lacked any special sense of an era for the 1920s but also denied the existence of rampant prejudice. As might be expected, shared "public" (Protestant) history ignores this motif and its variations as well.

The second period of concern for white Catholics in Savannah was one which emerged from changes in the 1960s, coalescing religious reforms and the social upheaval of integration. Not only civil rights but also the reforms of the Second Vatican Council, beginning in 1962, forced a rethinking of Catholic culture. While Catholics shared integration with other Savannahians, the link of changing beliefs and contested behaviors separated Catholic historical memory, reaffirming their community identity but separating them from the "general story" (see Sieg 1985). Protestants spoke of integration in relation to their city and even their congregation but obviously gave little importance to Vatican II. At the same time, ethnic and class divisions played less of a marking role among the recollections of Catholics with whom I spoke.

Black and Catholic memory took on a different structure. An older woman succinctly denied the 1920s as a marker for group identity since "The Klan didn't care if you were Catholic, if you were black." To her, prejudice meant a very different tradition based on race. Ironically, the 1920s were critical years for the formation of black Catholicism; perhaps the lack of family continuity and public history has precluded its incorporation into memory. The 1960s became a primary marker for all blacks, in which black Catholics again connected religious and social developments. Yet their interpretation of events often contrasted with that of their white co-religionists. The closing of the black parish schools, for example, promoted by the white hierarchy as a gesture toward integration, struck painfully at the heart of the black and Catholic experience.

The formation of personal and group historical narratives is a form of resistance by which members of marked and subordinated categories provide meanings for their life and experience. These narratives nonetheless reaffirm the divergence of Catholics from public history within Savannah. They also differentiate ethnic and class experience within Catholicism, marked categories within the subordinate group. Finally, such narratives portray the tensions between the diversities of everyday life and the heightening of experience, belief, and actions that brings difference to the forefront. Whether Catholic or non-Catholic, black or white, those whom I have interviewed speak within a range of southern accents, eat southern foods at home and at parish fish fries, and strongly identify with Savannah as home. In their narratives, I did not ask for distinctive Catholic experiences, although I had explained my research interests. Yet this distinctiveness was iterated by experiences of public discrimination ritualized in the yearly football clash of Savannah High School (public, Protestant, and white) versus Benedictine Military Academy (private, Catholic, male, and white) (McDonogh 1988a).

Gender as a marked category raises questions even more difficult to approach in any systematic fashion, particularly if we attempt to separate Savannah from the general construction of female as a marked category in the South as a whole. Southern males and females have created particular cultural dichotomies of white females of purity and delicacy versus active males as well as in opposition to the black female of strength and sensuality (L. Smith 1961; A. Scott 1970; F. King 1975, 1977; Daniell 1980; Giddings 1984; Fox-Genovese 1988; Tucker 1988; Hooks 1990). As Elizabeth Fox-Genovese described for the slave period, "Gender, race, and class relations constituted the grid that defined southern women's objective position in society, constituted the elements from which they fashioned their views of themselves and the world, constituted the relations of different groups of southern women to each other" (1988, 43).

In contemporary Savannah, men dominate leadership, whether political, cultural or religious. Women have served for decades as leaders in fields that may be considered extensions of the domestic realm, such as education or "society," but they only are emerging in the 1990s in the public eye as mayors, industrialists, or religious spokespersons. Personal ornamentation, language, and interests also differentiate gender and class roles within urban life: both blacks and whites have evolved strong images of "ladylike" deportment for church and social realms. While males manifest a variety of styles from classic gentleman to southern yuppie to good ol' boy to black urban flash, these are less remarked upon than female roles. Even aspects of southern life that might challenge American roles accommodate to consumer images in films, television, and malls to reinforce an asymmetry of power. Rosemary Daniell, an acerbic female critic of Savannah life, notes: "Good ole girls are realistic and materialistic and loyal to the land. Being a good ole girl means you stand by your man and don't make waves. . . . All the women in country songs are frivolous. . . . Aren' they?" (1980, 193). Women and men who fight for changes still face widespread stereotypes of "how life is."

The coexistence of categories that are marked in relation to a dominant "white" does not imply a necessary sympathy among subordinated categories. Recent diocesan surveys, for example, have attacked white Catholics for their prejudice against blacks. With social mobility into more powerful economic and political positions, immigrant Catholics have assumed many of the attitudes of the dominant group who had once rejected them. Similarly, white women, though often sharing familylike ties with black domestic servants, also reproduced the behaviors of subordination that reaffirmed classifications: use of first names instead of honorifics, or categorization by stereotype. As Alice Walker puts it "Those women would act 'nice' to blacks, . . . but eventually their faces become their masks" (in Daniell 1980, 182). Historically, even some southern feminist efforts such as the quest for voting rights played gender against race, offering the consistent vote of the white woman, for example, to offset any potential gains by black males or females (Giddings 1984, 154-67).

The opportunities and actions of black males also have imposed limits on the lives of black women, forming a complementary dialectic of race and gender. Postbellum black females, for example, often held stronger positions of education, earning, association, or influence than their male counterparts (Giddings 1984). At the same time, black male leaders evidenced paternalist stereotypes in their resistance, as the *Savannah Tribune* headline, "White Men Should Leave Our Women Alone" suggests (Apr. 23, 1907). Moreover, in the volatile areas of sexuality, white images of black rapists were countered by black activists who "attempted to refute this assertion simply by reversing its assumptions, contending that whites, not blacks, were the rapists" (Friedman 1970, 140). Thus, Friedman notes that "Clearly, white Southern racists and black activists looked at women in similar terms. Both viewed the female as a second sex with distinctly limited privileges" (1970, 142). Such categories have since been criticized by academics as well as by the actions of southerners, yet they continue to be woven into the fabric of southern symbolic culture. Women, black and white, resist the culture of their subordination; from this resistance a strength has emerged that permeates the black and Catholic parish.

Both religious sectarianism and gender establish marked categories that have complemented the dominant ideology of whiteness and permeate discussion about classification. Despite the changes and nuances discussed in more detail in succeeding chapters, these cultural values have an enduring heritage. These categories clearly reveal hybrids, and even conflictive, ideas among themselves. Yet members of doubly marked—doubly subordinated—categories offer significant criticisms throughout the historical formation of the black experience (Hooks 1990). The unmarked categories of whiteness against which they are defined are also separable. By their very vagueness and domination, however, these categories tend to overlap in defining "whiteness" as a norm dominated by Protestants and males within southern life. Such overlapping, but not identical, classifications provide fundamental ambiguities that underpin Savannah life.

BLACKS AND THE RECREATION OF BLACKNESS

All these characteristics of "whiteness" constitute a shared public culture of the South (and areas beyond it), inherited for generations as a second nature. As noted, blacks throughout the United States have held the ambivalent position of learning to deal with these cultural categories while building positive identities of their own. If white reflection on being white evokes unease, for Savannah blacks, as a marked category, this question of self establishes a way of life. In their experience of growing up, they cannot afford ignorance, whether or not they resist domination. For blacks, "white" has become a powerful but marked category within their discourse, a strongly delineated portrait of one who defines.

Blacks have met exclusionary and public claims that whites have made in Savannah through a variety of means. The campaign for social equality, which has its roots in resistance to slavery, has since taken many active forms of response, both individual and collective. Collective actions such as the formation of strong church institutions and public morality in the nineteenth century or protests against ostensibly shared southern cultural texts like "Birth of a Nation" in the twentieth, belied white stereotypes (Dittmer 1977). Subterfuge, escape, irony, and begrudging but partial acceptance provided a rich palette of individual response for slaves and freedman (J. W. Johnson 1965; Genovese 1974; Levine 1977). The quotations from figures such as Turner and Du Bois illustrate the power of black rhetoric in cultural redefinition.

As noted in the discussion of public and private space, the creation of "separate but equal" urban worlds in Savannah epitomizes black collective adaptation to white dominance. When downtown was barred to local blacks (except as servants), East and West Broad streets, beyond the boundaries of the white core, harbored flourishing commercial and amusement complexes that served urban and regional blacks. Shops, movie houses, hotels, restaurants, clubs, and churches lined the thoroughfares, so that even today Pie Chisholm recalls that "some folk from Thunderbolt never got no further than East Broad." Such streets were also focal points for celebrations and parades, such as the great pageant that welcomed charismatic Bishop C. E. "Daddy" Grace to Savannah each year (Hervey 1939; Georgia Writers' Project 1940; SMN Jan. 17, 1960). This opposed a black downtown to the white zone, where most functions of the city—apart from government—were played out in black terms. Ironically, black downtowns collapsed in Savannah, as in other southern cities, with integration (see Mohlman 1991 on St. Augustine).

Other parallelisms were more somber, such as the division of neighborhoods into black and white or the duplication of parks, hospitals, churches, funeral homes, and cemeteries. Again, blackness overlapped with other social divisions: for a century, the Catholic cemetery was the only integrated cemetery in the city (with blacks in a distinct area for years). The alley also differed in power and freedoms from nearby streets. In many cases, blacks themselves created and sustained parallel institutions. Thus schools, whose separate but unequal status was established by state law, depended on black churches. Nonetheless, unlike Catholics, blacks could not *choose* to attend other schools.

The privateness of black life also has had a defensive value in terms of control of information. White life, for example, takes place on a stage of mass media coverage and gossip even among black servants. Black control of domesticated information would be able to exclude whites more effectively than any secret could be kept from a maid. Yet the public proclamation of whiteness has sustained apparently general cultural evaluations of white "civilization" (see Crapanzano 1985). Formerly covert black resistance to these norms has emerged in increasing general accommodation in such realms as music and fashion. Food represents a more ambiguous area, since many white families have accommodated to cultural knowledge of black housekeepers and since southern cuisines share many dishes.

Figure 5. Black alley residences in Eastside Savannah, 1991. Photograph by the author.

In culture and communication, negative controls by whites have taken on critical values in black communities. Denied public information in white-controlled and white-focused mass media, for example, blacks have maintained both separate newspapers and an active network to exchange information. As one mature woman in Saint Benedict's put it, "Somethin' happen in the Old Fort and they know about it in New York the next day." At the same time, black control of information could exclude whites: "White man come in your neighborhood asking for someone and you never heard of them, even if they live next door." White becomes the marked, foreign category in a black, private world.

Language also takes on different values depending on its racial context. "Nigger" as used by most whites is offensive in intention and connotation, although usage might signal class divisions among whites:

> *Nigger* was a word poor whites used, a term they hurled at blacks
> (whom adults in my family always referred to as "colored people") the
> way my childhood friends from less affluent families hurled pieces of
> granite from the railroad tracks at hapless black children their age or
> younger. Despite linguistic niceties, however, all whites knew that
> blacks were, really, servants. (McLaurin 1987, 31; see Holt 1972;
> Smitherman 1977)

When Geraldine Abernathy read this, she also noted "You left out *nigras*. . . . The elite whites used to call us *N-I-G-R-A-S*."

Within black conversation in Savannah, however, this emblem of opprobrium conveys a variety of nuances. In 1987, a male dismissed dissension in a parish by saying "they're just a bunch of crazy niggers there who like to fight," criticizing other blacks for inappropriate behavior. It also implies judgment of those who copy whites as a means of advancement: "Butler Presbyterian; that's where all the elite niggers go" (woman, sixties, Saint Benedict's). Finally, the term can be transmuted into an intimate, in-group term: "Heard you were in the hospital and said that old nigger done bought it" (woman, late sixties, to female in her cohort group, Saint Benedict's, 1987). Irony and affection refract white power to foster a counter-language, an alternate, marked reality (Smitherman 1977, 62).

The black manipulation of negative restrictions underpins many actions in segregated worship and education. Equally striking in conversations among blacks is a vivid emphasis on individuals in contrast to the collectivity created by white classification. This person resists the label imposed upon all who are defined to share phenotypic traits.

Most Savannah whites, historically, confine blacks to a fictively homogeneous category, broken only by specific roles: visible leaders, the eccentrics ("curious Negroes" in newspapers), or those who "reach humanity" by becoming "like one of the family." Blacks in Savannah use very different markers to divide and situate members of their social networks. Family remains a primary marker: both immediate family and the extended and diverse kinship ties that crisscross black neighborhoods and link city and countryside. Chains of cousins, relatives through marriage, godparenthood, and friendship, all confirm a chain of placement that begins with "Where you' family from?"

The *where* of such a conversation also embodies a rich topography unknown to most of the whites with whom I discussed neighborhood names. Local identifications spring from historical traditions of incorporation of slave communities or recognition of events or historical figures: Clarence Thomas's birthplace of Pin Point or rural communities like Sandfly and Nicholsonville are part of black life as are urban centers that were once identified with Savannah Irish such as Yamacraw, the Old Fort, or Frogtown (see Georgia Writers' Project 1940). Some neighborhoods had names like Brownville that have changed with new community foci: the area now takes its more general designation from Cuyler School. And some zones play with simple irony in nicknames like "Lover's Lane" and "Dodge City" applied to zones of violence in neighborhoods or projects.[8]

Blacks also situate other blacks via class, opportunity, and history. Such divisions can be phrased through association, living patterns, education, and style: as the last chapter noted, church membership exemplifies a grid of meanings over time in black Savannah including color as well as creed (Dittmer 1977, 59-75). Perhaps the theme most deeply representative of the problematic nature of black and white is that of color within the black community (Blassingame 1973a, 203-9; Genovese 1974, 413-31; Williamson 1980b, 1986, 1988; G. Wright 1985, 135-38; Dominguez 1986; see comparative data in Martinez-Alier 1974). To be light-skinned ("White, bright, yellow, mulatto") and to have "good" hair (long, smooth, and not nappy) has long been prestigious among blacks. In the past, these connotations represented ambivalent genealogical associations with whites and access to white power through inheritance, training, or favor. Stephen Ochs cites a case from Pine Bluff, Arkansas, in 1906, for example, when Creole (black) Sisters of the Holy Family rejected a darker-skinned priest since they "felt insulted at the prospect of receiving the sacrament from a black, rather than a white, priest" (1990, 150-51). Today, although positive attitudes toward a variety of skin-tone/feature complexes have developed since the civil rights era, color retains an association with class made evident in a 1990 discrimination case in Atlanta between a light-skinned black employee and a dark-skinned employer. Identification as an elite, in turn, tends to inform suspicion of color: any upper-class church is likely to be accused of being "light-skinned" by outsiders regardless of the phenotypes of its members.

These divisions are reinforced outside the local black community in ways that can disturb blacks. Mass media, for example, are perceived to favor fair-skinned females in their representation of black life: "Have you ever seen a really dark woman on TV?" lamented a stylish woman in her twenties.

Yet being close to white does not mean a destruction of boundaries. There is an interesting ambiguity in the interest in passing for white, however, that surfaces in various past and present comments. In 1907, for example, the *Savannah Tribune* noted that Pete Ziegler in Albany, Georgia, "was caused to leave town because he passed as a white man. He boarded with one of the best white families and went with some of the well known white ladies. He was detected by a visiting white lady who knew him in another city. He was fair, well educated and polished. Despite it all he was a Negro." Contrasting this with the case of another mulatto forced to move from the black to the white car on a train, the newspaper commented "Race prejudice causes many inconsistent acts" (Mar. 9, 1907).To pass as white, for whites, is a tragic abuse of boundaries, entailing claims to a position of higher power. To blacks with whom I spoke, to pass means to leave: "They take the train up to Washington and they gotta sit with us. Once they there, they white." Breaking local ties is critical to the break of racial boundaries: "Otherwise, they too much known about they family" (woman, Saint Benedict's, seventy). Not the risk of ambiguity, but the pain of denial, pervades this interpretation.

Finally, disparity in the imposition of classifications does not imply that blacks are ignorant about individual whites. Both the public knowledge that defines whites as a power-expressing group and the intimate knowledge that blacks have gained through domestic service have created a strong if silent analytic appreciation of whites. Thus, criticism of behind-the-scenes political machinations and of the social ties among whites forms part of conversations in black households, although domestic service poses a conflictive loyalty: some would never talk about "their family. It ain't right" (Childress 1957; Tucker 1988).

Stereotypes recur in evaluation of mass media. I was surprised, for example, by the appeal of nearly all-white and middle- and upper-class soap operas to the black women of the middle- and working-class population I knew. Yet there did not seem to be an identification with those in "The Young and the Restless" or "Dallas" so much as a longer tradition of watching the ways of the white folk.

Black classifications of black and white have long existed within the public dualistic system imposed by white power holders upon Savannah society, although documentation of oral and private traditions from slavery days remains sketchy. Blacks use this dual skeleton in creative and different ways. They may resist categorizations imposed upon them while working out placements for significant others within their social networks. Within this variety, blacks reinterpret the power of whites to categorize at all. While their projection may be private rather than public, it remains significant in understanding community and contradiction, as is illustrated by an examination of intermediate, combined categories.

BLACKS, CATHOLICISM, AND CATEGORIES

As I have noted, categories and systems intersect in time and space. The Catholic (white) understanding of blacks since the inception of missions by white (immigrant) clergy among native African-American neighborhoods in Georgia illustrates this process. The Society of African Missions of Lyon had been founded in France in 1856 to preach to native Africans; only after decades of experience in Dahomey, Nigeria, and Senegal did they seek new territories "on account of the political situation [in France] inimical to religious congregations and in order to provide alternate occupation for confreres unable to endure the African climate" (Vogel b; Bane 1959; *L'Echo des Missions Africaines*). Ignatius Lissner, the priest who renewed missionary efforts to Georgia blacks between 1907 and 1922, began his colonial career in the 1890s. His biographer, Josef Vogel, reconstructed the impact of Africa for his family:

> Maybe the girls trembled a little at the thought that Ignace would have to go to Africa; surely "maman" had a stronger faith. Africa was then much less well known than in the 20th century; its west coast was still denounced as the "White Man's Grave." Missionaries were heroes like the Paris Foreign Missions' priests martyred in Korea and

Indochina those last 50 years. Boys and girls in those days, no less than
their mothers, used to read those true, eye-witness stories of those heroes in the "Annals of the Propagation of the Faith" or even, in French,
in the wonderful "Missions Catholiques" from Lyons. (Vogel a, 13)

Such Orientalism underpinned early missionary efforts by bishops and
orders to blacks in the region, a tension which Stephen Ochs has similarly documented for the Josephites as well as the American hierarchy
(1990). European-born priests and nuns with whom I have talked who
worked in Savannah in the 1920s, 1930s, and 1940s had often not seen a
black before beginning work in Africa or the urban United States. Their
expectations for their missions varied from a view of the population as
needy and primitive to an admiration, in the 1950s and 1960s, for civil
rights leadership. A concept of mission Catholicism, embedded in Vogel's
text melded uncomfortably with the cultural category of blackness and
with a justification for paternalism.

American racial stereotypes could also cut through positive, if paternalistic efforts. Bishop Thomas Becker, for example, who worked to develop a Catholic educational system for blacks in Savannah, nonetheless
recorded this rationale in his daybook in 1891: "They are very prone to
vice and when fallen are almost incapable of being raised up. The girls
are apt to go wrong at a very early age and their surroundings, even
among whites, are very bad" (cited in Peterman 1982, 198). This imagery, in fact, permeated early Catholic educational programs for blacks
throughout the United States and suggests a reason for black resistance
to them. Yet northern blacks wrote similarly about their post-Civil War
missions to the South (Levine 1977).

Categorization by race, albeit in a more positive and attenuated form,
haunts the discourse of contemporary Savannah Catholicism. Even
though the hierarchy promoted equality as a policy, it used language
that separated blacks, as in a 1939 addendum to diocesan statutes: "Inas-
much as there is no part of the flock dearer to Us than our colored brethren, and as there is no task closer to Our heart than the conversion of
the colored race, We earnestly exhort all Our priests to interest themselves deeply in the spiritual welfare of this people." This document pre-
supposes a logic of social and worship separation: "Especially in places
in which there is no colored parish church, our priests shall make known
to colored people that they are welcome in the local Catholic church,
and that there will always be special places reserved for them." Finally,

the instructions to priests, after forbidding reference to blacks "by names that are common among vulgar people," ends with the economic realities of class categories: "All who employ Colored help are reminded that they are bound in conscience to pay them a decent wage" (Diocese of Savannah-Atlanta 1939, 54).

The attitudes of white churches and communities were complex in practice and language in the pre-civil rights era, as an Italian American born in the 1940s recalled: "It was an event when a black came to church. You'd hear parents say 'Look at that nigger.' Maybe he's from up North. Comes down here and thinks he can get away with it." Yet this same man noted "If the church would have taught us, we wouldn't have suffered the anguish the day we woke up."

Indeed, attention to categorization may lead to a paradoxical elimination of the impact of race, as racially formed questions are rephrased outside their historical context and meaning, as if race were really not the question (Reeves 1983; Essed 1990). The 1987 Savannah Diocesan Report included a reference to black ministry:

> *Black Catholics* form a small but *significant* minority in South Georgia.
> The Office of Black Ministry serves *their* needs with educational programs, supports the work of a Black Catholic Council and sponsors meetings from the parishes which *are identified* as *black*. (*Southern Cross* Jan. 1, 1987, 4; emphasis added.)

The italicized words pinpoint key assumptions and metaphors underlying the consciousness of church leadership. From the beginning, black Catholics are treated as a unitary group with shared collective needs (*their*). They are few but *significant*, an undefined term. *Identified*, a seemingly neutral word, elides the processes of segregation and disfranchisement that led to missionary efforts within a segregated church, as if the parishes were so designated by interest. Finally, *black* parishes may have white members, as blacks may attend *white* parishes, the presumed contrast; in both cases they face a *white* priest. This office, nonetheless, has been a strong voice in revindicating black culture within the local church, part of a movement among blacks identified by reference to "Black Catholics" (as in the National Office of Black Catholics, NOBC).

This political stance is only one of the redefinitions of blackness within the church, however. Other friends in these parishes insisted that "There ain't no such thing as no *Black Catholic*; I am a Roman Catholic—ain't no special religion called *Black Catholicism*." Even if race was adduced as a socially powerful factor in their lives, such Catholics want to leave these divisions aside, symbolically, at the door of the church. Therefore I have chosen a more neutral, if awkward, reference to *"black and Catholic"* throughout the text.

The complexities of this dialogue within contemporary Catholicism also pervaded a flyer distributed by a white priest, Michael Smith, at his 1988 departure after nine years at Saint Anthony's. His text builds on a metaphoric framework central to the history of black religious expression: the use of Israel's captivity in Egypt as a symbol of oppression and slavery to be relieved by the deliverer, Moses (Genovese 1974, 252-55; Levine 1977): "Moses was raised in the House of Pharaoh, in the Courts of the great king, who thought he ruled everything. But even then he was training the very one God had chosen to be his undoing, the man who would deprive him of his slaves." Here, however, a white speaker uses the metaphor to reflect on Pharaoh as a representation of whiteness and domination: "Pharaoh loved to lord it over the Hebrew slaves. It made him feel so great and powerful. In fact, he was inferior to them for it was they who built the pyramids, not he."

Moses found "the people who were his own though he knew it not." Thus, Moses becomes a symbol for the personal development of Father Smith from his own white middle-class background to a wider understanding of the world: "All I had hoped for was to make money and advance in the ranks of Pharaoh's house." Yet for him, white as a personal world, as a public presence, and as a form of domination came together in learning from blacks: "I barely knew what the struggle was, but I was beginning to learn. I learned not in Pharaoh's house with all its fancy degrees. I learned by joining hands and making friends with the people of color, the people who knew."

Pharaoh also signifies the Church, in a key turning point of policy, at the closure of the local black high school, Pius X:

> I was sent there in April 1968 by "accident". A leader of Pharaoh's house had made some bad calls against the priests of the people of color and he needed someone quick to try to cover up the problem. God used this bad call of a leader of Pharaoh's house to set me free. I went to Pius to teach the story of Moses and the children of Israel to the people who were still slaves in our day. Teaching them, I began to grasp for myself for the first time what that story of Exodus is all about: about the struggle to be free. Soon we had to struggle together as the leader of Pharaoh's house closed the school. He won the battle. But the struggle made us strong. The more Pharaoh tried to put down the children of Israel, the more they multiplied and the stronger they got.

After this, Father Smith moved completely into black ministry at Saint Anthony's. Here his critical stance toward white as a category opens up the category of black and the meaning of the black experience:

> God has given me this nine years to learn this crucial factor: That we are brothers in the struggle, in the struggle to set all people free from the House of Pharaoh.
>
> For centuries now the white race has been trying to prove it is superior to all: in the years of colonizing and oppressing people all over the world, in the years of slavery here, in the world war begun by the Nazis, in South Africa and in the country clubs of the USA. This modern house of Pharaoh has been and is now trying to put down people of color all over the world, even though often they know not what they are doing.
>
> But now, as in days long past, God is preparing a people for himself. The more Pharaoh tries by every trick and torture to ravage and reduce this people, the more they multiply and become strong. All over the earth the people of color are singing songs of Zion even as they continue to eat the bread of affliction. All over the earth, people of color are coming together and getting stronger, preparing for that great day of the Lord. That day when God will use the "despised ones"—purified and made strong in the fiery furnace—as His chosen servants to set all people free to live as brothers. . . .
>
> God is using the ones who have been so despised by the house of Pharaoh to undo the world of racism and slavery that this House has created. God is raising up the lowly to put down the mighty from their thrones and make this world become His Kingdom where all people of all races and creeds and nations sit down to eat together in peace. . . .

This leads to a final reflection on Father Smith's next assignment in a white university parish. He sees this not as a simple redivision so much as a newly informed opportunity, again changing the meaning of white as the bounded category that must be opened up "Like Jesus in his native place, perhaps not to work many miracles, but to spend my time teaching what I have learned in the camps of the people of color, about the struggle to be brothers in the shadow of the pyramids." Thus, the document stands in contrast to normal use of racial categories, seeing black and white as experiential categories that become mutually redefining and redeeming. A religious pilgrimage winds through race to a new vision of humanity, while individual experience undermines categories.

This chapter has suggested the fundamental generative cultural values that have underpinned the classification of rights and privileges in Savannah. While it has sought chronological specificity in relation to my general process-oriented analysis, many traits are important precisely for their endurance; often, they are myths that remain central to southern identity or background for everyday choices. Given my upbringing and experience, such an analysis seems at once obvious and difficult. Yet the attempt proves crucial to understanding the dynamics of change occurring even within "white" and "black."

As the examples from observation, conversation, interviews, and texts have suggested, the category of white has been fraught with ambiguity and lack of clarity, an unmarked category defined by what it is not rather than by its content or limits. Yet this has facilitated its endurance. Black has a different complexity, in being an identity both imposed from above and a critical and creative identity established through resistance, which includes a delineation of whiteness. Historical events, as I will show, have dramatically changed the possibilities of black life, but the asymmetrical dichotomy of white and black still retains its force in Savannah life.

Other classifications of class, religion, and gender echo these fundamental distinctions as they intersect with them. Protestants and Catholics, for example, have been divided in sect and class interests. Yet their divisions have not coincided with the black and white dualities of society. Gender relations, while linked to the central themes of this division, still allocate power primarily to white males in contrast to all others.

The interdependence and differentiation of categories underpin the idea of contradiction that is central to this entire book. To be black and Catholic has been a profound transgenerational experience of building a community against real limitations of opportunity and power as well as the "shared" ideas of urban life. The success of black Catholics has also challenged cultural assumptions, especially in more open dialogues since the 1960s. In order to understand these broad and slowly changing cultural values, however, I continually anchor this framework in the social historical detail of the emergence of black religion. Thus, the next two chapters will discuss both Catholic movement into black Savannah as a hierarchical gesture and the formation of black and Catholic individual and collective responses, while subsequent discussions will look at specific issues of leadership, social life, and ritual as arenas of cultural formation and conflict.

3. Catholics Enter the Black Community: Race, School, and Missions

Veni Creator Spiritus, Mentes tuorum visita
Imple superna gratia Quae tu creasti pectora.
(Come Holy Ghost, Creator Blest
And in our hearts take up thy rest;
Come with thy grace and heav'nly aid
To fill the hearts which thou hast made.)
— *Rabanus Maurus (776-856 A.D.), Veni Creator Spiritus*

In 1929 the Josephite missionary John Gillard expressed his faith in the school as the basis for Catholic entrance into the American black world: "Today no missioner properly visualizes his ultimate field of success without planning for adequate school facilities. The school factor is the very hope of future mission stability" (147). Six decades later, each traditionally black parish in Savannah has a school building beside it, yet none holds classes. The empty brick shell of Saint Benedict's school speaks as eloquently to white missionary zeal for the formation of a black and Catholic community as it epitomizes the misunderstandings between that community and the ecclesiastical hierarchy.

While blacks were among the earliest Catholic immigrants to antebellum Georgia, the place of worship did not become a continuous core for black and Catholic life until the twentieth century. The parishes of the present arose from the schools that immigrant priests and nuns offered to all blacks, whether Catholic or not, after the Civil War. Hence, Sister Julian Griffin began her history of black Catholics in Georgia with a local echo of Gillard's assessment from half a century before: "Throughout the whole story, from its earliest days, one important element stands

96

out—and that is the role of the Catholic schools for black children. Over and over again, wherever a missionary effort was launched, a school was opened. Long before there were many people at Mass, the classrooms were full. For many parents and children, the school was the first contact with Catholicism" (Griffin and Brown 1979, 7). Although black parishioners built their own identity, the church began in the classroom.

Moreover, education provided the path through which a predominantly white church, represented by foreign-born nuns and priests, evangelized a black community it did not understand. For blacks, in turn, it provided mobility and strength of resistance as well as belief. The initiative to which blacks responded sprang from a policy decision so central to the organization of American Catholicism that it was made by plenary council of American bishops and implemented by a succession of Savannah bishops. Nonetheless, despite the strong hierarchical interest in Catholic schools for blacks, black and Catholic education diverged from white schools in three key ways. First, the majority of students enrolled in the black schools were always non-Catholic. That is, these schools did not serve a faith community but instead opened up the nucleus of such a potential community to outsiders. Second, while schools reflected their neighborhoods, they also became urban centers for dispersed black populations. In white Savannah, European immigrant Catholics and their descendants have built a series of parochial and private schools that have mirrored the evolution of class and residence patterns. Finally, black schools differed from their white counterparts in that teachers and students belonged to different races. Integration sought to breach this gap, yet the hierarchy often missed black voices in white planning. Hence, the commitment to inclusion of blacks in Catholicism, made against all the contradictions of race and class of the 1860s, resulted a century later in the most traumatic crisis of those who are black and Catholic in Savannah: the closing of the black parish schools between 1968 and 1977.

Both southern society and the changing values of Roman Catholicism have constrained black Catholic schools. In antebellum Georgia, the white-dominated state foreclosed educational opportunities for blacks, slave or free. Emancipation, however, brought a dramatic national reentry of Catholicism into black neighborhoods amidst an intense black interest in education as part of the very meaning of freedom. Yet as black competition threatened, many white Catholics acceded to the segregation of southern society despite their religion's universalist ideology and its missionary action. After Reconstruction, black Catholics again became separate and unequal.

In the twentieth century, three major Catholic schools for blacks in Savannah became nuclei around which parish life coalesced. Since the 1970s, however, educational reform has transformed the mission of the Catholic church in the black community. After the closure of all-black schools, inner-city interparochial schools were set up to reproduce an integrated *Catholic* community rather than an ecumenical *black* one. In practice, these schools have become as much as 70 percent black, including Protestants seeking what they perceive to be a better, more disciplined education for their children. Private Catholic high schools, however, still do not reflect these ratios.

The style and content of education also took shape within critical debates over black education epitomized by the positions of Booker T. Washington and W. E. B. Du Bois. Washington championed practical education following his own Hampton and Tuskegee experiences; Du Bois favored an education completely equal to the academic range offered whites (Washington 1895 (1965); Du Bois 1903 (1965); Anderson 1988). Savannah Catholic nuns and clergy in the nineteenth century attempted a vocational curriculum with little success; academic models, including families and neighborhoods, have triumphed in the twentieth.

Blacks with whom I spoke, finally, recognized the paradoxes of Catholic education in Savannah. A successful lawyer from Saint Anthony's reflected on his own experience:

> The Catholic church and school, in educating minorities, have caused their own dilemma. Those persons would go to college—At that time it was a miracle in West Savannah to graduate from elementary school. They got higher self-esteem, became more aggressive. They were the first to realize what they could not do in Savannah. If they cared.

This chapter pursues the roots and resolutions of such a dilemma, beginning with the fragmentary sources on the white church and black education in antebellum Savannah, through Reconstruction into the first decline of such initiatives. Here, historical ethnography reflects the "top-down" initiative of Catholicism in this period. Since 1900 mission and community have reformed under the aegis of specialized foreign religious orders in conjunction with local black educators and families. With richer documentation and oral traditions, I analyze this period of stabilization from 1907 to 1968 to encompass values, style, and content as well as the special problem of secondary schools. The final sections explore the closure of black Catholic schools and the current Catholic programs, cooperative and parochial, that reach black children. This reveals a shift from education *for* the black community to education *by* that community, which the emergence of parish identity reinforces in the next chapter.

RELIGION, EDUCATION, AND MISSION, 1800-1900

Early French Catholic immigrants in Savannah soon sought Catholic pedagogy to reinforce their faith. They began with a school run by a Father Charles and his relative, Madame Cottineau, in the early 1800s, which closed when both returned to France (Powers 1956, 9-10). No records exist to indicate participation by slaves or free persons of color who had arrived with the plantation owners, although such free blacks might have received some education in Haiti (see James 1963, 19-20).

The Sisters of Mercy established a permanent private Catholic school for whites in the city in 1845. This separation from public schools was typical of the emergence of American Catholicism (Ellis 1956; McNally 1987). By this date, however, government restrictions, enacted after widely publicized slave rebellions in the Carolinas and Virginia, had curtailed black access to education. Bishop John England had been forced to close a school for free blacks in nearby Charleston. In Georgia, in order to "prevent the circulation of written or printed Papers within this State calculated to excite disaffection among the Coloured People of this State, and to prevent said People from being taught to read and write," an act had proscribed that

> If any slave, negro or free person of colour, or any white person, shall teach any other slave, negro or free person of colour, to read or write, either written or printed characters, the said free person of colour, or slave, shall be punished by fine and whipping, or fine or whipping at the discretion of the court; and if a white person so offending, he, she or they shall be punished with a fine, not exceeding five hundred dollars, and imprisonment in the county jail. (Foster 1831, 316-17)[1]

Savannah oral traditions nonetheless suggest exceptions to the public acceptance of discrimination. Older nuns interviewed in the 1950s maintained that Sister Jane Francis of the Sisters of Mercy had run a clandestine school for blacks (Ahles 1977, 138, 490).[2] Better known today is the legacy of Mother Matilda Beasley, who later founded an orphanage for black girls that became part of the Saint Benedict's parish complex. Her descendants and later historians recalled the New Orleans-born woman as a teacher for blacks in the secrecy of her home (Powers 1982; interview with Veronica Arnold 1985; C. Davis 1991). Her 1903 obituary does not mention this endeavor.

These fragments suggest only that individual Catholics, sharing a special vocation, may have cut across the barriers of slavery, race, and education that Southern Catholicism as a beleaguered public institution did not strongly challenge.[3] On the whole, outside of enclaves of intense cultural Catholicism, priests and nuns proved unsuccessful evangelists among most slaves (Green 1972; Woods 1972; Miller 1983a, 1983b; Mills 1983). Later efforts redefined the school as the arena for evangelization as much as a service to the faithful.

Schools took on renewed importance after the Civil War, when American Catholic bishops perceived the collapse of the Confederacy and Emancipation to provide the challenge of a new mission field. American bishops, including southerners, saw the newly freed slaves as a receptive audience even if it was unclear whether the bishops' primary goal was the salvation of blacks or the growth of Catholicism as an institution. Augustine Verot, third bishop of Savannah and a former supporter of slavery, anticipated episcopal actions in letters to the Society for the Propagation of the Faith in 1865:

> The Catholic religion is eminently favorable for attracting and winning the admiration of the Negroes, because of the pomp, variety, and symbolism of its ceremonial ritual. Unhappily, we do not have enough clergy in these parts to give the ritual its full magnificence; let us hope this situation will improve. For the present, we must make a beginning by establishing schools—a necessity. The [northern] Protestants have anticipated us here: they have opened free schools which the Negroes attend in great numbers. Masters and mistresses have come from the North to superintend these schools, and the high salaries paid the teachers will attract many more. The Bible Societies, which, as we know, are quite wealthy, provide amply for school expenses. We must, therefore, prepare for the contest . . . in procuring religious instructions for this simple and docile race. . . ." (in Gannon 1964, 117)

100

Verot portrayed blacks as a non-Catholic target population whom a white hierarchy and its agents should recruit. His first choice for evangelization was the liturgy, corresponding once again to an Orientalist idea of all black values.[4] Schools proved simpler since they relied on sponsorship and employment of teachers rather than scarce ordained leaders. Verot, from his Savannah vantage, explained his necessity in terms of competition with Protestants as well as service to blacks.

Verot championed this cause in pastorals to the Catholics of Georgia and Florida as well as at general meetings of the American bishops in 1866, when he urged priests and leaders "to devote to this work their efforts, their time, finally, if possible, their lives" (Gannon 1964, 118-24). Despite local protests, he founded a Savannah school for blacks in 1867 under the aegis of the Sisters of Saint Joseph, whom he had invited from France. By 1870, this school taught sixty to one hundred students (Gannon 1964, 133-34). His proposal met resistance even among white Catholics: "On Sunday when Bishop Verot announced in the [Saint John's] Cathedral the opening of a school for colored children by French sisters, a whispering of disapproval was heard throughout the congregation, but the Reverend Bishop pushed on" (Stark in Quinn 1978, n.p.).

Yet the impetus for the growth of postbellum American Catholicism came from European immigration—which rose from 1.3 million in 1840 to 6 million in 1880 and 12 million in 1900—rather than native conversion (Greeley 1967, 67, 152; see Ochs 1990). Not only was the demographic presence of European Catholicism solidified, but resources proposed for American-born blacks were channeled to meet the needs of newly arrived Irish, Germans, Italians, and Poles. Whites, although foreign and poor themselves, dominated blacks. In Savannah, as more Irish immigrants streamed into the racially mixed ghettos near the port, Saint Patrick's and the Cathedral's School competed with black schools and chapels. However, the immigrants were already Catholic and produced priests, nuns, and funds for their own institutions.

The Savannah school system reached an accord with the Catholic hierarchy through which the city provided buildings and staffed them with Catholic lay teachers, an arrangement that lasted until 1917 (Powers 1956; Ahles 1977). The administration was less generous with any schools for blacks and made no religious accommodations. East and West Broad Street schools, founded after the war, scarcely met the needs of the newly freed children and adults. Hence, as noted in chapter 1, religious groups, both northern missionaries like the Congregationalists and local Methodists and Baptists, sought to fill the remaining demand with their own schools.

Verot saw these Protestant efforts as effective competitors to his building of Catholicism without crediting the fundamental differences implicit in their grass-roots initiatives. Meanwhile, he distributed his resources around an increasing white flock. Although he left to become bishop of the newly created diocese of Florida, his biographer, Michael Gannon, notes that his dioceses stood out among southern churches in their programs for blacks, despite strong local opposition and limited resources. Yet by his death, Verot saw his effort as a failure, with few conversions outside cities where he had built schools (Gannon 1964, 142).

In Savannah, the record of black and Catholic schools after Verot is incomplete, but it suggests the same trajectory of missionary intervention by white outsiders with minimal development of local black support. In 1874 European monks of the Order of Saint Benedict (Benedictines) arrived at the invitation of Bishop William Gross. They established an urban parish for blacks at Harris and East Broad—the origins of the modern Saint Benedict's—and a school on Perry Street that began in 1875 with fifty students (Oetgen 1969, 168). Within a year, they left to establish a school and monastery on Isle of Hope, about nine miles from the city core, a foundation wiped out by yellow fever in 1876 (Oetgen 1969, 168-71; 1976a, 13-14). Gross favored monastic colonies as a scheme for black conversion and control. He formulated a plan for a national missionary collection that would, in 1884, become the Negro and Indian Collection of the American Catholic church (McNally 1987, 137). The Benedictine mission was refounded as an industrial school for blacks on Skidaway Island, but this, too, was abandoned in the 1880s for a new urban parish, Sacred Heart.

The Benedictine initiative also shows how missionary action in the emancipated black community forced Catholics to consider what blacks wanted and needed from schools. Yet despite the debates that raged among black intellectuals for decades, American bishops took a distanced stance, wondering whether freed slaves would be willing to work at all and even regretted the lost opportunity of a more gradual emancipation (Gannon 1964, 125). In 1865, Bishop Verot had addressed emancipated blacks in a pastoral letter with the admonition, "We think it likewise our duty to remind you that labor, nay constant and serious labor is the lot of all men without any exception" (Gannon 1964, 119). In 1869, he expressed further concerns:

> Wicked men and unprincipled demagogues, abusing their simplicity, their ignorance and credulity, have promised them rich spoils, coming either from the Government or from the estates of their former masters, and have thus made them dupes of their own malice and crafty rapacity. Immense gatherings of colored men, women, and children have often been seen in our midst. What have these deluded creatures found in these meetings? Nothing but additional want and poverty can bring misfortune and punishment upon them. Oh! would that we could see such gatherings [for Redemptorist missions later that winter], where they will learn industry, love of labor, obedience to God, submission to the laws of morality and religion!" (cited in Gannon 1964, 137)

The Benedictines tried such vocational education, but found that the blacks of Skidaway rejected it. In addition to urban religious rivalries, Father Oswald Moosmuller also complained that:

> my plan of having a Manual Labor School for colored boys does not please the majority of the Negroes. The first reason is that most of them have a horror of farm work. The second cause seems to be that they want their boys to get an education which fits them for positions of clerks, bookkeepers, anything else but farmers. They told me that if we open a regular college for colored boys, we will have plenty of students who can pay for their board and tuition and at the same time can have a manual labor school for poor boys. I answered that such a plan is impossible because at present we have neither the buildings nor the professors for such an institute. (Moosmuller to Wimmer, Aug. 18, 1878, cited in Oetgen 1976a, 15)

The Skidaway school started in 1878 with twelve students and bright prospects; by November, only seven boys were left. Both program and discipline proved problematic: "The students' schedule was unusually strict. They rose at five A.M., had Mass and meditation, worked four hours during the day, received instructions for two hours, and recited the rosary twice daily with the brothers. As one historian suggested, the routine was more suitable for postulants or novices than for Negro students" (Oetgen 1969, 175).

When a public school for blacks opened on the island, Father Oswald encouraged a black postulant to become the teacher and thereby to convert more children. He learned to be flexible enough to use a band to "get the good will of our Negroes with such music as the Jesuits succeeded so well with the Indians of Paraguay" (Oetgen 1969, 176).[5] Moreover, while the Benedictines introduced new trees and planting methods, they also turned to locals for advice, indicating more sensitivity to black involvement.

Later, at Sacred Heart, the Benedictines tried to integrate their school but achieved little success against hardening opposition, white and black, and lack of local funds:

> To raise money for the parish, which operated two schools—one for white and the other for black children—Moosmuller began publishing a German historical monthly, *Der Geschichtsfreund*. From 1882 to 1883 he published 24 numbers of the journal, and from the proceeds he managed to cancel the debt of the church and begin constructing a school for the Negro children of the parish. Within two years, however, subscriptions dropped for the journal and he discontinued it . . . with the end of the publication a major source of income for the Negro school was cut off. As a result, Moosmuller had to close the school for blacks and the church eventually became one for whites only. (Oetgen 1976a, 17-18)

This black school never had more than fifty students before closing in favor of the segregated white school in the 1880s (Peterman 1982, 203). Ironically, this parish school became the first in what would later become the dominant pattern for Savannah Catholics: a school run by and sustaining the parish.[6]

Both Verot and Moosmuller read the aspirations of blacks from the standpoint of European peasant or American yeoman populations that valued farm labor as a way of life. Visible through their complaints are the feelings of another community that had been forced into such labor without honor or security. The blacks asked for recompense from their masters or advancement for their children with a logic born out of resistance (Oetgen 1969, 173-74; 181-82; see Bourdieu 1972, 1975). On the whole, Catholics seemed uninterested in drawing blacks into their own educational and religious planning. As late as 1885, no Catholic college in the United States accepted blacks, and thirty-five Catholic elementary schools held fewer than 3,000 black students in contrast to 800,113 in public schools (Ochs 1990, 63).

Despite the problems of the Benedictines, Savannah's next bishop, Thomas Becker, betrayed continuing prejudices within his commitment to blacks:

> Experience teaches us that negroes need to be taught to work, that they easily learn a smattering of the three Rs. To teach them neatness, industry, truth, honesty and decency, Religion must be brought to bear on their sensual nature. They are very prone to vice and when fallen are almost incapable of being raised up. The girls are apt to go wrong at a very early age and their surroundings, even among whites, are very bad. (Aug. 1891, cited in Peterman 1982, 198)

In correspondence with the Josephites, whose order had taken primary responsibility for Catholic ministry to blacks in the United States, Becker suggested that regional bishops still favored large industrial schools run by religious orders (Ochs 1990, 67). In 1893, he wrote to the Josephite newsletter, "It seems to me that colored people need to be taught less in schools, and a great deal more in individual work. They have the notion that the sovereign panacea for all their woes is to be able to read and write a little, and learn something of figures. They believe that such knowledge would somehow keep them from being obliged to work" (Peterman 1982, 199). Pastoral decisions coincided with and reinforced the impositions of Jim Crow.

This paternalistic and culturally biased interpretation of an education offered to blacks recurred among other northern and white philanthropists. In 1903, for example, the General Education Board did not wish to support Savannah State College, since under the leadership of the great educator Richard Wright, it "was too much under the 'false atmosphere' of Atlanta University [bastion of Du Bois], which stressed that 'higher education' only is of importance to the Negro Race" (Anderson 1988, 123). In 1919, after a summer of bloody race riots, Thomas Wyatt Turner of the Committee for the Advancement of Colored Catholics complained to Archbishop Giovanni Bonzano that Catholic University no longer admitted black students, even teaching sisters. In all the Catholic educational establishments in the United States, "the Catholic colored child has been well-nigh excluded from these benefits as though he were not a Catholic" (in C. Davis 1991, 218; see 214-21).

On the whole, the thrust of Catholic education among blacks until the end of the nineteenth century was still perceived as a white Catholic

105

mission to a non-Catholic black community, which sought unsuccessfully to impose an external understanding on the experience of local blacks. Mother Beasley was an exception, yet she followed the spirit of Catholic industrial education in advertising her Saint Francis Industrial and Boarding School for Girls, offering "all the elementary branches . . . also Dressmaking and music" as late as 1889 (*ST* Oct. 19, 1889).

As Michael McNally has noted, the effort to convert blacks was primarily an effort of the American bishops and foreign missionaries: "no popular groundswell was forthcoming in the white or black communities for these episcopal efforts" (1987, 139). Meanwhile, although black Catholics had produced priests and a bishop and organized Catholic Afro-American Congresses in Washington at the turn of the century (1889-94; C. Davis 1991), this consciousness seemed to have little impact on Savannah. Instead, white Catholics as well as black Protestants resisted challenges to their cultural and religious categories. As whites reestablished racial restrictions, Catholic intervention collapsed from a lack of support from blacks or whites.

EDUCATION AND COMMITMENT, 1899-1968

A revolution in Catholic church presence in the black community emerged with two religious orders committed to work alongside blacks: the Franciscan Missionary Sisters of the Immaculate Conception, and the SMA Fathers. The former, arriving in Georgia in 1885 and in Savannah in 1899, became the mainstay of Catholic education among blacks for ninety years. The latter, while not generally in the classroom for more than catechism, developed a statewide framework for education and ministry, based on their African experience, that challenged the foundations of power in the diocese. With these groups, a newly conscious black and Catholic community took shape, in which students, parents, and lay teachers participated.

The agreement between Mother Ignatius Hayes and Bishop Gross for the Franciscans' 1885 mission in Augusta specified both the target—poor colored people—and the content of the order's work: "The said sisters are especially to teach and train young colored girls in those domestic duties, such as washing, ironing, cooking, mending, etc. which form the daily occupation of women. While at the same time, they (the said sisters) will give the colored girls a simple and plain English schooling" (in Ahles 1977, 141). Bishop Gross, in turn, urged the sisters to teach "the negroes a great horror and hatred for impurity—to which they are fearfully addicted" (Ahles 1977, 143). This Franciscan foundation became a nucleus for a black congregation despite the lack of a regular priest: "They have a little Chapel in their house, a Secular Priest says mass there 3 times a week; and it has already all the appearance that this is the beginning of a Negro Parish in Augusta." (Moosmuller to Wimmer in Ahles 1977, 144).

A short-lived Franciscan mission to Savannah's Isle of Hope, companion to the Benedictine school for boys, had failed in 1879. The Sisters of Saint Francis did not agree to return to Savannah until 1896; in 1899 they took over Mother Beasley's orphanage. In 1907 this project, in conjunction with the SMA fathers, was extended to the formation of Saint Benedict's day school in the only remaining black parish in the city.

The arrival of the SMA fathers catalyzed the reorganization of Catholic educational opportunities for Savannah blacks. Father Ignatius Lissner and his companions raised money in Europe and the United States to follow an African missionary model of building many schools to foster parishes with indigenous leadership. From 1909 to 1910, they established Saint Anthony of Padua school in a frame house in West Savannah and opened Saint Augustine, again on the west side, in Springfield Terrace. These schools, first staffed by lay teachers, served three hundred students in 1910 (*ST* Jan. 10, 1910). By October of that year, two more schools had been added, including a night school for working boys under the direction of Robert Gibson, a black graduate of the Hampton Institute (*ST* Jan. 22, 1912). The SMAs recognized the needs of working blacks, while accommodating academics and involving black teachers.

The success of this educational mission was magnified by the city's failure to provide for black education, especially after the abandonment of Reconstruction. By 1913, more than 75 percent of the 8,655 white school-aged children in Savannah were in school; among black children, only 4,086 of 10,699 (38 percent) attended school (*ST* Oct. 15, 1913). Ten public schools existed for whites—including two Catholic institutions. Religious orders also ran two private Catholic secondary schools. Meanwhile, only five public institutions existed for blacks. When one closed in 1914, 2,918 black children jammed the four remaining public schools open to them, while over 1,500 found space in private institutions, with 442 in Catholic schools (*ST* Oct. 17, 1914). The SMA fathers noted with pride: "many of these children would be without any schooling if they had not found admission in the Catholic schools" (*ST* Oct. 15, 1910).

The SMAs also aimed for educational showplaces. Although Saint Anthony's continued to use its farm buildings until the 1940s, the historic Saint Benedict's gained a new three-story brick structure, including a stage, in 1916. Vogel observes that "usually Negroes could use or build only frame-houses. Father Lissner had to insist with the town council on this point; he did not want his school to be burnt down or otherwise destroyed by Ku Klux Klans or other so-called White Trash or other Georgia Crackers of this region" (Vogel [b], 52). Most Pure Heart of Mary, in middle-class Brownville, also provided a public relations coup:[7]

> It will be a magnificent building of the latest and most durable and pressed brick and its dimensions will be forty-three by seventy-three feet. It will be two stories on a basement with the first floor containing four large rooms twenty by thirty feet, while the second will consist of two rooms, a library and an auditorium.[8] The entire building will have all modern improvements such as baths and other conveniences and will be steam heated. (*ST* Feb. 4, 1911)

The SMAs avoided the error of the Benedictines and offered academic programs in black neighborhoods. At the same time, this article portrayed this project as a *gift* from Catholics to blacks, who thus should feel a return obligation: "When completed, it will be a most inspiring looking structure there in the middle of one of our most thickly populated Negro settlements. . . . For this new and magnificent structure the entire Negro population of Savannah is deeply indebted and it will stand as a fitting monument to the Catholics in their untiring efforts to better the advancement of our people in this city." Nevertheless, Marie Williams, a strong leader in Most Pure Heart of Mary during the time I was active there, recalled in 1987 that "they didn't want Catholics to build here in 1907-8. The KKK used to ride here and try to burn the place down, people used to tell us."

SMA publicity from this period provides insights into their philosophy of teaching as well as their sense of mission. They claimed to spare "no trouble and no expense to bring their schools up to a high standard. Not only is a solid secular education guaranteed, but also a good moral training is given to the children. Whilst all religion is eliminated in the public schools, half an hour is set aside in the Catholic schools, during which the great principles of Christianity and of morality are taught and thus the children are better prepared for the great battles of life" (*ST* Sept. 28, 1912). While emphasizing academic and moral education in opposition to either industrial education or secular learning, the SMAs re-

Figure 6. Most Pure Heart of Mary School and original convent and chapel, 1990. Photograph by Cindy Hing-Yuk Wong.

assured wary Protestant parents that "children of all religious denominations are admitted, and their religion is not interfered with. But every student must learn the principles of Christian doctrine and a short summary of Bible History" (*ST* Sept. 28, 1928). The "summary" of the Bible, rather than direct contact, indicates a Catholic slant that was evident to students in later classes who recall religion classes as undiluted catechism.

Another apparent innovation was also introduced: tuition. At this point, the SMAs charged five cents a week for kindergarten and ten for other grades. Funds, however, were available for those who could not otherwise afford to attend. This did not pay for school expenses, but it signaled a new participation by blacks in the school and parish.

A final striking adaptation in building community was the SMAs' use of black lay teachers, heretofore untapped in formal black and Catholic education in Savannah, although it may have reflected their Africanist strategies. In 1912, three of the four schools were staffed by unmarried black women, probably not Catholic according to a document in the diocesan and SMA archives (Lissner n.d., 2). When Robert Gibson left, however, the working boys' school closed. Other impacts of schools as an arena for lay involvement will be discussed in chapter 6.

In 1916, the SMAs faced a threat to their expanding teaching, especially at Saint Benedict's, as laws appeared in the South forbidding whites from teaching in black schools. In nearby St. Augustine, Florida, for example, Sister Mary Thomasine of the Sisters of Saint Joseph was "arrested and jailed for violating a 1913 state law forbidding white teachers to 'teach negroes in a negro school'" (Gannon 1964, 142). As rumblings grew in Georgia, Lissner formed an order of black nuns, the Handmaids of the Most Pure Heart of Mary, whom he hoped eventually would take over the school system. This order became one of only three successful black orders of nuns founded in the United States (Raboteau 1978; Ochs 1990; C. Davis 1991; see chapter 5).

Lissner conceived the order as social as well as educational: "It is not to be an exclusively teaching institution. The sisters will have to be instructed in Religion in order to be practical catechists and settlement workers" (n.d., 4). Their program would include domestic works as well academics. Mother Mary Theodore, the Louisiana-born superior, gathered five other black women around her and moved into the Most Pure Heart of Mary building, outfitted with dormitories, sewing room, community room, and classroom (Lissner n.d., 5). There seems to be no indication that these women were from Savannah, and no family connections remain there. In their convent, though, they were visited by the Sisters of Saint Joseph, who had previously taught blacks in the diocese, and by the Little Sisters of the Poor as well as by Bishop Keiley.

A pamphlet published by the Handmaids summarized the fate of their educational mission: "the proposed Bill to outlaw the teaching of Black children by White teachers did not pass. The White Sisters continued to teach in the schools of Father Lissner, except, Saint Anthony. Here the Handmaids of Mary taught. The meager earnings received from teaching were not enough to supply their needs. In order to survive, the Sisters conducted a laundry" (Franciscan Handmaids of the Most Pure Heart of Mary n.d., 4-6; Vogel [b], 72-76; Lissner n.d.; Ochs 1990). Their teaching received little local publicity, and the Handmaids' work threatened to become primarily domestic, thus replicating the stratification of race and gender within the larger society. In the 1920s, these nuns accepted an invitation to move to New York (Franciscan Handmaids n.d.; Vogel [b], 72-76; *NYT* Mar. 1, 1981).

SMA plans also moved beyond the city. In 1909, at a mission parish in Augusta, 120 miles northwest of Savannah, the SMA fathers again established close relations with the Franciscans who had preceded them (Vogel [b], 273-74). Our Lady of Lourdes in Atlanta was opened in 1911, with a school staffed by Philadelphia philanthropist Katharine Drexel's Sisters of the Blessed Sacrament, an order devoted to black and Native-American missions (275-76). In 1914, Saint Peter Claver in Macon was opened, likewise staffed by the Sisters of the Blessed Sacrament, who remain there (277-78). This expansion stopped by 1920 after conflicts between Lissner and Bishop Keiley. Thereafter, the American SMAs focused on consolidation, although they constructed a motherhouse in New Jersey and opened new parishes in Los Angeles and Tucson.

Black and Catholic school enrollments in Savannah after 1922 show a steady growth in schools and parishes [9] The early Depression years seem to have continued this consolidation, but a precipitous drop appeared in the mid-1930s. Oral narratives suggest that blacks again found this a good time to migrate north, following the route blazed in earlier decades. As then, this might have emphasized divisions among blacks and Catholics torn between values of community and individual strategy, especially for those now educated for better opportunities.

Isolated school figures from 1947-48 suggest a postwar boom in education, where enrollments nearly doubled in each of the schools, putting pressure on teachers and facilities. A letter in Saint Anthony's archives from 1947 talks about Franciscan and SMA concerns for a new school with a room for the sisters and an added classroom (Canavan Aug. 15, 1947). This school was constructed in 1949 by the SMAs with diocesan and some parochial aid, indicating a renewed dependence between missionary orders and the diocese as black and Catholic schools were incorporated into active parishes.

With the exception of the founding of Saint Pius X High School in the 1950s, this educational steady state operated in Savannah for five decades. School enrollments in 1958-59, on the eve of integration, show the extent and meaning of black Catholic education. Catholic elementary schools served 834 black students, while 119 older students were enrolled in Saint Pius (table 1). Of the younger pupils, only 259 (31 percent) were Catholic. High school enrollments inverted these ratios, with 70 percent of the students belonging to the Catholic church, indicating both childhood conversions and selection for reproduction of the Catholic community as factors in secondary education. Overall, blacks accounted for 27 percent of all students in the Catholic system, probably twice the proportion of blacks among active members of the Savannah Catholic church.

STYLE AND CONTENT

Although the classrooms of all traditional black and Catholic schools have been abandoned or converted to other uses, the schools themselves still convey messages that the SMA and Franciscan period represented to black and Catholic education in Savannah. All three are imposing buildings, incorporated into religious complexes. Both Saint Mary's and Saint Benedict's tower over their surrounding neighborhood. The symbolic weight of Saint Benedict's was augmented by its imposing rectory and the adjacent Franciscan convent. Saint Anthony's, a later building, is set apart by its parklike ambiance in an urban area; hence its nickname, "Saint Anthony's Country Day."

As students and teachers remember these educational spaces, classrooms were complemented by a general meeting room for assemblies, without facilities for hot lunches. Statues and religious markers decorated the halls and main areas, intensifying the religious ambiance of the educational mission. Outdoor playgrounds served the school and neighborhood.

The school represented temporal and spatial discipline. Bells rang in each neighborhood for early morning mass and later called children to the school. Upper level students at Saint Benedict's recall walking miles across the entire city, trying to beat the bell to avoid punishments from the sisters. Uniforms also became part of school life, although these were not present in the 1920s, perhaps because of expense—"we barely had enough money to buy books." Later, they became a badge of Catholic distinctiveness within the city. Saint Pius X High School, for example, adopted maroon and gold uniforms distinguishable as Catholic yet clearly differentiated from other, white Catholic high schools as well as black public schools.

Inside, the classroom was always characterized by its continuous linkage with the religious space of church. A crucifix, a distinctively Catholic key symbol of the Christian message, hung in every room. Pictures and statues marked Catholic space and were reintegrated in the calendar through the year. The nuns, as religious specialists detached from the secular world, became themselves both teachers and symbols. Parish priests visited frequently, teaching catechism or distributing small gifts. Mass in the church attended by the school children affirmed this blending of parish, school, and community.

Table 1: Savannah Catholic School Enrollment, 1958–59

School	Total Students (+K)	Black*	White*	Male	Female	Catholic	Non-Catholic
Elementary Schools							
Blessed Sacrament	644	0	644	317	327	637	7
Cathedral Day	421	0	421	230	191	412	9
Nativity	210	0	210	111	99	202	8
Sacred Heart	356	0	356	178	178	333	23
Saint James	445	0	445	234	221	427	18
Saint Michael's	143	0	143	77	66	94	45
Saint Anthony's	175	175	0	85	90	69	106
Most Pure Heart of Mary	333	333	0	167	166	114	219
Saint Benedict's	326	326	0	155	171	76	250
Secondary Schools							
Benedictine	303	0	303	303	—	241	62
Saint Vincent's	200	0	200	0	200	195	5
Saint Pius	119	119	0	47	72	83	36

Source: Diocesan School Board Archives

*Race is not specified, but we can presume a division by segregation

Figure 7. Early ca. 1930s kindergarten classes at Saint Anthony's School. Photograph courtesy Gloria and Evelyn Daniels.

The parish and orders also supported the school. By the 1930s tuition remained minimal—twenty-five or fifty cents per month—although priests and nuns waived even that for those who could not pay. Collections in the 1930s, 1940s, and 1950s remained similarly minuscule. Saint Anthony's, with the poorest physical plant, relied on laymen to raise money and repair buildings; in the 1930s, its students were charged with fueling the pot-bellied stove that provided heat. Money from the diocese, the Bureau of Indian and Negro Missions, and Northern philanthropists continued to supplement school and church. The teaching sisters received minimal salaries as well: Saint Mary's records, for example, show an increase from $30 to $35 per month in 1948. Scarce resources shaped pedagogy. In 1947-48, records show Saint Mary's collected $4,350 from tuition, books, supplies, and extra events as the basis for its budget for 263 students. Some teachers faced the demands of two concurrent classes; this may have meant fifty to sixty students each.

114

School and parish came together for special events like first communion and confirmation. At holidays and school closing exercises, students put on shows, of religious and secular themes, to which the parish and neighbors came for a small admission charge, a tradition shared with black public schools. A stage was included in the physical plant of each of the schools, including the transformed farm buildings of Saint Anthony's. In 1916, the *Savannah Tribune* described the festivities at Saint Benedict's:

> An immense throng attended last Monday St. Benedict's commencement exercises at Beach Institute. The whole event was a profound success. The music and singing were most charming, the recitations and speeches perfect. The little dramas were rendered with great skill and the flower drill was lovely. Gladys Rodriguez made the valedictory address and Mary Gridiron pronounced the opening speech. Four graduates received diplomas and their parents and friends rushed to shake hands and to present them with sweet bouquets of flowers. Genevieve Mills obtained the highest marks in graduating examinations, an average of 98 per cent. Nelson Cuyler and Mary Gridiron came next with 97 percent. Gladys Rodriguez carried an average of 96 per cent. (June 12, 1916)

*These events included some role for everyone, from the youngest children in flower drills to the final speeches. All graduates were recognized by name. At the same time, the ceremony drew together the school, the parish, the secular black community—in the use of Beach Institute—and white Catholicism, via Father Foley, the guest speaker from the cathedral.

Schools also responded to neighborhood families in which mothers worked by beginning classes with preschool or primer. Father Martin, for example, established this program in Saint Anthony's in the 1930s, as Mrs. Georgia Mae Tanxley Lucas recalled for a parish anniversary: "I was young and hardly knew what I was doing, but I needed a job. I was surprised how easy it was, but I had always dealt with children. But there were so many who had never been to school. . . . The older ones were embarrassed."

Primary education covered basics of reading, writing, and numbers; the SMAs and Franciscans favored an academic program, which may have increased their support among blacks. Some Saint Anthony's parishioners recalled an additional WPA-sponsored program that supplied after-school programs in basketry, sewing, and music, taught by neighborhood women. Latin was also taught in the upper grades of Saint Benedict, less as part of a classical education than as a means of incorporating children into the liturgy.[10]

115

Figure 8. Saint Benedict's School and rectory, 1990. Photograph by Cindy Hing-Yuk Wong.

Religion and morals were central to the program—"It began with catechism and ended with catechism." The priest supplemented the teaching staff, or at least came by to impress upon the students the seriousness of the activity. This also reaffirmed a male domination over the nuns or lay teachers of the classroom and the discipline imposed on students. A modern educator, reflecting on her schooling in the 1950s, criticized the methods: "St. Benedict's was like robots, rote education. . . . Father came in, we stood up. Mother Superior came in, we stood up. Missed mass on Sunday, we were strapped. . . .Whatever they said was law. . . ." Still, she noted "it was probably not different in public education."

As this and other memories suggest, discipline was a major value in the Catholic classroom. Parents valued it, even though nuns enforced learning with corporal punishments. At the Saint Anthony's seventy-fifth anniversary celebration, discipline was a frequent topic of recollections. A businessman in his forties recalled how his first day at school began with joy, "Then I got up here and I seen the nuns (Laughter). In other words, all hell broke loose: I hollered, cried. And that lasted about 10 minutes, until

Sister Margaret Mary got tired of it. I guess she got one of her number three switches and sanctified me a little bit (Laughter). I learned then she meant business, and I have a lot to thank her for that." Reflecting later, this same man concluded: "a house built on weak foundations cannot stand. And the education and discipline I received here took me all through life. . . . [I] regret that a lot of kids didn't get what I went through, didn't have the joy of those times."[11] A sense of order, and Catholic symbolism, pervade a vintage photograph of a classroom in Saint Benedict's (Figure 9).

Discipline permeated the ambience of the school without generally reaching these extremes. For example, Pie Chisholm recalled that nuns "had rulers, sticks in their hands. They made you stand in the corner. Made you write something over and over." But she recalled none of the threats of divine punishment—"Jesus is hurt when you lie" that McClaren (1986) has documented for other Catholic schools. Discipline was more firmly ingrained in the order of uniforms, class exercises, and activities that extended from the school to the neighborhood, as in Saint Anthony's bell. In contemporary discussions, the importance of discipline has been exaggerated by new problems of drugs, crime, and fragmentation that are perceived to threaten the black family (Hunt and Hunt 1975, 1976; Howze et al. 1984).

The "mystical" presence of the nuns reinforced their control. Nuns, while more accessible than priests, were set apart by their distinctive habits and cloistered life. At the Saint Anthony's anniversary, Sister John Frances also joked about the nickname that students had for her: "The Little General"; nicknames students recalled for others were sometimes much less complimentary. But students more often recalled awe at the sanctity that set the nuns and priests apart and made their word more powerful: "The priests were next to God, the sisters were next to God." Black lay teachers' power was reinforced instead by their importance in the parish community.

Yet for all the compassion and values of the parish schools, students became aware of the contradictions of Catholic education in Savannah. The commitment of missionaries to the black community could, itself, reproduce inequalities. One student, who went from Saint Mary's to Benedictine, complained that the nuns had overcompensated for black education, that they had not brought him to the level of the white schools. In part, he blamed this on a lack of contact between the teaching sisters and whites, emphasizing their status as "our sisters," whites who were sociologically black. Others complained that nuns favored old and active families: "some families were always right, others always

Figure 9. Classroom at Saint Benedict's, ca. 1948. Photograph courtesy of the Georgia Historical Society, Cordray-Foltz Collection.

wrong." A few echoed Geraldine Abernathy's Louisiana complaints of favoritism for fair-skinned students.

Schools replicated the prejudices built into urban society, including social and economic factors that limited educational performance. The inequality in academic performance between black and white schools became a primary focus of outside analysts in 1969. It is difficult, however, to weigh the holistic experience of the black and Catholic school by culturally biased academic measures alone (see Griffin and Brown 1979, 76-80). Those who transferred to segregated secondary public schools, by contrast, often found it easy.[12]

Other divisions within the church and school system seem more trivial but prove still painful as memories among alumni with whom I have spoken in the 1980s. Black schools curtailed sports programs since they could only play against other black schools. Black children, among all Catholic school children, were denied rights to march in the Saint Patrick's Day parade, a major affirmation of local Catholic identity, until

1968 (Fogarty 1960). Ultimately, problems in style and content sprang from the fundamental contradictions of the Catholic church as a whole in the black community:

> Unlike the German or Irish parish schools, the teachers in black
> Catholic schools were often not from the same ethnic background as
> their students, that is, not black. Unlike the student population of the
> European ethnic schools, most students in the African Catholic schools
> were Protestant. Unlike the other Catholic ethnic schools, which were
> designed to preserve language, culture and ethnic pride, black Catho-
> lic schools exposed their pupils to the prevailing white American
> Catholic culture and tradition, including racism. . . . The black Catholic
> schools did not communicate to their students a very positive self-
> image or a strong sense of self worth, or a pride in one's ethnic heri-
> tage, all of which are so necessary in the fulfillment of one's human
> potential. (McNally 1987, 183)

McNally's harsh global evaluation should be nuanced by both practice and memories within black Savannah. Yet the formation of Catholic education in the black community had faced such contradictions from the beginning. Despite or perhaps in response to this ambivalence, the school emerged as a part of the community, where the classroom was intrinsically bound to the family, the neighborhood, and the parish.

SECONDARY EDUCATION

Saint Anthony's and Saint Mary's offered limited programs that eventually extended to the eighth grade. Students could then complete ninth grade at Saint Benedict's. After this, generations of black and Catholic students continued in public schools, such as Beach Institute or Savannah State College's program. Hence, until the 1950s, blacks again had a comparative disadvantage in Catholic education.

White and Catholic high schools were private schools under the direction of religious orders rather than the diocese. The SMAs and Franciscans showed an early interest in such a secondary project in the black community as well: in 1912, the *Savannah Tribune* mentions a visit of Father Dahlent to Belmead College in Rockcastle, Virginia, an industrial school where three Savannah youths were graduating and ten others enrolled (June 6, 1912). In 1916 Father Lissner proposed a contro-

versial seminary for black priests, which could have offered higher education for at least some males, and he encouraged training for the
Handmaids. The Franciscan Sisters, by the 1940s, opened a black high
school associated with the SMA parish in Augusta.

Savannah's black Catholics also argued for a high school in the 1940s.
A 1951 Bureau of Indian and Negro Missions report, cited by Sister Julian
Griffin, emphasized demands for a "Colored Catholic High School in Savannah at the earliest possible time, in order to preserve the faith and morals of our Colored Catholic children." Sister Julian added that "parents had
been asking for a high school for some years, and some were reluctant to
send their children to the public high school, which they felt might constitute a danger to the morals and faith of their children" (Griffin and Brown
1979, 71). Retired SMA priests also recalled concern for loss of blacks to
northern migration and to other religions associated with public schools.

Money for the school finally was raised from the Bureau of Indian
and Negro Missions, who funded construction of a basic building with
four classrooms, science room, library, cafeteria, and offices at a completed cost of eighty-five thousand dollars (Griffin and Brown 1979, 72).
Local blacks raised money by buying bricks; priests sought donations
from whites in Savannah and the North. Savannah black and Catholic
support continued to be a mainstay of the school throughout its career,
furnishing the library and constructing the gymnasium-auditorium in
1955. Clearly, this showed a stronger community taking charge of its
actions and education rather than merely receiving missionary donations.

The school opened in 1952 with ninth and tenth grades and graduated its first fourteen students in 1955. Franciscan nuns and SMA fathers
joined local blacks in teaching at the school. A 1962 dedication program
for a new wing listed an SMA father teaching religion and Latin while
four nuns shared mathematics, English, music, French, typing, biology,
and social studies. Diocesan priests later joined as teachers and modera-
tors while local black laymen taught athletics and home economics
(some teachers at Savannah State College acted as volunteers in parish
schools). This program included thirty-four seniors, with their college
choices ranging from Savannah State to Spelman in Atlanta; Xavier in
New Orleans; Nazareth in Bardstown, Kentucky; and Hampton Institute.

A Pius X self-study in 1967 assessed the success of the program as
uniquely suited to a distinctive student body that had "suffered at the hands
of a cultural and economic system which has made academic progress difficult and thereby deprived them of the opportunity of progress in other

areas of society." The tuition, at $120, was a third that of the other Catholic high schools, and scholarships were available. While non-Catholics continued to attend, more than two-thirds of those enrolled were Catholic in 1958-59, twice the proportion of Catholics in black elementary programs.

Two programs coexisted, resolving the Washington-Du Bois debate. The college prep program had "a strong-emphasis on remedial work and/ or bringing bright students up to potential." This included four years of religion, two of history, four of mathematics, four of science, four of English, and three of French, and options of contemporary problems and typing. A general program had "strong emphasis on practical courses geared to foster an adequate self-image and good social and moral traits." The school also had a newspaper and programs in debate, leadership, and teen living. A report on the graduating class of 1968, included in the brochure, "Welcome to St. Pius X," noted that of forty-three graduates, two were in the Air Force, six were employed, one was deceased, and thirty-four were in college and nursing school. Between 1963 and 1968, 72 percent of graduates attended college (DS School Board Archives, Saint Pius X file).

Saint Pius developed the spirit of the parish schools in combining religious and moral education with practical skills. It also emphasized the ties of school and community, as "Welcome to St. Pius" notes: "We believe that the Catholic school provides but one portion of the educational experience. It shares the education of the total person especially with the family, the Church and the various private and public agencies set up for that purpose" (1967-68 [?], n.p.; DS School Board Archives). The school's ideal was reiterated in a 1967 position paper by teachers, students, and parents for the Notre Dame study. It described Saint Pius as an educational institution and a cultural symbol, observing that:

> Education of a child involves the complex of experience which enables him to enter adult life whole, uninjured and ready to face life's challenges. Part of this education takes place in the school. It does so because the home is not equipped to provide the variety of experiences necessary to prepare a child for the world in which he will live. This is true not only in the academic world but in the world of personal relationships. . . .
>
> Catholic high schools, too, must reflect real life. They must bring together boys and girls, rich and poor, Catholics and non-Catholics, black and white, the highly intelligent and the less so. Until they do, they cannot provide quality education. (DS School Board Archives, Saint Pius X file)

While calling for integration, this statement demonstrates a holistic concept of education, transcending categorization, in opposition to the traditional formation of Benedictine and Saint Vincent's, which enshrined divisions of race, gender, religion, and to some extent class. The answer to such contradictions, from the standpoint of the black community, was the use of Saint Pius as the nucleus of a new integrated educational system.

Saint Pius represented the first diocesan high school and the first coed program.[13] Yet it never achieved more than a trickle of movement across the rigid boundary of race. By the time of its closure in 1971, only two whites were enrolled; Saint Vincent's and Benedictine had enrolled as many blacks in their programs in the early 1960s. Today, for example, there remain complaints that Bishop Frey did not send the white Catholic orphans of Saint Mary's Home to Saint Pius to help integrate it. Saint Pius also failed to increase vocations to the priesthood and the religious sisters. Black vocations, after limited success in the nineteenth century, had disappeared, despite Father Lissner's concerns. As the community became large and stable in the 1960s, black vocations were encouraged by the integration of the minor seminary, Saint John Vianney, founded by Bishop Thomas McDonough to train priests. No black students completed their training for ordination, however.

Saint Pius X could have become divisive, as it marked the social and economic selection among elementary students that limited those who would complete high school. Instead, judging from all my conversations in Savannah, it became a source of pride in the Savannah black and Catholic community. As one student reflected on its closing, he lamented, "It was the only institution that we had been able to hold onto and say it's ours. Various people who hold leadership positions do so because of Saint Pius." This symbolic as well as educational role made the closure of Saint Pius in 1971 an agonizing moment for the community as a whole.

THE TRAUMA OF SCHOOL CLOSURES, 1969 TO 1977

In 1969, a study commission under the aegis of the Office of Educational Research of the University of Notre Dame was invited to review the parochial school system of Savannah: "The research team studied population and area growth, school enrollment and growth, faculty and staff, academic and religious education outcomes, parents' attitudes, and finance" (*SC* Nov. 26, 1970). The SMA fathers were already departing

122

under the slogan of a newly unified diocese. Civil rights activism and Vatican II also challenged long-standing assumptions about the correct organization of Catholic education.

The Notre Dame commission recommended closure of several schools, primarily those in black parishes. Their reasoning included facilities and academic programs, as well as the meaning of racial and class division:

> Students of average to low ability who do not have an academic orientation or an achievement orientation usually come from homes of low socio-economic circumstances. In Chatham County this is true. Cathedral Day, St. Benedict's, St. Mary's and Pius X—in comparison with other schools—did poorly especially in Science, Social Studies, and Math at the elementary level, and Reading, Science and Social Studies at the high school level. . . . People of lower socio-economic backgrounds, black or white, are not born dull. They are made dull and kept dull by a self-perpetuating circumstance which more than likely is a result of the economic system. Chatham Catholic schools need to take steps to remedy this situation. (cited in Griffin and Brown 1979, 78)

While taking account of the socio-economic system of the county as a whole, other vital questions of meaning for the black community were unheard.

Ironically, a minimal breach in the barriers of race and education had already been forced. Enrollments for Savannah Catholic schools in 1964 show a handful of black students in three suburban white elementary schools, as well as three blacks in Benedictine and one enrolled in St. Vincent's. Equally striking from table 2, however, is the barrier defined by white domination of the black (marked) category: as far as I can ascertain, no whites ever enrolled in the traditionally black elementary programs, despite St. Pius's "tokens."

Saint Benedict's was recommended for closure on the basis of student safety. Since renovation of the 1916 building was considered too expensive, the school was closed in 1969. An older male recalled in 1986: "Blacks went crazy. It had been there 100 years. At Tybee, they didn't have three black Catholics. Or Nativity. The priests said leave us alone." The newer Saint Anthony's also closed, after recommendations that its four grades be transferred to Cathedral Day School. Again, protests erupted; parishioners marched on the chancery. At the 1985 Saint

Anthony's anniversary, Gwendolyn Goodman, a public school principal, recalled the emotion of the period:

> When the Notre Dame society began its work, it had several of the representatives from the white Catholic community but there were basically no representatives from the black community. Some of those representatives today still agonize over having served on that committee and recall it as one of the most difficult periods in the history of Catholicism in the diocese of Savannah. . . .
>
> When the communicants and the parents of Saint Anthony's heard the news, it was a community that was deeply distraught and deeply embittered. A community that felt a sense of betrayal, if I might use that word, about what was happening in our community and our schools. . . . We approached the Bishop . . . and asked him to reconsider. . . . [Father Cuddy] consented to meet with us in the parish hall, to discuss, hopefully, the fate of the schools. Many of us came with open minds and open hearts and with prayers hoping that the schools would survive. I can remember, very vividly, one of the most heartrending situations that occurred when many faced reality in the parish hall that night that the schools would close. We were told that the buses were going to be sold. We appealed as to how we were going to get the children from St Anthony's to other schools that would remain open and I am very certain I heard Father respond "We will use Our Lady of Lourdes bus [a white parish] and we will ask them to stop and pick your children up." A long period of agony. Some historian said if you forget the mistakes of the past you are destined to repeat them in the future.

Closure, thus, suggested a painful new dependence on a white parish and school. Other actions also evoked the specter of closure of the parish or disruption of the community as Goodman noted, when some schools informed parents that "you will pay for the tuition as would a non-Catholic unless you attend this church as a parishioner. Some of you may remember that; I experienced it." The responsibility of Catholic schools to non-Catholic parents surfaced as a problem as did questions of black and Catholic identity itself. Reflecting on this incident in 1986, for example, a black educator in her fifties told me "when they closed the Catholic schools, it was my first rude awakening of just being talked down to as an adult and professional adult. Father ———— talked as if 'Let me tell these ignoramuses what they will do.' I became angry. . . . That was the turning point. I was a professional."

Table 2: Savannah Catholic School Enrollment, 1964

School	Total Students	Black	White	Male	Female	Catholic	Non-Catholic
Elementary Schools							
Blessed Sacrament	524	—	—	—	—	—	—
Cathedral Day	250	0	250	123	127	235	15
Nativity	305	1	304	153	152	289	16
Sacred Heart	351	2	249	175	176	370	11
Saint James	668	4	664	337	331	663	5
Saint Michael's	130	0	130	71	59	117	13
Saint Anthony's	152	152	0	74	78	71	81
Most Pure Heart of Mary	398	398	0	193	205	145	201
Saint Benedict's	—	—	—	—	—	—	—
Secondary Schools							
Benedictine	270	3	267	270	0	225	45
Saint Vincent's	268	1	267	0	268	265	3
Saint Pius	165	165	0	72	93	106	59

Source: Diocesan School Board Archives

Saint Pius X closed in 1971. This closure was gradual, stopping admission to new classes while allowing juniors and seniors to graduate. This remains today a more painful decision in terms of the feeling of the black community, which was keenly aware of the recent struggles that had been carried out to build up the school as a collective project:

> A Christian man loves God and doesn't worry about men but I still feel pangs when I go by there. Blacks get lost in white schools and parishes. But that group came in from Notre Dame and closed them down. Bishop Frey came in, closed Saint Benedict's, Saint Mary's, Saint Anthony's, and Saint Pius X, and then left. He was a hatchet man. (Male educator, thirties, 1985)

> I understood closing the elementary schools, but not Saint Pius, which was so new and meant so much to us. Not just because it wasn't integrated; . . . it might have become so in time the way people move. Everyone worked so hard. First they told us that the library wasn't good enough, so we found donors and raised money through sales, etc. Then they said it wasn't integrated. But 98 percent went to college—better than Benedictine. Do you close a school like that? (woman, forties, 1985)

Again, the hierarchy and the white schools came to the forefront, although this time many blacks perceived their bishop as a villain.

An official statement on the closure referred to the master plan of "amalgamation whereby our integration process will be accelerated so that the results demanded by social justice and the tenor of the times will soon be effected and realized" (DS School Board Archives, Saint Pius X File). In response to a motion of the Black Clergy Caucus in Atlanta that condemned the closure of black schools and charged southern bishops with "gutlessness," an editorial in the diocesan newspaper reaffirmed that closure intended to "further integrated education." It summarized the closings by noting: "In every case cited, reasons for the closings were very prosaic and very pragmatic. In no case was 'racism' the cause" (*SC* Nov. 26, 1970).

The public statements of those who opposed closure agreed with the ideal of integration but objected to "the continuing withdrawal of the Church from its traditional service to the black community and this at a time of great crisis and even greater promise." Furthermore, protesters strongly objected to "the manner in which this decision was reached.

Neither school administration, faculty, parents, students nor school board was consulted." (DS School Board Archives, Saint Pius X File). White hierarchical action, caught up in the civil rights movement, reduced the problem of black and white to a single variable based on their vision of the dominant racial paradigm. Their criteria and their imposed process appeared to override concerns of holistic and community education in which blacks had taken initiative. The clash of two distinct if well-meaning paradigms produced a tragic process that scars the black and Catholic community to this day. As the black bishops observed nationally in 1984, "We even dare to suggest that the efforts made to support [black parochial schools] and to insure their continuation are a touchstone of the local Church's sincerity in the evangelization of the Black community" (Howze et al. 1984, 28). Closure also had an impact on black enrollment and even more salience in the long-term decrease of black Catholic baptisms. The decrease in high school enrollment is particularly notable

In 1989 an administrator mentioned to me an alternate plan that had been discussed to deal with integration of the high schools, involving the consolidation of all three high schools and the minor seminary into a single diocesan campus. This was precipitated by a crisis at Benedictine, where the monks of Belmont Abbey found themselves unable to maintain their commitment to the campus in the mid-1960s. The Sisters of Mercy agreed to the plan, postponing a fund drive. Yet no discussion or decision was made public while the chancery awaited an outcome on the future of the dominant male school. A last minute agreement with the Benedictine community of Saint Vincent's in Latrobe eviscerated this plan, which apparently was never widely discussed. Here, however, the critical space of black and Catholic education could have achieved its status as a prophetic voice for systemic reform.

Most Pure Heart of Mary, in 1977, became the last school to close. When I asked parishioners if they had believed the school would survive, I was told "Not exactly. It wasn't that we believed it would not close, but we resisted, we tried to force the diocese's hand, to upgrade. We brought in some other nuns. Only two that time." Saint Mary's School Board felt they could not operate with a staff composed fully of laity. Alternative plans were proposed entailing the use of Saint Pius, clustering three grades there with other units at Cathedral and Sacred Heart. Nonetheless, principals felt clustering "would put all three buildings on the road to becoming all black institutions and we'd end up with three

Table 3: Savannah Catholic School Enrollment, 1971

School	Tuition	Total Students	Black	White	Male	Female	Catholic		Non-Catholic	
							Black	White	Black	White
Elementary Schools										
Blessed Sacrament	$127	536	48	485	269	267	46	474	2	11
Cathedral Day	$249	249	80	165	105	144	60	120	20	45
Nativity of Our Lord	$165	286	19	262	144	142	9	246	10	16
Sacred Heart	$150	228	102	125	115	113	62	107	40	16
Saint James	$191	658	4	638	342	315	2	610	2	28
Saint Michael's	$144	86	0	83	42	44	—	60	—	23
Most Pure Heart of Mary	$185	262	262	0	115	147	86	—	176	—
Secondary Schools										
Benedictine	$532	376	23	339	376	0	17	—	6	—
Saint Vincent's	$327	302	23	273	0	302	17	248	9	25
Saint Pius	$200	124	122	2	—	—	87	1	37	1

Source: Diocesan School Board Archives

Table 4: Savannah Catholic School Enrollment, 1975

School	Total Students	Male	Female	Black	White	Other	Catholic	Non-Catholic
Elementary Schools								
Blessed Sacrament	465	220	245	61	404	—	435	30
Cathedral	259	109	150	80	119	—	181	78
Nativity	285	145	140	10	275	—	262	23
Sacred Heart	260	131	129	100	141	9	182	78
Saint James	622	323	295	4	595	23	620	2
Saint Mary's	258	123	135	258	0	—	64	194
Secondary Schools								
Benedictine	498	498	—	37	452	9	341	157
Saint Vincent's	399	—	399	50	348	1	364	35

Source: Diocesan School Board Archives

Saint Mary's rather than one" (résumé of a meeting with principals of Cathedral, Sacred Heart, and Saint Mary's, Oct. 25, 1976, Most Pure Heart of Mary Parish Archives). Notes on another meeting between the diocesan superintendent, Father Seikel, and the group that sponsored social studies in Saint Pius X, raised a further problem:

> The Board indicated that they would be much more in accord with the idea of utilizing Pius as a school if the closure of St. Mary's meant that there would be 250 Catholic children unable to attend a Catholic school. But inasmuch as we are talking about closing down the present two programs in order to accommodate 190 non-Catholic children in a Catholic school, they were less sympathetic. (Nov. 15, 1976; Most Pure Heart of Mary Archives)

Catholics were guaranteed acceptance at another Catholic school while others were accepted on a secondary, space-available basis. Hence the hierarchy reenacted the dominant pattern of integration without appreciating the historical circumstances of the black and Catholic school.

During my fieldwork in Savannah, a decade after the closure of the black parish schools and Saint Pius X, these events still evoked an almost unanimously pained reaction among blacks who experienced them as students, parents, or members of the parish communities. Closure became a call to action, linked to other social convulsions, in which the black and Catholic community showed a strong identity and took on their previous benefactors.

Nonetheless, a comparison of school enrollments in tables 3, 4, and 5 suggests how groups survived these mergers. In 1964, 557 black elementary students, of whom 282 were Catholic, attended two of three schools. In 1971, 535 were enrolled, with 262 in the all-black Saint Mary's school. The proportion of non-Catholics, 290, was slightly higher. In 1975, 532 black students, with 265 non-Catholics were enrolled. Only in the 1985-86 figures did a significant new trend emerge, with 337 enrollees, only one-third of whom (133) were non-Catholic (table 5).

High school data show a clearer drop in black enrollment. Figures from 1964 show 169 blacks enrolled (including 3 not at Saint Pius), of whom 59 were not Catholic. This remained almost constant in 1971, the year of Pius's closure. In 1975, however, the black secondary school population had dropped to 103, and in 1985-86, it sank to 95. The last year shows an increase in black non-Catholic high school students, especially at Benedictine, where proportions are almost even.

Table 5: Savannah Catholic School Enrollment, 1985–86

School	Tuition	Total Students	Black	White	Male	Female	Catholic Black	Catholic White	Non-Catholic Black	Non-Catholic White
Elementary Schools										
Sacred Heart	$840	237	115	117	120	117	73	—	43	—
Saint Michael's	$830	98	0	93	49	44	55	—	38	—
Blessed Sacrament	$850	306	71	231	155	151	53	197	18	54
Saint James	$858	537	16	494	—	—	14	481	2	13
Nativity of Our Lord	$900	292	5	282	—	—	5	—	0	—
Cathedral Day	$790	272	130	137	152	120	60	74	70	63
Secondary Schools										
Benedictine	$1,875	470	30	434	470	—	14	—	16	—
Saint Vincent's	$1,250	443	65	375	—	443	40	305	25	70

Source: Diocesan School Board Archives

Other negative responses have dealt with the new social and cultural ambiance of integrated education, as one Saint Mary's parishioner recalled:

> The worst thing for blacks was integration. . . . Black kids found themselves with classes with nothing but whites. They didn't want to go, weren't prepared to keep up. Black teachers used to pick 'em and poke 'em. With no one to push them, they couldn't keep up. The way they did it wasn't the best, even if it's working out now.
>
> Each group took on the worst habits of the other groups: they used to fight every day. Then they started getting along together. Now they're together.

One cannot simply condemn the intentions or actions of the closure. Sister Julian Griffin carefully assessed the decisions:

> In numerical terms, fewer black children are being taught in Catholic schools. For those who have shifted to integrated school situations, the academic picture seems to have improved. Studies at Sacred Heart, while rather unscientific in nature, show that the level of Black children rose rather dramatically after integration, while St. Vincent's has made special efforts to encourage the Black girls there to make strong academic progress. . . . At the same time, for those who turned to the public schools, opportunities were much improved in a unitary integrated system, with various special programs to assist the bright child as well as the slow learner. (Griffin and Brown 1979, 79)

Yet it is the pain that remains most present, the sense that the heart of the black and Catholic experience was cut out through decisions in which black voices were not heard.

AFTER INTEGRATION, 1977 TO 1990

The decade since the closure of the black and Catholic parish schools has seen the channeling of religious and educational socialization within the community into two complementary pathways: institutional education in integrated professionally managed schools and catechism in community-based volunteer parish programs. While these provide an interesting cohesion and development to the educational tradition, they also represent a fundamental shift away from the early missionary spirit of Catholic education in black Savannah. Many black and Catholic elemen-

132

tary students in Catholic schools in Savannah attend one of two inner-city interparochial schools combined in 1990 into a single downtown program. Cathedral Day School, located next to the cathedral and staffed by Franciscan Sisters and lay teachers, was the primary assignment for students from Our Lady of Lourdes and Saint Anthony's as well as the cathedral. Nearby Saint Benedict's participated in a similar program at Sacred Heart along with Saint Mary's. Enrollment figures show that these two downtown schools reached black-white parity by the mid-1980s, while Blessed Sacrament had also recruited a large black population. The more suburban schools had a total of twenty-one black students, which did not reach 3 percent of their total school population; one school had no black students (Table 5).

The early years of integration showed predictable problems of adjustment. One black parent recalled white complaints, voiced in meetings, that blacks were lowering the educational standards of the school; however, these parents were confronted with blacks who made the highest scores on achievement tests. On the whole, incidents were less striking than those in the newly integrated high schools, apart from concerns about parish closure.

These schools' composition today reflects both parochial and inner-city realities. In 1982, of the 289 students of Cathedral Day School, 63 percent were Catholic and 37 percent non-Catholic, 45 percent were black and 55 percent white. In the past years, the black and non-Catholic population has grown; blacks now constitute more than 70 percent of the students in these two elementary schools. More than half the Cathedral school students in 1990 were non-Catholic. This contrasts with the largely white and Catholic populations of suburban parish schools. Many Catholic families, black and white, also send their children to public schools for a variety of reasons.

Both social change and the inner-city setting complicate the economics of the school system. Tuition has reached a thousand dollars per year per child, with reductions for multiple children and for Catholics. While producing "tuition converts," this can also exclude black families. This contrast with the minimal tuition of the black parish schools, however, represents shifting economic realities rather than a different orientation. "Sisters worked for nothing, subsidized from up North," a retired nun noted to me; a fully qualified lay teacher received only $8,500 in 1980. Today, salaries are the major budgetary item, as Catholic schools seek to maintain a pay scale at least 75 percent of the public system.

Financial aid is available for poor black students, although it may be more difficult for poor white families.

A Cathedral school self-study in 1982 identified the mission of the school in terms of education in values: "The teaching of religion is core to the curriculum as the staff tries to build community and to serve. . . . The faculty and the students serve one another by recognizing the Christ in all and letting that vision of Christ grow and mature" (Diocese of Savannah, School Board Archives, Self-Study, 5). Teachers and parents stress this moral component—combining religion, values, and discipline—as a major distinction between parochial and public schools. Catholic schools are thus seen as an answer to religious demands and personal and academic concerns. At-risk students are also incorporated because of the personal attention that has characterized the schools and the discipline that is offered. Other children are from single-parent families.

The setting of such schools resembles most American public schools, although public holidays and seasonal concerns are mingled with religious statuary, images, and references. Discipline continues in the spatial arrangement of the classroom as well as elements peculiar to the parochial system, such as uniforms. Lines and silence are also enforced by all teachers and by the principal, a nun in modified habit. A strong personal element pervades teacher-student interaction and the community of teachers and staff; children are generally known by their family and name. While nuns represent only a fraction of the integrated teaching community (which also includes Protestants), strong bonds are encouraged among teachers.

Catholic doctrinal education is fundamental for all students, whether Catholic or not, but this can be a complex content ranging from prayers or slogans on papers to discussion of moral issues. A nun spoke of this complexity in her own experience, valuing "being free to teach a code of ethics and moral law in the light of the Gospel. There is a lot of focus on the beatitudes. You're free to teach the Gospel and Christ's likeness. Peacemaking." Here, a sophisticated theology of liberation underlies education, rather than the rigid Baltimore Catechism. A white former student interviewed by Don Moore, a New College student who worked with me in 1984, also agreed that religion at Cathedral School was taught with liberal attitudes, encouraging personal understanding of God and faith and individual orientation within Christianity. She found that this made the transition to Saint Vincent's easier for her than for graduates of parochial schools who had focused on catechism; they "could not deal with

134

it as it was not dogmatic." Moore found a shocked suburban graduate in agreement: "I was used to spitting out rote, and this lady was asking how we knew God existed."

The relationship of school and parish differs in these interparochial schools from earlier black schools or larger white church complexes. Parish priests may still encourage children from their congregation; one pastor visits a different class each week. Yet the role of the pastor as absolute ruler cannot apply to these mixed schools, run by principals and boards. This is not the perception of those in suburban parish-school complexes.

The 1989 closure of Sacred Heart for fire code violations introduced a new element in this system. A decision was made to combine both downtown schools to serve all three black parishes and four white parishes, including Saint Frances Cabrini, twenty miles from downtown. Kindergarten through fourth grade is in the Cathedral building and fifth through eighth grades in a refurbished Sacred Heart. School supporters praised its enhanced facilities in languages, science, and computers and stressed both the church's and the Franciscans' commitment to inner-city schools. Nonetheless, the shadow of history was present in comments from Cathedral's Sister Nancy Craig about parents' difficulties in "letting go of the past" and the statement of Sacred Heart's Principal, Elise Gordon, OSF, about the closure: "In the past, when there have been closures here, the majority black schools have closed and black students have had to move to the white schools. The community is all pulling together this time" (B. King 1990, 1-2).

Gender expectations and congregational policies prove more influential in the transition from elementary and middle programs to high schools. The Benedictine military academy accepts students strictly on the basis of academic testing. Saint Vincent's, on the other hand, follows religious guidelines: first accepting all Catholics from Catholic schools; then, Catholics from non-Catholic schools, followed by non-Catholics from Catholic schools, and finally non-Catholics on a space-available basis.

Integration was more difficult at high schools than at elementary schools, according to reports from black students and parents. In Benedictine, blacks challenged the embattled identity of "Irish (Catholic)-military-football complex," as one priest labels it, which had taken on a key symbolic value for white Catholics within the Protestant city, epitomized in the rivalry of BC and Savannah High. In the early years of integration, racial incidents erupted at sports events and in the classroom. Subsequent black students with whom I spoke seemed more comfortable there. A 1985 black student praised the discipline and values: "when you are at private schools you do what they say. You'd be surprised at what they get away with in public schools. . . . Going to BC is just like going to work: if you are late, you pay the price. . . . They treat you like you'll make it in the future. That's what I like about it." Later, however, he complained "in some of my classes, I'm the only black person." After integration, black students have been caught in role ambiguities that their white colleagues do not seem to recognize.

The integration of Saint Vincent passed without major incidents. Some of the first black women to graduate felt a need for clearer role models, which they have provided to black students who have followed them. Saint Vincent's has now graduated over three hundred black women and has integrated classroom materials and historical awareness, although this still can raise contention among black students. Blacks nonetheless are not an active presence in the alumnae association. These alumnae, in turn, are eclipsed among Catholics by the Benedictine male alumni.

As students move into adult worlds in the Catholic high schools, all the social and cultural contradictions of their roles as black and Catholic permeate their experience. Recognition of African-American history or literature as a "concession" to the presence of black students reaffirms their participation in a marked category while meeting personal and developmental needs. Disciplinary actions that were valued in choosing Catholic schools may be misinterpreted within this unequal division of categories and differences of personal styles. Expectations within the school community of the limitations of "inner-city" schools may undervalue the experience of middle-class blacks or stigmatize through care. Equally striking is the unmarked consciousness with which white participants who have "owned" the schools move into them naturally. While whites may reflect on what these inheritances *mean* for the newly arrived blacks, I found no demands to consider integration along the lines suggested by Saint Pius. The disjunction of world views among black and white proves as crucial as policies within the schools themselves.

Parish educational programs represent the other phase of religious education for contemporary black Catholics, a reinforcement of face-to-face community in contrast to an integrated faith and educational experience. Such programs for children usually run from day care through reception of the near-adult sacrament of Confirmation. They are staffed by volunteers who usually organize their classes in available meeting space between or after masses on Sunday. Such programs are thus less intensive than earlier religious education in parochial schools and Protestant Sunday Schools. They also differ from the latter in their orientation to child development without stressing any continuity for adults and older youths.[14]

A laywoman and teacher who has coordinated programs for a black parish viewed the development of Confraternity of Christian Doctrine (CCD) or Sunday School programs as a direct response to the ambivalent situation of the black and Catholic parishes: "The evolvement of CCD came with black Catholic schools closing the door and the kids going to public schools. There was no place to talk about religion. Black Protestants had Sunday schools and were able to talk about religion, but our children couldn't talk about their religion, didn't even know about it."

Some such programs outside Catholic schools began as voluntary programs among the teaching nuns of the black parishes. Nuns also helped construct extra-institutional programs in these parishes in the 1970s, including Sunday schools and summer programs, which often use the familiar Protestant title of "vacation Bible schools." The summer Bible school at Saint Benedict's, for example, began in 1972, staffed by the Sisters of Mercy, the order to which the associate chaplains of the parish belonged. A 1978 report noted forty children, aged six through twelve, including parish and neighborhood residents. Their activities included "field trips, Bible study, training in reading and math, story telling and recreation. The highlight of each week was a trip to the beach." (*The Light* 3, no. 2, Aug. 1978). Today one nun is involved as a volunteer coordinator, while another supervises all diocesan CCD.

Parish programs focus on traditional Catholic education, complementing the public school programs that many students attend. The early years teach basic prayers and familiarity with the church. One young teacher vividly recalled a tour of the church with her class, explaining statues and parts of the sanctuary that she found they did not know. First- and second-grade programs focus on penance and first communion. Parents are generally required to enroll their children in order for them to receive sacraments in the church. Later grades mingle moral, biblical, and civic issues. The CCD format tends to be looser than day schools, without report cards or strict lesson plans, even though these bureaucratic elements are increasingly used. Tension may result from the volunteer teachers' own preparation. While many "use basics and let

137

lessons relate to everyday life," some teachers are described as "die-hards—they really believe in the Baltimore Catechism." Sacramental themes reemerge in prominence as teens prepare for confirmation.

Such programs revitalize the links between education, family, and community. Even students enrolled in interparochial schools are expected to join to learn to live with their future fellow parishioners, as priests stressed in their sermons. Parishes have recycled their school building at Saint Mary's and invested in a new educational building at Saint Benedict's. Community-building also includes outreach to parents, who must become actively involved in their children's education: teaching them prayers, sharing Bibles, demanding regular attendance. Priests and teachers see parental unconcern with a multiyear education as a major hurdle.

This community focus underlies an awareness of black history and identity that differentiates this program from earlier educational models. In Saint Anthony's 1985 Confirmation programs, students dealt with traditional saints and historical leaders in many fields who were both black and Catholic. Older adults in the community also shared their experiences with the teenagers assuming adult sacramental roles. Saint Benedict's also has developed historical and community references, as a teacher explained: "Ours is personal development, relating religion to it. We pull this out into black history in February. We have used certain themes for certain programs—celebrities, black Catholic saints. We let children write their own play, mostly centered around Martin Luther King, Jr. One celebration focused on our own church community, on role models whom they interviewed."

While parish and interparochial education as complementary processes seem to continue the rich tradition of black and Catholic education, both demonstrate a reorientation of focus toward *black and Catholic* community, in contrast to the tradition of Catholicism emergent from schools introduced into the black community. This reflects the autonomy of the black parish, which has taken over much of the parochial educational task formerly maintained by white outsiders and which sends students to metropolitan centers as representatives of black parishes within a universal church. Yet it also means that the missionary expansion of the Catholic church through education has been limited to scattered evangelization. Maintenance and reproduction, rather than conversion, have become the goal of schools and socialization.

In a 1967 memo in the Diocesan School Board Archives, Father William Coleman, one-time superintendent of the school board, summarized the problems that he saw black parish schools posing for Savannah:

On the one hand, their continuance seems to perpetuate the pattern of segregation and brand the church as insincere in its desire to abolish this practice in its own household as well as in society at large. On the other hand, we cannot help but recognize the incalculable good being accomplished by the Missionary Franciscan Sisters among the negro in general and among the poor negro in particular. To close these schools would undoubtedly remove the church from effective contact with Savannah's poor. In a word, the Church in Savannah faces a dilemma.

Dilemma, the very word used by a black lawyer drawing on his own experience at the beginning of this chapter, thus became the judgment of the Savannah Catholic hierarchy at a crucial point of transition.

Through more than a century of black and Catholic education in Savannah, individuals and groups have faced a series of interlocking contradictions which spring from the cultural categories and social and economic history studied in previous chapters. The definition and domination of blackness in Savannah denied blacks adequate educational resources for centuries. White and foreign Catholic missionaries crossed this divide, for conflicting reasons, to establish schools. Here they faced further contradictions in not comprehending the values of education as resistance that had grown up in the black community, which wanted academic knowledge as well as industrial skills. Above all, education came from outside without cultivating grass-roots support.

Once the Catholic system took solid foundation, a new sense of education emerged, which drew on the culture of the marked group as much as the ideals of white missionaries. This education linked parish and school, classroom and community in its goals and practice. It became the foundation of the modern black and Catholic community, which made active contributions to the school, yet this creation could still be dominated by white society. The agony felt when white administrators closed black schools showed the continuing conflict between blacks and whites embedded in urban and religious culture. These events appear more tragic since everyone, apparently, tried to meet their publicly professed Christian ideals, yet all were caught by contradictions in their society and culture.

The aftermath of the trauma has entailed new programs and a new awareness of black and Catholic agency. Education in Savannah, whether among blacks, Catholics, or more-inclusive communities, still faces complex issues of race, gender, class, and philosophy. Nonetheless, a critical dialogue informed by the past now participates in decisions and thus reforms the process by which those decisions can be made. My analysis of the parish extends and develops this theme.

4. Parish, Neighborhood, and Community

Amazing grace! how sweet the sound
That saved and set me free!
I once was lost, but now am found
Was blind, but now I see. . . .
When we've been there ten thousand years
Bright shining as the sun,
We've no less days to sing God's praise
Than when we'd first begun.

—Lead Me, Guide Me:
The African American Catholic Hymnal

As we left Saint Mary's one day after mass, a college-educated man in his forties stopped me and said, "I don't know what I'd do if they closed Saint Mary's. I guess I'd just stop going to church at all." For most American Roman Catholics, the parish has provided their fundamental experience of worship and association with other Catholics. In the United States, the parish and school complex in an immigrant yet ethnically divided society converted a European territorial institution into a deeply social and symbolic community: "These monuments to the neighborhood God became the people's cathedral, striking reminders to them as well as to their American neighbors of the Catholic presence in the city" (Dolan 1987, 2-3). In the white Protestant South, the parish took on an even stronger role through responses to its sociocultural context, which underscored

141

> its missionary character (a poverty of resources, population and person-
> nel, yet a flexible, even creative response to pastoral challenges); an
> evangelical, Protestant cultural milieu; a historical consciousness and a
> Southeastern cultural heritage; the prevailing presence of black Ameri-
> cans whose poverty and unjust treatment constantly call forth a pastoral
> response; the rural values of people over things that have permeated
> Southern culture; and the constant need for institutional building.
> (McNally 1987, 218)

These traits characterize Savannah as well. Yet the comments on Saint
Mary's convey a different and troubled loyalty, suggesting how urban
black parishes have shared southern and Catholic values while marked
in contrast to them.

In Roman Catholic ministry to American blacks, religious community
usually has followed educational facilities rather than preceding them as in
most immigrant parishes. White parishes, especially in the South, grew from
cradle Catholics, often beleaguered by their evangelical environment, who
came together to worship and to build schools to pass on their faith, making
their own demands on the episcopal hierarchy. In black Savannah, despite
some old Catholic families, it was primarily converts via schools who came
together to build the parish. Their roles, investment, and presence have
been stronger in their congregation than in the schools, where missionaries sought little grass-roots initiative. A dual promise of schools and salvation has been reflected in the response of black Catholics, individually and
collectively, to their hierarchy. This heritage is expressed today in the spirit
of predominantly black parishes as well as the wider integrated church.

While schools established ecumenical networks throughout the black
neighborhood, the worshipping black parish emerged as a separatist institution in its relation to surrounding religious communities. Hence, the
parish has fulfilled its Greek etymology, *paroikia,* a "dwelling in a foreign land." As this chapter further develops the dialectic of cultural symbols and face-to-face communities that have established and reproduced
identities, its vision of active agents and autonomous community complements the top-down activities that led to the formation of schools, while
it prepares us for more detailed examination of social structure and leadership in the chapters that follow.[1]

To understand Catholic parishes among blacks, ethnohistorical data
must mesh with the basic contradictions already elucidated in this study.
Black participation in antebellum Catholicism, unfortunately remains
relatively obscure from surviving documentation. By Reconstruction,

however, black Catholics had achieved a separated equality for parishes and schools that echoed the achievements of other religious or civil groups, while American bishops debated the meaning of racially segregated parishes in the context of widespread concern over nationalist exclusion (Gillard 1929; Dolan 1987; Nelson 1987). Debates over integration and difference continue today, although their premises and coalitions have changed. Thus, a division that once marked subordination can now be asserted as a social nucleus for the future.

The formation of black and Catholic parishes also highlights the divisions among blacks made present by the opportunities of a new faith. Since 1907 the three Catholic schools for blacks in Savannah have become centers for distinctive experiences of parish and neighborhood life. Their shared experiences—nuanced by class, gender, and age—provide significant continuities of belief, action, and leadership. Yet as social networks and face-to-face communities, these parishes are both deeply united and actively differentiated among themselves, whether in softball rivalries or liturgy, foci for neighborhood service or gossip.

Changes of Catholic and southern life in the past twenty-five years have challenged the distinctive identity of each parish in itself and as a black organizational unit. In the 1960s, civil rights, the Second Vatican Council, and the departure of the SMA fathers after sixty years altered parish life, as did school closure. Recent decades have witnessed a stronger assertion of black identity and power within the Catholic church associated with such national associations as the National Office of Black Catholics (NOBC) and local dissemination of black Catholic theology (Howze et al. 1984). Meanwhile, integration, secularization, feminism, lay assertion, and declining numbers of priests and nuns continue to change the Catholic experience.

The black parish in the modern era has not been the exclusive domain of black Catholicism, however. Whites have attended black parishes since their formation, usually without formally joining. Since integration, a small number of whites have chosen to identify with the traditionally black parishes or with their white priests. More significantly, blacks have moved into previously segregated white parishes. Both policy and practice suggested that blacks technically could always participate in any Catholic service, especially in rural areas that lacked separate churches. Only since the 1960s, however, do previously all-white urban parishes seem to have acquired a small but challenging black membership.[2]

Above all, this chapter balances the initiatives of a white Catholic hierarchy—bishops as well as priests and nuns—with the black responses that have constituted parish lives. At the same time, it completes the historical and social framework through which we will explore, in subsequent chapters, governance, worship, and belief. To do so, the discussion begins with an analysis of the earliest formation of black and Catholic citizenry in Savannah and proceeds, in the 1900s, to a general history of the three black parishes. Rather than repeating elements from previous chapters, I have stressed major differences before highlighting aspects of setting, community, and leadership that have constituted the unique identity of each parish. After these portraits, I consider those who cross long-standing boundaries: whites who attend black parishes and blacks who go to white churches. Together, these establish a discussion of communities that constitute the black and Catholic experience.

THE EARLY EXPERIENCE OF BLACK CATHOLICS, 1800-1900

Lack of documentation plagues portrayals of early black Catholic worship in Savannah, perhaps even more than education. All documents except basic records belonging to the cathedral—the only center for Catholic worship until the Civil War—were destroyed in 1898; and only a rare family, even in the black and Catholic community, traces its roots so far back as the nineteenth century. While this discontinuity indicates the ambivalent postbellum policies that shaped the black and Catholic experience, it gives little clue to faith, worship, or community.

The cathedral baptismal and marital registers show numerous black members of the Savannah Catholic community from its origins, whose inclusion in the register suggests de facto inclusion in the congregation. Indeed, slaves were among the first people baptized in the parish, and only in the 1820s, with Irish immigration, did white baptisms begin to exceed the West Indian blacks of the early church. O'Connell's unreliable *Catholicity in the Carolinas and Georgia* (1879) included scattered comments on blacks as worshippers and the problems of the church, but the author insisted that he knew only one black Catholic, "an old woman." Hence, his observations betray the attitude of the hierarchical church in the nineteenth century rather than an ethnographic sensibility:

The salvation of the negro race, both before and after emancipation, in the Southern States, has been a subject of deep solicitude to the Church. Special missions have been established for this object, churches were opened for them exclusively, but the harvest of souls thus far has not been as abundant as expected. There are many causes for this on the part of the negroes, which will always be an obstacle to their conversion to Christianity. They are naturally a sensual race of people, and their former condition of servitude aggravated the fatal propensity. (O'Connell 1879, 222)

The antebellum church was caught within a world divided by more than castes of color and liberty. The Catholic church, as an organizational structure, was primarily urban while much of the South remained rural. While a Catholic plantation owner might bring a priest to deal with his family and slaves, other rural white immigrants drifted from any ties to formal Catholicism (Baptismal Register, Saint John the Baptist Cathedral; M. Mitchell 1936; Chalker 1970; R. Miller 1983b; McNally 1987, 124). Older priests recount folklore about such rural families clinging to rosaries or statues through generations as marks of family identity whose religious meaning had been lost. Urban life offered more religious organization, but faith was shaped by the range of choices available as well as by nativist attitudes toward immigrants and competition between white Catholics and blacks in the working class.

The biracialism of other established denominations in Georgia offered several models for early Catholic blacks: separate spaces within churches, distinct congregations within a denomination or an entirely differentiated space and practice. American Catholicism never adopted a formal racial separation, whatever the attitudes of its members, but segregation became common in practice (see Raboteau 1978, 273). Catholic slave owners in Georgia, however, first arrived from mixed societies, such as Saint-Domingue, and only later from more homogeneous European churches. In the absence of concrete Savannah data, we must extrapolate from the practices of such areas and the Catholic South. In New Orleans, for example, mixed black and white congregations continued until well after the Civil War (Woods 1972; Blassingame 1973b; Mills 1983). Black Catholics in Kentucky were primarily slaves, but joint family prayer services were recorded in the 1850s (Green 1972, 37). In Georgia, Sister Julian Griffin notes a small frame chapel on Jekyll Island, on the southern Georgia coast, built "by the negroes on the island, who form the principal part of the congregation" (Griffin and Brown 1979, 18). Hence, it is not unlikely that joint services were part of a divided Savannah Catholicism in this antebellum period. Yet blacks were included in a sense of patriarchal plantation family as much as one of parish. The free persons of color in the register, however, suggest independent black participation as well.

The life of James Augustine Healy, the first American black bishop, illustrates the complexities of antebellum Georgia Catholicism. Healy was born in 1830, the son of an Irish father living near Macon and a slave wife. Healy and his siblings grew up without baptism or Catholic practice, and were sent North to Quaker schools. Only in 1844 were the Healy children baptized, after Bishop John Fitzpatrick of Boston took an interest in them. Later, with the Jesuits of Holy Cross College, the Healy brothers developed a stronger commitment to Catholic life. James Healy was ordained in France and became bishop of Portland, Maine, before his death in 1900. The family also produced a president of Georgetown University and the superior of a convent. Yet it seems critical to note that their religious life took form outside the South and its Catholic life (Foley 1954; Hemesath 1987; Ochs 1990).

In the decades immediately prior to the Civil War, when white immigration challenged black participation in the minuscule Catholic community, it prepared the way for a change in black and white relations, or for the departure of blacks from the Catholic church (R. Miller 1983a, b). A later bishop, Thomas Becker, came to this conclusion in an 1886 letter: "I have not data enough to go on but my certain impression is that we have in Savannah retrograded. There was formerly, and in slave days, quite a congregation among the old, good, and pious colored folks. They were put in the hands of an uneducated German priest by Bishop Gross, and the snows of last winter have not more fully disappeared" (cited in Peterman 1982, 202).

The renaissance of distinctive American black and Catholic communities across the United States arose from the post-Civil War councils in which the American bishops met to plan the future of the national church and called for evangelization of the emancipated black community. This initiative nonetheless suggests an important rupture in the hierarchy's attitude toward blacks that shaped Catholic parish life for a century: the tension between the maintenance of a reproducing congregation and the attraction of new (Protestant) converts. Gillard (1929), for example, complained that the Catholic church had not held on well to those who had joined the religion as slaves even while it supported drives for conversion in the cities (33-34). Certainly, investment in schools rather than parishes suggests a Catholic perception of passive but non-Catholic blacks as local and national objects.

Racially separated parishes also were debated within American Catholicism as an evangelical opportunity more than as a concession to postbellum southern whites or blacks. In the early postbellum years, independent black parishes emerged alongside other institutions such as Matilda Beasley's orphanage. As Jim Crow restrictions prevailed, however, these parishes collapsed. Evangelization still brought black and white together: Redemptorists conducted missions in 1868, 1875, and 1884 that included black conversions and specific missions to blacks within a generally universalistic message (Dolan 1978; Griffin and Brown 1979, 30). Yet the British Cardinal Herbert Vaughn, touring Savannah and the South in 1871-72, "witnessed such scenes as a priest refusing communion to a black soldier in cathedral and noted in Catholic churches the low, backless benches marked with signs that read 'for Negroes'"(Ochs 1990, 44).

The Baltimore Plenary Council's ambivalent goals, already glimpsed in education, seem nonetheless to have been met by Bishop Gross. Records of a separate black parish for Catholics in Savannah appear in the 1870s, within a decade after the first formal consecration of such a parish in Baltimore in 1864. The earliest recognized Catholic project for blacks there was the Benedictine industrial school on Skidaway Island, discussed in the last chapter. Within eight months, these monks also began a chapel on East Broad and Harris streets, only a block away from the Congregationalist Beach Institute and near other major black churches as well as the cathedral. Bishop Gross inaugurated Saint Benedict's with the Benedictines and his own Redemptorist order on January 3, 1875. The procession mixed black folklife and Catholic practice while mapping an umbilical link between the cathedral and Saint Benedict's:

> Although the weather was extremely inclement the various white and colored societies assembled at the corner of Drayton and South Broad streets, accompanied by two bands of music. The procession was formed with a band in the lead, followed by carriages containing the Bishop and eight clergymen. . . .
>
> A large number of colored people, men and women, followed in line and the procession, under Captain W. F. Black as Marshal, moved up Drayton street to Liberty, thence to East Broad and the Church. The edifice, which is a neatly constructed frame building, was densely crowded, whilst large numbers gathered on the outside on East Broad street.

147

> The dedication was the finale of the mission for colored people
> that had been in progress during the past week at the cathedral. . . .
> In the evening the dedication sermon was preached at the Cathedral
> of St. John the Baptist by Rev. Father Smoulder of the Redemptorists.
> The church was densely packed, one-half being occupied by whites
> and the other colored people. The latter participated with much unc-
> tion in the vocal exercises. (*SMN* Jan. 4, 1875)

The mixed and musical procession evokes black urban funeral processions (Georgia Writers' Project 1940; Calderon 1981), even though a white bishop led it. The opening march paired the cathedral and Saint Benedict's, but blacks followed white associations (see map 2). After the dedication, blacks and whites returned to the cathedral for a shared but divided mission. The construction of Saint Benedict's, however, marked a clear trajectory of sepa- ration. In 1876, after yellow fever had decimated the Benedictines, this church received a diocesan priest (Oetgen 1969, 168-69). It attracted a small but steady flow of baptisms, fading at the turn of the century but renewed by the new church (1899), before the SMAs arrived (table 6).

The year 1877 witnessed a more enigmatic event in black and Catholic history, with the inauguration of a third local black Catholic religious center. The new cathedral on Abercorn and Harris had been completed in April 1876. In March of the following year, the older cathedral building, refurbished and remodeled, was handed over to "colored Catholics" as the Cathedral of Saint Joseph (*SMN* Mar. 19, 1877). While the idea of a hand-me-down parish conveys the asymmetry of power relations between races (Lucas 1989, 69), the label of a second cathedral is probably inaccurate. Debates over a second, separate bishop for blacks raged between 1916 and 1920, but Saint Joseph's seems to have acted as a separat*ing* but unequal facility, perhaps removing any remaining blacks from the cathedral. Local white news items cite it as an object for white charity amidst the many church fairs that raised money for the Sisters of Mercy and the Westside Irish parish of Saint Patrick's (*SMN* Apr. 23 and 28, 1879). Another report mentions it as the "densely packed" site of an 1877 confirmation for thirty-five black Catholics of whom "about half were adults" (*SMN* Dec. 24, 1877); it was also used for the funeral of Abram Beasley, husband of benefactress Matilda Beasley (*SMN* Sept. 4, 1877). The parish school, of which even less record remains, was conducted by the Sisters of Mercy. Baptisms from this period show a healthy evangelization at Saint Benedict's, including numerous adult converts. Between 1875 and 1879, baptisms averaged nearly forty per year, numbers not regained until the 1920s. No records, however, seem to be available for Saint Joseph's.[3]

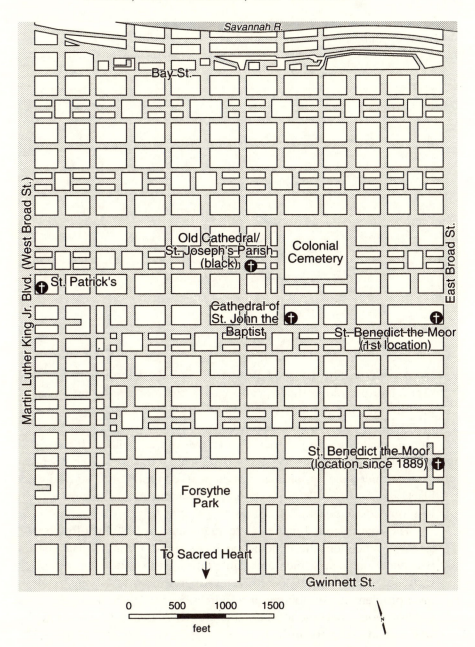

Map 2. Downtown Savannah Parishes, Black and White, in the Nineteenth Century

Table 6: Baptisms at Saint Benedict the Moor Parish, 1875–99

Year	Baptisms	Year	Baptisms
1875	60	1891	8
1876	52	1892	20
1877	44	1893	13
1878	29	1894	7
1879	28	1895	7
1880	25	1896	20
1881	2	1897	10
1882–89	—	1898	8
1890	26	1899	11

Source: Parish Registers, Saint Benedict the Moor Parish

An 1886 letter of Bishop Becker clarified the fate of Saint Joseph's: "They had the old Cathedral, and whites crowded them out. Financial reasons, viz., lest the new Cathedral might suffer by whites going to the old—among other reasons closed it to the colored congregation and they were relegated to the galleries. . . . They lost their Faith with fatal facility!" (cited in Peterman 1982, 202). Local white pressure and competition already limited the opportunities of the marked group of those who were black and Catholic. To the bishop, lack of attendance appeared equivalent to a loss of belief.

These mainland churches were augmented in 1880 by a fourth missionary foundation, the Benedictine Sacred Heart Church at Habersham between Saint James and Saint Paul streets. At that moment, the black Catholic missions outnumbered white congregations in the city, suggesting a problematic distribution of resources. Sacred Heart, however, stood in what would become a predominantly white area outside the city; by 1886 parish membership had become clearly white (Oetgen 1969, 177). Joseph Mitchell, priest and historian of the diocese in the early twentieth century, added details concerning this transformation:

Figure 10. Detail of a 1855 lithograph of the old Cathedral of Savannah, later the black parish of Saint Joseph. Photograph courtesy of the Georgia Historical Society, M. H. and D. B. Floyd Collection.

> Under Bishop Becker it was decided to found a parish in the city for the colored people. They already had a small church, but the work among them was not very satisfactory. So the Sacred Heart parish was established on Habersham Street, across the street from St. Mary's Home property. You remember this little frame church building, established for colored people, but which became a white parish because the colored people did not move into the section. (Letter to Thomas Gamble, Feb. 2, 1938; Gamble Collection CCPL)

The failed integration of Sacred Heart is manifest in baptismal records that include twenty-one blacks and three whites for 1881, followed by a long gap for both races. Nonetheless, records may be missing, (e.g., those of an 1884 confirmation of twenty converts at Skidaway) (*SMN* July 21, 1884; Oetgen 1969, 177).

For Benedictine historian Jerome Oetgen, Sacred Heart's change indicted the Benedictines and the white church:

> Perhaps some of the difficulties met by those early Benedictine missionaries among the Negroes were caused by their using methods related to or similar to those employed by the Spanish in dealing with the Indians. . . . In both cases the white man tried to impose his own culture upon the inhabitants without allowing for a sufficient and justifiable development of the native culture. When the predictable rebellion to this form of Christianization ensued, the Indians became "savage," the Negroes "unruly and lazy." (Oetgen 1969, 182)

Actions in this period seem to have led to the collapse of Catholic interest in the urban black population. Saint Benedict's has only blank pages in its baptismal register from 1882 to 1889; it disappeared from the city directory until 1888. Saint Joseph's vanished from the city directory after 1882, although the school remained until 1884. The pastor, Father Eckert, appeared at Saint Benedict's, as well, suggesting a combination of parishes. In 1886 and 1887, neither city directories nor newspapers referred to any black Catholic parish.

This historical decline belies the pronouncements of Savannah bishops amidst increasing segregation. Following Verot's efforts in schooling, Bishop Gross issued an 1884 pastoral to promote black evangelization, a position that he supported despite rumors among SMAs to the contrary and the comments of his successors. These reports nonetheless still envision blacks as pawns in Catholic debates over integration.

Gross's successor, Bishop Becker, focused on the need for a *new* black church, whose cause he pleaded to northern benefactors (Peterman 1982, 202-6). One 1886 letter vividly portrayed the process by which blacks had been excluded as white and immigrant Catholics accommodated to local racial categories in a church caught between antagonistic whites and blacks who doubted the sincerity of Catholic commitment: "The moment you allow your congregation in the South to be mixed, you must lose caste with your blacks. They see you are not solely for them. They feel their inferiority. We need not antagonize the whites— far from it—but in this case we must work for the blacks" (in Peterman 1982, 202). Becker thus accommodated to local cultural and social patterns that separated blacks and either made decisions for them or followed the interests of the dominant whites. Yet he and other bishops also saw blacks as an essentially passive flock who had not produced local leadership apart from the Beasleys. Indeed, United States bishops still opposed the ordination of blacks (Ochs 1990). In this ambiance, both slave descendants and Reconstruction black Catholics faded away.

The 1889 dedication of the new Saint Benedict's Church on East Broad and Gaston, its present site, provided a new historical and religious landmark for black Catholics. Table 7 shows the growth of Saint Benedict's in baptisms and other sacraments from 1900 to the 1970s. According to Oetgen, this parish, too, sprang from a project of Moosmuller in 1887 (1969, 180). Moosmuller left for North Carolina in the 1890s, although Benedictines retained formal control of the parish until 1907. Yet reports suggest the continuing decline of black Catholicism in the city: "the church will start with a membership of 200 but there are 500 colored catholics in the city who will worship there. Heretofore, service for the colored people has been held in the *chapel* of the Sacred Heart Church" (*SMN* July 15, 1889; emphasis added). When the mission to Skidaway closed in 1889, Father Reichert took over the new Saint Benedict's.

The new parish maintained its special relationship with the cathedral. Shortly after its foundation, for example, James Cardinal Gibbons, primate of the American church, visited Savannah and toured the church and orphanage, where he "expressed himself as highly pleased with the work that has been done." Bishop Becker also noted "the great joy he felt each time he celebrated vespers at 'St. Benedict's *pro nigridis'* when he heard the singing of 'the heavenly choirs and all together, in praise of God and St. Benedict'" (Peterman 1982, 204). At the same time, the new Saint Benedict's centered missionary efforts in a core of urban black life. The first location at Harris and East Broad had been near elite black centers. The new location placed it south of the poorer black and Irish neighborhood of the Old Fort but well within the boundaries of a strong and respected black area, today a focus of black historical preservation. As a longtime resident said, "We didn't have any neighborhood name, we've been too nice."

An 1891 Saint Benedict's parish list, made up shortly after the inauguration of the new building and the closure of other parishes, gives a unique glimpse of the parish. It lists 350 members: 130 males and 220 females. Of these, nearly half belonged to families of from two to seven members; some of these families are annotated in a later hand as having departed the city among the forty who later left.[4] Unfortunately, it is difficult to locate many of these families in city directories. While some

Table 7: Baptisms at Saint Benedict the Moor Parish, 1900–75

Year	Baptisms	Year	Baptisms	Year	Baptisms
1900	18	1929	42	1953	46
1901	9	1930	78	1954	85
1902	14	1931	42	1955	73
1903	12	1932	42	1956	41
1904	11	1933	45	1957	42
1905	32	1934	25	1958	21
1906	14	1935	53	1959	45
1907	14	1936	29	1960	57
1908	34	1937	61	1961	75
1909	39	1938	62	1962	107
1910	43	1939	38	1963	77
1911	41	1940	26	1964	90
1912	35	1941	29	1965	86
1913	29	1942	30	1966	108
1914	31	1943	32	1967	131
1915	43	1944	29	1968	76
1916	40	1945	33	1969	14
1917	34	1946	37	1970	26
1918	29	1947	16	1971	31
1919	35	1948	51	1972	49
1920	32	1949	32	1973	65
1921	47	1950	24	1974	40
1922–27	—	1951	44	1975	50
1928	23	1952	69		

Sources: Parish Records, Saint Benedict the Moor Parish, and SMA Reports, *État des Missions Africaines*

lived close by, others lay outside the city in Thunderbolt: the wide range of localities suggests that Saint Benedict's combined all earlier missions, including the islands and Sacred Heart. Family surnames show an even more complicated history. Along with families who would emerge as mainstays of the parish for the next three to four generations, such as the Beasleys, the Campbells, the Cuylers, the Dowses, the Nelsons, and the Scurdys, other names that have since disappeared retain a clear

French heritage: Deau, Dejoiner, Dezere, La Ris, and Mirault. Some left the city while others probably changed to other local churches.

Baptismal records show only limited growth each year, despite Bishop Becker's claim that the number of black Catholics in the diocese reached 1,300 in 1893 (Peterman 1982, 204). Becker nonetheless continually worried about black opposition to Catholicism and looked into the establishment of local black "colonies" with a resident priest of the Josephite order (Peterman 1982, 205).

Given the documentation, the discontinuity of religious and secularized foundations is difficult to follow. Yet records indicate the tenuous commitment and resources available for black ministry and black inclusion in the Catholic fold throughout the nineteenth century. After Reconstruction, a black and Catholic community that had once boasted three or four churches and schools had been reduced to services in the chapel of a white church. Despite the intermittent statements of the bishops, blacks obviously did not accept white promises of faith or community. The discontinuity of oral tradition and genealogy that separates the past also affirms the rupture between these early experiments and modern black acceptance, at least in terms of parishes as living communities.

THE FRANCISCANS, THE SMAS, AND THE REBIRTH OF BLACK CATHOLICISM, 1898-1920

The arrival of the Franciscan Sisters in 1898-99 proved a major stabilizing point for those who were black and Catholic in Savannah. Although these nuns did not immediately become associated with any parish, they provided the foundation for the complex of convent, orphanage, church, and school that became the nucleus of a Catholic renaissance among the city's blacks.

More revolutionary for parish life was the arrival of the SMA fathers in 1907. Father Ignatius Lissner, sent to locate opportunities for evangelization outside Africa, saw the Savannah church as much weaker than one would have imagined from episcopal claims: "The Catholic negroes numbered only twenty-five persons and the collections were poor in proportion. I was told that if I did not get friends to help me we must face the alternative of starving or abandoning our attempt" (in Elliott n.d.). With Bishop Keiley's permission he began an apostolate *exclusively* to black Savannahians; evangelization revived at the price of segregation.[5]

The SMAs were not so readily accepted by local clergy and white congregants as by the bishop and the blacks. The Benedictine switch from black ministry to white remained a thorn for diocesan priests, who employed this example to argue against admission of the SMAs:

> The Benedictines came to the diocese under these false colors: to minister exclusively to the colored people. How did they do it? They ministered to the colored people exclusively by encouraging first the white people to come to them, then they went actively to work under cover to induce them to come and finally wound up by abandoning the nigger and securing the prospectively best white parish in Savannah. (Fr. Schlenke to Keiley 1906, Keiley Correspondence, Savannah Diocesan Archives)

Nonetheless, Keiley supported SMA activities in their early years, although he, too, ultimately fought with them over the nature of their mission.

In conjunction with the Franciscan Sisters and a few established families, Lissner made Saint Benedict's his base of operation and expansion. Growth in the congregation soon was supplemented by two urban parishes[6] and statewide missions. Lissner founded his second school-church, Saint Anthony of Padua, on former rice lands in West Savannah, where he had purchased sixty lots for over five thousand dollars in July 1908. The surrounding area included truck and dairy farms, while lumber, fertilizer, and cottonseed oil plants were located along the nearby riverfront. The Central of Georgia railroad divided West Savannah from downtown. The solid industrial base and proximity to the city made it a candidate for growth that the SMAs extolled:

> Lots are being sold there everyday. A few beautiful homes have already been erected by colored men, who are being moved by the praiseworthy ambition of having their own sweet home! Soon a nice colony of colored citizens will be established on that beautiful healthy spot where peace and happiness will reign supreme. Near enough to the city for the workingman, Fellwood tract is an ideal spot for our children, who will be sheltered from the evil influences of the city and at the same time get all the advantages of the city children. (*ST* Aug. 17, 1909)

This passage exudes a pastoral, middle-class ideal of family, recalling nineteenth-century interest in colonization as a means of forming stable black and Catholic communities. Indeed, rural lands around the church

Figure 11. The old Saint Anthony's Church. Photograph courtesy of the Georgia Historical Society, Cordray-Foltz Collection.

and school were urbanized in the early 1900s by blacks and whites who found regular employment in the industries there. This stability, affirmed by urban boundaries, has been maintained by key families, producing a small but closely knit parish.

Father Lissner opened Saint Anthony's school on October 1, 1909, within months of the purchase. His fellow Alsatian, Martin Pfleger, a missionary with experience in Ghana, became the first pastor. This haste did not allow for new buildings; instead, existing farm buildings functioned as school, church, and rectory for decades, and local black lay teachers were hired for the school. Although a white school later opened down the street, West Savannah lacked a black school until 1938. Hence, the school and parish became a symbol of racial and religious division as well as interracial commitment for the whole area.

Lissner intended more projects for West Savannah, which could have become as large a complex as the senior, Eastside Saint Benedict's. In the local black newspaper, he expressed his hopes to use the mission lands to build a home for elderly and infirm blacks, arguing that "There is a grand and beautiful home for white folks under the care of the Little Sisters of the Poor. But where is there a similar institution for old colored men and women? What a grand and noble charity it would be to provide with food and lodging our old people, who are often without a home and without a friend!" (*ST* Aug. 17, 1909). Nothing appears to have arisen from this project to balance social services according to race. The SMA fathers also proposed an orphanage, probably the male equivalent to the female orphanage run by the Franciscans at Saint Benedict's and to a white Catholic facility in Washington, Georgia. Bishop Becker had proposed this but failed to implement his idea (Peterman 1982). In 1923, 130 orphans were listed for the parish. As late as 1926, thirty orphans resided there, but no living parishioner recalls the project.

As the school reached out to the Protestant neighborhood, the parish began to grow. Mass was first celebrated at Saint Anthony's on Christmas morning 1909, followed by Christmas exercises and a party for the schoolchildren (*ST* Dec. 28, 1909). On May 27, Father Lissner baptized the first convert, nine-year-old Henry Debro. At the end of the first year, a note in the baptismal register concludes, "In that time, houses were few, and two people who had been otherwise were joined to the flock of Christ" (Saint Anthony's Parish Archives).

In its early years, Saint Anthony's grew through the conversion of entire neighborhood families, with eight baptisms in 1911, twenty-one in 1912, seven in 1913, and nineteen in 1914. Nonetheless, the parish was constrained by its poverty, forcing the priests to grow vegetables and raise livestock, selling their produce in the city market (Begley 1965, 17). Despite the nearby opportunities for work, out-migration was also frequently noted in the register in decades when Georgia lost 10 percent of its black population. Despite 167 baptisms in the parish's early decades, Father Jean Martin found only fifty-three parishioners when he arrived in 1929. This raises a continuing dilemma in the black parishes, where the cumulative number of baptisms never corresponds to the growth of community. Migration, unprepared or "insincere" conversions, and family opposition denied the commitment of baptism, especially at the inflated numbers some priests like Father Martin recorded.

The third SMA school-parish was Most Pure Heart of Mary, built in 1911, whose proud construction notice appeared in the previous chapter. Here the SMA fathers established their complex in a different kind of neighborhood, which would shape the distinctiveness of the parish community. In the 1930s, the Savannah Unit of the Georgia Writers' Project described Brownville, as it was then called, as the zone bounded by West Broad Street, Laurel Grove Cemetery, and railroad facilities:

> Brownville, more prosperous of aspect than the Negro communities usually fringing business and industry, spreads westward along the edge of Savannah. Though on its Currytown boundary it, too, contains the inevitable shacks in lanes, several of its streets, paved and tree shaded, are lined with good frame and brick houses which are occupied by the more well-to-do Negroes, among them teachers, doctors, lawyers and business men. A substantial school building and the Charity Hospital speak of advanced social consciousness. (1940, 46)

A modern neighborhood activist confirmed this image of her community in the 1920s when she was growing up there: "Over on Bolton there were doctors, seamstresses, teachers, postmen. After the war, there were new houses north of 37th street. The area north of the cemetery was a field and houses were built there. After the war, people moved out. . . . Houses used to be beautiful, used to be mixed. Whites lived on Ogeechee Road. German Jews had businesses."

The neighborhood influenced the composition and activities of the early parish. The 112 members who joined in its first two decades, while records were still kept in Saint Benedict's, included the teachers, postmen, barbers, elevator operators, and glaziers mentioned by the resident quoted above. While not the elite of the black community, this was a relatively stable middle class within a caste of limited opportunities. Many of these were linked to families formerly in Saint Benedict's (the Cannals, Kings) while others began to establish major families in the new parish, such as the Davis-Tompkins, the Williams, and the Millers. These families provided leaders for subsequent development. The residential distribution of those early parishioners who can be located (25 percent) shows a strong sense of the westside neighborhood within a ten-block radius of the chapel, although black parishes have had no territorial boundaries, unlike white congregations.

Despite the school and chapel and the short-lived order of religious there, the parish remained small and local in the first decades. It had no resident priest or records apart from Saint Benedict's until Father Wassler added the rectory in 1929. Even the origin of the present church that replaced the tiny schoolhouse chapel is unknown, although it may have been a barracks or Protestant church before being brought to the site.

159

Some parishioners recalled it being used there as a stage for school presentations before becoming a church.

After this initial consolidation, the SMAs turned to the formation of new schools and parishes in Augusta, Atlanta, and Macon. A rural parish was also attempted but destroyed by arson, suggesting the power of rural nativism and segregation. As Father Adolph Gall recalled in 1985, Lissner "built the school and was always watching the church. He went to lunch and came back, the school was on fire. KKK. That's why all the schools are in town: we were protected." A clash between Ignatius Lissner and Bishop Keiley and the overextension of facilities and personnel as the First World War cut into recruitment, changed the general SMA direction by 1920. Thereafter, parishioners, working with a series of long-term priests and the school sisters, consolidated each parish.

CONSOLIDATION AND EXPANSION, 1920 TO 1960

The major themes of parochial life in the next four decades present an interrelated growth in community, leadership, facilities, and mission. Each mission grew in numbers. This expansion translated into social organization, identity, and institutions, including the construction of new church buildings. At the same time, all of these contributed to a change in the meaning and orientation of the congregations from missions to parishes which could undertake their own missions to urban blacks. Blacks emerged increasingly as leaders and shapers of the community. These Savannah changes echoed other national developments, as Josephites shifted toward conservation of urban black Catholics rather than rural evangelization and the recruitment of black priests (Ochs 1990, 214-46). National black Catholic lay consciousness also became more evident in black criticism of the hierarchy, especially that led in the Washington area by Thomas Wyatt Turner (Ochs 1990).

While I do not equate the church edifice with the worshipping community, buildings nonetheless pervade community participation and identity. As noted in the discussion of schools, Catholics long have recognized symbolic representation as a means of teaching, focusing devotion, and expanding the metaphoric meanings of the liturgy. Paintings, stained glass, statuary, and ornamentation have both decorative and pedagogic functions. Architecture creates a special space for worship: it focuses the congregation on the Eucharist at the front. Pews and aisles order seating and movement, while congregants create a social geography within this setting by their repeated choices of place. Placement patterns follow the social structure of the black community, although this varies among parishes.

The splendors of masses in a totally furbished pre-reform church or a modern parish also emerged for blacks from the realities of poor missions. Black parishes began in bricolage, a do-it-yourself ethos which meant using space in buildings not designed as churches until adequate facilities could be constructed. New facilities, in turn, became symbols of parish strength and pride.

Saint Benedict's had been the first major church building constructed for blacks, and continued in use for nearly seventy-five years. Contemporary black newspaper accounts noted:

> The building is one of the tastiest in the city and presents an elegant site viewed from the streets. Its interior workmanship and appointments are in keeping with the outward appearance. The style is gothic, the archways, ceilings, etc. being of highly polished yellow pine, the windows being of varied colored glasses. The seating capacity will be 400 with ample choir facilities. The basement has five comfortable rooms which will be used for school purposes, under a corps of good teachers. . . .

These presumably Protestant reporters nonetheless portrayed the church as a rich gift from whites to blacks: "The entire cost of the church is $10,655 including the lot, all of which were contributions from the two bishops (Becker of Savannah and Haid of North Carolina, Benedictine Abbot) not one cent having been collected here" (*ST* Nov. 30, 1889).

Although no photos of that church's interior exist, Pie Chisholm recalled it in conversations with me in 1987:[7]

> In the sanctuary, we had a beautiful marble altar; it had two angels on the side, one on each side, with candelabra. You've seen the altar in the cathedral—it was similar to that. The tabernacle was in the center. We had a bookholder—bibleholder—that was pretty; it was brass, and we used linen scarves.
>
> On each side, we had the Sacred Heart side and the Blessed Mother side, with a statue of the Blessed Mother and of Jesus. They sat on small altars.
>
> We had an altar rail, but I forget if it was wooden in the old church.

Up to this point, Pie followed the Eucharistic focus of the building rather than general mappings—a common interpretation among lay Catholics. The description also captures physical focal points of Catholic belief: altar, angels, Bible, Sacred Heart, and Virgin Mary. This changed with a question about pews:

> *Q:* What about seats?
> *A:* We had a capacity of two hundred people, with pews made like they are today. They had a rail down the middle. We had a center aisle and two aisles on the side. On the far right side, white people would segregate themselves. We had two black ladies always sat on that side.

Here, the description drew on other conversations that we had held concerning the social history of the church. People, rather than architecture, amplified her spatial vision. She added other sacramental details:

> There were two confessionals in the back of the church. Stained windows.
> *Q:* With pictures?
> *A:* No.
> *Q:* And the choir?
> *A:* The choir loft was in the back of the church, upstairs. We had an old style pipe organ that you pull things out.

In keeping with its many functions, Saint Benedict's worship space was on the second floor of a multipurpose building. A question on this point situated worship with regard to other functions and buildings: "Downstairs used to be the school. Later, it was the kindergarten. In front of it was the orphan home, a brick building. It had a kitchen, living room, office—the children slept upstairs."[8]

The current brick edifice replaced this church and orphanage in 1949. Here, construction involved many parish projects to raise money and marked a new identity for parishioners, a pride in their own efforts resembling reports on Saint Pius. The current church seats about three to four hundred in a warm and hazy light centered by the rose arches of the side altars and the central arch above the altar. This focus, marked by light, luxuriant ornamentation, and seasonal plants, includes presidential seats for the priest and deacon behind the altar in the central light. The lectern to the congregation's left and the piano and choir to the right complete the frontal tableau; choirs were moved from back lofts to the front in the past decade in all black parishes as well as many white ones. Wooden pews in two islands with central and side aisles provide seating. Stations of the cross and statues punctuate the dark brick side walls, alternating with translucent windows.

This fixed religious landscape alters in relation to the Eucharist. The movement of the liturgy, for example, may be accentuated by placing bread and wine on a table at the entrance, greeting all who come to mass, or bringing the collection to the altar. Light comes into play in a liturgical sense at Easter, when the darkened church is relit by congregants' candles to denote the death and rebirth of Jesus. Incense also infuses the ambience.

Saint Anthony's, on the other hand, made do for decades with converted farm buildings; the original church was small, wooden, and uncomfortable. Two older parishioners whose families have belonged since the 1920s described it to me in 1987. They also had a strikingly different narrative style, which wandered through social and cultural characteristics:

Q: Tell me about the old church.
A(1): It had a potbellied stove on the left—that was all the heat we had. It seated about fifty people.
A(2): It was very small. . . .
Q: Was there an aisle in the center?
A(1): Yes and small aisles on the side. There were plain pews on the side for the children. They said they didn't have shoes to wear and couldn't come, so Father Martin said come barefoot. No one laughed—we fixed our attention on the altar.
A(2): The choir was on the right side in back. . . . On the left hand side we had a confessional box—If they just called somebody something mean they would go to confession.
Q: What about the altar?
A(1): We had a pretty little altar.
A(2): A wooden altar.
A(1): And a sacristy in back of the church, one little room.
Q: And the baptismal font?
A(1): I don't recall a baptismal font, but some white basin. . . .
Q: And lighting?
A(1): Chain lights, electric.
Q: Windows?
A(1): There were two beautiful house windows at front, and three on each side. And a porch out in front, underneath an A-Line roof. The breeze was different then from now—The church was set out in the open, only one building in front.

Intimacy, rather than an impressive liturgical space, characterizes memories of the older church. Again, construction of a new school, a new parish hall, and later a new rectory involved efforts of the entire community as well as aid from outside missions. The new church that replaced the farmhouse in the 1950s is one of the brightest and most open in the city. Its A-line roof flows down to short side walls with regularly spaced windows. The entire church interior is white with blue accents; the sanctuary has a dark blue backdrop and a simple crucifix. The altar is in front, a simple table, with white wooden chairs for the celebrant to one side and a lectern to the congregation's left. Side altars of the tabernacle and a Marian statue flank the central ritual space, and the choir is seated beside the priest.[9] This church seats over 150, although it rarely gives a sense of crowding. At the back, it has an enclosed vestibule as well as an upper balcony. The church stands on a rise and opens onto a lawn along the road that unifies the facilities, still rural in their use of space.

Saint Mary's, like Saint Benedict's, was built as a combination chapel and school in 1913. This first chapel was extremely small, primarily for the teaching nuns. The permanent building has a long and narrow frame that still shapes liturgical space. Because of its narrowness, the church automatically focuses sight on the simple sanctuary in the front, where ornamentation has been reduced to a minimum. A black metal crucifix against a gray wall dominates the small altar. The tabernacle was moved in the 1980s from a side altar to a spot behind the altar. This church has also seen continuous work. When Saint Patrick's church was destroyed by hurricane in 1940, SMA Father Adolph Gall begged windows for Saint Mary's. Hence, one faces the incongruities of Irish saints gracing a black church; these windows also filter light and dominate ornamentation. Parishioners refurbished the frame building in brick for its seventy-fifth anniversary in 1978; in the 1980s, they added a parking lot, indicating the needs of more suburban members.

After the 1920s, each building enclosed a growing community. The graph compares baptisms as an index of growth. Saint Mary's, after a slow growth in its first decades, grew to 150 in the 1930s, with roughly twenty-five baptisms per year. Hence, it is obvious that many of the baptized schoolchildren never fully participated in the parish. By 1947, it reported 227 members—roughly 60 percent of its current membership (see table 8). Saint Anthony's skyrocketed in the 1930s, when Father Mar-

Figure 12. Saint Anthony's Church, 1992, rectory and parish hall in background. Photograph by Cindy Hing-Yuk Wong.

tin baptized "almost anyone," in the words of a nun who worked with him. Baptisms oscillated between 130 and 250, while the parish grew to over 400, roughly its modern size. In 1948, however, a more cautious priest reported only 253 congregants. Clearly, Martin's actions and reports did not agree with the realities of black conviction. Table 9 shows parish register and SMA reports (in parentheses) of baptisms and other activities in the parish at the time.

Although Saint Benedict's had more baptisms than Saint Mary's, it reported relatively stable parish membership through the 1930s and 1940s, nearly five hundred people. After the war, this climbed to six hundred, and continued to grow to its current membership of more than twice that figure.

165

These figures must also be placed in context. In the 1920s, as we have seen, migration was important to all southern blacks. Catholic records indicate a second dip in the late 1930s, perhaps as a response to Depression or, by 1940, to war-industry opportunities elsewhere. The depression was hard for economically marginal parishes. World War II also drained males from the parishes, which slowly recovered thereafter. Their dependence on charity grew: one priest recalled living on gifts for mass intentions and donations from other parishes. In Saint Benedict's, Pie Chisholm recalled: "We were a mission. We used to get boxes of clothes from the North and [Father Obrecht] divided them up." Yet this was the period in which strong parish organizations took place and long-term leaders clearly emerge in community memory.

Reviewing the history of consolidation, the interplay of dynamic priests and strong families is also apparent. Lissner, for example, brought another Alsatian, Father Gustave Obrecht to Saint Benedict's, who would shape its character for decades afterwards. Obrecht, ordained in 1899, was one of the original SMA fathers delegated to American work (Vogel [a], 273). Obrecht stayed at Saint Benedict's for forty years, until his death in 1952, and was a patriarch in the Eastside black community.

When asked how to describe Obrecht, one older informant distilled the relationship of the priest to the parish: "He was like your daddy. Picture your father and write him up." Another woman in her seventies recalled, "Obrecht was a godsend to black people, he really treated us like humans." Even after his stroke in the 1940s, parishioners carried him to witness the dedication of the new church, and the program credited him as "the priest who has rendered the greatest possible service to the area."

A similar phase in Saint Anthony's was chaperoned by Father Martin, who had a rather more effusive but paternal style, as Mrs. Genevieve Woerner recalled at the seventy-fifth parish anniversary:

> Father Martin was a lover of children, . . . and naturally by knowing
> the children and being so good to them he got the parents to come to
> the little old wood church and it was a beacon light in this community
> for Protestants as well as Catholics. Fact we had more Protestants in
> there than Catholics. . . . I wouldn't say he was like Robin Hood,
> 'cause Robin Hood got from the rich. He got from anyone he could
> and he shared it.

166

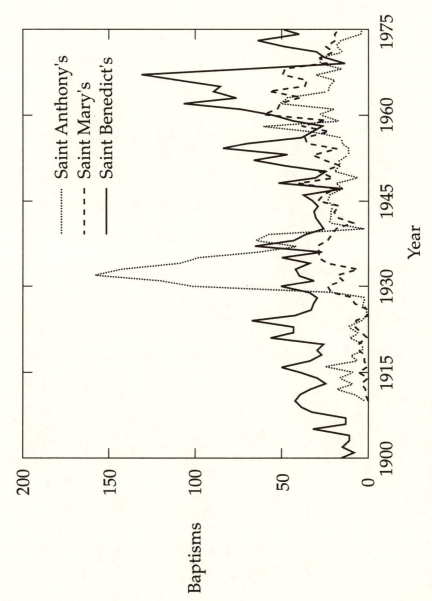

Figure 13. Savannah Catholic parish baptisms, 1900-1975.

Table 8: Sacramental Life of Most Pure Heart of Mary Parish, 1923–38

Year	Staff	Congregation	Catechumentate	School	Baptisms	Communions	Confessions	Marriages
1923	Peter	30	20	150	8 —	—	—	—
1924	Ludan/Antz/Gall	30	20	105	(8) —	—	—	—
1925	Gall	no report	—	—	0 —	—	—	—
1926	Gall	30	20	145	(0) —	—	—	—
1927	Wassler/Obrecht	30	20	145	(8) —	—	—	—
1928	Wassler	30	20	145	(9) —	—	—	—
1929	Wassler	30	20	173	13 (25)	595	—	—
1930	Wassler	50	20	254	24 (2)	1,050	1,020	—
1931	Wassler	90	15	225	29 (15)	625	615	3
1932	Wassler/Weiss	50	20	254	24 (19)	1,050	1,020	—
1933	Wassler	50	20	254	24 (33)	1,050	1,020	—
1934	A Gall	141	10	230	34 (6)	1,120	950	—
1935	A Gall	147	7	230	35 (24)	1,186	987	1
1936	A Gall	150	3	180	22 (27)	1,720	1,330	2
1937	Ramstein	170	5	180	20 (30)	1,750	1,350	4
1938	Ramstein	170	5	194	24 (23)	—	—	—

Sources: Parish Records, Most Pure Heart of Mary Parish, and SMA Reports, *État des Missions Africaines*

Table 9: Sacramental Life of Saint Anthony of Padua Parish, 1923–38

Year	Staff	Congregation	Catechumentate	School	Baptisms		Communions	Confessions	Marriages
1923	Riber/Imbach/Balthasar	70	6	90	12	—	orph.	120	—
1924	Riber/Marchall	60	26	90	4	—	—	—	—
1925	Riber/Marshall	—	—	—	1	—	—	—	—
1926	Riber/Marchall	94	26	140	1	—	—	30	—
1927	Riber/Marchall	94	26	140	3	—	—	30	—
1928	Wassler	94	26	140	2	—	orph.	—	—
1929	Wassler	94 (53)	26	134	4	(22)	307	—	—
1930	Wassler	107(128)	26	134	16	(104)	600	540	—
1931	Martin	128(268)	16	115	47	(120)	450	265	1
1932	Martin	107(350)	26	134	16	(159)	600	540	—
1933	Martin/Laugel	107(320)	26	134	16	(143)	600	540	—
1934	Martin/Laugel	328(403)	12	170	80	(110)	690	650	4
1935	Martin/Laugel	403(415)	18	248	75	(98)	867	700	—
1936	Martin	412(412)	8	122	40	(64)	1,235	900	2
1937	Martin	415	8	181	40	(43)	1,067	920	2
1938	Martin	415	12	157	54	(66)	—	—	2

Sources: Parish Records, Saint Anthony of Padua Parish, and SMA Reports, *État des Missions Africaines*

In Saint Mary's, Father Adolph Gall was the parish builder, and the only one of the founders whom I was able to interview, in his retirement in Tenafly, New Jersey, in 1985. Father Gall was an American-born SMA who had been raised in Alsace, whose health precluded African service. He had not seen a black person before his posting to Georgia, where he also had to learn English. In our interview, he immediately recalled the poverty of the parish when he arrived "There were fifty-nine people, including children. My first collection was $1.95. We were poor!" Father Gall established ties with blacks and whites in the city and built the parish in both liturgical and social life, adding a canteen/USO hall for black soldiers in World War II. He also invited a black priest in for a mission. Yet the division of the society in which he worked disturbed him still when we spoke: "It was the law of the land that there was no communication between white and colored. Drinking fountains were white and colored. Tramways had whites in front; colored, in back. Movies had colored upstairs; whites, downstairs. The law of the land. It was terrible."

While all of these priests encouraged the physical and numerical growth of the parishes, they also encouraged parish identity and active leadership on the part of blacks and Catholics as individuals and communities. After World War II, the changing climate of black identity and economic opportunity was met by another set of Irish or American priests. Father Joseph Feeley in Saint Benedict's, for example, told parishioners "we couldn't be no mission anymore, that we had to stand on our own feet." Father Feeley himself, in a 1989 interview, emphasized growth in sacramental life and preaching for vocations to the priesthood. Yet he felt that blacks had few opportunities for leadership outside the parish— "nurses, teachers, ministers." And if blacks were not accustomed to leadership, the city also opposed it: "It was simmering, but this was to come later." Under Feeley, Saint Benedict's completed its new building and began a mission to Savannah State College. This was relatively short-lived, drawing upon teachers and students. Yet it recognized an increasing access to higher education that shows the advancement of the community into the middle class. It also may have prepared the way for Saint Pius X in the 1950s.

This stress on independence characterized congregants' interactions with the SMA priests in the 1950s and 1960s. Saint Anthony's, as noted, also built a new church and continued to grow within its neighborhood context. In personal recollections at Saint Anthony's in 1985, educator Gwen Goodman attributed an important role to Father Dennis Begley, the last SMA to serve that parish:

170

Figure 14. Most Pure Heart of Mary Church, 1990. Photograph by Cindy Hing-Yuk Wong.

He instilled in us something that I think every priest that followed has helped us to capture as we should have many years ago. His sermon, almost weekly, was "Do not wait on someone to tie a gift for you with a big red ribbon and give you something free. It is time for you to stop being of a mission status and be of a parish status." Sometimes we didn't listen to him. But he preached every Sunday.

Father Begley himself described the parish and its life in a 1965 article seeking funds from benefactors:

The "Mission" has, gradually over the years, grown to parochial status, if only on a small scale. The new church, a miniature Cathedral compared with the old tumbled down shack it replaced, probably suggested the prestige preference of "Saint Anthony's Church" to displace the more indigent title, "Saint Anthony's Mission." . . . The truth is: "The poor we have always with us." So many of our parishioners are in the "low-income bracket" and struggle to rear their families in "low-rental" housing projects. Consequently, little can be expected in the way of Church support or in school tuition. (22)

171

Nonetheless, Father Begley and the congregation constructed a parish hall, as well as introducing such Vatican II reforms as the parish council and wider participation in governance and liturgy. At the parish anniversary, it was clear that those who worked with him continued to take active roles in leading the parish thereafter.

Saint Mary's underwent a different process of transformation. There was, ultimately, a flaw in its locality which Lissner had not foreseen. Much of the neighborhood property was rental housing, which has subsequently deteriorated as blacks have been able to purchase property in new suburban developments since World War II. This has led to an ironic reversal of neighborhood and status as Saint Mary's became surrounded by a problematic slum. While parishioners and pastors have led efforts for neighborhood revitalization, many of its middle-class parishioners live far away. Under Father Mulvey in the 1970s, a proposal was voiced to move the entire church complex westward to a new, suburban property. Property was acquired and plans drawn up. The rejection of this plan by Bishop Frey produced resentment that smoldered into the 1980s. The parish also acquired a convent on Thirty-seventh Street through the donation of Sophronia Tompkins, an educator and member of one of the oldest families in the parish.

In the SMA era, all three black and Catholic parishes showed steady growth, interrupted by depression and war. The correspondence of parish to school is evident as well, although the schools consistently served larger non-Catholic populations. While I have used priests to organize the depiction of historical growth, it must also be underscored that black Catholics themselves were central to this consolidation. Parish growth was evident in work on the physical plant, in the stability of families, and in the power of organizations that I will examine in later chapters. Individual parish identities, formed by parishioners, neighborhoods, and priests, also became clearer. These changes, in turn, encouraged subsequent dialogue over black identity and autonomy.

THE FORMATION OF THE CONTEMPORARY PARISHES, 1968 TO 1990

In the 1960s the dualities of southern Catholicism influenced black parishes in a new way: "What was going on literally in the secular society was interpreted literally by Catholic southern bishops. On the one hand, blacks were now on an equal footing in every Catholic church in the

South. On the other hand, the drive to integrate all but destroyed important black institutions—the black parish and the black school" (McNally 1987, 148). This original contradiction produced further ambiguities in integration, which McNally has highlighted as a general experience of southern parishes:

> Although black Catholics supported the move to integrate in the public arena, they did not wish to abolish or "consolidate" what they considered to be their parishes and schools. The move to close the black parishes, influenced as it was from events in secular society, did not come from the grass roots, but from the hierarchy, which was concerned not only with cooperation with the political climate of the times, but also with teaching the white Catholic community a lesson in social justice. The only problem was that nobody asked what the black Catholic might have preferred. (1987, 148)

Even before the Notre Dame report led to integration of schools, Vatican II, civil rights, and economic development impinged on black Savannah parishes. All were crucibles for black organization and self-identity as they challenged claims of traditional white authority. Problems arose not from reforms themselves so much as the channels through which they were imposed, which treated blacks as passive actors. As New York black priest Lawrence Lucas later complained: "Yes, Lord, white Catholics have not only twisted Your priorities, they have trained Negro Catholics to go and do likewise. They have made You completely white in Your appearance, Your thinking, Your interests, and Your concern" (1989, 95).

This ambiguous potential for imposition and response pervaded the civil developments described in previous chapters as well as liturgical reform. Yet the culturally recognized expertise of the priests and bishops here made their innovation more normal. The liturgical changes of the Second Vatican Council, analyzed in chapter 8, were generally well-received among blacks. Latin had always been part of a foreign culture, while black devotional traditions, especially music, had been denied by the European liturgy of the church.

Another complex change for the black parishes was the SMA departure, announced by Bishop Frey in May 1968. The bishop explained that it was his hope "that the staffing of these churches by diocesan priests, on the usual rotating basis, will help make our Negro Catholics believe us when we tell them that no distinctions are made in this regard, as far

173

as the Church is concerned" (*SMN* May 18, 1968). This transition was made with remarkably little discussion; neither SMA histories nor Sister Julian Griffin devote substantial analysis to this theme. The latter notes only that "during all these changes, the SMA Fathers—who had worked among the black population for about sixty years—withdrew from most of the Black parishes, and these were taken over by diocesan clergy" (Griffin and Brown 1979, 75). Members of the SMA and the Savannah diocese with whom I spoke have remained reticent, and no available official correspondence illuminates the departure.

Given the long history and deep affection demonstrated for the SMAs, it is striking that the departures did not seem to generate strong outcry. The parishes had strong and well-remembered leaders in such men as Father Dennis Begley at Saint Anthony's and Father John Mulvey at Most Pure Heart of Mary, who had encouraged the development of local leadership and community autonomy. These men continued to be respected and cherished. Minor protests over Begley's departure were mentioned in interviews with Saint Anthony's parishioners. Yet the departure, as the first of the major transformations of the relationship of blacks with the Catholic church, seems to have been felt only in a personal emotive way without sparking group reflection or reactions. Even though Father Begley was returned to Savannah for burial only a few years later, there was little rancor or imputation that the departure effected his health. Perhaps the parishes had indeed moved beyond a missionary dependency. Nonetheless, this transition removed active spokesmen for the black community at what proved to be a critical time for rethinking Savannah Catholicism. The SMAs were not available to contest Notre Dame committee recommendations, a job left to laity, young diocesan priests, and nuns. The departure of the priests also prepared reactions to future imposed decisions.

The presence of diocesan priests, and a new priestly relationship, thus was negotiated in the midst of school closings and post-Conciliar reforms. The three parishes between them had eight pastors between the SMA departures and 1974, and still another pastor by 1977 when Saint Mary's school closed. The ideal rotation in a parish is five years, with a possible second term. Between the restabilization and 1986-87, when some problematic personnel changes were made in the parishes, five pastors served in the parish, each with long tenure. These men proved deeply influential while being guided by dialogue with their mature parishes. Parishioners also tested their new priests: one, for example, was dismissed by a parishioner: "We thought he hated us, he was such a

174

mean man. But then he went and treated the white folks at _____ just as bad." But black and Catholic responses to priests were also questions about the very survival of the parishes. Saint Mary's, for example, commenced a cooperative relationship with Sacred Heart—ironically, a church that had begun to serve blacks—and merger loomed as a possibility in hierarchical planning. Parish protests blocked this, but the memories remained strong in the 1980s. A young black female educator recalled that closing the schools "plus rumors of parish closing made people down-hearted—'The church cares nothing about us.' If they had closed that church everyone would have gone Baptist or Methodist, even Old Catholics said so. No one would have gone to Sacred Heart." Baptisms reflect the shift of parish lives in these transitions as they have through the history of modern black and Catholic Savannah (Figure 13).

After the initial SMA-diocesan transition, each parish settled with new agendas and another long-term priest. The first of these priests to assume his role was Father Fred Nijjem, a native of Valdosta, who became pastor of Saint Benedict's in 1972. Nijjem proved to be a charismatic priest who introduced many of the reforms in the spirit of Vatican II that initiated more enthusiastic lay participation throughout parish life. Although he became the first white southerner to serve the parish, he ceremonialized the black heritage in Black History Month and the gospel choir. Saint Benedict's also began a newsletter, *The Light*, which explained parish activities and highlighted lay leaders and activities.

Father Nijjem experimented with leadership while others took on more active roles. He brought in Father Elmer Powell from Chicago, who became the first resident black priest in a Savannah parish in his year at Saint Benedict's. Dr. Prince Jackson of Savannah State became a permanent deacon. A more controversial innovation was Nijjem's shared ministry with two white Sisters of Mercy who handled peace and justice and social ministries. This team ministry, while surrendering priestly authority, nonetheless introduced more white leadership into the parish without clearly defining responsibilities to satisfy all parishioners. The arrangements became a source of tension after Father Nijjem's departure.

Father Nijjem was followed in 1981 by Father James Mayo, a Massachusetts-born clergyman who previously had served in a primarily white parish in Warner Robbins, Georgia. The attachment that parishioners had formed to Father Nijjem made the first year of transition inflammatory, but cooperation soon emerged. The parish now maintains a strong commitment to food banks and food service while continuing to encourage its black identity in history and liturgy. Saint Benedict the Moor today is the oldest and largest of the black Catholic parishes in Savannah, the "mother church," and the only black parish serving the east side of the city. Its 500 to 600 families overshadow the 180 families of Saint Anthony's or the 200 of Saint Mary's. In addition to age and size, its central place in black Catholicism was confirmed by its being the residence for the Franciscan Sisters who taught at all of the black schools, as well as the large rectory that sheltered visiting SMAs.

As a social group, Saint Benedict's can be characterized not only by its size but by its historical continuity, with various families tracing their Catholic heritage for generations. Many parishioners are middle class, having come up through schools and social formation, although the urban poor are present in church and neighborhood. While it retains a neighborhood anchorage, the church also has a large suburban membership. The variety of the parish is evident in the networks that form around individual masses—gospel, spiritual, or folk—and the bonds that constitute its active organizational structure. Saint Benedict's also provides a center for black heritage, as in music, and for political activity; among its members are the local state senator and candidates for public office.

In Saint Anthony's, a post-Conciliar era took form with the arrival of Sister Julian Griffin in 1971 even more than with the change of priests. Sister Julian, a black nun of the Vincentian order, worked with parishioners to sponsor projects ranging from a black history museum to the Westside Comprehensive Health Center and a credit union. A black youth ministry began, and Father Dowling and Sister Carmelita linked Saint Anthony's to the Diocesan Social Apostolate program. An Irish-born priest, Father Frank Higgins, became pastor in 1972, completing the physical reconstruction of the parish with a new rectory in 1973. By 1976 the parish was free from all debts, which it celebrated with a mortgage burning in 1976. Father Higgins was followed in 1979 by Father Michael Smith, an Augusta-born priest who had become active in social issues during the closure of Saint Pius X. Father Smith fostered increased neighborhood activism and ecumenism as parishioners became involved in service projects such as the Savannah Night Shelter and distribution of government food. Smith's own reflections on this time have been introduced in chapter 1 and will be discussed again in chapter 5.

As a social group, Saint Anthony's retains its West Savannah roots, although the parish includes a vast range of economic and social opportunities; Sister Julian suggested to me that it was the most complex of

176

the black parishes. In the past, members of the other black parishes denoted the mission by its "country" ambience. Today, members of both other black parishes view it as a warm, family place. Saint Anthony's members actively have promoted their history in parishwide anniversaries in 1985 and 1990, and they support activities ranging from young adults' work with the urban Night Shelter to parish suppers (Saint Anthony's 1990). The parish is small, with less than three hundred members, and the presence of several key lineages serves to promote unity and continuity.

In Most Pure Heart of Mary, the reforms of Vatican II, including the parish council and an increasing awareness of black history, were fostered by Father Frank Patterson. He was followed by Liam Collins, another Irish-born priest who also became an activist in neighborhood concerns. The 1978 Rededication Program noted how congregants viewed the priest as catalyst:

> He arrived just in time to direct us from apathy, a what's the use syndrome. Projections from project self study began to materialize. With each passing day St. Mary's becomes a more vibrant entity. We are a busy, happy, concerned and fulfilled people. This involvement takes place in the daily and Sunday masses, sharing of the body and blood of Christ our Saviour, prayers for the sick and those not in attendance at the service. Happiness is involvement in the choirs, Blessed Martin de Porres Guild, Bible Study Group, Youth Group, Sunday School, Holy Name Society, Parish Council of Catholic Women, Marriage Encounters, Cursillo, Liturgy Committee, Communion Ministers, adult education, supporters and friends.

Saint Mary's nonetheless has faced problems from its complex human geography, with parishioners spread among different neighborhoods—and classes—with the church almost isolated in the core, as a distribution. A list of parishioners in the 1980s shows this diffusion, which constituted social and even class divisions in planning projects such as MaryHeart. A 1985 survey I conducted there underscored the complexity of composition and belief among members. Handed out to all who attended mass, roughly one-third of parish adults responded. These parishioners identified broad concerns with unity, participation, and social and neighborhood concerns for the Cuyler community around them, including crime, poverty, and housing. They also voiced similar concerns of social and organizational natures for their own, often middle-class, neighborhoods. In response to questions about Catholicism as a whole, parishioners raised issues of ministry, including a strong voice for the ordination of women, as well as reference to racism and family issues. Finally, in response to questions of problems facing America today, economic and social worries clearly dominated. The survey showed a wide range of opinions in these responses, springing from the experiences and concerns of black Americans and Catholics. While responses reflected the social activism of the priest, they also moved in directions of both neighborhood concern and ministry. The laity of the parish went beyond their pastor to reflect on the church and its organization.

In each case, parishioners have reached accommodation with successful long-term priests and new religious and neighborhood concerns. This synthesis illustrates the maturation of the parish as an independent and self-conscious community, an identity that pervades lay leadership and sacramental belief. As I note in succeeding chapters, this maturation also means that parishes reject priests who violate local norms or practice, producing difficult transitions and continual questions about the future.

Identities as blacks and Catholics are also apparent in joint actions among parishes, ranging from missions to days of reflection. Blacks from the entire diocese come together for Lenten missions or participate in events sponsored by the National Office of Black Catholics. Since 1989 *The Julian* has appeared as a monthly publication for diocesan blacks. Invitations to choirs and members of other parishes are frequent for celebrations of events.

A consciousness of history has also been part of the maturity of parishes as communities: each church, since Vatican II, has celebrated major anniversaries, publicly proclaiming their historical identity and presence among blacks and Catholics. Saint Benedict's celebrated its centennial in 1975; while Most Pure Heart of Mary celebrated its rededication in 1978, noting that "Our work as Christian brothers and sisters has just commenced." Saint Anthony's celebrated its seventy-fifth anniversary with a homecoming mass and celebration in 1985 and renewed the celebration in 1990. Father Michael Smith explained his thoughts on the meaning of such historical consciousness in the parish bulletin of October 6, 1985:

> If we do not take time to remember, we will surely forget. The whole Bible was written to help us remember, remember how good God has been, despite our weakness, so we can be grateful and trust Him more for our future. And so, after seventy-five years, we set aside a weekend to remember. . . . In all of this we are trying to do for us in this place and in this time what the Bible authors did for God's family: to see the hand of God at work planting seeds, pulling weeds, struggling

178

through times of hurt and disappointment, finally seeing some seed produce a rich harvest.

Remembering is not just recalling the past. It is seeking to discover the God who is not past but ever present, ever now, so we can come before our God with grateful and trusting hearts. We will do this especially on this first Sunday of November with Bishop Lessard for Mass.

The comparisons with the historical consciousness of First African Baptist church in the commemorative volumes analyzed in chapter 2 are illustrative, as are comparisons with the lessons of history brought out by parishioners in this celebration as they are cited through this current study.

In addition, parishes have sponsored testimonials for priests and raised money to care for retired Franciscan Sisters in Tenafly, assuming responsibility toward those who once ran the parishes. Liturgy, action, and belief within each parish reaffirm these identities, just as their histories underscore the formation of social groups that hold together despite contradictions.

Parish identities also have been shaped by their rivalries with each other. As noted above, Saint Anthony's is generally characterized by its location and isolation, which is seen to produce parish intimacy. Saint Mary's, on the other hand, as a traditionally middle-class group, often is characterized as "uppity" or "cold" by members of both other black parishes. It maintains a rivalry with Saint Benedict's as a "daughter" parish; even communication between these parishes seems relatively weak by contrast to that of Saint Benedict's and Saint Anthony's. Saint Benedict's is characterized by its size, activity, and access to the cathedral, although Saint Mary's members may object to its domination. A Saint Mary's parishioner who had started in the other church noted to me in 1986 that "We had more of the higher element—teachers, doctors, educated people in my day. Trying to get souls, don't be choosy. Families died out. St. Mary's has a different class: cultured people. The higher element now goes to St. Mathew's Episcopal."

Black parishes, even if relabeled "traditionally" black, are also set apart from other diocesan units. Aside from their racial composition, they are also much smaller than other urban parishes, although all downtown parishes have now faced demographic decline. They are not territorial since their geographic range, in fact, overlaps with that of prior white mappings of the city. Finally, they are linked by social organizations that set them apart within the city, the diocese, and the nation. This tension of integration and separateness within the community is echoed by individual choices that have crossed traditional racial-parish boundaries.

CROSSING BOUNDARIES: WHITES IN BLACK PARISHES,
BLACKS IN WHITE

In decades of de facto segregation in the South, Roman Catholics none-theless were trained in the unity of the Mass. While neither whites nor blacks formally joined churches chartered for the other category, they would attend mass in such churches, at times with regularity. This penetration of barriers has both affirmed and challenged categories.

Both blacks and whites recalled whites who attended the black churches in the pre-1960s period. For Saint Benedict's, these were often Irish-American families in the Old Fort area. The alternative for such families, their geographic affiliation, was the cathedral parish, which some felt to be too elitist and wealthy to accept working-class immigrant families. Several Irish families attended Saint Benedict's faithfully, although SMA agreements with the diocese precluded their membership; some have retained ties with the parish over generations. Within Saint Benedict's, nonetheless, whites would sometimes claim prerogatives of class that they had been denied in their formal white parish, including separate seating to one side of the church. Pie recalls:

> We used to have a whole gang of whites who sat on the right, friends
> of the S.M.A.s. But Mrs. R———, a real dark lady, sat in the front row
> to let the others know it was her church. And another tall, light-
> skinned lady dressed in old-time bustle and all would sit there, pull
> out her rosary and missal and spread it around.

Both priests and parishioners addressed this separate presence of whites as a problem, even to the point of a priest's asking the whites to attend the parish to which they belonged. Other whites used Saint Benedict's as a downtown convenience in the case of schedule conflicts or waited at the back while fulfilling their Sunday obligation; this was a frequent identification among white Catholics whom I interviewed in the 1980s. The problem of such white congregants, who sometimes brought in financial support, also puzzled Josephites (Ochs 1990, 45-46).

Most Pure Heart of Mary and Saint Anthony's had fewer whites in regular attendance, although both were close to white neighborhoods. Whites were oddities even more than problematic. A white woman who lived near Saint Mary's in the 1930s did recall frequenting the parish, especially for daily mass, a voluntary action that follows convenience patterns more than the social and obligatory Sunday service. Gloria and

Evelyn Daniels of Saint Anthony's remembered a white man who attended each Sunday in the 1930s as an eccentric apparition: "There was a German man named John Coply and he used to attend church every Sunday and bring his dog and tie it outside. During that time it was a state law that whites sat in front, but his heart wasn't in it." Although West Savannah was integrated in the early years of the church, the insistence of urban segregation could be emphasized by physical proximity—especially when the western suburbs had few other Catholics beside a Cajun colony, with its own parish of Our Lady of Lourdes.

Since the more insistent integration of the Catholic church in the 1960s, Saint Anthony's and Most Pure Heart of Mary have gained a few white members. Saint Benedict the Moor, on the other hand, has had a strong white contingent as regular members. None represent neighbors even in the limited territoriality of contemporary black parishes, much less nearby white districts. Generally, they follow the white priests or seek the life, witness, and style of the congregation. Those whom I interviewed cited the liveliness of services, especially the gospel choir at Saint Benedict's, and the intimacy of the small parishes and their personal bonds.

This association of racial bonds between priest and people is called into question when a priest is transferred. Blacks expect the whites to follow; their actions become a proving ground for loyalties within the congregation: "All of them leave after they priest go" observed one black congregant; while another commented "I thought we go to serve God, not to serve the priest." Whites may serve as lectors, ushers, or members of the parish council; they generally lack informal power, which tends to be based on network, social knowledge, and presence. Neither have parishes registered white infant baptisms or marriages,[10] which would indicate a commitment to transgenerational presence within the community.

Blacks in formerly all-white parishes rarely mentioned casual attendance at white Catholic churches prior to integration. Since the 1960s, three main routes have led blacks into white parishes. One is a conflict with their own parish (or parish priest) which causes them to transfer membership. Generally, the circumstances of such a move are well-known within the black parish whose members share critical anecdotes about the "uppitiness" of such movers or relish their social failure in a white man's world. This response is more extreme than transferring to another black parish, although it may be "logical," since the transfer usually involves a white parish near their home.

Physical mobility also challenges affiliations. One of the oldest parish-ioners of Saint Benedict's in the 1980s came from Liberty County, an hour's drive from the church. Eventually she alternated this trip with Saint Anne's, a closer parish in Richmond Hill that, through the Benedictines, suggested a historical connection to her family's ties to Skidaway. Other suburban blacks, including both descendants of old black lineages and migrants, have chosen to attend the nearest church in the outer reaches of the county rather than the central black parishes. Saint Frances Cabrini, for example, serves the mixed congregation from new suburbs, rural areas, Armstrong College, and Hunter Army Air Force Base (which also has its own chaplain).

A third factor in recruitment of blacks to white parishes has been the integrated school. Black parents have been encouraged to become involved in the parish at which the interparochial schools were situated, although one noted, "I attended mass there because of the kids but I wouldn't join because it's such a segregated parish." This route often leads to prominence in the public roles of the newly integrated parish.

Ironically, some blacks are married in white parishes, especially the cathedral, since "Our church too little for the big crowd they gonna have." This comment confirms the images of social mobility—and cri-tique thereof—which many blacks associate with movement to an inte-grated but formerly white church.

Black integration of formerly white parishes diverges from white entry into black parishes. It entails a move toward power and a rejection of tra-ditional sources of black strength and identity, even if these are not explic-itly developed, with consequences for both family and community. Whites, however, have always been able to enter black churches by the front door, to represent their public power. Integration both ways appears more accepted at daily mass, as a voluntary pious action, than on Sunday, when it refers to a home community. In both cases, however, crossover incorporates in-dividual strategies rather than transforming urban cultural categories; no Savannah Catholic parish has achieved the integration of the day-to-day worlds in which Savannahians live. Nonetheless, Catholic integration seems unique in Savannah Christianity, reflecting upon its own complex history.[11]

Gillard, in 1929, reviewed the advantages of separate parishes, which to him included black responsibility for leadership, adaptations of educa-tion and liturgy, culturally valued patterns of social life, and avoidance of a continual confrontation over color. Nonetheless, he, like the Josephite order, remained paternalistic and ambivalent:

Experience has amply demonstrated the need and advisability of churches which the colored people can call their own. Without gainsaying the fact that it were better for both races to worship in unison, under the existing social order it is evident that this ideal is not realizable. The Catholic Church is not committed to the policy of separatism, but were a missioner to remain loyal to the best interests of both races, he cannot with safety ignore present racial antipathies and consequent demands for separation. (1929, 69)

Savannah's present-day black and Catholic parishes have taken form within this dialectic of black and white, of reproduction and evangelization. Despite the efforts of the Catholic church to convert blacks in the nineteenth century, any sense of community-building was caught in shifting hierarchical and religious emphases as well as a lack of accommodation to black habitus. In the twentieth century, the SMAs adopted a more cooperative strategy, in which race, neighborhood, priests, and people took on particular forms expressed in the contemporary parish identities. The aftermath of the 1960s has tested these emergent identities and ultimately strengthened them, as parish traditions, values, and social patterns constitute foundations for the interpretation and incorporation of new events. Each parish, despite a drop in baptisms, was able to survive the closure of the school that had provided its origins. Parishioners may, at times, express concerns over the future plans of "the Church," yet they are surer of their ability to respond as blacks and as Roman Catholics among other communities.

Indeed, we can now situate black and Catholic parishes in regard to McNally's survey observations on Catholic parishes in the South and their response to changes in the past two decades:

On the one hand, the laity is more deeply involved in parish life and more critical of it than ever before, yet, on the other hand, the majority of Catholics either are not involved intimately in parish life beyond Sunday Mass or have stopped going to Mass altogether. Moreover, the church has taken a much more benign view toward American culture, though it finds itself in conflict with that culture in its stands on marriage, abortion, contraception, capital punishment, and nuclear war. One could go through a litany of contradictory signals in the post-Vatican II age. . . .

And yet, in spite of all these rapid alterations, other aspects of Southeastern parish life demonstrate continuities with the past, continuities that give a sense of stability and identity (that is, something that endures through change). (1987, 218)

The maturation and identification of black parishes represent a slow process of group formation, of individual and collective commitments. Informal groups with contrasting identities, linked like schools to a larger black community and individual experience, now embody both symbolic representation and political action. Individual crossovers reflect on both the possibilities and limits of a more holistic integration, and the fundamental contradictions of southern Catholicism itself.

5. Priests and People: Organization, Power, and the Church

Spirit of the Living God, fall fresh on me.
Spirit of the Living God, fall fresh on me.
Melt me, mold me, fill me, use me.
Spirit of the Living God, fall fresh on me.

—*Lead Me, Guide Me:*
The African American Catholic Hymnal

On May 20, 1988, Robert Eugene Chaney, a black Savannahian who had been baptized in Saint Benedict the Moor Parish as a child, was ordained to the priesthood by Bishop Raymond Lessard in the Cathedral of Saint John the Baptist. Father Chaney became the first member of Saint Benedict's to join the priesthood and only the second black priest to be ordained in the history of the diocese; the first, Divine Word Father Bruce Greening of Columbus, Georgia, preached at Father Chaney's first mass at Saint Benedict's the next day. Nearly a century had lapsed since Charles Uncles became the first black priest ordained on American soil in Baltimore in 1891.

The ordination assembled bishop, priests, sisters, and laity from the entire diocese to witness the historic event. The bishop's sermon conveyed general themes of preaching which he developed across several ordinations. Attendance was drawn from all over the diocese, including all parishes where Father Chaney had served. His extended family and Saint Benedict's parishioners were highlighted, and the Saint Benedict's choir provided gospel music. As in the reinauguration of the cathedral, this ritual made present the hierarchy and continuity of the priesthood within Roman Catholicism.

185

The contrast of Father Chaney's first mass in the more familiar ambiance of his home parish proved striking. At Saint Benedict's, while the white pastor concelebrated, the preaching was characterized by rhythms, emphases, and humor ("We *know* what he's giving up!"). Father Greening also discussed the mission of the *black* church instead of Roman Catholicism, which the cathedral service had emphasized. His examples ranged across denominations from slavery to the present. At the end of the summer, Father Chaney went to Holy Trinity in Augusta, a parish that had formed by combining three parishes, two white and one black. Since then, another Saint Benedict's parishioner has followed his example in beginning work at a minor seminary.

Later in the summer of 1988, Father Michael Smith, who had served nine years as the priest in Saint Anthony's, sent his farewell letter to his parishioners. Smith meditated on his experience as a native-born white Georgian confronting black history, in a letter that I have analyzed in chapter 1. Using the metaphor of Moses emerging from the House of Pharaoh to examine his pilgrimage to a new sense of priesthood and commitment, he recapitulated his development from college and seminary through his work with various civil rights movements in Savannah in the 1960s and 1970s. His conclusions merit review:

> I thank God for giving me this past nine years with you and the past two months with the dark brown native people of Mexico, to learn more what the real struggle of God's people is all about, and to learn how to survive and overcome, singing Zion's songs as we struggle together.
>
> Now this same Lord is sending me back to the House of Pharaoh, back to the other side of the tracks, back among my own kind and color.

Smith's departure, then, showed his identification with a new vision of racial diversity as well as his sense of whites as a marked category for missions.

The ordination of Father Chaney, like the departure of Father Smith, raised questions of ritual leadership among those who are black and Catholic. As Catholics, blacks participate in a hierarchical institution that subordinates laity to consecrated specialists (priests and nuns); to bishops, who act as regional overseers; and to the pope, conceived of as the Vicar of Christ in the official historical continuity of New Testament foundations. Contradictions in the history of these parishioners are condensed in the social and symbolic interaction of priest and people.

186

The topics examined in this chapter also evoke basic questions about the nature of the priesthood in contemporary Catholicism regardless of race, gender or class. Priests, nuns, and brothers of the Roman tradition have been set apart from the secular world and their fellow clerics by their vows of celibacy, by cloistering or isolation, and even by clothing. Thus the pyramid of ritual and authority in the traditional Catholic church has flowed downward to the priests but has floated above the average layperson. The extreme monarchic structure of the pre-Vatican II church and the gulf dividing lay members of the church from consecrated ones were enshrined in tradition, sustained by control of knowledge and ritual efficacy, and continuously iterated in practice as simple as the clerical title, "Father." This divergence has eased with conciliar reforms that underscore the priesthood of all believers and the varied ministries that constitute a congregation. Yet distance is still clear: if not clothed in a soutane, priests generally wear collars or other indicators of religious specialization and their sacramental ordination.

Priestly status implies many repercussions in the parish. The priest, for example, is an appointed and transient power-holder in a stable, transgenerational community, an outside father to a family. As Father Smith had noted several years before his departure, in an article in the *Southern Cross*, "I feel that if we are called 'father' we ought to practice hospitality to our family and neighbors to make them welcome. Ultimately most of the people are there when you come and they will be there when you go. The parish is much more theirs that yours. You meet people who have been in the same church for sixty years, and it is rather humbling—so much of their time and energy and money has gone into it". (G. Brown 1984, 9). Not all priests, past or present, so easily relinquish power.

The priest is also a clearly differentiated figure in a relatively coherent community. He enters as a man set apart into a context whose rifts generally have been tempered by cross-cutting ties of family, friendship, and everyday experience among competing groups. He may not share the same social or cultural formation, especially in an earlier era when priests entered the seminary in high school. The priest may remain aloof and isolated, or he may galvanize the divisions diffused throughout the parish.

Moreover, the priest represents power, both religious and secular, as the holder of an office who can enforce his decisions through a range of sanctions. Others in the community hold authority on the basis of their knowledge, service, piety or longevity, which I will analyze in the next chapter. When claims of power and authority clash, they threaten the very existence of the entire parish.

The Catholic priesthood diverges sharply from the leadership of other denominations in black Savannah. While Episcopalians, Lutherans, Presbyterians, and Methodists have a similar system of overseers or directors, none has a bureaucracy so monarchic as that of Catholicism. Other black Christian denominations emphasize the charismatic rather than institutional selection of leadership, calling their ministers or accepting leaders who arise within the congregation. Deacons are elected in the Baptist church, ordained in the Catholic tradition. Deaconesses are women of power in some Protestant traditions; in black Catholicism, the title ironically labels similar women of informal but ironclad authority—a woman may not be ordained.

The most striking question within Savannah's black and Catholic community—which distinguishes it from other black churches—lies in the racial division between priest and people. Congregants have been primarily black; priests and nuns, almost exclusively white. The social personality of missionary priestly leadership has nuanced color categories, but the ordination of blacks has been a point of tortured debate for American Catholicism for a century, as Stephen Ochs has shown in careful detail (1990).

Savannah has produced a few black seminarians; more women have been involved in religious orders, including one order founded in the city. Visiting black priests have led missions and served as short-term pastors. However, since the death of Sister Julian Griffin in 1985, there have been no black members of religious orders in the city, and no black priests work there as of 1993.[1] Yet while the traditionally black parishes of Savannah have been served by white priests, nuns, and brothers, these leaders themselves often have become anomalous, as Father Smith's reflections suggest. Priests and nuns have been foreign-born specialists recruited from abroad rather than from the population with whom they work and are therefore marked as foreigners. SMA fathers and their diocesan successors and the Franciscan sisters also recounted numerous incidents in which they were reclassified as "blacks" by their congregation as well as by whites in Savannah with whom they deal. To work with blacks over the decades was to be a "nigger priest or sister" in the eyes of other Catholics, even other priests and nuns.[2] More than one cleric cited his own reorientation, either by identification as part of the community or through a search for the meaning of the black experience; hence Father Smith could write "God is using the people of color in our world to strike a blow for His name." The priests' and nuns' lives did not give them the everyday experience of blackness so much as it placed them painfully "outside" white.

To situate the politics of Savannah Catholicism in the context of intersecting dimensions of power, this chapter begins with a brief review of Catholic organization. Such a schematic presentation, however, demands popular and polemic elaboration as well as official tenets. Bishops, for example, exist not only in the abstract, as a category, but also as persons who were loved and hated by Catholics and non-Catholics. The chapter next extends the dialectic between those who primarily guide and teach and those who primarily learn and follow. The archetypal conduit of power from heaven to earth, from pope to bishop to priest and nun to people can be neither simple nor unidirectional. Informal leadership and lay authority, changes in clergy, and the particular witness of black and Catholic parishes have made structures of power ambiguous, especially since Vatican II. On this basis, I turn to the black and Catholic experience of ritual leadership, weaving together themes from social history with the memory, experience and reflections of modern communities. This discussion encompasses both white experiences in black ministry and black recruitment to institutional leadership positions. This chapter also explores the continuing contrasts in gender roles between priests and nuns. Finally, it returns to the beginning of the century to explore an alternative ecclesiology that would have divided Savannah blacks even more from characteristics of the white immigrant church. The confrontation of Bishop Keiley with Father Lissner illustrates the conflicts of race and power implicit in black ministry.

THE LITURGY OF HIERARCHY

Liturgical texts recapitulate in public prayer the order of authority in the Catholic church from God to people through time and space. Even if most Catholics have little personal contact with upper members of the hierarchy and forget the intricate etiquette to address them that they learned in catechism, ritual repetition constantly brings order and power alive through the words and actions of the priest. The prayers begin with a recapitulation of salvation history and Trinitarian doctrine, which the priest speaks from a position of inclusive yet elocutionary power: all members of the church participate in the Eucharist with him, yet his statement is perceived to particularly crystallize the miraculous presence of God. Eucharistic prayers unite the life of Christ to that power of the priest to make present and transcendent the Eucharist and the community that receives it. Time fluctuates between the past (the death, the Victim) and the future ("ready to greet him when he comes again," Resurrection), held in the tension of the present re-presentation.

The emphasis of the prayer shifts gradually downward through a supernatural hierarchy in Heaven, invoking the Virgin Mary and the saints. As Roman Catholics often explain, this intermediate level does not imply the veneration of statues of which they are accused, nor does it suggest that Mary and the saints are coequal with God. Saints represent past humans now in God's presence who act as intercessors for other Catholics before divinity. In the practice of the faithful, the distinction between veneration and intercession may not be so clear. Most Catholic churches today have deemphasized the saints in ritual and teaching, although modern parishes use black saints as role models for new generations. Savannah black churches have statues of Mary, of Joseph, her husband, and of their individual patrons as well as black saints like Martin de Porres.

Knowledge of saints, nevertheless, is often limited in use to biblical figures or extremely prominent patrons. Few blacks seem to have the statues in their homes that I associated with Catholicism in my childhood. Prayers to the Virgin Mary appear in daily mass at all three parishes as well as special devotions during the "Marian months" of May and October. Mary rarely arises in conversation about religion or worship, however, except with devout or elderly parishioners or in funeral rosaries.[3]

The Eucharistic prayer then changes in both focus and tone, moving from an other-worldly to a temporal order. It restates the order of those who are being prayed *for* rather than prayed *with* as in the case of the saints:

> Lord, may this sacrifice,
> which has made our peace with you,
> advance the peace and salvation of all the world.
> Strengthen in faith and love your pilgrim Church on earth;
> your servant, Pope John Paul, our bishop Raymond, and all the bishops,
> with the clergy and the entire people your Son has gained for you.
> Father, hear the prayers of the family you have gathered here before you.
> In mercy and love unite all your children wherever they may be.

Offices are rapidly introduced. The pope is presented by his pontifical name, the only designation by which many Catholics will know him. Although the current pope has become well known as a mass-media figure, few Savannah Catholics will meet the pope—other than the busloads who went to Columbia, South Carolina, to attend a mass during his 1987 American tour. Banners and photos recall this trip, but there seems to be little casual discussion of policy or orientation. Generally, pontifical decrees are filtered slowly through canon law and episcopal, priestly and mass-media interpretations of morals.

Bishops represent more immediate, personal figures. The historical outline of the action of various Savannah bishops has described only partially their human contact with blacks or black perceptions of them. Saint Benedict's, as noted, maintains a "special" relationship with the cathedral in the minds of many parishioners, which is reflected in frequent episcopal visits. Saint Anthony's members, on the other hand, have perceived the bishop more in terms of official visitations for Confirmation and examination of records. Members of all three parishes unite in condemning a bishop they hold responsible for closure of their schools, entwining narratives of personal contact and appeal with their statements of disapproval. Whites generally seem more positive about bishops, although class issues arose in one case I discussed (McDonogh 1988b).

Clergy and people follow bishops in the prayer sequence, although the second approved Eucharistic prayer does not mention the people, while the fourth approved version has a full stop after "*N.* our bishop, and bishops and clergy everywhere." This prayer also elides the significant categories of religious such as sisters and brothers within orders and the deacons who, in practice, form important intermediate categories in the hierarchy of the church. Some of these have not received the sacrament of ordination; they are laity who have made special vows to set them apart. Yet they are not priests. Deacons are bound sacramentally, but this aspect of their ministry seems ambiguous, as do many others. Some individual priests in black and white parishes recognize intermediate categories as they say the written prayers.

Finally, the Mass returns to the bonds of past and future, natural and supernatural, expressed in terms of mortal and immortal life rather than in divine history. This leads to the concluding acclamation:

191

Welcome into your kingdom our departed brothers and sisters,
And all who have left the world in your friendship.
We hope to enjoy for ever the vision of your glory,
through Christ our Lord, from whom all good things come.
(International Committee on English in the Liturgy, 1968, 1969, 1973)

These liturgical prayers, or an approved variant, are repeated daily throughout the Roman Catholic church. In a sense, liturgical prayer as enunciated by the priest and followed by the congregation becomes automatic; it neither demands nor receives reflection. Yet it insists on structured power descending from God to man that lingers, ultimately, at the priest as a fundamental channel of interaction between hierarchy and people.

THE CONSTITUTION OF THE PRIESTHOOD

Historically, the relationship of priest, nun, and congregation in black and Catholic Savannah arose as antebellum European immigrant priests ministered inconsistently to slave and free congregations. Since the paucity of available information of early missionaries already has been explored, I will only insist here that it was not clear, even in the nineteenth century, that local congregations would not supply priests. Oetgen mentions the recruitment of blacks by the early Benedictines, including three black brothers from the early mission who stayed to work with Father Moosmuller. In 1877 Moosmuller wrote that "two of them . . . would be able to teach ordinary branches in school, the third do housework." "I hope that soon we get more," he continued; "these brothers received the habit from the Bishop" (Oetgen 1969, 170-71). In 1878, Siricius Palmer, another black, became a candidate for the priesthood. Palmer then entered the public school on Skidaway as teacher and convert missionary, only to ask dispensation from his vows in 1883 (Oetgen 1969, 175-78). There is no evidence of later recruitment, nor was it a major thrust of American Catholic evangelization (Ochs 1990).

The paternalistic dichotomy of white leaders for black congregations stabilized after the decline of Reconstruction's independent black voices. Both the Franciscans and the SMA fathers had backgrounds in missionary work. Mother M. Ignatius (Elizabeth Hayes), who founded the Georgia Franciscan missions, had sought to work in Jamaica and with American Indians before turning to the South as "a vast uncultivated vineyard of souls, lying idle for want of laborers" (Ahles 1977, 123; see 29-37,

44-48, 53-60). Her cooperation with the Benedictines recruited an early black postulant, Frederica Law from Savannah, who died in Rome on December 30, 1883, after making a deathbed profession and receiving the name Sister Benedict of the Angels (Ahles 1977, 152-53). The Law-Campbell family continues to be active in Saint Benedict's Church. Yet, as with the Benedictines, no local blacks subsequently entered the Franciscans, although some joined other black orders.

The SMA fathers were committed to work in Africa (Vogel a and Vogel b; Bane 1959; Fabian 1986). Yet they were immigrants, divorced in race, language, and background from their parishioners and students. Hence, critics accused the early Alsatian ministries of garbled accents and erratic behavior, although the memories of parishioners focus on warmth and commitment within an authoritarian framework, reflecting the church as a whole prior to Vatican II.

After 1907, the Franciscans and SMA priests committed *uniquely* to blacks in the Savannah diocese. SMAs served only in black parishes while no others entered there; Franciscans specialized in black education, although they shared this task in Georgia with Sisters of the Blessed Sacrament and dealt with inner-city children in other parts of the United States. This commitment became a barrier even to their colleagues. One elderly Franciscan sister painfully recalled to me her years in the novitiate when a friend in the Sisters of Mercy, well-patronized by Savannah whites, said "I understand how you can give up your life, . . . but for *them?*"

Nonetheless, this also was an era of clear divisions of office and authority. The priest as representative of the church offered minimal consultation on finance, liturgy, or moral affairs in the parish. Nor was there much open disagreement: "If the SMA fathers made a rule, it stuck." Parishioners described the SMAs as "matter-of-fact." However, Father Obrecht stayed at Saint Benedict's for forty years, and others developed long and deep attachments to their parish.

A male parishioner who had served fearfully at the altar with Father Dennis Begley distilled the SMA years as he remembered him in a more touching fashion at St. Anthony's anniversary. He came to know Begley differently during the years that he explored a possible vocation with the priest:

> He sort of took me under his wing. And I realized that he was flesh
> and blood, that he was human. And I realized that some Sundays
> when he may have been impatient with some of the members was
> because he had this great fathering instinct. Saint Anthony's, the mem-

bers, everyone else, became his children. It was like our yard. We used
to go around planting hedges around the church. And he was talking
about, always talking about the future . . . when these hedges grow
up. . . . Everybody was a child . . . and the teachers were his mothers.

Paternalism here blends with commitment—building for future times
rather than priestly transience—and caring. Through compassion, Begley
bridged the structural distance from priest to layman and layman to
priest, synthesizing both roles. Not all SMAs were so successful, as some
proved unable to adjust to the isolation, attitudes, or responsibilities of
their mission. Yet long-term priests provided continuity for younger
priests and congregants.

The changes in priestly leadership fostered by Vatican II coincided
with the departure of the SMAs, blurring the apparently eternal divisions
of priest and people by awkwardly opening lines of discussion and dialogue. As we saw, the changes occurred amidst the agonies of the closing of the black parish schools. Had the school closure been done arbi-
trarily by the SMAs, for example, it might have been accepted more easily than the decision made after skewed consultation in a more seemingly democratic era. Uncertainty was renewed thereafter by the reas-
signment of the Franciscans. Both parish and sacramental leaders were
on the verge of new definitions.

PRIEST AND PARISH IN CONTEMPORARY SAVANNAH

Since the end of the 1960s, black parishes, like all other diocesan parishes, have participated in a regular rotation of leaders decided by the
bishop in consultation with the priestly synod and the desires of candidates to move into different ministries. In these decades, a dominant
scenario of adjustment and conflict has emerged in painful repetition
from parish to parish. I describe this model from the arrival of the priest,
through adaptation and recategorization, to end with reflections on departure.

The arrival of a new (white) priest in a black parish stimulates more
testing and mutual adjustment than similar circumstances in white parishes that I know. In the white parishes, an assumption of a shared
(white) heritage and expectations underpins the confidence of the
"unmarked" term. In black parishes, an assumption of difference, marked

by color, must be overcome. Furthermore, the transition is more likely to be absolute: since the SMA departure, black parishes have had a single priest rather than a rectorial household in which one member can be replaced while others remain. Finally, unlike the process of black Protestant churches, parishioners are not consulted in the choice nor are they likely to know the appointee well. Hence, "We gotta have some time to blackenize him."

Prior consultation in most of these transfers has been minimal. Ten years ago, Sister Julian Griffin called for special prior training, a goal that many leaders still try to achieve:

> 1. . . . It is recommended that priests and sisters who are assigned to
> Black parishes should receive some form of cultural orientation, to
> acquaint them with minority ways, and that Black lay people as well
> as priests or religious be involved in the orientation procedure. . . .
>
> 2. . . . It is recommended that seminarians . . . be encouraged to
> spend a summer working within a Black parish. . . . They should also
> be encouraged to familiarize themselves with the neighborhood in
> informal ways. . . . (Griffin and Brown 1979, 82)

While the second recommendation has become relatively commonplace, the first rarely holds. Priests undergo some self-selection and preparation for black ministry as well as examination by the synod, but never to the extent that Sister Julian commended or that interaction would suggest to be important.

At the transition, as a time of uncertainty, the most stereotypical models of black and white behavior surface. Hence one hears comments like that of an adult black lawyer, that "I used to think of blacks as a whole lot more spiritual than whites." An older parishioner was more critical in her expectations: "These new priests. . . . Some of these priests won't take no time to study no niggers." "Niggers" here draws a sharp boundary between the in group, for whom the term is acceptable, and the outsiders with whom the priest is associated. The future worries many parishioners, as an older long-time member expressed it: "Once we get complacent and set in our ways, here comes somebody who's gonna change, and your fear is that they're gonna change everything we're doing and they'll upset the whole apple cart."

In the transitions I have witnessed, the attitudes and actions of the first few weeks prove determinative. Since priests arrive with very little knowledge of the parish, consultation is critical, although channels are not readily apparent. The permanent deacon may act as a transitional figure, yet a priest commented that there simply were no guidelines; like parish employees, the deacon was extremely vulnerable in a transition. Would he be consulted? "If he [the priest] had any kind of sensitivity, pastorally. . . ." Parish councils, well-known leaders, self-studies, or open fora may be in place to develop understanding; parish records are more idiosyncratic.

The speed and manner in which the priest begins to make *his* mark is also critical. In an unsuccessful transition that I witnessed, the priest immediately began to assert his authority under the guise of his own interpretation of church orthodoxy in all realms of parish governance and ritual. This produced a clamor from many parishioners used to consultations. Rumors and misunderstanding soon poisoned the atmosphere.

Father Smith, by contrast, had entered his parish in the late 1970s with a self-effacing humor. In 1989 a parishioner shared the autobiography Smith had serialized then, including this portrait of his first week:

> Monday I ended up meeting with the Mayor and City Manager with the Hudson Hill Community Association and then attended the groundbreaking for the new Westside Recreation Center. Tuesday I was on a panel for TV. Wednesday I cooked my first meal for Frs. Collins, Otterbein and Bishop Lessard. Then I had an inspiring briefing on all that's happening and really got a feel for how the parish works. Thursday I tried my hand at weeding and found some weeds tough to attack right on unless you dig under them—maybe like some of our sins and weaknesses. Friday and Saturday I was in Macon at the Intern Training program for our new permanent deacons. It wasn't relaxing but sure enjoyed it and am feeling right at home. (Parish Bulletin, Aug. 1979)

Smith followed this excerpt with vignettes of his family, education, and experience as a priest, conveyed in a similar tone. He insisted on humanizing himself to his parishioners while he learned from them. This introductory portrait has much the same spirit of the farewell letter that has nevertheless incorporated a renewed sense of race and social justice.

Another priest reflected at length on his experience of the transition: "It was a great challenge to me personally. I had no idea where to start, where to go. . . . I knew the history of black/white relations, but I was totally ignorant of what it meant to be black. I wished to do a good job, not wishing to say the wrong thing. . . . I was keenly aware that I was white and they were black. And they shared the same sentiments. In time they no longer saw me as a white man and I no longer saw them as black." This priest's personal scenario saw deep division give way to an eclipse of fundamental categories. He did not have the same feelings or fears in adapting to a white parish. Ultimately, the scenario that underpinned his formula for transition was one of slow accommodation: "People ask, "What do you want us to do?" "Do what you normally do; let me experience personally what you are doing. If it's working, good; if not, let's look for change." Nonetheless, his position as the dominant actor in change was clear throughout the interview, as it was in his actions in his first years in the parish.

Almost all other priests with whom I spoke and worked had similar experiences of accommodation. They were keenly aware of social and cultural differences and their multiple implications as marked figures within the marked community. Diocesan advisors such as Sister Julian or black leaders acted as their counselors. While parish officers and councils offered important voices, identification of informal leaders was a more complex process that might inadvertently link the pastor to parish factions. Such identification, with the traditions of the parish, proved crucial to their effectiveness.

Parishioners, too, remain wary in the first few weeks. The presence of a powerful newcomer challenges the integrity of the community. This represents more than a potential disruption of the customs of identity in a conflictive world. It also threatens the compromises through which various social, regional, and ideological factions constitute a united parish. The lawyer cited above schematized the transition in terms of a competition for power: "Don't expect it to be smooth. First, he got to be accepted. The faithful few will rush in as saviors; others sit back and wait. Finally, the personality will blend in."

Pressures force the parish to adjust at the same time. While a single incident may not have any repercussions, repeated conflicts between priests and congregations label the members of a parish as "difficult," "uppity," or "troublemakers" As an older parishioner in one church said of the controversies in another black parish, "These people so damned hard on they priests, and he such a nice fellow." The ultimate threat, in any case, is to shut down the parish completely or to combine it with a predominantly white jurisdiction.

Blacks additionally face a cumulative effect of many transitions since the SMA departure, which situates parishioners between independence and detachment. Through history and lay leadership they have become more aware of their ownership of community yet perhaps more distant from the tight parochial family that once existed. Thus, after a rocky year of adjustment, an older leader expressed his cynicism about a new priest expected at the end of the summer: "Old, young, don't make no difference. All you can do is read your Bible and try to listen to what they say."

After an initial liminal phase, priest and parish generally build on their relationship. Here, stylistic variation among priests influences their relations with the parish and neighborhood. Inclusion and exclusion emerged at a level as obvious as the discussion of race and class as "our" concerns or as "your" concerns. Rarely would a priest slip into direct reference to himself by a color-crossing term, yet long-term priests tend to be inclusive and associative in their preaching about "our parish," "our neighborhood," or even distant references, for example, the use of "an important day for all of us" in reference to the ordination of Eugene Marino as archbishop in Atlanta, the Metropolitan see as well as the first archdiocese ruled by a black.

Such stylistic adaptation carries over into liturgy and sermons, where priests may interpret and change the custom of the parish. Here little evidence beyond adaptation to scarce materials exists from early missionary days; sermon outlines are generally dogmatic and syllogistic. Today, white priests in Savannah sometimes have adopted forms from traditional black Protestant preaching ("Let the church say Amen!") or have encouraged Gospel music in their congregations (Southern 1971; H. Mitchell 1979; Howze et al. 1984; Davis 1985). Here, however, it is often difficult to distinguish personal style from an adoption of perceived black mores, especially since the process often remains unconscious and collaborative. Thus one priest admitted that he could no longer separate his sense of justice and spirituality from the experience of working with poor blacks inside and outside his parish.

Language and style can establish separation as well. In more difficult cases, I was struck by the formal distance that the priest maintained, spending little relaxed and informal time in the parish or neighborhood. Complaints surfaced about how hard it was to find "Father." This was echoed in sermons that were strictly scriptural and dogmatic rather than drawing on the personal anecdotes and neighborhood concerns of long-term priests.

Preaching epitomizes this adaptive process. Preaching, while central to the liturgy of the word, remains the prerogative of the priest and deacons

198

as ritual leaders, more than of the community as a whole. The permanent deacons, drawn from leaders in the community, along with the invitation of black priests and preachers from outside as visitors or revival leaders, have expanded the black voices heard from the pulpit. Yet foreign priests also live within their community, listening to and interpreting their feelings and experiences. In a sense, the very awareness of distinct backgrounds may have forced more conscious synthesis than in comparable white parishes where the priest is just as likely to come from outside the parish, rotated through the diocese. (This symbiosis reappears in the analysis of preaching and worship in Chapter 8).

Neighborhood involvement plays a special role for any minister in the black community. In praising their white priests, black Catholics would often use a formula like "You can't get anyone more involved than him." A black priest noted "people expect the minister to lead. A white priest may find it a burden; there is more community work than actual parish work."

Obviously, adaptation toward collaborative goals of harmony and worship erases neither the institutional power of the priest nor the enduring authority of the community. One of the clearest areas of adaptation involves the extent to which the priest relinquishes control. Here, the potential of his position is almost without limit, except for the mandated foundation of a parish council and a finance committee, whose roles are discussed in the next chapter. More difficult is the identification of "real" parish leaders and the solicitation and acceptance of their comments in a dialogue rather than an authoritarian monologue. I asked a long-term priest in a black parish who would tell him about mistakes he made:

Fr.: I could always rely on *X* [an older, female resident community leader] to give me a clue. I could always rely on Sister Julian on another level. I used to touch base with about six black men quite a lot, have breakfast with them and all that kind of thing. . . . They never knew, I'd say how about breakfast some morning, I had no written agenda. . . . the thing was social, it was really a listening thing just to see what was hidden between the lines.
McD.: Would the deacon tell you if you made a mistake?
Fr.: Yes. Only, though like after two or three years. [He] and myself became best friends.
McD.: What about if you're doing something wrong liturgically. . . .
Fr.: Nobody would ever say it.

199

Even within the multiple capacities of the priest, social and political aims were more easily criticized than ritual actions:

> McD.: . . . The priest is presumed to be the expert in many areas.
> Fr.: He is. Without question. He is *presumed* to be. And unless he does something that is obvious, a very obvious violation of the rubrics, . . . there is no question raised.

By the end of a five-year term, or a double term of ten years that reaches the limits of diocesan practice, the accommodation of the priest and parish is generally much more intimate and extensive. The testimony of Father Smith highlights the interstitial position of the priest in any parish, but perhaps especially a black one. In reading it as a friend, I recalled the almost folkloric identification that he had achieved with his parishioners. That is, when asked in a religious education class to talk about black heroes in their community, black junior high students readily identified Father Mike. Similarly, small children from the neighborhood would swear that they did not know any whites even as they were playing with him. Acceptance into the community is expressed in his ambivalence of identification on both sides of the city's fundamental racial divide.

Similar stories, however, have been reported for earlier generations in Savannah. They were echoed by Geraldine Abernathy, a senior member of Saint Benedict's, from her childhood in New Orleans:

> A lot of them feel that if they had a black priest, they could better relate to him than they could a white priest, although the contradiction was with the sisters, the Franciscans. . . . Little black boy would say, "I hate white people," so sister say "Don't you hate me; I'm white, I'm a nun." "No Sister. You one of us, you not no white."

This process of identification, however, transcends the individual case of one priest as a recurrent theme among the priests and nuns in black ministry with whom I talked. Although white, they have in most cases developed an identification with the political and religious cause of the blacks as a subordinate group in the South and as a model for other subordination that they feel the church must confront, whether economic or social.

What does it mean to become "sociotypically black?" The response of one priest to my query, "When did you find out that you were white?" teased out some of the feelings associated with this status in confrontation with the values of the South. We pursued whiteness as a concept:

McD.: What does it mean to you to be white?

Fr.: (Pause) That's as complex as it is obvious. . . . I think what it does is I can't even begin to grapple with it: you know why? I think because I (Pause) a sense of separateness, a sadness in that, a breaking down of one's own world so to speak. A kind of a calling of—I don't know how to put it.

McD.: I don't know either and I have a chapter on it. . . .

Fr.: I think there is a sadness in the realization of separateness.

McD.: I think that's your being white because you're dealing with blacks. How would you characterize being white in Savannah?

Fr.: Separate. And a certain working at keeping the separation. And there's a way in which by virtue of the fact that you are white and you're part of that ethnic dimension there's a way in which the pain begins to enter in the sense of the deliberateness of the separateness, when you begin to absorb some of the pain there. You know what I mean?

McD.: Yeah. I think it means you're not white.

The priest holds a dual position: while deeply set in the black community in friendships and work, priests often spoke of their continuing sense of separation from the historical suffering that has also constituted blackness in the South. A fear of hurting through overfamiliarity and a sense of unease in the midst of loving community were all overtones to conversations—evoking feelings familiar to me as a white anthropologist who seemed and felt himself an adopted member of a black community.

The departure of a long-term priest, by contrast to his arrival, is more agonizing than the transitions in similar white parishes that I observed. Stress on the formation of family and community combines with uncertainty about the future to create anxiety. As noted, the departure is also an absolute and unmediated shift, although parishioners will try to find out information on new appointees. An older woman phrased it in basic terms of the psychology of black-white relations:

McD.: Why do you think it's so difficult in the black parishes to change priests? It seems that every time the priests have changed there's been some sort of blow-up. . . .

W.: Well, I think what it is, is the loyalties of the people. And the priests endear themselves so much to the community, because I was shocked to hear the things about Fr. *X,* I couldn't believe the people actually disliked him that much, but that was some few people because there was a lot of people over there who dearly loved the ground he walked on, and this is what it is. . . .

201

This respondent noted that white parishes did not have the same transitional anguish and sought some explanation in her experience:

> *W.:* Maybe they don't have the closeness or they don't get as close, maybe they don't *allow* themselves to come that close to the people. See, we tend to go all out just like a girl. You meet her for the first time and she can make me her footstool, she can walk all over me because I *love* her, . . . and then when she leaves you guys are so upset it may take you twenty years to get over it. . . .
>
> *McD.:* Why do you think blacks get so much closer to the priests?
>
> *W.:* That feeling of insecurity that most of us possess because all of our lives there's been something been lacking in terms of security, I think that's what it is. And I think this is the chance we get, a way to find some of the security that you realize. Now this is just me personally talking. . . . Suddenly here comes someone who says they're gonna help me and gonna dedicate themselves to deliver me, and most of the priests do—they come in and they dedicate themselves to the parish. . . . Here's somebody I can confide in and you're not gonna go down the street and tell Miss Jones. . . .

The anniversary testimonials of Saint Anthony's parishioners to their SMA pastors also poignantly underscore the identification of priest and community. While I would hesitate to extrapolate the psychological rationale of my informant, the process of adaptation and familiarization that proceeds from dramatic cultural differences suggests that the separations take on a drama not apparent in a parish where the priest is, in racial if not family ties, "one of us." The energy of breaking down racial walls, as we shall see again, erupts when these new bonds are threatened or appear to be lost.

Even so, ambivalence remains in the white priest-black congregation relationship, epitomized by two non-Savannahian commentaries. The black bishops' pastoral begins with an acknowledgment of early white teachers: "When we as Black Catholics speak of missionaries, we shall never forget the devoted services that many White priests, vowed religious and laypersons gave to us as a people and still give to us daily. We shall remember and never forget that this ministry was often given at great personal sacrifice and hardship. The same holds true today" (Howze et al. 1984, 3). While recognizing past contributions, the bishops clearly project whites into the past by contrast with the "Black men and women who have gone before us" that follow. Black priest Lawrence Lucas was more bitter in his description of a white priest with whom he worked in Harlem:

The Negro's *need* of him, whether it be of the social, intellectual or economic order, is the basis of the relationship. When the relationship is firmly established and accepted (that is, the superior white man doles out patronage out of largess to the inferior Negro) he is at home. He is happy; he is cheerful; he is well. He is extremely kind and generous. Everything is in its proper order. . . . That's the way God wanted it between white and black. (1989, 215; see Ochs 1990; C. Davis 1991)

So far, however, this process of parish-priest interaction has been analyzed from the standpoint of a white priest in a black parish in reflection of historical experience. The potential for a black priest in either a black or white parish demands reconsideration of both historical background and cultural expectations.

THE MARKED PRIESTHOOD: BLACKS AT THE ALTAR

In the past, the absence of consecrated black and Catholic ritual specialists has led Protestants, black and white, to decry Roman Catholicism as a "white man's religion." Accusations range from overt discriminatory paternalism to suggestions that whites have failed to develop or have discouraged black candidacy for the priesthood. Only five American blacks had been ordained by the end of the nineteenth century, including those, like the Healy brothers of Georgia, ordained abroad (Gillard 1929; Foley 1954; Ochs 1990). In fact, few were ordained before the segregated Divine Word Seminary in Bay St. Louis, Mississippi, began to produce candidates in the 1930s; and only seventy-four black priests were ordained between 1854 and 1954. In 1925, W. E. B. Du Bois excoriated the leadership of the Catholic church because

they are unable or unwilling to produce leaders for the black race. In over 400 years, the Catholic Church has ordained less than a half dozen black Catholic priests either because they have sent us poor teachers or because American Catholics do not want to work beside Black priests and sisters or because they think Negroes have neither brains nor morals enough to occupy positions open freely to Poles, Irishmen, and Italians. (Reply to Father Joseph B. Glenn, March 18, 1925, in Du Bois 1973, I: 309).

203

Stephen Ochs (1990) has documented the long and painful struggle of the Josephites to recruit and use black priests in their evangelization of the black community. In particular, the liberal caution of Superior General John Slattery at the end of the nineteenth century coincided with the reluctance of bishops to accept black priests and resurgent racism throughout American white society. Papal encyclicals in the twentieth century, however, demanded more "native" clergy, spurring attempts to draw blacks into integrated or segregated seminaries. Nonetheless, sociological and ecclesiological literature has suggested the failure of the American Catholic church to promote meaningful black leadership, especially by contrast to the dynamic actions of Protestant ministers in the civil rights era. This theme has been expressed to me as a recurrent preoccupation among white clerics who work with the black community, while it dominates national black and Catholic discussion in congresses, monographs, and journals.

This situation has changed in recent decades. There were by 1990 12 black bishops in the United States, including the archbishop of Atlanta, Eugene Marino, who was installed May 4, 1988 (although he subsequently stepped down, only to be replaced by another black prelate). Most bishops serve as auxiliaries in metropolitan areas with significant black populations, such as New York, Detroit, or Baltimore; eight of the twelve belong to religious orders that have specifically promoted black priesthood. Collectively, they have issued a major statement on the African-American experience in Catholicism (Howze et al. 1984); individually, they have sponsored discussions and revivals throughout the United States, including various visits to Savannah. By the mid-1980s, there were approximately 300 black priests and a similar number of seminarians, 265 black deacons, and 700 black nuns in the United States. This represented one black priest for every forty thousand black Catholics. As the ratio of priests to people has increased in the church as a whole, it decreases within the black community. Still, it does not converge with the white and Catholic experience.

Obviously, not all black priests serve black parishes, raising other questions of marking and universality. As discussed in terms of parish formation, black priestly entry into a white community might subvert rather than invert power categorizations. Yet the immediate question that strikes any outsider in looking at the history of Savannah's black and Catholic parishes is that of Du Bois: why have there been no black priests over one hundred years, or at least over the consistent mission of the past eighty years? There is no clear-cut answer, and perhaps none generalizable from the special case of Savannah, which has not produced enough priests even in its white parishes to maintain mission programs, resulting in the continuing importation of foreign priests.[4] Blacks and whites cite factors that have damaged recruitment, including prejudice, lack of social support, and lack of cultural awareness.

Prejudice clearly holds a primacy as an explanation. As one older community leader recalled of the 1960s: "There was lots of discrimination. My son and ———— wanted to become priests. They wouldn't accept them at Saint John Vianney. The priest tried to get them to Black Creek, tried to get scholarships but no go." At the beginning of the century, Bishop Keyes did not even wish black SMA priest Father Joseph John to visit the diocese, much less stay there (Ochs 1990, 272-76). Father John's mass was well-received by parishioners at Immaculate Conception in Augusta, although SMAs recounted black complaints in the *Echo des Missions Africaines* that others ignored the event: "If yesterday at 10 AM a colored man had committed a murder at the church door, all the United States newspapers would have published the news with giant headlines, but when, at that same time, a priest of color sang the mass it was not considered worthy of attention" (April 1924, 75).

Prejudice also subtly permeated other scenarios confirmed by priests and nuns, black and white, as well as ex-candidates. Prejudice often was enshrined in selection or limitation at the seminary or convent, implicit in such statements as "Wouldn't you be happier with . . . ?" Unconscious prejudice had become apparent to older priests and nuns in their reflections when I met with them in the 1980s. A Franciscan sister who had served in Savannah in the 1930s regretted: "We didn't encourage vocations. Didn't want them? ———— is an Oblate now in Carolina who would have come with us, very devoted, but we didn't want her. . . ." An SMA who had worked in Savannah also recalled "I was always very keen about that; I don't know how many times I preached it. One went from here to the SVDs (Divine Word Fathers) in Bay St. Louis. But it was very hard; they tested black vocations more. That's still prevalent today, too."

Another white priest responded more directly to my question about the reasons for the lack of blacks in the priesthood:

> One is the history of racism in the church. Until 1950 there was no seminary for black priests. I think that the requirement of the mandatory celibacy is a major, major obstacle. The whole notion of call, to serve the people of God is something that is in the most profound way central to black spirituality, the whole place of the man of god, the minister, the sense of call that people feel is obviously a very living part of their faith.

Reports on Clarence Thomas's passage through local and national seminaries again evoked racist jokes and expectations that created an unsupportive climate for black candidates. A relative of a black in the seminary at the same time as Thomas felt blacks "almost had to walk on water to get there." Thomas's experiences, as they came to light in his confirmation hearings, chronicled both blatant and subtle racism. A white friend, for example, recalled that Thomas, a Saint Pius student who entered the seminary in 1964, fit in well: "There was a great deal of closeness and camaraderie among the students." Yet Thomas remembered otherwise "'Not a day passed that I was not pricked by prejudice.' He once told an interviewer that when the lights were doused in his dorm room, one of his classmates would crack, 'Smile, Clarence, so we can see you'" (Lancaster and LaFraniere 1991, 7).

Later, in a seminary in Missouri where he was one of three blacks,

> Thomas recalled that the final straw came when he overheard a white seminarian's response to the news that the Rev. Martin Luther King, Jr. had been shot: "Good—I hope the SOB dies." Later, Thomas wrote to O'Brien [a friend] that he had left Catholicism entirely—a decision he changed several times—partly because of O'Brien's pastor in Kansas City who "can call himself a Christian and a [George] Wallace man at the same time." (Lancaster and LaFraniere 1991, 7)

The lack of a fostering atmosphere in the social structures of the black and Catholic community has also contributed to the lack of seminarians or their decision to leave the seminary. Many families are religiously mixed, where distinct Christian traditions may clash in the approbation of a career of differentiation. Moreover, Savannah black Catholics lacked religious secondary education until the 1950s, thus missing an important period in the decision of vocations (although the church was no more successful in recruitment in Augusta, where such an institution existed). Finally, few role models exist, perpetuating the problem from generation to generation. Sister Julian Griffin noted: "If vocations among young Black people are to be encouraged, there is a need for them to see Black priests and sisters and to take an interest in their work" (Griffin and Brown 1979, 84). As it is, a black cleric notes, black priests are "few in number, facing high stress and loneliness," and potential candidates must ask themselves, "Why do this when I can do another career—doctor, lawyer, teacher, and be successful?" (see Ochs 1990).

Lack of cultural adaptation and support is mentioned by both black and white priests. Where white culture is dominant to the point of being unconscious and unmarked, few black questions or sensitivities are incorporated into recruitment and training. This absence permeates early incorporation, seminary training, and the emergence of the priest into the wider Catholic community.

Within these processes of cultural adaptation, celibacy, too, is referred to as an issue. It was certainly alluded to in a humorous reference in the sermon preached for Father Chaney's first mass. Yet black and white leaders generally told me that it was no more an issue for blacks than it manifestly is for contemporary whites. There is, however, a strong emphasis on the pastor's wife and family in almost all black Protestant congregations, which has led black nun Sandra Smithson to criticize celibacy:

> But the Black family in general, and the Black man in particular, having been successfully destroyed by the terrible circumstances of slavery, need to be restored to their rightful place and honor through the pastoral and redemptive grace of Sacrament. In Black psyche, it is family and community that are the repository of religion and culture, not an isolated eunuch called *priest* nor a building called *church*. (1984, 53)

Here the priest relates more deeply not to sexuality or marriage but to the entire community, as both church and family.[5]

Once a black priest is recruited and trained, he will not be sent immediately into a black parish. Various members of the black and Catholic parishes with whom I have spoken have highlighted the potential difficulties they perceive for someone who is actively involved in the social networks of the black community. Another male leader criticized his perceptions of community expectations:

> It's the message not the messenger; if they have the message it's worthwhile to listen. Most black Catholics are more defensive when a white tell them to be more concerned. . . . [But] some feel they can't get anything done unless there is a white in charge. A black priest . . . would need a strong will and faith. He would have to understand criticism and goals and realize that's a fact of life—any black faces that.

Catholics also face a dilemma going back to the Cahenslyist controversy, which arose over demands for "national parishes" among German

Catholics, and other ethnic debates throughout the twentieth century (Dolan 1985). Does providing a black priest for a black parish establish identity or promote segregation—if these can be separated? The implications are as challenging in the present as they were for ethnic nationalists eighty years ago but are made more difficult by posing the unmarked question: is it bad to put a white priest in a white church? Here, the factors that mitigate against a black priesthood are related to the more general dilemmas of blacks in the church, as a priest noted:

> *McD.:* Why do blacks leave the Catholic church?
> *Fr.:* The most obvious reason: lack of cultural affirmation. I know black Catholics who have left the church. I brought some of them into the church and there was an initial euphoric kind of romantic experience of loving aspects of the faith and all the rest of it, . . . and then that wears off and there is always an incredible pain felt, at least I felt it as a *white* priest in a black parish.
> *McD.:* Why?
> *Fr.:* By just the sheer reality of being white and knowing that there is a need . . . spiritually, a need to, in some authentic way, to touch the soul of people and in the deepest, most profound way to allow it to happen—not that I do it—the touching. But to facilitate, you know, an openness and . . . I just don't think white people can do it for black people on *any* level.

This priest, despite a successful career in black ministry, foresaw the need for more extensive cultural and social relativism:

> *McD.:* Do you think black parishes should have black priests?
> *Fr.:* I do. I feel very, very . . . and I know that's argued, and I know that's argued by black leaders, you know, that it's not a necessity. I feel very strongly about it. . . .
> *McD.:* . . . People don't make the argument that *women* should have women priests. . . .
> *Fr.:* Oh, but I think there are situations where it cries out for a woman. . . .
> *McD.:* But I don't hear that being mentioned.
> *Fr.:* You don't but it's apples and oranges. In the social context we're speaking in race as a factor is incredibly significant. . . . It makes a major difference. It's unique and uniquely explosive and carries so much with it in society.

Other priests who had served with black parishes in the pre-Conciliar era, as well as older black parishioners, nonetheless mentioned reservations about a black priest in the parish. Whether because of cultural training with regard to white authority or discomfort with the networks implicit in black social life, these objections focused on an inability to talk as freely with a black priest. No one felt that such a priest would be rejected, however.

This stands in striking to contrast to expectations for a black priest assigned to a predominantly white parish. Identifying two of the most conservative parishes in Savannah as possibilities, a white priest asked, "How would he [a black priest] be welcomed? How many protests, how many would change parish, stop using the offertory. . . . How many wouldn't drink from the chalice?" Blacks, too, wonder about expectations and reactions, although there have been few problems when the actual situation has arisen.

In reviewing the role of the black or white priest, however, it is also important to see them not only as leaders of their parish, but also in relation to the structure of the diocese. They are involved with fellow priests and parishes, at the level of black ministry and the regional synod, and they are answerable (an ambiguous term) to their bishop. Apart from these bureaucratic roles, they also act as teachers and distillers of knowledge for the parish and beyond it, bringing the concerns of a larger church into focus through doctrinal teaching, spiritual reflection, or involvement in causes ranging from Habitat for Humanity and the local food bank to missionary work in the third world.

Priests have professional and collegial bonds with other priests emphasized by their lack of family ties. One pattern, set in SMA days, established the priests and nuns who worked with blacks as closed and self-sustaining communities, generally divorced from other priests. Certain relations followed from the Irish presence among the Franciscans and later among the SMAs. This also established a bond with Irish immigrants in diocesan priesthood. Nonetheless, a wall of experience and discipline divided secular and religious priests. Yet the rectory of Saint Benedict's provided a compensatory meeting place for an SMA community amidst priest rotations.

After departure of the SMAs, white priests in black parishes were merely in a different circuit. Some had experience in other, predominantly white, parishes and residence in multiple-priest households. Their age cohort as much as their parishes have shaped friendships and support. Neverth\`eless, the lives of priests in black parishes are different. They live alone instead of sharing a rectory. They have strong ties to their parish and, over time, to the black community. Those whom I questioned felt that the majority of their local friends were black parishioners or other Savannah blacks. Parish participation determined personal lives.

The relationship of priests and bishop combines personal and structural strain. In so far as the priest identifies with the concerns of the black and Catholic community, he will be caught up in the contradictions that it experiences and even those that blacks come to symbolize for whites, such as the exploitation of the third world peasantry by owners sustained by local Catholic churches. Advocacy springing from the contradictory situation of blacks within the church as a whole may oppose them to the projects, concerns, and governance of the bishop. In a less conflictive sense, such priests have also led discussions of social concerns and campaigns for parochial unity.

Finally, priests form part of a larger church. One of the continuing advantages for me of conversation with the priests has been their own processes of reflection and involvement that have raised general questions of social and cultural transformation beyond my ethnographic interests. Here again, priests seem to be guided by concerns of the parish and black culture toward their own exploration of various aspects of Catholic structure and action.

These concerns have been introduced throughout this chapter as dialogues with named and anonymous figures, reflecting the limited number of priests with whom I have talked and our personal relationships as public and private figures. Perhaps closure to this section can come once again from the midterm report of Father Mike Smith. Here, after years of work with Christian life and formation, he faced the prospect of application of principles to a real community: "They always laugh when you don't put into practice what you had been telling them to do." Thus he built a bridge between his participation in Caritas, an international fraternity of priests inspired by Charles de Foucauld, and his parish work. Smith explained that de Foucauld "saw himself as a brother to all people, and he practiced what he called universal hospitality, trying to make everyone feel welcome. He thought this was the way to show God to people, by simple friendship and brotherhood." Father Smith translated this to his parochial role: "If you are present to God in prayer you will also be present to people in friendship. I guess I have found this way of life a good base for parish life, giving the enrichment of prayer, the sense of God, the vision and strength that God provides" (G. Brown 1984, 9). Here the priest acts as a leader in and of the community, transcending historical and categorical divisions.

THE NUNS AND SUBORDINATION

My preliminary focus on the priest reflects accurately the patriarchal structures of the formal church—to be challenged, as we shall see, by the structures of community leadership. Yet it does not fairly reflect the historical continuity of Catholic ministry to blacks. While bishops, priests, and orders have offered inconsistent response to the needs of the black Savannah community, religious women offered an earlier and more continuous service in that community. The first and most dangerous missionary efforts recorded to blacks were the antebellum schools in which Sisters of Saint Joseph were involved. The longest career of service in the black community has been that of the Franciscans, who began to work with black schools in the era of Matilda Beasley and have taught blacks in segregated and integrated schools to the present.

Nuns form a marked category with regard to both lay women and the sacramental marking of the priesthood. Nuns (and lay brothers) function under vows of chastity, obedience, and poverty within a reinforcing community.[6] Gender has been a hotly debated bar to the formal priesthood in the Catholic church, but nuns are not female priests. Traditionally, their lives have been defined by service, generally in such "domestic" areas as cloistered contemplation, teaching, and health care. The life of the nun, nevertheless, has often provided autonomy, power, and prestige to women, whether exemplified in leaders of the pre-Conciliar church (N. Davis 1975; Bossy 1985; Keightley 1988) or contemporary leadership in a variety of fields. In Savannah, sisters of various congregations have contributed more than a century of service by hundreds of women, in schools, hospitals, social services, and care for the elderly. Recently, a nun has served as chancellor of the diocese, and Sister Virginia Ross currently heads the Diocesan School Board. Sister Julian Griffin headed the Office of Black Ministry until her death; the position is now occupied by a black deacon, Frank Mathis, from Saint Mary's.

White nuns in the formative period of black parishes and schools experienced many of the processes of separation and adaptation to ra-

211

cial categorizations that priests underwent. At the same time, they were locked into related expectations of gender and service. Nuns were continually subordinate within the parish and even, in some ways, within the school. This situation has only begun to change with the disestablishment of schools as a primary commitment for the sisters, as well as the radical changes in religious life since Vatican II.

The contact between nuns and blacks, as already noted, centered on the school, even as this school was a pervasive institution of Roman Catholic life. Hence contact was more intense and more intimate than that of layman and priest, although it might also be less enduring as faculties changed from year to year. For most of the history of the black schools, nuns provided the entire teaching and administrative staff, which brought them into day-to-day contact with generations of black children. Discipline is as important a component as warmth in parishioners' memories of the sisters. Their role also included nurturing beyond the classroom, in work with families and children, as well as their dramatic symbolic presence in the classroom.

The presence of the priest, however, remained dominant. In the school, while nuns might teach a vast range of subjects, religion was generally the domain of the missionary priest. Hence, children were taught that this subject, as well as the teacher, was set apart. The priest also acted as the ultimate administrator—paying the bills and settling disputes, even if it meant tension between rectory and convent. Even if a nun objected, like the earlier critic of Father Martin's baptisms, she could not dispute his power.

Within the church, nuns also held subordinate positions of service. At the pre-Conciliar Mass, they watched children, contributed music, and performed similar tasks in addition to participating as communicants. Convents often had the responsibility for cleaning altar linens, until this was taken over at Saint Benedict's by laywomen. Here, in an unintended parallel to the thrust of Vatican II reforms, an area of domestic but sanctified responsibility became another service role for the laity, generally lay females.

Nuns had corollary limitations in their social life. Those who taught at Saint Anthony's and Saint Mary's had to be picked up by the pastor or a parishioner and transported to the school. Indeed, travel was restricted for religious women: some orders were not allowed to leave the convent except in pairs; nuns were expected not to be out at night. Another nun who served in Savannah in the 1930s bitterly recalled her inability to protest the segregation she hated, even in so simple a matter as sitting with her students and coparishioners on caste-divided buses.

212

The attitudes of the black community tended to reaffirm subordination. Blacks speak protectively of the sisters, with repeated expression of concern for "the poor nuns" or declarations that "they're my dolls." Parishioners would take care of them with gifts of food, and in the 1990s black parishes have become active in raising money for the Franciscan sisters' retirement home in Tenafly.

The differences between nuns and priests become more interesting in the area of black recruitment and presence. The Franciscan sisters had their first postulant shortly after their arrival in Georgia. In subsequent years, each of the parishes has produced nuns, although all have joined orders away from Savannah, favoring traditionally black orders. A number of these nuns have also left the convent for various reasons, as have many white women. Hence, the recruitment has been ambiguous, as has the role of black nuns themselves.

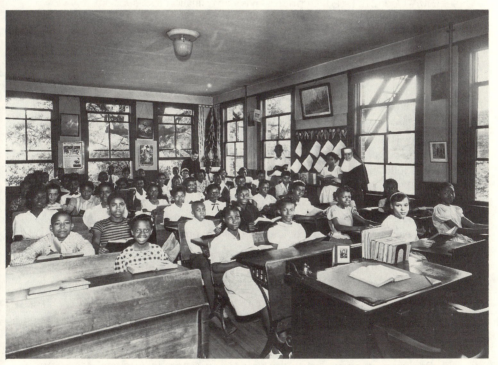

Figure 15. Classroom at Saint Benedict's, ca. 1948. Photograph courtesy of the Georgia Historical Society, Cordray-Foltz Collection.

Matilda Beasley has already appeared as an enigmatic figure in the analysis of schools and churches in the nineteenth century. Her status as a lay or religious leader, however, indicates the ambiguities of such categories in the early missionary church. Matilda Beasley was a New Orleans immigrant, with mixed Creole, Indian, and black heritage (Ahles 1977, 138; Veronica Arnold, oral history interview, 1984) who became the second wife of the prosperous black merchant Abram Beasley. After his death in the 1878, she committed herself and her wealth to religious work (*SMN* Dec. 21, 1903). She became involved with the Benedictines and contributed to the construction of Sacred Heart. In 1887, with Father Moosmuller, she founded a Catholic orphanage for black children near Sacred Heart parish, as I have already noted.

Here her status becomes more unclear. According to Sister Charlene Walsh, who worked as a pastoral associate at Saint Benedict's, Beasley took vows in the Third Order of Saint Francis in London and founded a community in Savannah in 1889, with herself as Mother Beasley (Powers 1982; see *SMN* Dec. 21, 1903). Cyprian Davis's investigation also supports this view (1991, 110-11). Others see the name as an "attempt to give permanence to her work," noting the lack of documentary evidence (Ahles 1977, 139).

A biographer of Bishop Becker notes his paternalistic plea in 1891 to Mother Drexel to incorporate Beasley and her group:

> Why not try to have a sisterhood here which might envelope Sister Matilda and her poor assistants in some lowly grade and utilize them. This, or something similar might ward off the obloquy which is charged against the Church that she either does nothing for the colored folks or does it in a very slovenly manner!
>
> Mathilda has two black women as helpers and quasi-Sisters to attend some thirty girls ranging from two to fifteen about. At fourteen or so they can safely be put into service, having made their Communion, etc., and learned to cook and sew a bit, provided we can find decent places for them. . . .
>
> If she had good Sisters from the north whose heart would be in this work—in a few, a very few years, many Southern girls would join them. (cited in Peterman 1982, 197)

Beasley herself wrote to and visited the Blessed Sacrament motherhouse and continued to seek their financial support (C. Davis 1991, 111-12).

Becker next appealed to the Franciscan sisters in Augusta, receiving an offer of their assistance in January 1896. At this point, Beasley may have joined the Franciscans, as Sister Julian Griffin claims (Griffin and Brown 1979, 44; Peterman 1982, 197). Her group remained somewhat separate; Ahles talks of its dissolution under Bishop Becker, although there is no documentation (1977).

The orphanage moved to Anderson Street in 1894, with help from Mother Drexel, and to East Broad in 1901 (Peterman 1982, 198). Sister Charlene Walsh noted the decline of her community until Mother Beasley was found dead in her cottage near Sacred Heart in 1903 (Powers 1982). Her obituary in the *Savannah Morning News*, while treating her as a benefactor to the black community and a religious, does not actually identify her as black, speaking instead of her French and Indian heritage. Mass was held at Sacred Heart, by then a clearly white church, with pallbearers from Saint Benedict's.

Yet despite historical silence thereafter, her order may not have disappeared so quickly. A *Savannah Tribune* article of April 9, 1910, reported the death of still another local black nun associated with Mother Beasley who had apparently maintained her vows in isolation, at least apart from the control of white superiors or church authorities. Perceptions of race, class, and secularization mingled in the denigration of the black female.

Subsequently, black nuns have been extraordinary even to black parishioners, as Father Lissner noted in responses to the Handmaids of the Most Pure Heart of Mary:

> Never before had they seen one of their own dressed up as Sisters. "I am very glad" I overheard one saying to another, "to see these Ladies. I believe now that there are also real good religious women among our people, just like white folk." "God Bless them." . . . During the week the ladies visited them and brought them provisions of all kinds and even arranged a house for them. But the White sisters, I am sorry to say, kept away. As real Southerners they could not believe that a colored woman could make a real Religious Sister. I was blamed for the mistake. "It is a shame" they said. Father Lissner will soon find out his mistake. "He may give them the veil but will that prevent them from stealing chickens and telling lies?" (n.d., 5)

A kaleidoscope of black and white imagery contributed to interpretation of a new categorization. To blacks, the black nuns marked advancement, even to the denigration of the virtue of the laity. To whites, they were suspect according to the most marked stereotypes of black repression.

Fifty years later, when Sister Julian arrived at Saint Anthony's, parishioners still registered strong surprise: "I *have* to go see a black nun."

The changes of Vatican II and the general roles of women have had
no more striking impact in Catholicism than on the religious life. The
change from medieval habits to simple everyday dress, for example, challenged established stereotypes of otherness and sanctity. A decline in
vocations since the 1960s, as women have pursued other new opportunities, meant a change in both the religious and the economic life of
schools, as nuns have left and lay teachers demanded real salaries. As
numbers declined, however, more creative roles were recognized for
women who had years of experience in administration and service as
well as education. This is evident in the coordinate ministry in Saint
Benedict's and in diocesan administrative tasks.

The role of nuns in the black and Catholic community, however, poses
central questions about the role of women in that community, as well as
about race and gender in Savannah as a whole. Since the 1960s, these
relations have changed somewhat, both in the evolving role of nonordained
religious and the gradual but widespread disappearance of sisters and their
orders. Yet the issues of gender and race may be completely understood
only after consideration of the formal and informal roles of lay leadership
that the matriarchs of the community have assumed.

PRIESTHOOD, ECCLESIOLOGY, AND THE MISSIONARY CHURCH

The evolution of priests and nuns in the black community as figures of
power includes all the central ambiguities of the Catholic church in South
Georgia as a whole, between Christian ideology and racist society. Yet an
alternative model was also proposed and contested by the SMA fathers at
the beginning of their tenure. This model was linked to the experience of
African churches and the development of independent and self-sustaining
missions.

A document in the Savannah diocesan archives, presumably by Ignatius
Lissner (on the basis of internal autobiographical evidence), suggests an
intriguing vision of the situation of Georgia when the SMAs arrived:

> Now the State of Georgia has a colored population of about one mil-
> lion, two hundred thousand souls. White priests and Sisters are able to
> start missions and schools in the cities and larger towns. But no Soci-

ety could furnish enough teachers for the numerous rural population. . . .
In proportion Africa has more colored Catholics and missionaries than
Georgia. . . . To supply more workers and produce greater results
Father Lissner had planned for several years a Seminary for the formation of colored priests and a Convent for the training of religious Colored sisters. It is without doubt the real spirit of the Church and the
only logical method practiced by the Church from Apostolic times until now. Why should America be any different? (Lissner n.d., 1)

The author establishes his authority by an anecdote of a conversation
with Pope Pius XI in which the pope complained about failures in the
Indian missions and said, "the Protestants are in their formation of a Native clergy, more Catholic than the Catholics themselves" (Lissner, 1).

Another indication of Lissner's missionary zeal came in the enigmatic
naming of the first parish he founded in Savannah. Saint Anthony of
Padua has no relationship to black history or to Lissner's own Alsatian
background, yet he chose the name for both the parish and the
motherhouse in Tenafly, New Jersey. In Vogel's history, he mentions only
one other Saint Anthony's, the patron of Elmina, on the Gold Coast, established by the Portuguese in the sixteenth century. When the SMAs
redeveloped the African missions in the nineteenth century, Father Max
Albert as prefect apostolic of the Gold Coast dedicated this critical mission diocese to the Saint. "St. Anthony was much honored by the Portuguese and his statue in Edina or Elmina was saved by then baptized but
soon re-paganized converts as a fetish. Well, Bishop Albert loved him
too and dedicated his 'diocese' to him" (Vogel [a], 55). This may well
have been a connection within Lissner's cognitive and intellectual framework in planning the Savannah African-American church.

In 1915 Lissner used laws under debate in Atlanta that would have
forbidden white teachers for blacks to develop his first larger missionary
project: the creation of a black female religious order. Again, the African
heritage is clear: "I explained my plan to the bishop who was well
pleased and encouraged me, saying, 'Yes, Colored Sisters for Colored
People and in time also Colored Priests.' 'Thank you, Bishop, it was my
plan for a long time.' 'Convert Africa by the Africans themselves,' was
my cry when I was a missionary on the West Coast of Africa" (Lissner,
2).[7] In Washington, D.C., Lissner located Elizabeth Williams, a black
woman who had entered a short-lived Marist-sponsored community in
Missouri and was later working as a servant for the Notre Dame sisters.
He found her promising, if headstrong. She replied, "Even before I met

217

you I saw you in a vision and the good Lord revealed to me that somebody would accept my offer to be one of the Sisters" (Lissner, 3). In November 1916 Williams remade her vows as Mother Mary Theodore and began the community in a furnished house in Savannah. Lissner's emphases follow the needs of a colonizing African church as much as any local ideals:

> It is not to be an exclusively teaching Institution. The Sister will have to be instructed in religion in order to be practical catechists and settlement workers. I expect the candidates to be instructive and [illegible] in all domestic works, in order to give the girl schoolchildren a practical knowledge in housekeeping and home economics; at the same time to give the knowledge that they would receive in the corresponding standard of the Grammar School grades. It must be understood, however, that there are to be no exclusively manual working sisters. Candidates must first of all be trained to teach the various grades in the Grammar school so that the members of their own race could not look upon them as being uneducated and so trying to subjugate the Colored race. They were to be uplifted and to improve the condition of the Colored people intellectually, Spiritually and morally. (Lissner, 4)

Lissner here adopts a paternal tone of concern for blacks, which underscores his sense of mission from above vis-à-vis both blacks and women. This entails an inverse class prejudice in the rejection of manual labor as a plan of uplift, although Lissner was more keenly conscious of his role as a white than entering directly into Washington-Du Bois debates.

The meaning of the sisters becomes clearer in the context of another controversy that emerged from Father Lissner's expansion of the black Georgia missions along the lines of an African church, which Stephen Ochs (1990) has highlighted by comparison to Divine Word and Josephite attempts to recruit black priests. Lissner, too, had proposed a Savannah seminary. In 1919, however, he suggested to Rome the establishment of a separate bishop with special responsibilities for blacks in Georgia. Approved in Rome, the news was sent to Savannah (S. Congregazione de Propaganda Fide to B. J. Keiley Jan. 30, 1920; Keiley Chancery Papers, Box 5, SMA file, Diocese of Savannah Diocesan Archives). Bishop Keiley reacted quickly to Rome, explaining that there were only twenty thousand white and one thousand black Catholics in the state and "bigotry towards Catholics and blacks is truly rampant, and

I fear the effect of such a project" (Keiley to S. Congregazione Propa-
ganda Fide March 3, 1920; Keiley Chancery Papers, Box 5, Diocese of
Savannah Diocesan Archives). Keiley expressed his concerns to Cardinal
Gibbons, a leader of the American church:

> You remember that these Fathers have been here for a number of
> years and their provincial (who by the way is of Jewish ancestry and
> has many of the qualities of the "Chosen People") has raised a large
> amount of money, and has labored hard and with some success. He is
> anxious to establish a seminary for the training of colored youths for
> the priesthood here. I need not tell you what this would mean to us in
> the South. I placed the matter before the Consultors at one of our
> quarterly meetings and it was unanimously condemned. . . . We have
> had much trouble here and are gradually overcoming it owing to the
> Union of all our Catholics in our Laymen's Association, but this matter
> I fear would do incalculable harm. (Keiley to Gibbons, Feb. 26, 1920,
> Savannah Diocesan Archives)

Bishop Keiley's reasoning manifests both his personal animosity toward
Lissner and the delicate balance of black and white and Protestant and
Catholic. Keiley had himself been the focus of anti-Catholic prejudice
when, despite his Confederate service, he had been boycotted as a
speaker at a United Daughters of the Confederacy rally. Nonetheless, he
had spoken out against lynching and racism, although he also critiqued
Roosevelt's invitation of Booker T. Washington to the White House
(C. Davis 1991, 197). Keiley adduced the threat of an African Cahenslyism
to Gibbons, which suggests his concerns over the unity of episcopal power.

In the meantime, Lissner consulted with the pope in Rome about
the situation of American blacks and shared his thoughts with Cardinal
Gibbons, who realized the seriousness of papal interest in "native clergy"
(Ochs 1990, 260). Local concern became more evident after another letter from the Vatican pursued the appointment of a vicar-general for
blacks as an auxiliary bishop (De Lai to Keiley, Nov. 8, 1920). Keiley
scrawled in Italian a six-page handwritten epistle to Rome and adamantly
sought to enlist other American prelates in his cause. In another letter to
Gibbons, he expanded his personal attacks on Lissner: "This man Lissner
is personally very distasteful and is disliked by every priest in my diocese. He is the grandson of a Jewish convert and has all the objection-
able traits of the race." Keiley appealed to marked categories outside
Catholicism to denigrate his opponent. He also threatened to resign if

Lissner "is forced on me" (Keiley to Gibbons, Dec. 7, 1920). In a letter to Archbishop Bonaventura Cerruti, Keiley augmented personal bigotry in his arguments with an explicit attack on separatism: "The racial question would be more involved. Why not a Syrian V.G. and a Polish one, since we have Syrians and Poles here? Besides, it would be a great evil to the negroes themselves. You know how easy it is to cause prejudice and how hard to still it" (Keiley to Cerruti, Dec. 7, 1920, Savannah Diocesan Archives).

Bishop Keiley also contacted Cardinal O'Connell of Boston while rallying his diocesan priests around him. Moreover, he contacted J. M. Chabert, superior of the SMAs to ask not only for Lissner's removal but also for the replacement of all Alsatian priests with Irish ones (Nov. 23, 1920). Chabert replied that this would wait until his pastoral visit to Georgia in 1921 (Dec. 11, 1920). In December, Gibbons wrote Rome to suggest that the Vatican did not understand American blacks and adduced problems with both black priests and their reception in black parishes (Ochs 1990, 266).

Lissner's actions during this time are harder to document. Presumably, he argued his case with his superior as he had presented it in Rome. By 1922, however, he was removed from Georgia, devoting the rest of his efforts to the Tenafly motherhouse, with its seminary, and expansion into new states. No bishop for blacks was appointed, and the Handmaids soon followed Lissner north as local problems with Savannah whites and blacks continued. Mother Mary Theodore of the Handmaids complained after Bishop Keyes intervened to prevent Father John from joining the mission church:

> whites had stopped her on the street to voice their displeasure over the prospect of Father John's assignment to the city. . . . Even some of the Franciscan sisters complained that it was enough to have black sisters in Savannah without bringing in a black priest. Mother Mary Theodore suggested, however, that whites were not the only angry people in Savannah; many black Catholics were furious with the bishop when they learned that he had rejected Father John. She worried that these people would leave the Catholic church as a result. "The Japanese, . . . Italians, . . . Chinese, . . . Africans . . . have priests," she plaintively wrote to Lissner. "Why can't the American Negroes?" (Ochs 1990, 274-75)

In historical retrospect, Lissner proposed a church that did not accommodate to southern cultural values so much as it imposed SMA missionary values of an autonomous native church, honed in Africa, on the tenuous racial and denominational balances of Savannah life. White bishops and priests, as custodians of a predominantly white church beset by bigotry, rejected this option at many levels. Local blacks were not only caught in between but seem to have been silenced by their leaders however much they cared for them. The result was a church fraught with the contradictions of southern and Catholic life, embodied in the constitution of a white priesthood and sisterhood in a black church. As Ochs has suggested, this experience was not unique to Savannah, but a fundamental contradiction in American Catholicism and American society.

The constitution of the priesthood as church doctrine and the redefinition of these roles of real political, economic, and spiritual power in practice by both priests and nuns intensify historical contradictions of race, culture, and gender. Whether in the formative period of the SMAs or in the liberalization since Vatican II, the meaning of priesthood in the black parishes has faced an unusual set of challenges that has been met by adaptations both personal and institutional, involving priests, congregation, and authorities. Through it all, ambiguity and pain emerge from both the ordained leader and the transgenerational community.

In order to follow a dialectic rhythm established in the earlier chapters, however, external and clerical authority, transformed by action, must be complemented by the active authority of parishioners as realized in formal and informal roles within the parish and school community. Leadership, tradition, gender, and race can then be viewed from a different perspective.

6. Laity, Continuity, and Empowerment

We've come this far by faith, Leaning on the Lord
Trusting in his holy word, He's never failed me yet.
O can't turn around, We've come this far by faith.

—Lead Me, Guide Me:
The African American Catholic Hymnal

Reflecting on her experience as well as her work in Savannah, Sister Julian Griffin highlighted the centrality of black women as community leaders in a 1983 article: "In the past, the black woman was a power behind the scenes, in the home, on the farm, in the working world. Today she is even taking her place in the ordained ministry in some Churches, influencing, challenging and inspiring congregations of men and women" (49). In 1989 the multiple roles Sister Julian cites reappeared in a more quotidian fashion in a dialogue between a priest and an older black woman at a daily mass:

W: Thank you, Father.
Pr: Why are you thanking me; it's your parish—you let me work here.
W: Yes, Father. But we like you.

Here, the priest joked about his transient role only to be upstaged by a deaconess who treated his joke literally and affirmed the authority of her family position and years of service.

The pervasive power of the Roman Catholic hierarchy, of appointed priests and religious, long has limited the leadership roles for the laity in the black and Catholic community. Yet, as in all Roman Catholic par-

222

ishes, black congregations establish permanent social ties, group identification, shared expectations, and recognized figures of authority. These transgenerational processes diverge from the power of external and temporary leaders, the priests. Some lay roles may be recognized officially and even recompensed; thus they are linked to formal clerical leadership. Others, especially charismatic social figures, remain more distanced from the priest and may come to constitute opposition to him. Some roles, paradoxically, appear invisible—one man in Saint Mary's said many a real leader is "not visible, but is the hero who will paint the church."

Lay leadership also challenges the divisions of gender, race, and class reified in sacramental ordination and the hegemonic construction of marked categories. Thus the power of black Catholic women as "deaconesses"—a term borrowed with irony from Protestants—must be understood within the double marking and subordination of social and cultural heritage.

The interaction of priest and laity further illustrates the contradiction and community intrinsic to the black and Catholic experience. Some separation of priest and people characterizes all Catholic parishes, yet color and culture intervene in a special way in black congregations. As noted in the last chapter, the priest in black Savannah parishes, white and usually foreign, represents an anomaly among dominant whites while generally being isolated from the day-to-day formation of African-American experience. Blacks, in turn, have formed expectations for interactions with whites that the priest must confront. At the same time, black Catholics retain awareness of the traditions of authority among black Protestants. Catholic matriarchs, however powerful, thus may criticize ambivalent women's roles among evangelicals—such as the preacher's wife—or the emotional displays that confirm spiritual power among Pentecostals, while they borrow fund-raising ideas or weave different structures of control.

Leadership roles must also be traced through a historical perspective, although this is often difficult because of the evanescent personal qualities that have constituted status and network in the past. Early Catholic missions throughout the South, whether black or white, relied by necessity on laity, male and female (McNally 1987). The reforms of Vatican II increased lay recognition in the church as a whole (Abbott 1966, "Dogmatic Constitution on the Church," 56-65, and "Decree on the Apostolate of the Laity," 489-522). These bishops offered new opportunities in education, liturgy, parish government, and outreach projects to the laity, who eagerly took them. Today, declining numbers in available clergy, as well as the increasing empowerment of blacks in political and economic life and in questions of conscience, social justice, and neighborhood activism, have shaped new leadership in the black parish.

This chapter begins with an overview of practices of lay leadership from the vantage of both laity and clergy. A historical examination of formal public roles follows, balanced by an analysis of informal roles in parish life. The chapter concludes with a discussion of food as a nexus of service and leadership, where the table of the community mirrors the table of the altar.

THE DIALECTIC OF LEADERSHIP ROLES IN THE PARISH

The weekly bulletin of Saint Benedict the Moor Church lists nineteen lay officers, including the parish council president, music directors, home mass coordinator, soup kitchen coordinator, educational and liturgical coordinators, organization leaders, and the parish historian. The parish council president and members of the council are elected by the parish as a whole on a regular rotation. Officers of the Holy Name Society, the newly formed Knights of Columbus, and the Catholic Women's Club are elected as well, although positions actually rotate among long-term members. Two members of the parochial Women's Club have also been elected to interparochial offices; these, too, appear in the bulletin.

Other leaders hold rather more stable positions derived from particular interests and talents. These include musicians and altar personnel who require special training. The parish employs a trained, salaried director of education, who has expanded the previously voluntary post. Outreach functions, such as soup kitchen teams and the home mass coordinator, represent long-term service commitments as well, although these continually incorporate new volunteers.

Informal networks with their own leaders also take their part in the parish. Small groups that formed for the diocesan renewal program in the 1980s found their own organizers and hosts. Leaders have emerged temporarily to prominence for historical commemorations, diocesan retreats, or NOBC delegations. Moreover, many parishioners participate in extraparochial schools and social clubs while maintaining ties of friendship and familylike bonding that structure parish life.

Official roles incorporate many traditional "informal" leaders in the parish, although the authority of such leaders tends to be recognized by their office rather than created by it. The personal authority, experience, reputation, and service are evident in the deference paid to elders of the parish by formal leaders and priests and in requests for advice or support—"No one can beg like you!" Public leadership thus emerges through a continual dialectic of influence and position.

The range of leadership in the black and Catholic parish, however, cannot be reduced to an opposition between charismatic authority in the laity and bureaucratic power vested in the priest. Parish councils and finance committees may veto priestly actions; parishes even may force the removal of an appointed priest. Successful priests, meanwhile, evoke their personal presence and understanding of parish social interactions as well as their institutional power in order to lead. Black Catholics evaluate both the priest as a valued director and the lay leader by their ability to convince, to persuade, and to organize rather than by the trappings of office: the good leader does not order so much as he or she builds consensus. Personal character, long and sincere commitment, family history, service, and reliability overshadow public traits that may be recognized in white churches, including social status, wealth, and public piety.

Black and Catholic parishioners talked frequently about the qualities of leadership that would ensure their continuity as communities. Gloria Daniels, for example, a member of one of the oldest active families in Saint Anthony's, summarized the actions and qualities of a leader: "You got to know what you're doing. You got to know to meet the public, how far to talk, and when to cool it. You must be open and not possessive. Don't be stuck up." Pie Chisholm, herself a leader in Saint Benedict's, stressed similar characteristics: "How you carry yourself religiously and how you meet the public. I don't care how much education you got, sometimes you just don't get along with people. People don't like you and won't listen to you. You have to win their confidence. Get 'em told. Let 'em know what you mean. . . ."

Memories of past leaders sustain these evaluations of personal qualities in the constitution of parish authority and continuity. Thus a modern active worker in Saint Anthony's recalled those who had shaped her in her youth: "Mr. John DeCoteau, . . . he was a worker, a worker for Saint Anthony's until he died. . . . Jesse Smith lived around here. You would always see him work, cleaning and cutting grass, putting on chicken dinners, anything the priests wanted done. . . . Claudia Bryant—truly a leader; she would get things done." These same characteristics can be used to draw distinctions among parishes and priests, as an older male in Saint Mary's observed: "Father Lissner gave a lot to Saint Benedict's, and Father Obrecht was more outgoing. Saint Benedict's still has better leadership—fighting for things, togetherness, more unified." Nurture, suasion, and reputation underpin even parochial tasks that congregants and priests must undertake.

Priests and nuns who shared their experience in the black parish echoed these values, emphasizing strength, confidence, and responsibility as traits that they and the parish encouraged, especially among youth. Those who had worked in Savannah prior to civil rights also added concern for the lack of opportunities blacks had faced in everyday life outside the church: "the whole context of that time was against any leadership principles." While such guidance in the past was often aimed unsuccessfully toward religious vocation, youth fellowships today promote more active participation in the liturgy, the parish council, and other organizations. Moreover, where it was once seen as a primary task of the priests and religious, such fosterage is now evidently a task of the laity as well.

The stress on reliable service and strength in contrast to status, wealth, or public piety underscores an important contrast between at least modern black and white parishes. Indeed, the black parish tends to invert the values of an (unmarked) white and public city, where wealth, length of family association, and status are recognized. A black "undervaluation" of wealth probably arises from the objective and symbolic limitations on black economic success and display in the past. Many parish families lived in poverty only a few generations ago. Even as the school and church became avenues to increased status, differences among families have emerged slowly in public. While distinctions are visible within and between parishes today, as discussed in chapter 4, older blacks frequently lament materialism and display. Furthermore, long-time members and converts criticize any attempt to substitute cash or prestige for time and work (although they also note, "Lots of people leave when it is time to pay; they think the church can get along without money, but it can't" Male, Saint Anthony's, born 1950s). Community traditions formed in times of necessity and family service also are valued over the actions of white Catholics who join black parishes as individuals.

The question of piety is more subtle but seems to spring from the same symbolic relations. In each parish some leaders attend daily mass or lead the rosary, but this is not a prerequisite for recognition. Working parents have had obligations that have precluded active devotions; more than one black Catholic recalled his or her parents' attending a 5 A.M.

mass in the cathedral so as to arrive at work on time. Even within the sacramental dimensions of parish life, the leader need not be the "purest." Serious failings, whether alcoholism, sexual scandals, or work problems, disturb other parishioners, but forgiveness also is extended after reform. As one priest observed, the leader must "be authentic": private values triumph over public appearances.

Cultural differences of leadership may be threatened by the integration of the schools and parishes in the eyes of older parishioners. Defending parochial segregation, for example, one catechist in his forties complained: "Blacks choose it to be like that. They resent it when white people attend—don't want white leadership. It's threatening to them. That's not their church but our church. . . . They don't want whites to take over in authority." His addendum clarified one significant exception, "The priest is all right. The priest can tell them a lot of things."

In addition to differing from much white Catholic practice in significant ways, status in black and Catholic churches also diverges from evaluations of emotional demonstrations in many Afro-Baptist and Holiness traditions (Baer 1984) as well as other distinctions of lineage and color. In a Catholic parish, she who sings the loudest, shouts, wails, or dances is as likely to be chastised as to be followed. While color is recognized as a potential division among individuals within the community, it does not correlate with leadership in any of the parishes I know.

Finally, cultural categorizations beyond the parish may divide leadership. This is exemplified in the parochial roles of mature black women. While Saint Mary's long has had an active group of older males who advise the priests, in every parish older matriarchs have been the leaders to whom I was directed for information and who reappear in all organizations and projects. Their authority embodies the idea of the leader as experienced nurturer and networker rather than an appointed commandant. Sister Julian Griffin, quoted earlier in this chapter, emphasized the importance of the black woman in the family and the church:

> The black woman has long been the backbone and glue that held
> church communities together. She sang in the choir, taught Sunday
> school, collected funds and cooked for parish gatherings; she also
> reached out to the wider parish community, visiting the sick and
> working with youth groups. Countless black women today carry on
> the tradition that is part of their history in this country. (1983, 47; see
> Billingsley 1968; Stack 1974; Giddings 1984 ; Howze et al. 1984, 13-14)[1]

Yet the role of the black woman also epitomizes a constellation of limitations on all blacks, including black males (Giddings 1984; Gresham and Wilkerson 1989, 116). A Saint Anthony's woman recognized this as she reflected on the impositions of time and power that have constrained males: "Black men work so hard and have so little time; women have to take a role and carry it. . . . At one time, men couldn't get anything except hard labor. What time is there left to do anything physical for the church?" The black bishops also have argued that black men and women have suffered special burdens:

> For many historical reasons, the Black man has been forced to bear the crushing blows of racial hate and economic repression. Too often barred from access to decent employment, too often stripped of his dignity and manhood, and too often forced into a stereotype, the Black male finds himself depreciated and relegated to the margins of family life and influence. Not the least of the evil fruits of racial segregation has been the artificially fashioned rivalry between Black women and men.
>
> It is important, we believe, to encourage a reevaluation of the fundamental vocation to fatherhood that Black men must have in the context of the Black family. (Howze et al. 1984, 12)

The bishops do not note, however, that black males are constrained (as are white laymen) by the presence of a male power figure at the altar: the priest. This conclusion was substantiated by the memories of a male in his sixties with whom in 1990 I discussed this chapter: "Ladies could do things men couldn't do—they were so busy trying to get young boys into the priesthood, the only thing a man could do is take up collection. No leadership or nothing." Here, since there are no prescribed roles for active females in the parish (nuns generally being associated with the schools) and women are adamantly denied access to the priesthood, their opportunities are open to creation. A male lay leader must relate to an established role and presence and thus create his power, to some extent, in opposition to that role. His situation inverts the question of the last chapter: "If he wants to lead, why isn't he a priest?"

Generations, age, and length of affiliation may also appear in categorizations of parish leadership, especially in the explanation of historical developments. Older Catholics may be seen as participants who "have more respect, not so easy to tear up; they speak their own mind and go through with it"—as an older cradle Catholic in Saint Benedict's put it in contrast to new converts. A member of Saint Mary's felt that converts lack "a deep sense of sacrifice." In fact, almost all activities seem to integrate old and new, with recognition for the age and experience that favor cradle Catholics. Interpretations may also reflect the historical chronology of the parishes, where the oldest parishioners and families still evoke a direct connection to the historic age of Lissner, Obrecht, and Beasley.

Parish functions in which I have participated sometimes suggest a three-generational model, with the senior Catholics recognized for knowledge and historical traditions as well as organizing networks and the younger Catholics undergoing intensive selection and training. In between are those who take on more demanding work roles in the parish and often in their community, without obviously challenging the status of the "deacons" and "deaconesses" they will someday replace even as they are ordered around.

Lay leadership opportunities and actions in the black parish, then, reflect the construction of power in southern society as well as the structures and values of white and black denominations. Within this setting, parish lay leadership is more flexible in personality and position than it might be in either a local white parish or a black Protestant church. Yet it is no less vital for the continuity and identity of the social group.

FORMAL LEADERSHIP ROLES

By *formal* leadership roles in the African-American parish, I refer to positions that entail selection by priest, committee, or congregation, or involve remuneration, as in education. These roles tend to demand specific skills, in opposition to the general authority of informal leaders. Records of education and church-sponsored organizations permit us to trace formal offices through history into the expanded contemporary roles for the laity, including the permanent lay diaconate and other changes fostered by Vatican II. Nonetheless, formal roles may be occupied by charismatic leaders who will extend their activities and their position: the heuristic distinction between formal and informal roles varies among individuals and contexts.

Although education has been discussed at length in earlier chapters, lay involvement represented another ambivalent facet of black and Catholic life in Savannah, as Matilda Beasley's career has illustrated.

While other nineteenth-century initiatives relied on white religious, the Africanist models of the SMAs incorporated nonordained (and even non-Catholic) community workers. Saint Mary's employed lay teachers until 1916 and Saint Anthony's until 1938. The 1916 farewell to lay teachers at Saint Mary's allows a glimpse of their meaning to the parish at that time:

> Miss Gertrude Davis is a graduate of St. Francis de Sales Institute,
> Rock Castle, Virginia, where she obtained the highest marks in exami-
> nations. She has taught for five years at St. Mary's in the highest
> grades with great ability and success. Miss Carrie Elliott has been
> teaching for nearly ten years in the kindergarten and was much loved
> by all her little pupils. Miss Frederica Campbell taught first at St. Au-
> gustine school near the water works from where she was transferred
> last year to St. Mary's and she was also much loved and appreciated
> by her pupils and had made friends by the scores on the west side.
> (*ST,* June 17,1916)

All these women subsequently played other active roles in their parishes. Ms. Davis entered the public school system, but remained a parish leader until her death in the 1960s. In Saint Mary's first decade, for example, she served as godparent to twelve of the thirty-six new members; Carrie Elliott sponsored three more. Ms. Campbell, from one of the oldest Catholic families in Saint Benedict's, which had produced the parish's first nun, joined Saint Mary's by marriage and became an active member there.

In Saint Anthony's as well, multiple responsibilities reinforced and familiarized the formal role of the teacher. Ms. Bonnie Remiggio, an early teacher, played the organ each Sunday; Mrs. Georgia Tanxley Lucas has worked actively in neighborhood concerns and with foster children as well as contributing to parish fund-raising events. Eugenia Haig Daniels, who taught from 1933 to 1938, belonged to a family that has provided altar servers, home visitors, and many other day-to-day needs for the parish.

With one exception, all these teachers were women. This may reflect the higher access of black women to secondary education in the past century (Giddings 1984), although some of the women had little training outside their own family. It appears more likely that it springs from other, if inconsistent, demands for labor that took black men away from such commitments (Harris 1982). The dominant presence of women, however, reinforced the link of lay leadership and nurturing.

After nuns took over elementary education, lay involvement became parental support. Women participated in nursery and child care projects. Males and females volunteered as coaches and youth leaders. Black female lay teachers reappeared in parish schools in the 1950s; most teachers in the inner-city Catholic schools are laypeople, including non-Catholics. Saint Pius epitomized total community support among the parishes, not only for those who had children or siblings attending as students.

The closure of parish schools returned responsibility for religious education to the parish laity. Volunteer catechists, both male and female, have undertaken the formation of Christian and parochial identity. Parishes have raised money for facilities like Saint Benedict's new education complex, inaugurated in 1989. Here again, direction tends to be vested in women, including the nuns who guide educational programs for the diocese. Males support sports and youth groups in all parishes, however, and have worked with special neighborhood programs as well as national Catholic conventions. In all, these programs link parish, history, and leadership, as a teacher explained to me:

> Our aim is personal development and relating religion to it. We pull this out into black history in February. We have used themes for certain programs—celebrities, black Catholic saints—or let the children write their own play, mostly centered around Martin Luther King, Jr. One celebration focused on our own church community, interviewing role models.

This statement about Saint Benedict's could also apply to programs that I observed in other parishes.

These parish programs bring education full circle. Where once religious formation was the primary mission of an external church amidst a black Protestant population, it is now the task of the parish itself as a self-sustaining community. Teaching is a highly visible public role in each parish, although its specialized authority does not necessarily generalize to other realms. Yet volunteer teachers often have made their commitment one of many, thus affirming their leadership by their own personal dedication.

Voluntary associations to promote faith and to assemble resources for the parish also emerged soon after the first missionary interventions in black Savannah. In some ways, they provided an adult counterpart to educational services and constitutions of community among children. In general, these followed national organizations or models; most organizations thus have reflected the divisions of gender and race within the church as a whole. Even since the Second Vatican Council, for example, Savannah Holy Name societies were found only among the men of local black parishes, although this is not the case nationwide. The Teresians (named for Saint Teresa)—a woman's society that encourages vocations—meets jointly for all three black parishes without connections to similar local or national assemblies.

One of the earliest recorded black associations highlights the contradictory history of black and Catholic organizations. News reports from 1880s visits to Skidaway mention the presence of an honor guard composed of members of the Catholic Knights of America (*SMN* July 21, 1884). Another report elaborates that a "branch of the Catholic Knights of America, to be composed exclusively of colored men, has been very successfully established in the Cathedral and the sodalities for the women are truly a great edification for all" (*SMN* June 2, 1884). The Catholic Knights of America had been founded by Irish-Americans in Nashville in 1877 as a lodge and fraternal insurance society (Kauffman 1982, 7). Other organizations, including the Ancient Order of Hibernians and Georgia militias, organized Irish Catholic males in Savannah; it is striking that any such national association would be composed of blacks alone there. No reports appear on this group thereafter, however, which may mean it failed because of racism or declining missions.

Later Catholic military-fraternal organizations such as the Knights of Columbus, founded by Irish-Americans in New Haven in 1881 and introduced in Savannah in 1902, remained strictly white for decades. Although the Knights of Columbus encouraged national campaigns against racism, on the local level, their color bar was not broken until the bishop and priests actively intervened in the civil rights era (see Kauffman 1982, 269-73). Even so, a young black who joined the suburban branch recalled being asked if he were the janitor when he visited the downtown council. Attempts to strengthen black interests continue; an integrated council began in Saint Benedict's in 1990.

Among black national alternatives to the Knights of Columbus was the Knights of Saint Peter Claver, founded under the aegis of the Josephite Fathers along the Gulf Coast. Competition among missionary orders probably precluded its introduction into SMA-dominated Georgia. Efforts were made to organize a branch in Savannah parishes in the 1980s, with seemingly little impact.

Male and female mutual aid societies, perhaps heirs to the 1880 sodalities, participated in Saint Benedict's even before SMA arrival. The male Catholic Mutual Aid Society, founded in 1901, served in the funeral of Mother Beasley in 1903 (*SMN* Dec. 22, 1903). A later report notes that

> the object of this Society is the relief of its members in sickness and death; and the development in all that pertains to the best in morals, social and literary acquirements. . . . Besides the ordinary officers, the society has a sick committee of three members whose duty it is to visit the sick members and to render them whatever aid the society allows, to watch near their bed of suffering during the night and to give them consolation and comfort. (*ST* Jan. 30, 1909)

Burial and hardship societies of this type were common self-help efforts among all black denominations, the origin of some later black public insurance corporations.

Here, this hardship element was linked to pastoral duties, such as visiting the sick. It received public ecclesiastical approbation in the appointment of leaders (a tradition revived in modern black parishes):

> The newly elected officers are President, John Scurdy; Vice-President, James Dowse; Secretary and Treasurer, Joseph King; Sergeant at Arms, John Simmons; Chairman of the Sick Committee, John Boifeuillet. On Monday evening these officers were installed into office by their pastor, who in a few delicate words reminded each of them of their respective duties and responsibilities After the installation a delightful party took place, during which serious conversation was mingled with wit and humor. (*ST* Mar. 9, 1907)

These leaders include most of the well-known families of the parish at that time, some of whose descendants remain active. As evident in their installation, ecclesiastical and social functions were combined, resembling secular social clubs. This group supported money-making and social activities for the parish. Reports continue on its activities until the 1930s (*ST* Jan. 12, 1912; *État* 1935-36) when it seemed to give way to interparochial groups such as the Catholic Laymen's League.

In Saint Benedict's, the woman's equivalent to the Catholic Mutual Aid society was a service guild, the Saint Mary's Aid society, organized in 1908: "The aim of this society is above all to unite its members by the sweet bans of Christian charity and to help each other in times of sickness and of death. What we want in the lonesome days of suffering and sickness, is not only the financial help but also the consoling visit of good friends; we want a cheerful word even more than a dollar" (*ST* Jan. 23, 1909).

Nonetheless, this society did not strictly parallel the male guild. The news report stresses visiting over financial aid, which the men's group fostered. Saint Mary's also employed a male officer, J. M. Dowse, "by a special privilege, . . . certainly a great compliment to Mr. Dowse, who is the devoted and talented secretary of some other societies attached to St. Benedict's" (*ST* Jan. 23, 1909). By 1912 membership reached fifty-four, including nineteen new members (*ST* Jan. 22, 1912). At this point, with a congregation of less than five hundred, this society probably played an important role in bringing together all women leaders of the parish.

The gender-defined tasks of this society were recalled by members active in the 1930s and 1940s:

> They picked up slack. . . . They paid for the cleaning of the church.
> They would give a shower every year for Father's house. Thanksgiving
> shower. If you were sick, out, they would give you $2.50. They went
> to communion the first Sunday of every month in a body. Put on ben-
> efits to raise money and help and support the church and school.
> Anything that was needed. . . .

Male and female societies also organized social life outside the parish. At a 1910 trip to Charleston organized by the Mutual Aid Society, "they were most cordially received by the Catholic men of St. Peter's Parish [a black Charleston parish]" (*ST* Aug. 26, 1910). Meanwhile, picnics at Saint Anthony's reaffirmed values of family, while proselytizing schoolchildren: "Over 300 children and grown up people visited the beautiful grounds of the mission in the afternoon and evening. So pleasant was the outing that a request was made to have another picnic before the closing of the season" (*ST* Aug. 26, 1910).

By the 1930s, a Catholic Women's Club similar to that of white parishes appeared in Saint Benedict's, where it became the forerunner of the primary contemporary women's organization. Saint Mary's Aid was closed acrimoniously in Saint Benedict's in the 1960s by a priest who felt it was "a coterie of old ladies." The Catholic Women's Club remained separate from the all-white diocesan organization until such segregated societies were replaced in the civil rights era by the Council of Catholic Women, in which Saint Benedict's women have held local and diocesan offices.

Other parishes have formed similar organizations since the 1920s. SMA reports for the 1930s mentioned Confreries for the Propagation of the Faith, Saint Anthony's Mutual Aid, and the Apostleship of Prayer for

Saint Anthony's (*État* 1935-36, 103-4). An Altar Society prepared flowers and altar cloths while the Legion of Mary, an international organization founded in the 1960s, later took on home visitation. Reports from the 1930s show that Saint Benedict's sponsored a Converts Club and the Children of Mary, whereas Most Pure Heart of Mary had both a Mutual Aid Society and a Ladies Club (*État* 1935-36, 103-4). While there is little specific information on groups that have not survived, their focus seems clearly to have been mutual aid, prayer, care, and domestic tasks, with women's groups predominating but perhaps less powerful.

Men's clubs were organized and augmented in the 1930s by the Catholic Laymen's League. This diocesan association paralleled the white Catholic Laymen's Association of Georgia, a lobbying group that had been founded to combat anti-Catholicism in the state a decade before (Cashin 1962). The Laymen's League lacked this focus, since virulent anti-Catholicism had died down and blacks felt that the Klan did not distinguish religions within its racism. League membership became synonymous with parish membership: "You became a member of the church and joined the Laymen." The association, which had ten to fifteen active members per parish, "gave entertainments, handled pallbearers, ushered" and met yearly in diocesan conventions. It was converted in the 1960s into the Holy Name Society, which still acts as the major men's organization in each parish. One Layman's League member reminisced, "they changed the name because they didn't want to integrate. But that was all right with blacks." One informant recalled a Council of Catholic Men that may have been a short-lived 1960s organization among all parishes. According to him, this organization collapsed when whites refused to deal with racism and volatile issues: "they just decided not to meet again; that's the way whites will do if they don't want to deal with something."

Other social clubs for men were never formalized in the church, although they included many congregants. A 1933 yearbook for the city, in fact, complained of the influence of all such clubs on urban stratification:

> As time passed, these groups became clannish and separated themselves entirely from the masses. This separation became marked and gave rise to an aristocracy that exercised *almost* as much caste as the people of India. For years, these small groups functioned exclusively but with the spread of education and the influx of a different type of people, there is to be found only a semblance of the old caste. (Smalls 1933-34, 53)

Especially prominent in this regard throughout black Savannah are the Masons. The presence of Masons in black and Catholic parishes (even without formal ceremony) is striking given the violent rejection of this group by the white Catholic hierarchy. Yet the historian Cyprian Davis has noted that compromises were discussed for black Catholics as early as the turn of the century. In 1913 a report from John Burke of the Catholic Board of Negro Missions suggested that "the ban regarding membership be retained for black Catholics, but permission should be obtained from the Holy See allowing prospective converts to retain their membership in such societies for the sake of their financial benefits. Burke noted that black secret societies did not present the same threat to Catholicism that the white societies did. He also urged that the church should create societies with similar financial benefits for black Catholics" (1991, 201).

Members today remain proud of their association, and have explained it as a bridge to interracial unity that does not conflict with their religion. One remarked that he saw problems dividing older white Masons, but that they did not separate authentic black Prince Hall Masons from reconciliation (Cass 1957). Nonetheless, some other Masons suggested that the order taught them "things they did not know about Christianity."

The organizational structure of the Catholic church in the pre-Conciliar period embodied the primary contradictions already outlined as well as their solutions within parish groups. Associations mirrored both white Catholic and black Protestant practice although, with the exception of the Masons, they were adamantly separate from both. Self-help clubs synthesized black tradition and missionary emphasis, while social and religious functions became more prominent with the stabilization of parish communities. Since the 1960s, many of these organizations have merged into integrated diocesan organizations while still retaining their parish base. Other national groups have encouraged a new racial awareness. Although there has been no permanent National Office of Black Catholics affiliate in any Savannah parish, their conventions and literature have stimulated discussions. NOBC interests can be socially identified in part as a political stance—those who are "Black Catholics," referring to racial activists, in contrast to black *and* Catholic.

These organizations also tend to divide functions on the basis of age as well as gender. All are adult and are often dominated by the oldest members. Youth groups and programs exist in each parish, but they tend to be organized by older leaders *for* youth and are generally more short-lived. Men's clubs tend to hold more prestigious and public roles while women are confined to prayer and service, which may represent the imposition of missionary and diocesan models on the black community. Above all, no such organization could challenge clerical policies. Instead, they became service and social extensions of the priest and church in the city and organizers for parish life.

AFTER VATICAN II: SHARED LEADERSHIP AND SHARED LITURGY

Since the 1960s, Catholic reforms have created new positions for the laity in governance and service as well as liturgy. Yet calls for increased grass-roots involvement, as in the case of integration, have filtered through the episcopacy and priesthood. Hence, while leadership in these new roles has changed the visage of the black parishes, it retains an ambiguous quality. That is, lay parishioners may create strong and vocal offices, but their roles exist nonetheless within the constraints of priestly control.

Parish councils were put in place in the late 1960s as a reform of priestly governance. In general, parish councils are responsible for planning, financial affairs, and some internal questions of the parish. Special review boards may be set up to deal with personal dilemmas, such as the validity of marriage, although councils do not generally assume spiritual leadership. The council may also act as a coordinator for organizations and social events. Generally it coexists with an independent finance committee, mandated by the diocese, which oversees long-range planning. Council elections are parishwide, although the priest often maintains some appointive leeway, either vetoing nominees or adding board members "who should be recognized." In general, elected members are already recognized figures; no one gains power through his or her position on the council.

As a formal leadership body, the parish council functions within limits set by the individual priest of the parish, who also has direct access to the bishop as a final arbiter. An extended interview with a leading woman in her sixties who has served in her parish council teased out problems she had seen. On the relationship of priest and council, she complained: "I think the priests ought to give them more authority in terms of doing and being a part of the parish. I don't think that he should be the director and . . . I mean the sole dictator. He ought to give them more responsibility and more authority." The question was immediately framed in terms of power held by the priest, doled out to the parish. She elaborated this by specific references:

McD.: Well, do you think priests have been sort of sole dictators?
A: Yes. They don't, I mean I can distinctly remember some issues that
we have been called to vote on and the decision has already been
made and all we had to do was sanction the decision, you know.
"And of course I'm gonna do so and so and so but now I want to hear
how you feel about it or what you have to say." You are saying "Go
along with me." It's sort of like praying and saying "O Lord let your
will be done but let your will be my will."

Here, the woman depicts the actions of the priest and parish council
as a charade of consultation. The priest, she recognizes, must act, yet to
her it appears that his actions can be oblivious to the values and will of
the parish as an enduring community. When asked if this had changed,
she became even more specific:

No, not too much. We still don't have a voice in a lot of things and
policies. For example, I know that there are some things that are contrary to the law of the church and I'm not saying that we have a right
to change them, but it seems to me that if it's a law that can have an
exception or ruling, then it ought to have a discussion or something.

This woman faces a dilemma arising from her knowledge and experience as an educated, middle-class, lifelong Catholic. The laity accepts
priests and hierarchy as experts, whose rules cannot be changed. Yet
this clergy generally has offered little recognition of the knowledge that
lay members have gained, much less allowing them to oppose priestly
practice that the congregants feel to be wrong.

Nor are appointed leaders necessarily sensitized to implications of
their actions as expert leaders. A priest, for example, reading this manuscript, labeled this passage tragic but wondered if he did not in fact rep-
licate the same patterns of control, of doing what was best "for them."
Indeed, this pattern of thinking recurred unconsciously in some priestly
discussions on planning or liturgy. While many priests see guidance as
their major vocational responsibility, rarely are they trained to share it.
The conflict of roles, as much as a gap of sensitivity, exacerbates the
ambiguities of power. And race, in turn, shades any conflict.

Given the councils' foundations, it is understandable that priest and
council rarely oppose each other publicly. Nevertheless, each black parish
has witnessed major confrontations since Vatican II. Usually, these spring
from a new priest's attempt to change customs that preceded his appoint-

ment or his misinterpretation of public will, as well as the patterns of inter-change that follow. Diocesan policy has also been a touchstone for re-sponse, as we have seen in the debates over integration. Some of these confrontations continue to smolder personally and professionally; hence, I have chosen to focus on a simple confrontation between Father Liam Collins and the Saint Mary's parish council, over their MaryHeart property.[2]

Saint Mary's acquired the suburban MaryHeart property originally for a new parish, which Bishop Frey overruled with a "general rule" against new buildings that was later controverted for white parishes. Hence, disposition of the property represents a mythically sensitive area of concern for parish elders. Father Collins, in a decade at Saint Mary's, had devoted himself to programs for his depressed neighborhood, including Habitat for Humanity and the Cuyler Community Program, in which his middle-class suburban parishioners supported him. In the late 1980s, Father Collins, along with a resident lay brother, became involved in the foundation of a local Catholic Worker house to shelter those in need within a Christian community. In-spired by this, he sought to turn the MaryHeart into a Catholic Worker farm. Despite his enthusiasm, the parish council rejected the plan.

Here, the parish council did not see Saint Mary's concern for the neighborhood as committing all parishioners to the same concern for the urban poor to the exclusion of other problems. MaryHeart also en-capsulated both past disappointments and future hopes. Some members still held to the hopes of creating a new, exemplary, suburban black and Catholic shrine. Giving it away, to those outside the parish, abrogated that dream. Since Father Collins had already gained wide acceptance in the parish and was known to be a listener rather than a racist, the situa-tion did not escalate. Nor did Father Collins press when the proposal was turned down. Members of other black parishes were nevertheless shocked by this interruption of the smooth relations of an established priest. Yet when the priest is new, or when issues escalate, conflagra-tions have erupted where power is debated through the idiom of race, class, and discrimination.

The parish council, therefore, has held a potential authority that re-mains ambiguous. While formally a governing body, it is chartered from above and limited by the sensitivity of the priest. As a ratification of the character of its members, a council may oppose the priest, but this be-comes agonizing for all involved. Nonetheless, this seems a path through which the parish members may change leadership as they face short-ages of priests.

Not unlike governance, the active roles of laity in worship prior to Vatican II, apart from music, were designated as stages in preparation for the priesthood. Thus, only males could serve as acolytes (altar boys), since only males could be ordained, even if girls served in scarce times in outlying missions. The reforms of the 1960s brought laity into the sanctuary, expressing a collective conception of the church as a body rather than deriving lay activities from those of the priest. New positions include the lector, who reads the non-Gospel readings and may also act as a master or mistress of ceremonies for the mass, and the minister of communion, who distributes communion during the mass and assists in visiting the sick (Wallace 1981). Liturgy committees have also been established to discuss worship. Like the parish council, these are highly public roles that generally have ambivalent expectations. Perhaps the most challenging innovation is the lay deacon, an ordained liturgical and social specialist, whose position has notably increased a black presence behind the altar.

The liturgy committee, which may be constituted around elections, appointments, or interest, is generally the most independent voice in terms of parish worship. Several priests and parish participants mentioned active committees that planned songs, identified themes for preaching, and discussed issues, although this seems to vary according to clerical disposition and possibly education of participants. The committee has the power it is given, but may develop over time, with knowledge, especially as representatives of community continuity (Baker and Ferrone 1987).

Lectors are appointed by the priest or the liturgy committee and are trained in reading and scripture. Over my years of observation, most lectors have been women, as in many predominantly white parishes. While priests do not see this as a conscious pattern, they associate it, on questioning, with a desire for a more egalitarian female presence in the sanctuary, in contrast to conservative clergymen who dismiss any female presence. The choice of lectors also recognizes special groups like youth who, while not leading, are cultivated for future participation. These choices emphasize the lector's symbolic presence rather than extraliturgical authority: the role can become a stage rather than a platform.

Communion ministers also represent a controlled position within the church, since they must be approved by the diocesan chancery. The priest chooses candidates on the basis of previous service or recognition, thus usually promoting older men and women already recognized as leaders. They are expected to maintain respectability—marital or conduct problems may result in their removal—but their authority is limited to functions of the Mass. In fact, they may add prestige to their position rather than gaining anything more than a title from it.

Within this list of officers, ushers play a minor but intriguing role. Ushers greet entering parishioners, control movements at collection and reception of Eucharist, and distribute bulletins at the end of mass. Before Vatican II, they often were strong male leaders in white Catholic churches. Black Catholics also draw on the model of Protestant churches in which usher boards constitute formal and uniformed social groups. No black and Catholic parish asserts this level of formality, although semi-uniforms (dark slacks or skirts and white shirt) have been adopted at Saint Benedict's and Saint Anthony's. Saint Mary's uses only males, generally senior, who wear a special insignia; men and women serve in other parishes. Again, these tend to be positions of recognition, not leadership, differentiating black Catholics from both white Catholics and black Protestants (G. Smith 1980).

The most ambiguous of the lay roles revitalized after Vatican II is that of permanent lay deacon. Theologically and historically, deacons represent "to the Church its calling as servant in the world. By struggling in Christ's name with the myriad needs of societies and persons, deacons exemplify the interdependence of worship and service in the Church's life." (World Council of Churches *Baptism, Eucharist and Ministry*, cited in Kwatera 1985, 13). The black permanent diaconate had been discussed at the turn of the century as a way of providing black clerical missionaries while maintaining a segregated white clergy (Ochs 1990, 152, 178; C. Davis 1991, 204). The 1984 black bishops' pastoral also devoted attention to this new status:

> The permanent diaconate provides an opportunity to utilize those
> men who are natural leaders. Furthermore, it makes use of an institu-
> tion that is familiar to most Blacks, since deacons are part of the con-
> gregation in many Black Christian communities.
>
> The permanent diaconate sacramentalizes this reality which is
> already present and gives it a prestige which cannot but be realized to
> the advantage of the Church in proclaiming the Good News to the
> whole community. Incorporated into the hierarchy through the sacra-
> ment of order and yet part of the community in whose life he shares,
> the black deacon has a role of mediator which is truly unique.
> (Howze et al. 1984, 24-25)

241

Several points in this programmatic passage capture attention. First is the contrast between the burdened black male of the bishops' earlier description and the natural male leaders to be recognized sacramentally. Furthermore, incorporation through ordination of the diaconate "sacramentalizes this reality which is already present." Here, a formal office is conceived in bureaucratic terms to rest on communal recognition and personal charisma.

Like religious life for sisters, the diaconate is marked in contrast to the priest and to other laymen. The deacon must be a layman, a member of the parish, who occupies a normal job and may be married with a family. He is a parish employee, receiving a stipend for expenses, but he may move depending upon a job or circumstances. His training and ordination resemble that of the priest—who must first be ordained as a deacon in the process of becoming a priest—but classes are generally more abbreviated and sacramental roles are limited. A deacon may preach, conduct baptisms, marriages, and funerals, but he may not consecrate the Eucharist.

While the subsequent effort to recruit black priests has been arduous and contradictory, Savannah black laymen joined the diaconate as soon as it was reestablished and have changed the racial configuration of the altar in all three Savannah parishes. Deacons are sponsored in their candidacy by priests who recognize them as leaders in their community. Prince Jackson at Saint Benedict's, for example, was a senior parishioner and past president of Savannah State before he began his training. Frank Mathis at Saint Mary's was a civic and school leader. Once ordained, the roles of the deacon in the parish vary according to community needs, individual personality, and the expectations of the priest. In Saint Anthony's, deacon George White assists at the Mass but does not preach. In Saint Mary's and Saint Benedict's, deacons have taken on both pastoral and liturgical roles. While these deacons' concerns in preaching have tended to coincide with those of the pastor, their cultural heritage as blacks and members of the parish can also differentiate their style and approach in the sanctuary and the parish. On the whole, deacons outside of Mass tend to be more informal than the priest, reflecting their local origins. Since 1990 Saint Benedict's has had a white deacon, an intriguing extrapolation of race and lay roles.

It remains impossible to generalize about the development of the diaconate, given the recency of its revival and the few who have begun to give meaning to the role. A role conceived for lay participation nevertheless increasingly appears to be an extension of priestly ministry. Yet deacons, despite their training, ordination, and permanence, lack the autonomy of priests and may be marginalized by hierarchical power within the parish, especially in transitions from priest to priest. Hence, their position distills all the ambiguities of formal lay leadership.

In sum, public lay offices in the parish, both prior to the Second Vatican Council and in the period of democratization that has followed, have been constrained by the formal and hierarchical structures of the Roman Catholic church. Even when planned as democratizing divisions of priestly power, lay leadership roles are still generally perceived and enacted as concessions rather than positions that arise from the parish. The priest, rather than the congregation, controls them, although he *may* listen to parishioners' ideas. Yet other crucial aspects of leadership and structure remain vested in the actions and will of the parish community in contrast to and even in opposition to the transient priest and external authority.

INFORMAL LEADERSHIP ROLES

I characterize as *informal leadership* the actions of those whose authority rests on personal influence and community support. The contrast in criteria from role to person is critical: informal leadership is both more personal and more pervasive than formal office, being tied to actions, attitude, and record instead of a single job. This does not imply that such people eschew formal offices, which they may even enhance through their charisma. Nor does it imply that informal leaders are less able to execute their decisions. Instead, informal leadership subsumes those aspects of decision making that spring from the history and traditions of the parish, from long-term habitus. As such, these figures represent a more decisive contrast with priestly rule than those who hold delegated positions.

Unfortunately, such personal charisma is often even more difficult to trace historically than organizational roles. People in Saint Anthony's, for example, remember "Papa" Dan Washington, who guided many into the church, or Mrs. Claudia Bryant, who founded parish societies in the 1960s, yet it is difficult to construct biographies that manifest the personal force of earlier leaders. Still, a sense of early personal style penetrates Father Dennis Begley's report of the conversation with a parish

243

matriarch at Saint Anthony's, Mrs. Bell Pringle. When the pastor scolded her for attending non-Catholic services,

> "Miss Bell" shook her head and mused that there must be something amiss. Then she drew herself up in a pose of dignified defense. She pursed her lips, and with dramatic tilt of grey head, in mock serious tones of one more sinned against than sinning, she blurted out: "Ah, sure, Father, I get lonesome for the singing' and the clappin' and that movement of the spirit all over.—So, I go along for the fun of it". With an all-embracing gesture of comely old hands, as if she held "the whole world, the whole world in her hands," she declaimed: "What's the difference, Father?" "They only give you a bit of bread and warming mouthful o' wine. That's no harm, is it?" She finished with a pious joining of the palms, and such a disarming twinkle of eye—as close to "blarney" as Father himself could get. (Begley 1965, 20)

After editing the "Celtic lilt" from black voice in this telling, Mrs. Pringle evinces a notable if indirect resistance in her response, more reminiscent of contemporary deaconesses than of the parish council or similar formal positions. As in the conversation that introduced this chapter, humor comes at the expense of the priest, who becomes reproved instead of reprover, the transient missioner to be taught the knowledge and ways of the community.

Informal leadership took shape amidst the poverty of early missions and their constituents, in a pattern analogous to many white parishes in the early Southeast (McNally 1987). Parishes unable to pay for repairs or expansions or to raise money for them from wealthy members called upon volunteer labor, whether for mowing lots, paving a parking lot, cooking for a fund-raiser, or cleaning the church. In each case, certain parishioners and families were identified as responsible servers, from which their voice in the community took shape. Leadership by service thus became the basis of alternative authority which in white parishes would be more quickly challenged by wealth or political power. Such structures of power in the black and Catholic world can be defined, to judge from examples who were pointed out to me and with whom I interacted, by three primary characteristics: presence, network and organizational skills, and knowledge.

Presence includes participation and visibility at the center of parish activities. In all three parishes, at least one major focus of such power resides with the rectory's closest neighbors or most frequent visitors, who can take messages or control activities in the church for the priest in his absence. Some families chose to settle near churches; others were neighbors converted to Catholicism. This role overlapped with that of the housekeeper as a more formal role. Traditionally, the SMA fathers hired black women of their parish for cooking and cleaning. This contrasted with white parishes of the city, who might employ whites (or blacks) but did not have the same parish association. Although salaried, these women had roles and reputations that eclipsed their jobs. Since the black parishes lacked secretaries, the housekeeper's role extended to scheduling and errands in which she, too, became an extension of rectorial authority. This was particularly evident in transitions from priest to priest, where the housekeeper often proved one of the most vociferous defenders of parish and rectory traditions. Today no black parish employs a housekeeper (in contrast to white parishes who generally have varied and larger staffs), although invitations and gifts of meals to the priest remain common.

Yet physical immediacy expands in a true leader through voluntary service in multiple arenas: as Sister Julian noted at the beginning of the chapter, a leader is one who sings *and* cooks *and* cares for the parish, etc. Even housekeepers are remembered for the extension of the rectory in other ways. At Saint Anthony's, for example, the housekeeper distributed special treats; reminiscing about the 1930s, Gloria Daniels recalled that "On the first Friday when all the Catholic children received Holy Communion, making the nine Fridays, Mrs. Jennie Bell Brown, who was the housekeeper, would make flapjacks." Other leaders establish their centrality by repeated volunteering, promoting availability and reliability as the basis of recognition.

Network and organization constitute a leader on the basis of those whom he or she can rally to any activity. Again, this gives priority to established families with extended household support on whom to draw, including matriarchal extended families within each parish. Such leaders act as coordinators, maintaining reciprocity with other families who can be counted upon in times of crisis. When formal groups raise money, they turn to network leaders for sales or distribution instead of seeking individual buyers. This provides the coordinator with leverage over future arrangements.

Knowledge—both historical background and day-to-day gossip—is a third primary source of power for informal parish leaders. A leader should be able to talk about the development of the parish; here, he or she can defend the social and cultural traditions established over generations in contrast to the priest or religious. Such a sage may identify people who claim connections with the parish in funerals for northern emigrants or clarify the contributions of past priests and nuns who return for visits. Yet a leader must also be in touch with the concerns of many parishioners in order to identify and act upon problems as they arise. As such, this informal power is recognized by priests who may consult the elders of the parish for advice without going through the established channels of formal parochial authority.

These qualities of informal leadership can be held by males or females, yet private and domestic arrangements of reciprocity and information tend to favor the latter. Women live longer and are more actively involved in family socialization and social networks, despite active work lives. Males may also be channeled into formal roles as well as limited by the eminent male role of the priest. Both men and women in their thirties and forties are often suggested as "upcoming leaders," especially if they have family support. Whites who belong to black parishes are unlikely to command transgenerational ties, although they may occupy formal positions.

Formal positions, by their very structure, tend to be conciliatory. Informal authority, by contrast, whether or not associated with formal status, becomes apparent in periods of conflict, in which networks oppose each other. Leaders contest general recognition, ecclesiastical approbation, and reputation—in which case opponents may even be described as propagators of lies, deceptions, or misconduct. Such conflicts are not present in everyday parish life, but they are galvanized by external stimuli, especially associated with the uncertainties of transitions between priests (or traumatic events such as the school closings). When enmities come to the surface, they may result in deep-seated chains of conflict, or, in serious cases, in departures from the congregation. On the whole, though, such crises are minimized by decades of coexistence and the intervention of other neutral leaders.

This suggests some of the limitations of informal leadership as well. While able to respond to crises such as the closing of the schools discussed in chapter 3, no continuity of institutions or policies seemed to grow out of these mass meetings. The same people would be leaders in the future, but they did not create enduring formal institutions so much as they continued to influence those around them, speaking out in times of stress through personal authority coupled with knowledge of the past.

FOOD, FAMILY, AND LEADERSHIP

Given the limitations of resources for the reconstruction of lay leadership as process, the meaning of informal organization can be depicted more fully through the analysis of an everyday modern domain in which it is exercised, such as food. The table has been central to the black family as a living symbol of unity, as a place of welcome, and as a center for discussion, prayer, and teaching. In commenting upon the black bishops' pastoral at the 1985 NOBC meetings, for example, Greer Gordon addressed changing food ways as a representation of both social and religious meaning in flux: "If the table at home is not a source of fellowship how can the altar be a symbol of fellowship?" (July 24, 1985). In my years in Pie Chisholm's house, the table has been the heart of family and community, as it was in oral histories that I gathered. At the same time, the table epitomized urban divisions to many blacks: segregation of food was a bitter indignity.

The week at Pie's begins on Sunday morning with a breakfast for any in the parish who want to come over after nine o'clock mass. Pie started these breakfasts in the early 1970s, when her aunt was homebound, in order to provide company and conversation. They began as communion breakfasts, when all would receive the Eucharist and then join for breakfast. Later, more stopped by to inquire after her aunt's health and stayed to eat. In practice during my fieldwork, these breakfasts have assembled a group of twenty to thirty regulars who share a meal of grits, biscuits, and meat—smothered pork chops, sausage, corned beef hash, liver, or some special treat like crab. Some are family or godchildren; others have become like family. Priests and deacons visit between masses, and new visitors, including my friends and family, have been welcomed. Pie purchases and prepares food each week, although people also come by with contributions, and Jimmie Reynolds, who lives in the house with her now, handles much of the cooking. Women help in serving and cleaning up, and men may do various household tasks while visiting. The group that emerged also recognizes Pie's work in other ways—in food or staggered visits during the week or with a new railing on the front steps as a Christmas present.

The staple of Sunday morning, though, is the conversation that continues for hours around the table which Pie presides over in the breakfast room, surrounded by plants, religious hangings, and calendars and memorabilia from friends. Topics range from discussion of sermons to current events. Marriages, deaths, and illnesses are pieced together in terms of family connections or past experience with the individuals involved. Laughter often erupts through the house from verbal duels or running jokes.

Breakfasts also become a crucible for parish operations. Here, plans and reputations are discussed, volunteers are at hand, and tradeoffs are arranged. Pie acts as both provider and coordinator, a role that she extends through the frequent visits of the week. My role as an anthropologist was also legitimated through these meetings, with inquiries ranging from "How long are you going to be with us this time?" to "When is that book of yours going to be done?" By one o'clock, Sunday dinner is ready—another heavy meal where other friends may drop by. During the afternoon, people not in the breakfast crowd may come by and be offered food—or some of her godchildren who live in the neighborhood may stop by to eat.

Throughout the week, food is a token by which fellowship is expressed. Friends drop by for coffee, grits, and conversation in the morning. During the day people come by with shrimp, fish, pecans from their trees, or home-baked treats and stay to sample whatever may be in the oven. Pie's aunt or neighbors may call to have me pick up a dish, or I might deliver something to their house. For all the cooking in the house, there never seem to be leftovers: food is meant to be shared, not stored. At night, someone in the neighborhood might enjoy a treat or send over crabs from a church social. Food is currency, not capital; it is an expression of family, not an investment in networks. With food come plans, information, and questions that circulate through the same network.

On Saturday morning, finally, Pie's aunts, Annie and Sweet, her friend Geraldine Abernathy, and other old friends come for breakfast and dinner, staying on at the house until the 5:30 vigil mass. Other regulars come by later to talk, to share drinks or a light meal, or to play Pokeno.

The weekly cycle of food and family is intensified by special events, where more dramatic leadership is needed. When Pie prepared the priest's birthday party, planning began weeks beforehand, as tasks were allocated around the community by a central coordinator. The Holy Name society was solicited for beer; the Catholic Women's Club, for sandwiches; others, for deviled eggs, cakes, or salads, while Pie fried chicken for 150. Everyone assembled in the hall for Eucharist and a short program. The priest recognized those who had prepared the meal, and dining with conversation followed.

On other days, the meal turns outward, as the parish feeds the less fortunate of the community. A soup kitchen staffed by parish volunteers every Monday serves over fifty individuals. The largest such event is Thanksgiving. This project started under the aegis of the worship committee in the time of Father Nijjem in the late 1970s. Like breakfast, it has become a parish tradition. In 1985, the parish sent out over 400 dinners and 150 food baskets to the poor and lonely, while serving many more in the hall itself under Pie's supervision. Numbers continue to grow each year, including those who may be away from their family—retired elderly or service workers—as well.

When I participated with Don Moore in 1985 and Cindy Wong in 1990, work began in the first week of November, eventually enrolling four hundred to five hundred people via contributions, preparation, and distribution of the food throughout the city. By Thanksgiving week, turkeys were constantly coming in to the rectory or to Pie's house and being sent out to those who would cook. Food baskets were packed with goods the priest had bought and collected, and hours were devoted to assembling requests and dividing names into viable routes. On Thursday morning, the first workers assembled at 8:00 A.M., and others joined them in the parish hall after mass. Cars delivered food that came out of an assembly line that lasted until 3:00 P.M. Residents were often waiting on their porches for the gifts; Saint Benedict's is widely known for its charity. Only by early evening did the primary workers go home to celebrate Thanksgiving with their own families. Even so, cakes, pies, and delicacies were sent around in the evening among friends, while highlights of the day were discussed by phone.

While these uses of food reflect the particular role within the community of one leader, they are not atypical of the black and Catholic experience. Special meals like Christmas Eve—whether a turkey basting while the parents attend midnight mass or Pie's sixty pounds of chitterlings that represent her Christmas present to the Sunday family—are part of the rhythm of seasonal life. Sunday dinners have their own traditions of food and family. Food also seals life passages. At death, for example, the household becomes the focus of food brought for wakes and to maintain the family. Close friends, neighbors, and relatives not living in the household will come by with dinners, liquor, and other supplies. Organizations bring a dinner or host a meal in the hall after a mass, while distant friends might drop by with a cake, a single dish, or some sodas. This would also be true in the black Protestant community: indeed, religious lines are not drawn in food-sharing, although racial divisions may still be maintained.

Food ways change as well. As black Catholics have moved to the suburbs, distance and privacy have limited their exchanges. As families develop multiple careers or children build interests around school, peer group, or cars, the daily rituals of the table are also lost. Foods may also be added: after my wedding in Saint Benedict's in 1990, my wife's fried wonton was a requested plate for another special event. In this sense, Pie is unique in maintaining traditions lost even in other black parishes. None of the white parishes or even the other black parishes equal the Thanksgiving efforts of Saint Benedict's—although dinners have been served at the Social Apostolate, other black churches, and a local chicken franchise in conjunction with a black radio station. Yet her actions and planning knowledge are intimately linked to her standing and power within the parish.

Even though food integrates family, parish, religious, and secular communities, it can also segregate. Until the 1960s, downtown Savannah restaurants either denied service to blacks or sold food from the kitchen for them to eat outside—humiliations that sparked sit-ins and boycotts. Ironically, as many have noted, those who cooked and served whites in the restaurant and the home were often black, yet they were not considered equal at the table, reinforcing cultural categories. For black domestics, an area of recognized power within their "white family" and their black community was thus portrayed as an area of submission.

The presence of white priests and nuns has integrated the black and Catholic table, as have white parishioners of the congregation. Bishop Lessard has come by Pie's house for breakfast and shared Thanksgiving dinner. A cleric's visit may call for the formal dining room, but often these dinners are simply incorporated into the family. Clerics, in turn, may now invite black parishioners to dinner in the rectory or a restaurant. This establishes friendly contacts to mold encounters between hierarchical power and the enduring leaders of the parish. But it does not change enduring divisions of urban culture, either: a black would not be expected to have a white servant, nor are mixed-race parties well accepted in all restaurants.

Food and family are both real and metaphoric in the black Catholic experience. This is as true of the kitchen table and the domestic family as the altar and congregational family in the sanctuary. Family and food bind and sustain the religious community and the secular one, at once constituting and representing a leadership based in service, knowledge, and network. Yet they also participate in the divisions of church, culture, and society that condition Savannah life. This, too, is a fundamental part of the black and Catholic world.

In a conversation a few years before her death, Sister Julian Griffin spoke to me about the need to develop "black Catholics strong enough to be a witness of the church, very conscious of who or what the church is about." In looking at how that process has been fostered and constrained, these last two chapters have continued to explore the dialectic between white and black, public and private, powerful and subordinate, in the constitution of the black and Catholic community. Here, the processes of marking and subordination emerge in new combinations represented by the white priest and the black woman leader, who epitomize different realms of symbolic action and political power. Yet they also produce concrete people and groups who continue to shape the future of each parish as leaders, clerical or lay. Formal and informal power cannot be an absolute dichotomy, either. Those whom I place in disparate roles within the parish generally do not conflict so much as they embody the continuous tension from which community emerges.

This chapter does not speculate on whether the laity could take over the Catholic church without substantially altering it, even if such proposals have existed in theological discourse. Instead, the laity have actively defined their role in such a way as to adapt formal relations. Nonetheless, in the past two decades, crises in education, in the dwindling priesthood, and in issues of conscience such as birth control and divorce have spurred individuals in the laity to develop their roles—even if the Catholic hierarchy seems unready for such empowerment.

A 1989 decision on liturgical rites for parishes without priests indicates the continuing bureaucratic wariness of the national Catholic hierarchy concerning leadership. American bishops approved a measure establishing services for such parishes, found in one-third of the nation's dioceses. Episcopal reservations included the appearance of equality between lay presiders and priests and the "protestantization" of the liturgy. Critics asked why the Eucharist, rather than the priesthood, should be reconsidered. Bishop William E. McManus, retired bishop of Fort Wayne, expressed his view of the dilemma of the situation: "Every pastoral instinct in me warns that approval of the document could be misunderstood, misinterpreted, in some situations misused. . . ." He added, "By adopting this statement, will the U.S. bishops seem to make a value judgment that it is better to have a priestless prayer service on Sunday than to ordain married men or women to celebrate the Eucharist?" (Steinfels 1989). Many lay Catholics, black and white, could ask similar questions.

These chapters started from questions of organization to look at operation, at how parishes work in a range of crises as well as everyday activities. Through this analysis, community increasingly emerges as the product of individual and collaborative actions, of the creation of religious responses to social and cultural contradictions. The following chapters continue to examine social structure and culture through the examination of the individual and collective roots of belief.

7. Life Cycle, Family, and the Sacramental Order

Blessed assurance, Jesus is mine!
O what a foretaste of glory divine!
Heir of salvation, purchase of God
Born of his Spirit, washed in his Blood.
This is my story, this is my song
Praising my savior all the day long.
This is my story, this is my song
Praising my savior all the day long.

—Lead Me, Guide Me:
The African American Catholic Hymnal

In their 1984 pastoral letter, black Catholic bishops eloquently set forth their perception of the intrinsic relationship of family and church:

> This sense of family in our own African-tradition can easily be trans-
> lated into a richer sense of Church as a great and all-embracing family.
> In our parishes we should truly look upon ourselves as brothers and
> sisters to one another. The elders among us should be a living re-
> source for the young, for they have much to tell and teach. Our cel-
> ebrations should be the affirmation of our kinship and our common
> bond. The words of the third Eucharistic Prayer, "Father, hear the
> prayers of the family you have gathered here" are not a pious fiction
> but a sacred reality that defines the meaning of the Catholic commu-
> nity. (Howze et al. 1984, 11-12)

Nonetheless, this document also recognized the trials that the black family has faced because of racism and economic exploitation: "For many

reasons, the black family has been especially assailed, despite the importance that families still have within the black cultural and spiritual tradition" (Howze et al. 1984, 11). As scholars, novelists, politicians, and theologians have pointed out (Billingsley 1968; Genovese 1974; Stack 1974; Gutman 1976; Morrison 1987; Gresham 1989), the formation of the black family itself often has entailed a creative response to social challenges rather than the simple reproduction of ideal models, whether secular or religious.

A year later, Deacon Prince Jackson of Saint Benedict's assessed the pressures on the black community and families he saw around him:

> The grave crisis engulfing the black community of Savannah is not entirely one of economics. The robbers are not buying sandwiches and paying rent with the loot they gain illegally. There is also a moral aspect of the crisis. More than 50 percent of the black babies born this year will be the result of unmarried unions. There is a growing disregard for the value of a human life in some parts of the black community. Recently, we experienced the killing of a black by another black which stemmed from the possession of a recyclable aluminum can whose worth is about 1 1/3 cents. . . .

Jackson's solutions evoked values that his Catholic church has championed: family, church, schools, and government cooperation in youth formation.

> We must deal with the home because parents are the first and foremost educators of their children. Thugs are not born. They are made, fertilized, weeded, and watered by parents. We must involve our churches because of the tremendous influence they have on the moral development of people. We must involve our school system because of the importance of education in the total development of children. We must involve our criminal justice system because its laxity in many cases contributes significantly to the commission of crimes. (*SMN* July 23, 1985)

Jackson's comments suggest how the black and Catholic *family* embodies the historical contradictions and challenges of the black and Catholic *church*. The family enshrined in Roman Catholic doctrine has idealized a household developed in the Mediterranean and Europe, transmitted through immigration and evangelization. The American Catholic hierarchy has emphasized the continual renewal of the church as society and culture through this family's centrality to reproduction, religious preparation, education, and social life. From birth and baptism, through schools and confirmation, to the choice of Catholic spouse and the teaching of the faith to children, the family has sustained the life of the Roman Catholic church (Dolan 1985, 241-61; *New Catechism* 1972). The sacraments have both marked a family cycle and linked it to an underlying logic of faith and truth for Catholics.

Catholic models have not necessarily suggested experiences to which blacks have had access, nor have they encompassed all key values of black life. The history of the black family in America has been one of creation, synthesis, and resistance. In some cases, education, migration or dual-income families have stabilized aspirations to middle-class practices and values. In others, extended families have permitted survival after the loss or departure of individuals. Blacks have learned to deal with unwed mothers, adoption, and problematic environments as facets of an enforced experience of poverty, just as they have also learned to deal with problems of middle-class life, integration, and mobility.

Catholicism brought an idealistic model of family to blacks while it disrupted the family itself through evangelism and conversion. Often children were the first to join the church, although one of their (non-Catholic) parents might follow. This process exchanged the unity of family and religion for other values of education and mobility. Even the oldest Catholic families repeat marriages generation after generation in which one spouse is not Catholic. If all members of one branch are Catholic, the extended family—cousins, grandparents, and neighbors—may be associated with other churches from which Catholics have been isolated by dogmatic exclusivism. By incorporating everyday reactions to these problems, the family remains rich as both practice and metaphor, springing from the experience of those who are black and Catholic rather than being imposed upon them.

This chapter develops the symbolic and historical tension between the sacramental cycle and family, society, and culture in Savannah's black and Catholic parishes. Baptism, Eucharist, reconciliation, marriage, and anointing of the sick seem to chart the lives of individuals and communities within the universal Catholic church. Beyond being rites of passage, they also represent belief—signs, to all Catholics, of God's presence in the world. Yet they have also been changed by the experience of human life in Savannah. Between church and society, black Catholics have sought to use and interpret sacraments to synthesize ritual and belief in response to contradictions.

255

SACRAMENTAL VISION AND CATHOLIC EXPERIENCE

Roman Catholic worship and belief center on seven sacraments that are conceived as manifestations of God's presence in human life. According to Vatican II documents, "the purpose of the sacraments is to sanctify men, to build up the body of Christ, and finally, to give worship to God. Because they are signs, they also instruct. They not only presuppose faith, but by words and objects they also nourish strengthen and express it . . ." (Constitution on Sacred Liturgy in Abbott 1966, 158). These sacraments comprise the Eucharist, holy orders, baptism, penance (reconciliation, confession), confirmation, marriage, and anointing of the sick. The Eucharist, as the most continuous, frequent, and communal sacrament of the church, represents a special area for adaptation and experience of community; as such, it is the sole focus of the next chapter. Ordination (holy orders) has been treated among questions of hierarchy, leadership, and gender. It is the only sacrament limited to males, although it constitutes the foundation of the ongoing formal structure of leadership in the church. Of the remaining sacraments, four—baptism, confirmation, marriage, and anointing of the sick—demarcate in a both symbolic and social fashion the life course of any Catholic from birth to death (*New Catechism* 1972; McBrien 1980). Indeed, these are often the landmarks of Catholic life narrative. The fifth sacrament, that of reconciliation, is a lifelong process that nonetheless can be treated in its introduction to children at a crucial rite of passage: first participation in the Eucharist.

Four basic aspects of shared symbolic action in the Catholic church guide this analysis. First, all sacraments are conceived of as constitutive of and universal to Roman Catholicism, a mythic charter among the people:

> The heart of Roman Catholic faith and life is not the authority of the church organization, however formidable that may be, nor the relation of church and state, however complex that may be. Roman Catholic life is centered in the seven sacraments of the church. By these sacraments the faithful live and die. The church organization is there to administer the sacraments and to guarantee their proper administration, but it is the sacraments that carry the life-giving grace of God to the believers. (Pelikan 1959, 110; see Abbott 1966, "Constitution on the Sacred Liturgy," 137-78; *New Catechism* 1972, 252-55)

Theologian Lawrence Cunningham affirms the meaning of this vision in the personal notes with which he prefaces his overview of Catholic faith:

> As a kid growing up in the deep south I rather envied the simpler church style of my overwhelmingly Baptist neighbors. They had a church, a preacher, a Bible, a few doctrines, two ordinances, and a straightforward service: sing, pray, listen to the Bible readings and the preacher's sermon, and go home. We, by contrast, had this bewildering array of clergy (bishops, two kinds of monsignors, pastors, curates, monks, nuns, etc.), churches (cathedrals, shrines, parishes, missions), a complex set of beliefs (they had heaven and hell; we added limbo and purgatory), seven sacraments, and a very complex worship service that was all in Latin to boot.
>
> So our first question is this: Is there something beneath (or behind) this complex phenomenon called Catholicism that holds it all together and gives it a certain logic? Is there something like a set of Catholic first principles from which everything else flows or, at least, which helps to make sense of everything else? (1987, 7)

Cunningham points to an array of features of Catholicism as a distinctive religious and social identity in the South. Yet his final question is even more essentially Catholic to me, echoing the belief in first principles, the Catholic imagination of the truth that reverberates in documents of Vatican II as well as in everyday interpretation and practice. Cunningham finds the answer in the Christian traditions and community that constitute a church. A sacramental imagination, as belief and practice, encompasses both socially embedded actions and a way of making sense of the world. On the basis of the cultural and social processes and structures that I have examined, therefore I evoke black and Catholic belief, individual and collective, as embodied in concrete sacraments while nonetheless looking beyond them (McDonogh 1991).

Sacramental universalism thus implies both an embracing belief and an international extension of community. For example, all Catholics must attend Mass wherever they are on Sunday. Yet they expect to find there an accepting community of similar beliefs and practice, despite linguistic or cultural differences. The limits on this have already been plain in black history.[1]

In order to maintain Catholic claims to universalism, hierarchical institutions, sustained by traditionally valued knowledge, supervise the administration of sacraments. The nature of preparation for the ritual, the structure of the ritual, and the wording of prayers and participation form Catholic tradition and the theology that builds on this tradition. While distance from a hierarchical center, local poverty, or irregular training may have permitted more variation in the past, especially in missions, supervision is readily communicated today from central authorities through intermediaries to the parish community. Bureaucracies supervise implementation of rituals worldwide. At the national level, offices of the United States Conference of Bishops approve texts and applications of sacramental rites. Dioceses set guidelines through formal rules or by discussions among clergy and laity. Specific prayers for local interests, for example, may be supplied for Sunday Mass. Finally, each parish and its priest develop its practice within these guidelines. Multiple voices interact within a hierarchical frame.

Second, the sacramental *order* uniquely defines Roman Catholicism, as Cunningham points out. Many of the sacraments, of course, are shared with other Christian traditions; dialogues since the 1950s have clarified common elements of belief among these churches (McBrien 1980, 766). Analogous rites of communion, cathartic purgation, and separation are more general to religious life. Yet key shared rituals such as baptism and Eucharist vary widely among Christians. Catholics see baptism as the inauguration of human religious life, properly administered even to infants, a decision shared with Orthodox, Lutherans, Episcopalians, and Presbyterians. For the Evangelicals who dominate black religion, however, baptism is a sign of commitment entailing mature conversion and direct, individual contact with God. Whether received in adolescence or later, it must be a personal response to a divine call to faith. Pentecostal traditions speak of a second "Baptism in the Spirit," or in Holiness, that may be uneasily incorporated into Catholic theology and worship. Catholic law also distinguishes the validity of Catholic baptism from parallel Christian rites. Before Vatican II, those baptized in other denominations were rebaptized on entrance into the Catholic church; today, other baptisms are recognized by a "provisional" baptism or simpler reception into the church.

Eucharist meanwhile represents to Catholics the *real* rather than *metaphoric* presence of the body and blood of Jesus in the bread and wine of the altar. Catholics reenact the ritual each day; potentially, all the community may share in it. Despite ecumenical dialogues and confluence, the Roman Catholic hierarchy excludes outsiders from full participation in this rite, even at services involving multiple denominations. While Episcopalians and Lutherans share some of these ideas, evangelical Protestants generally see communion as a symbolic representation rather than a real presence of Christ. Most Protestant traditions celebrate communion less frequently. Nonetheless, they may do so more inclusively: Catholics may receive communion in many Protestant churches, though Catholics generally are not encouraged to do so by their own priests.

Funerals also evoke widely shared ritual patterns throughout the West. Catholicism, however, emphasizes anointing of the sick, formerly known as extreme unction, as a key sign of God's presence in crisis. The Mass of Christian Burial may include the sacramental presence of the Eucharist, but it does not represent a specific sacrament for death. Within these separation rites, other practices such as the collective rosary that seeks the intercession of Mary differentiate Catholic funerals from other Christian rites.

Other sacraments become signs of discord among Christians. Confession evokes debate over the nature of a sacrament and the power relations it implies, as does sacramental marriage. Limitations on sacraments such as priesthood also differentiate Catholics from other denominations.

Beyond comparisons of individual rituals, the *set* of rituals recognized as a unity also distinguishes Roman Catholicism from other religious traditions in Savannah: "What is essential is not the number seven, but the affirmation that there are certain ritual actions through which the saving presence and activity of God appear, on the one hand, and the sacramental nature of the Church, on the other hand" (McBrien 1980, 744). This set is further embedded in a wider range of sacramentals, dependent on the faith of those who practice them rather than on inherent power and presence. This wider set includes many of the most familiar attributes of distinctive Catholic practice: holy oils, candles, palms, crucifixes, statues, and medals (McBrien 1980, 745). These subsidiary aspects of the church are often more vivid in anti-Catholic responses than the sacraments themselves.

Third, and critical to any understanding of contemporary adaptation is an awareness that Catholic rituals, like all rituals, undergo historical transformations despite an aura of timelessness. Some sacraments originated in the Biblical community, including New Testament revisions of Old Testament precedents manifest in the Passover imagery pervading the Eucharist (Dix 1945; Jungmann 1959; McBrien 1980; Feeley-Harnik 1981; Meeks 1983, 140-63). Others developed in form and character in the Middle Ages (McBrien 1980; Bossy 1985), reaching "final" form in the Council of Trent. The Latin liturgy, for example, through which most older black Catholics of Savannah experienced Sunday Mass as an apparently immutable act, was only reified in the sixteenth century. In the Tridentine church, tradition often became valued as an inherited representation of power rather than a creative force.

The adaptation already examined in social and structural realms thus has been equally present in worship and belief, especially since the Second Vatican Council encouraged renewal. In Eucharist and baptism, reform has centered on clarification of the historical essence of the ritual and on the participation of the entire community. In other cases, such as confirmation, major changes in guidelines for preparation and reception have ensued which offer new understandings of the rite. In the anointing of the sick, the theological focus and action of the ritual have changed more deeply from a marking of imminent death to a sign of the presence of Christ in suffering and healing. Ironically, today, the reformed rituals of the 1960s have taken on the authority of immutability to new participants.

A final theme summarizes the first three with regard to the life and experience of black Catholics: the recognition of a long popular and transforming response to the sacramental order by all members of the church, not just the official leadership. This has been perhaps more readily recognized by students of history than by anthropologists working in the present (N. Davis 1975; Ginzburg 1980, 1984; Bossy 1985) Nowhere is this clearer than in reconciliation, which, while transformed in intent and structure by ecclesiastical councils, has been more seriously altered by popular reevaluation. In the 1950s, prior to Vatican II, confession of serious transgression was a necessary prerequisite to any reception of communion and therefore to full membership in the church, making it a sign of exclusion. Today, frequent reception of the Eucharist depends on individual reflection and collective penance within the context of the liturgy. Individual confession has all but disappeared in some parishes, echoing national trends. The Vatican however has expressed intense concern over parishioners' choice of communal penance, and their neglect of the individual sacrament.

This disuse of confession is a general phenomenon within American Catholicism. Other adaptations reflect more clearly the intersection of black social and economic experience and the history of Catholicism with a predefined ritual order. The predominance of adult over infant baptism reflects historical patterns of recruitment; the relationship of marriage, divorce, and nonsanctioned relationships emerges from both recruitment and socioeconomic circumstances. Even beyond these factors, parishes have developed innovations around rituals that supplement without transformation, such as funeral meals at Saint Benedict's or various Eucharistic innovations at the parish level. Sacramentals, historically, have also been a rich area for popular expression that shape everyday Catholic devotion in the home through statues, holy water, and crucifixes. The sight of a body dangling from a cross or a palm frond blessed in a Palm Sunday procession tacked to a wall are clear markers of Catholic identity for outsiders. Yet among the black Catholics whose home life I know best, these are not especially salient within an array of decorations, photographs, and memorabilia; indeed, they represent a stronger statement of autobiography than of devotion or reflection.

As in other areas of history and experience of those who are black and Catholic, then, the sacraments as rites of passage define and sustain individuals and community in their choice of identity while differentiating them from others black and white, Catholic and Protestant. These rites represent individual and collective performances against a shifting backdrop of both possibilities and constraints. Analysis of each, in turn, structures our understanding of contradiction, ritual, and the building of community and belief.

BIRTH, BAPTISM, AND ADULTHOOD

Rites of entrance and membership are critical to religious institutions and exclusivity. Modern American Catholicism generally treats baptism as a rite through which an infant is absorbed into the beliefs of his or her parents. While Savannah blacks are marked at birth by race, until the 1960s black Catholics tended to join the church as children or adults. The formation of a convert church thus transformed a central ritual even as it recaptured many facets of the early history of baptism as a Christian rite.

Baptism is the only ritual action mentioned in the Nicene creed, which underlies the doctrinal unity of Western Christianity: "We believe in one baptism for the forgiveness of sins." Old Testament precedents (Isaiah 42:1) and the scriptural example of the baptism of Jesus by John the Baptist (Mark 1:11; Matthew 20:22; Luke 12:30) charter it as a central religious event of Christianity. Catholics celebrate and reenact this perceived historical origin at the Feast of the Baptism, in which the story is retold and baptismal vows renewed. Easter and other masses during the year also situate new baptisms in a ritual renewal of vows with a symbolic sprinkling of the entire congregation.

Baptism elaborates a simple action of cleansing in water, coupled with the illocutionary pronouncement, "I baptize you in the name of the Father, the Son and the Holy Spirit" over the initiate. Since the early church, rich metaphors have expanded this act, identifying immersion with death to sin and to the world, and associating emergence with new life with the resurrected Christ (Meeks 1983, 141-57). In its first three centuries, Christianity relied on adult conversion and baptism. Infant baptism emerged later, in response to the theological perception that infants were conceived with original sin, although non-Catholic Christians do not necessarily adhere to this tenet. In Roman Catholicism, baptism became an urgent ritual for any infant, who would otherwise face a sort of damnation. Hence Catholics remain acutely conscious of the possibility of emergency administration of the sacrament, de-ritualized from its family setting, to protect a child from the dangers of an unsanctified death: "He's being deprived of the right of being part of the Body of Christ as priest, prophet, or king." This remark, by a black and Catholic laywoman, is remarkable in its mix of ecclesiastical diction and everyday belief. It also reflects the empowerment of baptism as a sacrament that can be administered by anyone, regardless of preparation, age, or gender.

While it is no longer common to baptize within two or three days of birth, this rite normally occurs within a few months of birth in a Catholic family. Masses are scheduled on a monthly basis in most parishes as parts of a community mass. While older white elite families occasionally boasted of their privilege of baptism in the cathedral, no significant variation in timing or ritual distinguishes infant baptisms in black and white parishes.

As those who view baptism primarily as an adult faith commitment argue, the infant has little part in this rite or decision. However, for Catholics, infant baptism demonstrates the commitment on the part of parents and godparents—ritual sponsors who act as spiritual guardians for the child—to raise the child within the Catholic faith. Furthermore, it represents a bond between the family and the community:

> Christ made his salvation a community matter, a social thing. He did not give it to individuals in isolation from each other, but to a people. Just as the herd has its calves, each living people has its children, beings whose existence as men is totally sustained by the adults around them. Hence the baby is not baptized because it believes, but because we naturally want to pass on our faith. We bring the children within the circle of our own faith, into the faith of the Church. (*New Catechism* 1972, 250)

Current Catholic practices emphasize this corporate responsibility, removing baptism from settings that treated it as a private ritual for family and friends celebrated outside the normal liturgical spaces and times. Baptism is especially important in the general renewal of the Easter Vigil.

However, the Catholic church in the black community has not been a biologically reproductive church so much as a church based on adolescent and adult conversions. Saint Mary's, for example, recorded 1,735 baptisms between 1912 and 1984. Of these, 545 were infant baptisms, reproducing the community through the Catholic family; 650 represented school-age children, recruited through the elementary program in most cases and divided equally between males and females. The remaining 540 were adults: 366 females and 174 males. The female predominance may be attributable to conversions at marriage and to a higher general involvement of black women in religious life.

These divisions follow clear historical trajectories. In the early days of the Catholic missions in black neighborhoods, baptisms grew out of the schools. While some children left both school and church thereafter, priests and nuns also worked closely with children, expecting parents to follow their offspring. The decrease in baptisms in the 1970s, seen in figure 13, indicates how close the relationship of school and baptism became. School closures had an immediate as well as continuing impact on conversions and reproduction of the parish.

Apart from such parental conversions, other blacks attribute their shifts to Catholicism to the delayed influence of Catholic education. Still others have converted because of marriages. In the 1980s, the hierarchy has stressed evangelization by neighbors, mentors, and friends, although individual and parish activism in black neighborhoods evidently have long attracted converts: "We knew this neighbor woman" is a prologue to many conversion stories among old families. The increased Catholic acceptance of other Christian traditions since Vatican II, however, may also undercut a Catholic sectarian drive to convert and rebaptize Protestant adults.

Since the 1970s, infant baptisms have come to predominate in all three black parishes, even though adult baptisms have been given a new liturgical prominence through inclusion in the Easter Vigil mass. In 1987 less than ten adolescents and adults joined the church in all three parishes combined. Nevertheless, the Bishops' Pastoral of 1984 and meetings of the National Office of Black Catholics in 1985 fostered evangelization and the Rite of Christian Initiation for Adults (RCIA) as central foci for the black church. Evangelization regained prominence as part of the 1980s diocesan renewal program.

If baptism in the RCIA becomes an adult decision, it still is not equivalent to the adolescent and adult baptism of black Evangelicals. An emphasis on commitment is developed in black Protestant churches through trial and education in the community before formal baptism. Yet the thrust remains toward spiritual and emotional conviction. Narratives of black Catholic conversion talk of guidance toward membership by friends and clergy rather than an emotional catharsis or a salvation experience. This is not a lesser belief, but one expressed through a different logic of truth, a sacramental vision. Catholic conversions also include a shift of community—from one or more Protestant churches to a Catholic one in most cases, rather than focusing on formation within a single congregation:

> I was going to different churches: Baptist, Holiness (raises hands and shakes); it's like going to a concert. There's only one thing that counts—you're praising God and worshipping God. Who cares how you do it, . . . there's just different methods. (woman, fifties)

> I guess Catholic is just more me. I was kind of young and didn't know what it was all about. The Catholic church had its advantages; it was shorter and it didn't go from 8 to 8. Once I started understanding and compared it to other types of churches, I liked it. (male, twenties, interviewed by Don Moore)

Baptism for a mature Catholic follows catechesis, whether in schools or parish classes. Again, logic and proof receive more emphasis than catharsis. Reception of the sacrament requires the examination of knowledge, faith, and behavior that is generally formalized in the penitential period of Lent, the forty days before Easter. Inauguration of life in the parish comes with the continuing interaction of individual and group. Catholic adult baptism also tends to be more restrained than that of low-church Protestant denominations, black or white. Generally, it involves a minimal pouring of water and a symbolic new garment rather than the total immersion and full white robes emphasized by some Protestants. While it represents a particular forgiveness of sins, other procedures for absolution supplement it, rather than representing a one-time commitment to salvation.

The historical demographic predominance of mature baptism in black Catholicism also has differentiated godparenthood from immigrant white Catholic groups, as well as black Protestant traditions, which generally lack such formal sponsors. Black godparents reinforce the unity of parish, extended family, and church. Sister Thea Bowman, a black nun,

Figure 16. A Holiness baptism by the Reverend C. M. Grace, United House of Prayer, ca. 1930s. Photograph courtesy of the Georgia Historical Society, Cordray-Foltz Collection.

emphasizes this extension of family and church: "In the traditional black community, the church is more than a body of believers in the Lord—it is an extended family. Many members may be related by blood, but all elders are 'mothers' and 'fathers' in the church. Godparents are especially respected in daily as well as church life. Informal adoptions abound" (1987, 10).

In white Catholic praxis, focused on infant baptism, godparents tend to be relatives or friends of the parents who reinforce their relationship with the parents through shared ritual responsibility; this process shows a wide variation among cultural groups.[2] Adolescent and adult initiation among black Catholics, however, allow the candidates to reinforce their own bonds and experience. Adult converts select a single sponsor instead of the male and female parental surrogates present at infant baptism. The godparent may be a person who encouraged one's entry into the church, a

teacher, a community leader, a friend, or a spouse. Or he or she may provide even more fundamental linkages, as one elderly woman recalled to me
in 1984: "My godfather took me into Saint Benedict's. He was born Catholic,
and was seven years old when they freed the slaves." Yet choice is para-
mount; thus, I became godfather in my fourth year of fieldwork to Jimmie
Reynolds, an older man to whom I was linked through Pie's household.

Since all sponsors must be Catholic, in the early black missions, the
same members stood repeatedly as godparents or acted as sponsors for
whole families who would join the church. Even as the church grew, some
leaders continued to act as godparents far beyond the expectations of the
institution in white Catholic America or white Savannah: my adoptive
mother has become godmother to some eighteen to twenty members of
Saint Benedict's over the years, and other leaders have five to ten adult
godchildren. Trees of godparental relationships reinforce network and influence, thus accommodating the sacrament to both social structure and
values of leadership. Hence Percy Miller was qualified in a metaphoric fashion by a Saint Mary's member as "godfather to the parish."

Godparenthood also permeates the community to a greater extent than
all but the most ethnic and traditional American white parishes. Over the years
in which I have lived with Pie, I have met almost all twenty of her godchildren; some come by every week while others make special visits. "Godmother" and "Godfather" regularly appear as terms of address in conversation, while at Robert Chaney's ordination, the pew that held his extended
family included his own godparents and Pie, his mother's godmother. The
language usage can be extended to terms like "Godsister," although this
appeared to be an extreme case. Black Catholics baptized as infants appear
to be the only ones who may not know their godparents, although those
with manifold godchildren may not know "whether they all are dead or alive."
For adults, though, this proves a special bond, between *compadrazgo* and
fosterage (Mintz and Wolf 1950; Bloch and Guggenheim 1981).

The *practice* of baptism among those who are black and Catholic links
them to Catholic and other Christian traditions. Yet these practices also
define characteristic meanings and uses of the sacrament for black parishes
that separate black Catholics from most black Protestants. The predominance of adult baptism re-presents the emergence of Catholicism as a foreign religion in the black community and, with godparenthood, incorporates the values of this community into Catholicism, binding the parish
family together in opposition to other, white Catholics. These themes
are repeated in the social formation of other sacraments.

CHILDHOOD, FIRST COMMUNION, AND PENANCE

Most black Savannah children have been introduced into the life of the church community as they have learned about the social worlds of their city. Adult converts to Catholicism are confirmed and initiated into the Eucharist within the mass of their reception (baptism) into the church. For children within a Catholic family, however, this is a longer process, associated with intellectual maturation and parental guidance: "The child cannot know God through its own efforts. As it plays, cries, and sleeps, it feels at home in its own little world which is very great to him and in which goodness, omnipotence, and omnipresence are represented by father and mother. The way we have learned to know our parents is of immeasurable importance in our image of God" (*New Catechism* 1972, 383). Parents soon bring babies to church, and these may be blessed by the priest when their parents receive communion. Toddlers begin to learn prayers at home. Young children also learn proper behavior in church, although some squirming and distraction remain generally evident.

Within multigenerational black families, roles reinforce religious expectations as children raised Catholic develop a sense of the relationship they are expected to have with God. A woman in her seventies recalled:

> I don't know how old I was, but I had been bad in school and I had to tell Mama cause if I didn't tell her Sister would tell her. And I told Mama and she said, "Well I'm gonna get you in a few minutes." And I went outside to the privy and I began to pray. I began to say a Hail Mary and I was praying loud and Mama passed me up because she wanted me to feel my prayers had been answered. So, next time I did something bad I went running out there. Mama said, "No, no need to go out there cause I'm gonna tear your butt off right now."

When children reach school age, or that which the church considers "the age of reason," at about seven, they are ready for further incorporation into the sacramental universe. The child's training is taken over by religious specialists, either by the nuns of parochial schools or by lay teachers in modern Sunday schools. The Eucharist will be received at eight or nine.[3]

"First Communion" is not a sacrament so much as it initiates a long-term sacramental relationship to the Eucharist. Practically, however, the First Communion of a child has also been set aside in Catholic cultures as a special age-grade event. For non-Catholics in schools or neighborhoods, this visibility is a critical stimulus to interest and conversion.

267

In the experience of those with whom I have worked in Savannah, and for many other Catholics, First Communion for children has also been set apart by ritual, dress, and springtime festivities. In a typical First Communion, during a spring Sunday mass that I observed in 1988, for example, seven boys and seven girls entered the church in procession before the celebrant and sat apart at the front. All the girls wore white party dresses, symbolizing their purity; boys wore suits and white ribbons. They participated in lighting the paschal (Easter) candle, reserved for special occasions, and they read the intercessory prayers of the Mass to the congregation. At the liturgy of the Eucharist, they assembled around the altar. Afterwards, there was time for photographs and presents, including traditional prayer books and rosaries. The celebrant linked the event to the history of the parish: "as we are breaking ground for a new parish hall, so these are breaking ground for their future."

That ceremony evoked childhood memories in others. Recollections of First Communion ritual substantiate long-established associations of theological rites with special white dresses, ornamental prayer books, and parties, as Pie recalled from Saint Benedict's in the 1920s:

> Oh, I was excited, cause I was going to receive the Body and Blood of Christ. And then afterwards we looked forward to eating sweet rolls and drinking coffee.
>
> *Q:* Who gave you that?
>
> *A:* The sisters would make a huge pot of coffee with milk in it and the bakery shop would give us these large pans of sweet rolls. Sweet rolls and coffee that morning and it would taste so good. We couldn't get down in the basement fast enough. . . .
>
> *Q:* Did you have any special clothes that day?
>
> *A:* Oh yeah, I had white dress, white shoes, white veil, white socks.

Popular ceremonies emphasize gender divisions in dress and gifts. Dress contrasts age grades, too—innocent and pure versus later adult status—as part of initiation. White has a similar symbolic role, of course, at marriage and sometimes at graduation. In all cases, females are primarily marked, although males are generally "dressed up." Again, a daily part of belief is created into a special ritual tied to human development and family, neighborhood, and parish ties. First Communion as a ceremony precedes the major evangelical conversion event of adolescent baptism, although some black Protestant churches associate elaborate rituals with incorporation and passage in Sunday school.

Figure 17. First Communion, Saint Anthony's, ca. 1950. Photograph courtesy Gloria and Evelyn Daniels.

SINFULNESS AND SEPARATION

Preparation for communion involves reflection and penance. "Confession," as the sacrament of reconciliation is still popularly known, evokes many images of Catholicism and its distinctiveness for those outside the faith. Non-Catholics often have looked with curiosity and animosity at the sacrament. Some focus on it as a weakening of any commitment to lead a sinless life since it offers an escape from the consequences of sin. Others have seen it as a mysterious accumulation of power in the priest, who is the only one who can administer the sacrament.

Early Catholic missionaries to blacks felt compelled to explain and defend the sacrament in lectures to non-Catholics (*ST*1910), just as white critics luridly excoriated the confessional with images of sexuality and power.[4] The sacramental emphasis on repentance and forgiveness finds its Biblical charter for Catholic tradition in John 20:22-23: "Receive the Holy Spirit. If you forgive men's sins, they are forgiven them; if you hold them bound, they are held bound." Public penance emerged by the sixth century as a one-time, post-baptismal opportunity to deal with serious sins (McBrien 1980, 772-78). This action was generalized to less-serious offenses and more frequent examination in the early Middle Ages. Only in the later Middle Ages was sacerdotal absolution added. After Reformation debates over the penance as a sacrament, the ritual received its modern form at the Council of Trent.

In the past, priests and nuns linked penance to ideas of sin and of punishment, with the latter often taking on a vivid form (though perhaps not in comparison to Evangelical preaching) in depictions of hell and purgatory. An early SMA priest defended this doctrine to a skeptical newspaper audience:

> The doctrine of purgatory is clearly proved by the Old Testament, in Mach 11: 43. . . . It is insinuated in the New Testament when our Lord speaks of sins "which shall not be forgiven neither in this world nor in the world to come." Matt 12: 32. Reason itself tells us that a soul which departs life with a small sin cannot be condemned to the eternal torments of hell, and cannot enter into the Kingdom of Heaven . . . and that therefore there must be an intermediate place which we, Catholics, call purgatory. (*ST*1909)

The apologetic thrust of the text is clear, as the priest struggles to make sense of an abstract theological calculus of sin, punishment, and forgiveness. Punishment figured more directly in the sense of sin recalled by a church-trained woman now in her seventies: "Nuns gave you a lot of fear about certain things and priests would, too. They'd make you feel like if you'd go to a Protestant church, you'd go to hell, you were sinning. They gave you fear."

The Second Vatican Council, in the 1960s, produced deep changes in the theology of penance:

> The new Rite of Penance does bring out the ecclesial dimension of the sacrament more fully than does the traditional (i.e., post-Tridentine) practice of private confession. In the new rite, the effect of the sacrament is identified as reconciliation with God and with the Church. The minister functions more as a healer than as a judge. Emphasis is placed on conversion inspired by the Church's proclamation of God's word. And communal celebration of the sacrament is provided for and encouraged.
>
> The celebration of this sacrament is thus always an act in which the Church proclaims its faith, gives thanks to God for the freedom with which Christ has made us free, and offers its life as a spiritual sacrifice in praise of God's glory, as it hastens to meet the Lord Jesus. (Introduction to the New Rite, n. 7; McBrien 1980, 782)

This new theology emphasizes reconciliation of the church as a sinful community, while it also expresses individual growth of a moral sense of right and wrong. This dual emphasis has forced parishes to face the developmental question of the age at which children should receive confession.

Confession poses challenges to the interpretation of modern understandings of the life cycle as well. While confession long has preceded First Communion, for example, contemporary priests and educators in Savannah have suggested to me that children are incapable of understanding the issues involved in reconciliation, and some leaders wish to postpone this sacrament until later. For Catholics, as noted, the sacrament also has a checkered meaning: "Confession is an explosive topic, producing as it does a wide range of feelings, from rage to gratitude" (Donoghue and Shapiro 1984, 91).

The memories shared publicly in Savannah of childhood confessions and sinfulness tend to be banal. An elderly black woman recalled her sins as a child: "They taught you that you was supposed to tell all the sins, and my sin would be that I ate meat on Friday. . . . I'd curse, and you weren't supposed to get angry, but I'd suck my teeth. . . ." Such minor offenses satisfied the need to confess; but with adolescence, confessional memories become increasingly permeated by sexual guilt and other responsibilities. Confession also linked religious training and the school: "They took you out of class to confess: I ate meat on Friday, cursed, had bad thoughts. I worried about original sin and grievous sin against God. Purgatory: the picture would scare you. I haven't heard about purgatory since I left Saint Benedict" (female, late forties). A black male who has since left the church had different memories of adolescent confession in the 1960s: "I still made things up. Not sex. Not real sins: you knew that he knew what you were doing. But I still remember not telling him the biggies." Thus, confession could be an isolating as well as a reconciling phenomenon.

Outside the school ambience, confession has taken on other meanings for adult Catholics as a continuing part of religious life that not only distinguishes them from Protestants but divides contemporary Catholics. Some have continued it regularly in Saturday visits to the cramped confessionals at the back of the church. Others have moved away from it or to new interpretations of the sacrament. Even prior to Vatican II, authorities required confession only for a Catholic in mortal sin, a serious and conscious act against the spirit of God, who required absolution to receive communion in the Easter season. Furthermore, confession implied rejection of a past pattern rather than forgiveness of continuing states. The relation of practice and meaning, however, remains more dense.

Today, despite a wide range of transgressions known and discussed in the modern parishes, sin does not immediately call for cleansing. I have never heard anyone criticized for receiving communion; one priest insisted that he could not imagine turning someone away from Eucharist, a sign of forgiveness and unity, for any reason of sin. Moreover, many questions of sexuality, alcohol abuse, and language are often moot among both black and white Catholics as both have faced contradictory demands in the modern world (McNally 1987; Dolan 1987). In preaching that I observed in black parishes, sinfulness was often imputed to structures of exploitation or unexamined accommodations not so easily resolved by confession. Practice today also represents a different sense of sin, based on conduct over time rather than spiritual accountancy. For some individuals, it also seems to represent a move away from a spiritual sense of sin, a secularization of the Christian kerygma.

Revisions of the ritual of communion in the past decades have emphasized the long-term guidance implicit in reconciliation as well. Dark, secretive confessionals have been abandoned in favor of meetings in offices or reconciliation rooms with face-to-face contact. Priests have also discouraged use of confession for bookkeeping instead of as a time of individual growth. Among priests who have served in black parishes, some have abandoned traditional appeals to the sacrament, emphasizing counseling for the individual and community. Another told me that confession remains frequent, although not as practiced prior to Vatican II. Lay people, meanwhile, speak of advice and reconciliation as much as divine pardon.

Communal rites have also taken on more importance. The black parishes sponsor healing and reconciliation services to which other congregations are invited in Advent and Lent, the seasons Catholics traditionally designate for reflection and repentance. Here, several priests may be available for brief private confessions, while general absolution also is given. Chapels, confessionals, and sacristies are pressed into service for individuals while children are gathered around a priest at the altar. Symbolic acts and space stress communal healing to conquer suffering and separation. In this, black practice seems quite similar to white parishes while distinguished from black Protestants by the idea and practice of the rite itself.

These changes in confession reflect manifold changes in the Catholic church. Among those who are black and Catholic, as among whites, the shift of church ideals has converged with changing values of independence in such areas as sin and forgiveness. Black choices bind individuals and churches to the process of change underway in other parishes, while communion and confession separate them from Protestant liturgical traditions. These rituals also unite children to the life and growth of the community, the discovery and enactment of good, evil, and forgiveness. Yet Ethel Waters, the black singer and actress raised as a Catholic, found this vision lacking in the pre-Vatican II church. Hence, confession became a stimulus to conversion:

> My logic, my reasoning powers made me question much of the doctrine.
>
> For example, as a little girl I was told to ask God to forgive my sins. But what sins could a little girl commit?
>
> My search for God and my finding of Him were to begin in one of those Protestant churches where they were having a children's revival. It was there that I truly came to know and reverence Christ, the Redeemer. (1951, 220-21)

The divergence of Catholic and evangelical world views becomes more apparent as Catholics prepare for the next sacramental right of passage, confirmation.

CONFIRMATION AND ADOLESCENCE

Pie Chisholm recalled the next step in her sacramental incorporation into the church in the 1930s at Saint Benedict with Bishop Keyes:

> *A:* You do confirmation when you're twelve years old. I must have been. . . . I finished ninth grade when I was thirteen, so I must have been in eighth grade. During that time the bishop would only come like every two years, and we'd have a huge confirmation class for him. . . .
> *Q:* And what did you have to do to prepare for confirmation?
> *A:* Well, you'd better study real good, your catechism, because the bishop would ask you questions. . . . The bishop liked me because he and I had become personal friends. See, he lived at Cathedral and he'd walk down Harris Street, it's on Harris Street, and I'd always run out and greet him. So we were friends.
> *Q:* What did they tell you that confirmation was?
> *A:* [Don't ask me that.] It's the sacrament that made you strong, and they taught you that the Holy Spirit would come down to bring you this knowledge. . . . The sacrament that made you stronger in the faith.

This lay interpretation lies close to modern sacramental theology, again stressing the intrinsic relations of education, experience, and community:

> As a continuation and/or ratification of the Christian baptismal commitment, Confirmation expresses the essentially missionary character of the Church and its nature as the temple of the Holy Spirit. It is a community called to manifest "the spirit of wisdom and understanding, the spirit of right judgment and courage, the spirit of knowledge and reverence, . . . the spirit of wonder and awe in (God's) presence." (*Rite of Confirmation*). It is not only a sacred, grace-bearing sign for the good of the recipient, therefore, but it is also a principal moment when the Church reveals itself to itself and to the rest of the world as a particular kind of community, filled with the Holy Spirit and committed to the Spirit's release for the transformation of the whole of creation. (McBrien 1980, 757)

Despite this overall agreement on formal meaning, some confusion exists among priests and laity about what the sacrament does in practice. Confirmation is one of the most difficult sacraments to define in Catholic life, whether in the history of the black churches or the actions and understandings of the church as a whole. In general, confirmation is a rite of passage to adulthood for the adolescent initiate, ratified by the presence of the community and the bishop.

Guidelines for preparation and administration are more vague and variable today than in the past. Confirmation may now be received late, in high school or college; the priest himself confirms adult converts on reception into the church. Normally, only a bishop administers the sacrament to a group, sealing all candidates with oil and putting his hands on them or slapping them gently, evoking the presence of the Holy Spirit in a gesture that epitomizes as well the passing on of the tradition in ordination or consecration of a new bishop (Dix 1945, 125). More questions are raised about its function within the parish and life cycle.

The lack of clarity in contemporary confirmation descends from its historical relationship to the sacramental order and the life cycle as a whole. As early as the beginning of the third century, baptism and confirmation were part of the same rite in the Catholic church, a practice maintained by the Eastern Orthodox tradition (Jungmann 1959, 84-85). The separation of the two proceeded as more urgency was attributed to infant baptism and as bishops in growing communities became less likely to be present at every initiation. By the thirteenth century, confirmation was postponed until age seven, and distinctions were formalized in the early modern period. The rite became a ratification of baptism, strengthening rather than forgiving.

Adolescent preparation for confirmation focuses on preparation for adulthood through mastery of ecclesiastical knowledge (the catechism) and discussion of rights and responsibilities. Godparents are less critical at this juncture—"the Church has two sponsors for the whole group"— although individual sponsorship is permitted. The individuals also get to choose a new name, as in Baptism, generally drawn from favorite saints, family, or friends. The bishop's visit creates a short-lived cohort in the parish. Whites from other areas who associate confirmation with their high school activities suggest a framework that has been lacking for most Savannah blacks.

Confirmation as a sacrament focuses on the transitions of adolescence to adulthood. Yet as a one-time ritual with a limited impact, it does not meet the challenges facing those black youths who grow up amidst social and economic problems, whether caused by a lack of opportunity for lower classes or an abundance of opportunity for the upwardly mobile members of the parishes. These problems were discussed by members of the community and brought to public attention in a conference on parenting sponsored by Saint Anthony's in 1984, where panelists discussed difficulties in parenting and childhood present in the black community today. A male educator in his sixties noted: "Before, all cared, . . . now few reach out. Years ago we might be thirty guys on a corner. But if any parents came by, all the bad language hushed. There was respect. Now most adults are fearful and don't go out where the kids are—on the street. We stay behind our desks and our pulpits, in our coats and ties, being professional. But Jesus was always out there where the people were." This passage emphasizes the collective presence of neighbors and elders who have controlled child training within the black community. In action, discipline remains a part of the action of elders of the church who will reprimand any unruly child whether or not they have specific family authority. This same value was linked to family and religion by black educator Greer Gordon at the NOBC meetings of 1985: "It was understood that if you were acting out on a streetcorner, you would be corrected. You can't do that with black kids today? Yes you can!" (July 24, 1985) Ms. Gordon also emphasized the role this extended family and education gave to black women.

In the Saint Anthony's discussion, a male lawyer focused on middle-class concerns that he developed in contrast to his childhood need:

> It was so hot in those small homes . . . that we had to come out on the porches and the streets, so we got to know each other and formed strong neighborhood ties. Now people not only have air-conditioning that makes them stay in more, but cars to get out and about, not only around the city but families and friends are scattered all over the country. . . . It wasn't just air conditioning and cars we didn't have back then. . . . Really no one had anything much. So we had to look to God. There was nothing else to rely on, like we have our credit cards today. Because we all had nothing, there was nothing to be jealous of; whereas now, middle-class suburban life is constant competition. . . . We're both working. . . . We come home tired, so we tend to give our children nice clothes so they look good on the outside, rather than the time and attention and love that touches the heart and mind and really lasts. . . .

Other parishioners have spoken of the pains of affluence within the increasingly middle-class black parishes: lack of family time, reliance on material rewards, and isolation, or pervasive problems of modern youth, such as drugs and alcohol. In this they developed a concern for the vulnerability of youth that has preoccupied the black and Catholic bishops: "Today's youth in our Black community undergo many pressures. Especially in our urban areas—where disillusionment and despair, desires and drugs, passion and poverty entrap the young—adults and mature youth dedicated to Christ are needed to counsel, to inspire and to motivate those whom Jesus loved and placed first in his Kingdom" (Howze et al. 1984, 27).

Yet what is the meaning of confirmation in this context? In spite of the hyperbolic imagery of the bishops' vision, a parish priest I asked about confirmation summed it up: "We're afraid we're going to lose them." He added, "We need stronger youth programs; Protestant churches have more. With youth programs, we keep them in and help them choose. All I remember is a slap by the Bishop, a new name, and a party. Kids today get more."

Yet the bonds of family, school, neighborhood, and parish culture were formerly more interwoven for blacks—a gap that modern youth programs must attempt to fill. Today, when most black Catholic youths do not attend Catholic schools and many black neighborhoods are perceived as dangerous, this sacrament has become overly punctuated as a response to long-term problems. Scouting and other activities are used to maintain adolescent involvement, while the black bishops seek youth leaders as much as sacraments.

An incident at a Sunday morning mass at Saint Anthony's in 1988 evidenced continuing popular exploration of sacramental forms to meet socioeconomic challenges. During the intercessory prayers, a woman asked the congregation to join her in prayers for her teenage son and his difficulties. The theme hit home to many, and, led by the priest, they focused prayers over youths who were there and for the many who were absent. People came forward as if to an altar call, with an intense outpouring of concern, a call for a sacramental vision. Yet many of the youths prayed for were absent.

For adolescents growing up Catholic, then, Eucharist and reconciliation have been continuing parts of growth in a faith community. Confirmation, by contrast, is a unique rite of passage that demarcates changing life status. Yet as this life passage has been diffused in American society and in the black community, social challenges transcend a single transitional rite. As in the rest of the sacramental cycle, popular adaptation and theological evaluation are evoked in a crisis of faith and the world.

MARRIAGE

The mass readings of Sunday, October 6, 1985, point strongly toward discussion of marriage and sexuality. The first reading, from Genesis, establishes man and woman as partners (Genesis 2:18-24).[5] The responsorial psalm echoes the marital theme, with its refrain "May the Lord bless us all the days of our lives" (Psalm 128:5). The second (epistle) reading takes a somewhat different tone, emphasizing the issue of Jesus' divinity and humanity that permeates the Epistle to the Hebrews. Even so, the themes of suffering, of striving toward perfection, and of union with God have deep ramifications for discussion of sacramental bonds.[6]

The Gospel, finally, reemphasizes the theme of the centrality and indissolubility of Christian marriage (parentheses indicate materials which may be omitted in reading):

> Some Pharisees came up and as a test began to ask Jesus whether it was permissible for a husband to divorce his wife. In reply he said, "What command did Moses give you?" They answered, "Moses permitted divorce and the writing of a decree of divorce." But Jesus told them: He wrote that commandment for you because of your stubbornness. At the beginning of creation God made them male and female; for this reason a man shall leave his father and mother and the two of them shall become as one. They are no longer two but one flesh. Therefore let no man separate what God has joined." Back in the house again, the disciples began to question him about this. He told them, "Whoever divorces his wife and marries another commits adultery against her; and the woman who divorces her husband and marries another commits adultery."
> (People were bringing their little children to have him touch them, but the disciples were scolding them for this. Jesus became indignant when he noticed it and said to them: "Let the children come to me and do not hinder them. It is to just such as these that the kingdom of God belongs. I assure you that whoever does not accept the kingdom of God like a small child shall not enter into it." Then he embraced them and blessed them, placing his hands on them.). (Mark 10:2-12)

On that Sunday, those in Savannah's black Catholic churches where I attended mass heard sermons much more similar than the variations among congregations and leaders normally produce. Three themes dominated. First was the sacramental nature of marriage: the Catholic church considers marriage to be a sign of Christ's presence, and matrimony frequently is used as a metaphor for the relation of the church and God. This entailed specific reference to the indissolubility of marriage through divorce. "Failed" marriages arose as a second theme. These were made clear in portrayal of love and suffering as well as in the "ultimate" response of annulment,—a declaration that marriage never truly existed. Here the priests showed emotional concern for the problem of divorce and separation that have hurt not only converts but blacks within the Catholic tradition. Finally, all three priests spoke of the subordination of sexuality to Christian love. Here the presentation ranged from a more philosophical tone to direct discussion of "those of you who are shacking up." Another priest suggested that the next time he saw someone eating out in a fancy restaurant with someone who was not their spouse, he would come up and say hello. Indeed, the last sermon erupted not only into continuing comment throughout the parish but also became a topic brought up to me by members of other black parishes.

The publicity of the SMA fathers shows that a wedding at Saint Anthony's in 1913 called up a similar sermon:

> The congregation hushed in deep silence listened with a kind of religious amazement when the Rev. Gentleman, with the Bible in his hand, proved that the marriage contract has been elevated for Christianity by Jesus Christ to the dignity of a great sacrament. . . . Quite especial stress was laid by the Rev. Father on the sacred forever irrevocable character of the marriage tie as considered by the Catholic church. If once validly contracted, nothing short of death can sever that sacred bond. Nations may lawfully dissolve their treaties; merchants in companies may dissolve partnership; friends may part from each other; brothers may leave their parent's house and separate from one another but by the law of God the nuptial knot uniting husband and wife can be severed by death alone. "What God has joined together, let no man put asunder" are the words of the Lord, Matt. 19:4-9. . . .

The priest, Father Zimmerman, quoted Cardinal Gibbons to contrast the sacrament to Protestant teachings and perhaps to the social practice of his neighborhood:

> Are there some of you who think perchance the Catholic church severe on this point? If so; bear this in mind, it is not the church but our Lord who has given the law, and indeed this law is mercy itself compared with the terrible cruel consequences of the easy divorce as admitted by the Protestant denominations and governments. Think of the woeful anguish and miseries caused in families by divorce. Young children are deprived of the protection of the father or the tender care of a loving mother. Rudeness, quarrels, even adulteries are like provoked and encouraged in a dissatisfied husband or wife, as these very sins will provide a pretext for divorce. . . . (*ST* Oct. 25, 1913)

This 1913 wedding was a large and elaborate celebration before friends and family of the type idealized by most Catholics today. Nonetheless, in 1913 as in the present, homilies underlined potential contradictions of institutional values and social practice. Indeed, modern sermons had special effectiveness deriving from the awareness that divergences from stated Catholic ideals exist in the community. As one parishioner in 1985 said afterward, "It was so quiet that if a butterfly flown in you would have heard it."

Such contradictions are not necessarily more present among black Catholics than among whites. While most blacks have emerged from an economic and political history that has strained nuclear-family stability, middle-class whites and blacks both also have faced real challenges to the stability of their homes. Nonetheless, the priests to whom I listened in white middle-class parishes veered far away from the themes outlined above. One launched into a more general discussion of sacramental bonds. In another parish, the homilist focused on the optional verses of the Gospel (those concerning the children) to speak of the issues involved in the right-to-life movement. This may have reflected parish interests as much as social differences.

Teachings can also vary over time in the same parish. In 1988, using the same readings, another priest in a black parish stressed that the passages showed the equality of male and female, a point that had just been stressed in a Papal letter; he then used this to explain the sacramental cycle. He stressed, however, that one who had divorced and remarried lived in serious sin, and that one who had sex before marriage or after (apparently outside of matrimony), did so as well. The Church, however, still held out the promise of reconciliation. While I felt uncomfortable, I could not speak with congregants at the time. Nonetheless, others with whom I discussed the sermon had strong reactions. A priest flatly asked if anyone had walked out: other blacks asked if the homilist knew who he addressed. Even while questions were being raised in another parish about an ongoing divorce and remarriage, such a blanket prohibition was not well received, however based in hierarchical dogma.

Marriage, as an adult sacrament of commitment, usually affects the lives of both the cradle Catholic and the later convert. This is not to say that blacks do not join the church after marriage, divorce, and remarriage; here again, the prevalence of adult conversion alters the demography of a community that formally preaches the indissolubility of marital bonds. Nonetheless, blacks, whether raised as Catholics or converted in adolescence, often do not marry other Catholics. Thus at this critical juncture in the reproduction of the family, the social and historical contradictions to which black Catholics must respond become clear, a crisis increasingly present among white Catholics as well (Cahill 1987). Nonetheless, however critical it is in most world societies, sacramental designation of marriage and its incorporation into the life order have an ambivalent history in Catholicism. While rooted in an Old Testament view of union and regarding marriage as a symbol of man's covenant with God (Genesis 1:28; Psalm 127; Isaiah 54; see McBrien 1980, 788), the early church saw matrimony to be a less meaningful sensual state (Corinthians 7:32-35). Marriage thus prevented entrance into a holier sacramental state of the priesthood. Some later Protestant reformers denied its sacramentality, diminishing the church's authority. At Trent, however, Catholic bishops and theologians definitively affirmed the sacramentality of the ritual (McBrien 1980, 790). The theology of Vatican II in the 1960s shifted the active and interpretive focus of marriage from the wedding to the covenant, adopting love rather than ritual action as the sacramental seal of a processual bond (Abbott 1966; McBrien 1980). It became a model for the church rather than a single event in it.

Here, however, theology and praxis have an uneasy interaction. On the question of sexuality and sensuality, for example, one faces clearly different standards among communities. Even among leaders of the black parishes, jokes about desire, sex, and infidelity erupt in informal conversations. Their role is not to condone a looser sexual ethic; infidelity is strongly condemned. The graphic expression of the humor is part of a different aesthetic of laughter and fellowship (Levine 1977).

Other problems arise from the factors that may facilitate or permit continuation of marriage as process. In the early days, when the church appealed to blacks with limited opportunities in Savannah society, social

281

and economic roles conspired against long-term marital stability. Slavery frequently barred formal recognition of bonds or stabilization of the family. Later, poverty and migration disrupted families. Sporadic, unreliable, and low-paying employment condoned by segregation made it difficult to support families, as did poor housing conditions. As black Catholics have emerged as middle-class families, new pressures have been added.

United and enduring families are ideals in the black parishes, manifest in the celebration of golden anniversaries and the renewal of marital vows that become community events. In this, they are not dissimilar to other Catholic and Protestant churches. Yet broken families are very much a part of the life histories that I have heard in black and white communities. Illness and death have been consequences of employment conditions. Migration, jail, military service, and other experiences have torn apart black families. Separation and divorce also are present in the parishes, especially as priests have reached out as counselors to those who thought that such an action excluded them from the church, a particular problem in middle-class Catholics. The overriding value embodied here becomes the inclusion of the individual in the community and the building of the family even against odds.

Equally striking are the religiously divided families, where churches set boundaries. While mixed marriages of a Catholic and a Protestant might be expected in terms of adult converts, they proved equally present among scions of the oldest Catholic families. Most explained that the parish was too small to choose from. Furthermore, the parish was also only one of the communities in which blacks participated, and Catholics were a minority among urban blacks. Even Catholic elementary schools had predominantly Protestant children and parents, while high schools, colleges, workplaces, and neighborhoods were dominated by non-Catholics. Friendships formed along lines of race and neighborhood more than religion. Although some spouses convert after marriage, Catholics also join other churches.

Such a pattern would have been unusual in white ethnic parishes until the 1960s. In the experience of black Catholics as with other Catholics, ritual restrictions emphasized formal disapproval of such an arrangement. Prior to Vatican II, the couple could not marry in the church but only in the rectory. This implied that the marriage was not a complete celebration: an affair of families but not of the parish. The Catholic spouse was warned against attending the non-Catholic church and the non-Catholic spouse required to agree to raise the children as Catholics while conversion was encouraged. These pressures speak to an ecclesiastical concern with real issues of life cycle and the reproduction of community.

Yet across generations, black children experience religions other than Catholicism as practiced by grandparents, cousins, and even parents. Protestant values and customs are part of everyday life just as palm fronds and crucifixes may signal Catholic beliefs. Friends spoke of the Gospel hymns and prayers passed on by grandmothers or the celebrations of end-of-school gatherings with Protestant ministers. Compromises were worked out: one man remarked how much he liked the innovation of Saturday mass, which allowed him and his children also to attend his wife's Baptist church on Sunday. Such an arrangement would have been impermissible under older Catholic exclusivism, suggesting the depth of turmoil that conversion and choice could create.

Statistics are not available to say whether marriages in the Savannah community that is black and Catholic are more or less stable than those in other black groups or among white Catholics. What is evident instead in the black community is a more general sense of tolerance for problems that lead to divorce or of marriages that cross religious lines. A case recounted by a parishioner, whose details have been altered here somewhat because of the sensitive nature of the data, recalls the elements of judgment involved (names have been changed):

> You take Zachary Lewis. He married while he was away and brought his wife home. She weren't no Catholic but they were married in the church. Then he went North to work and she was unfaithful to him. He came back and wanted to get rid of her and marry Ellen. Father asked a council to look into it and we found out who was at fault and he was allowed to marry her.

Tolerance has limits, and flagrant infidelity is chastised by the community as a whole. Complaints roared about a man who showed up at a baptism with his wife and his "woman." A more humorous anecdote told of a woman approaching the coffin at a funeral with a group of children and announcing "Children, say goodbye to your father," shocking the widow and congregation. The underlying theme of the discussion was that sins in life, however well concealed, would come up and hurt the family after death.

Marriage vows, finally, stress reproduction through children "as God so provides." Black and Catholic family size seems to reflect general Catholic and middle-class tendencies toward two or three children, with a notable decrease in recent generations. While families reached nine or ten in the past, this did not distinguish black from white or Catholics from Evangelicals. Today, unwed mothers provide a point of concern in the black community which Catholics share; as Deacon Prince Jackson noted, Savannah ranks extremely high in its rate of teenage pregnancy. In one parish, the weekly bulletin announced all births, congratulating the mother regardless of her status, until concerned elders suggested to the white priest that this might be sending the wrong message. This parish has since sponsored meetings on teen pregnancy and similar topics. Yet those who have had children outside of marriage seem to be accepted if they raise the children well. In general, children are regarded as good and valuable.[7]

Marriage—in theology, sacramentality, and practice—is clearly valued in black and Catholic communities as part of their society, culture, and faith. But the definition of marriage balances ideals against old and new pressures on the family that spring from the economic and social situation in which blacks in Savannah encounter themselves. Their realization of marriage as a sacrament and as a symbol of the church has been creative and complex.

ILLNESS, DEATH, AND FUNERALS

As in the case of other life transitions, death evokes ritual, shared community action, and individual response, for which Catholicism prescribes proper religious forms. While the Mass of the Resurrection holds to long-established forms, other aspects of the funeral process have changed in the theological reassessments since Vatican II. Shared secular behaviors have also evolved, most notably in the citywide decline of the home wake for the deceased. While nearly universal in both black and white communities through the mid-twentieth century, this practice has declined in favor of the church or professional funeral home and has almost disappeared in the last decade. As with other sacraments, nonetheless, the interweaving of ritual practice and collective action most clearly defines the black and Catholic community.

The presence of illness and potential death is part of the fabric of black contact and information in Savannah, both inside and outside of church. Health is as common a topic in conversations as any scandals, news events, or shared projects. A litany of information and complaints ranging from blood pressure or sugar level to chronic problems flows freely around the table, in meetings, or via telephone networks. The dominance of the elders and the strong connections across generations further emphasize this topic in everyday speech; it is invariably a primary feature of every return I make to Savannah, reincorporating me into news and thus into community.

When a health situation becomes serious, parishioners bring it more vividly to the community in the shared prayers of the liturgy, which remind all who attend of those who are chronically ill or shut-in. Special prayers from the pulpit or from congregants highlight immediate crises, operations or accidents. These prayers also bring information to the general congregation about relatives and neighbors outside the parish itself and stimulate further discussion on the church steps. All three predominantly black parishes also have prayer lines, church members who unite to pray for special intentions and to call others to do so. This system unites the parish and disseminates information, especially among the females of the community who control it.

Visiting the sick is an obligation enshrined in Catholic teachings. Priests and deacons make regular visits to hospitals and "shut-ins," bringing the Eucharist with them to bind the sick person to the community. Lay ministers of communion aid in this task; one parish ceremonializes this participation with a special blessing for such ministers after the Sunday liturgy. Lay organizations took on this task from the early days of the church, as I have noted.

Visiting is also familiar and social. When Pie was rushed to the emergency room in 1987, this called forth her network of family and friends from around the country. Arrangements had to be made to notify those in other cities and host them during their visits. Since the hospital lies miles away from the city core, ride-sharing and daily reports were constant necessities, even as visitors crowded her room. Priests from other black parishes; nuns from the hospital; her former employers; relatives from Massachusetts, Florida, and South Carolina; neighbors and friends were brought together in the hospital and the home. These reunions were underscored by joint prayers led by a priest or deacon, as well as continual iteration at liturgy and through individual prayers. A home mass was celebrated around the dining room table, with friends and family, when she finally left the hospital.

In the past, the segregated structure of hospital care would have changed such health crises. Until the 1960s, Savannah blacks were barred as patients in white hospitals, probably including the Roman Catholic institution. Alternative institutions were closely tied to the history of the black community. The Georgia Infirmary, founded in 1832 by a wealthy white disgusted by his fellow citizens' treatment of slaves, was the oldest hospital for blacks in the United States. A black husband-wife team of physicians founded Charity Hospital in 1893 in prestigious Brownville; they sponsored nursing education and public health as well. These institutions were secular, although sustained by contributions from black religious and civic organizations. Blacks mentioned that whites might visit, yet this seems uncommon in white recollections. Both facilities were underfunded and antiquated by the 1960s and closed rapidly as blacks gained access to government, religious, and commercial hospitals. Most Catholics, black and white, favor Saint Joseph's, administered by the Sisters of Mercy. Religion more than race determines the cultures of care, although patients follow their doctors and must face economic limits on their options.

Care can be conceived of in both physical and spiritual terms. Prior to the Vatican II, sacramental theology focused on death and funerals: extreme unction was a prelude to the end that could inspire fear in the recipient by its very finality. Catholics have since amplified their perception of this transition to encompass both illness and healing. Theologians now insist on the transformation of the sacrament into the anointing of the sick as a recognition of suffering and healing. It becomes a sign more generally, and less ominously, administered. A 1972 catechism noted the shift:

> As soon as the sickness takes a grave turn, the priest should be called
> to anoint the sick. This is often put off too long, for fear of frightening
> the sick person. But the administration of the anointing of the sick
> does not mean that certain death is impending. It means that there is a
> possibility of death, perhaps only very slight. Very often, on receiving
> this sacrament, the sick person actually experiences a revival of
> strength. As well as being a preparation for death, the sacrament may
> in fact be a preparation for life. (*New Catechism* 1972, 469)

Preparation for life is now emphasized by more frequent anointing during an illness. Communal healing services in times of spiritual preparation such as Advent and Lent underscore the connection of renewal of the body and renewal of the spirit. These rites often suggest links between traditional sacraments and modern charismatic Catholicism.

When a death occurs, multiple networks and leaders must respond. Key rituals are controlled by the priest and deacon and entail conferences among the families, the professional undertaker, and the clergy in order to secure proper use of facilities such as the funeral parlor, the church, and the cemetery. Older female leaders provide background knowledge and family connections, especially if someone is being returned to the parish after living elsewhere. Rituals tend to be standardized with certain minimal variations (expense, choice of hymns, sermon) that echo variations evident in other areas. There are clear distinctions throughout between black Catholic and black Protestant services: the former are characterized by their liturgical structure, as well by their more subdued emotional tone. Racial distinctions are structured by segregated institutions and networks—funeral homes, churches, families, and neighborhoods—as well as by Savannah custom.

As planning continues, community involvement widens. Leaders telephone others in the community soon after the actual death. These, in turn, inform their networks; women dominate this flow of information. As the news ripples through the community, conversations detail causes and life history and often compare the deceased with others. Schedules must be communicated to the choir and the general community, while other calls assemble food, flowers, and money.

In the time of the home wake, family and friends sat with the body until its removal to the church and eventual burial, while food, drink, and memories were shared through the night. This disappeared decades ago among whites and more slowly among blacks in favor of funeral homes. Saint Benedict's has held no home wakes with the body present since 1982. The wake in Savannah, as in other areas of the Christian world, was a way of uniting the family and friends as both a memorial unit and an ongoing community. Because of the general social patterns of the city, these tended toward segregation, although black clients and servants would mourn separately in a white family, and even antebellum whites recognized major black public figures such as Reverend Andrew Marshall. Funeral homes today reaffirm segregations found in life; their clientele in Savannah remain largely divided on the basis of race and class. Jews and white ethnic Catholics have been strong enough to support funeral homes identified primarily with their denominations, although these homes generally served all whites. Black Catholics relied for years on a fellow black Catholic who ran a funeral home but did not devote himself to Catholics alone. Today, they share the major and predominantly Protestant black funeral homes; and these homes in turn advertise in weekly church bulletins (see Baer 1984, 171). Only for cremation are blacks forced to cross racial barriers to a white undertaker, although this process is frowned upon in the general black population and especially among Catholics.

The tenure of the body in the funeral home allows final viewing and meetings with the assembled family. Apart from more individual visits, there will also be a communal gathering to pray the rosary under the guidance of the clergy. In the past, the rosary marked all Catholic funerals with its repeated prayers and responses, clearly distinguishing Catholic and non-Catholic funerals. More recently, the rosary has been diminished as the primary prayer—only one decade (ten Hail Marys) was recited at a recent funeral—while the service has been augmented by a general Catholic liturgical wake service. After the evening rosary, the family may still provide food and refreshments for those who have attended.

The Mass of Christian Burial, generally the day after the evening rosary, brings everyone together in the church. This ceremony is directed more toward the family and community than toward the deceased, who is presumed to have already been taken up to God. Hence its theme is resurrection, and its liturgical color is a triumphant white rather than the red of suffering or the purple of mourning. Readings and songs reaffirm this belief.

In a typical mass I attended, resurrection permeated ritualization of the passage for family and community. The closed coffin, draped in white, was accompanied into the church by pallbearers drawn from senior males of the parish. The family and representatives of organizations to which the decedent belonged followed the casket and sat at the front of the church alongside the casket, which rested in front of the altar. The sermon spoke of the importance of the deceased for the community, relying on the black deacon's personal experience as a lifelong member of the community. Speakers linked the deceased member to ancestral participation of the family in the congregation, to other more recent deaths in the extended family, and to the continuation of the presence of the family in the future of the church. Children and grandchildren were addressed as both inheritors and future builders, and transitions in family leadership were emphasized within the continuity of generations. The congregation was referred to gospel admonitions to be prepared for death. Combined elements of all church choirs led the congregation in response to these themes with hymns including "Amazing

288

Grace" and "Blessed Assurance" as the service ended with communion and the distribution of mass cards, small remembrances containing photos or devotional pictures and prayers. The coffin was blessed with holy water and incense and left the church amidst family and friends for the cemetery, where a short service would be held. Overall, the emotional tone of the ritual is restrained in contrast to more charismatic black denominations, stereotypes of "black" events.

Black Catholics have a paradoxical position with regard to such black Protestant funerals. They attend them with frequency because of family, school, neighborhood, and professional ties within their segregated communities. Some who are black and Catholic enjoy the emotional release of the alternative format; others shun its prayers and shouting. Family lore is rich with stories of such funerals, which distance Catholic and non-Catholic. One speaker, for example, characterized Baptist funerals as "remarks from neighbors, deacons, church workers, friends. . . . They also pass resolutions that they will not forget the family and acknowledge all telegrams and important letters. Sometimes if there are not many they read cards, read all the verses. . . . Some people go to see what kind of show the family puts on." A humorist in another parish remarked: "I'll be happy with what Father says and no more. I don't need no neighbor saying like one did 'I don't care how much Sallie drank, or how many men she had, or how often she stayed out late and didn't come back till 6 A.M. She was good by me.'"

Some Catholics internalize a marking ideology by characterizing rural black funerals by "superstitious" behavior. Passing all the children over the coffin so that the spirit will not come back for them was cited as one example, sparking a discussion of calling the spirits of children out of the home when a family moves (see Morrison's *Beloved* 1987).[8] Even though blacks identified these actions with "primitive blacks," I later found other Catholics who knew about these traditions and practiced them. Funeral stories as folklore also deal with problems of community: divided families, people who have alienated themselves from the parish, and conspicuous display.

From the funeral, the body is taken to the cemetery, which embodies a final remembrance of institutional segregation, metaphoric division, and municipal neglect of the city's black heritage. The black section of the Colonial Cemetery, for example, was paved over and is now a playground; Laurel Grove, which replaced this burial ground in the nineteenth century, maintained divisions between races. Other small black burial grounds were sponsored by outlying settlements such as Woodville and Sandfly (Georgia Writers' Project 1940), or represent limited and undercapitalized commercial efforts. These also represent a legacy of Creole belief evident in the African figures found in a cemetery in nearby Liberty County. In contrast, the Catholic cemetery, founded in 1850, has been integrated for some decades, with some demarcation of a distinct racial section. Nonetheless, because of the continuity of family in burial and memory, many black Catholic converts join their Protestant ancestors in older, segregated cemeteries.

The idea of a shared community meal after the funeral, provided for the family and those who attend the funeral, emerged in Saint Benedict's and more recently in Saint Mary's as an extension and completion of the funeral process. In Saint Benedict's, this event began roughly a decade ago when the death of a member who lived in a small house forced the movement of the traditional post-funeral reception to the parish hall. In time, this reception was transformed into a parish-oriented event, replacing home meetings. Saint Mary's only began to follow this practice after 1986. It is not practiced at Saint Anthony's, nor is it found in white Catholic churches of the city. Similar events appear among black Protestants, generally, as in the case of Saint Mary's, under the sponsorship of a formal organization.

Such a meal provides a banquet selection of food associated with almost all collective meals at the parish. Turkey, ham, and fried chicken are the major meats. Green beans, potato salad, red rice, and rolls are the major accompaniments; iced tea, soft drinks, and pies or cakes complete the meal. None are particularly associated with death, although red rice is jokingly referred to as "funeral food" by some, since it is a substantial preparation suitable for any large gathering. At Saint Benedict's, all contributions are provided by members of the community who are generally within the network of the organizer of the meal rather than having particular associations with the family itself. In such circumstances, alcohol would only be served if the family or a church group provided it. Those who contribute to the meal are not expected to send flowers or money to the family as others will. Those who have gone to the cemetery return to the parish hall in thirty to forty-five minutes. The buffet meal begins after a short blessing by the priest, its only purely religious aspect. The family is not set apart; instead, individual members mingle with friends throughout the hall. All depart after the meal.

Figure 18. A black rural cemetery showing African influences, Liberty County. Photograph courtesy of the Georgia Historical Society, M. H. and D. B. Floyd Collection.

The meal does not erase the deceased from the community; condolence calls continue for weeks as the news travels. Anniversary masses and memorials in association with specific events may continue for years after the death. Advertisements in the program for choir concerts and special church events commonly recall deceased family members. The anniversary announcements frequent in local black newspapers, however, are rare among Catholics.

Within parishes, variation among funerals depends upon the size and wealth of the deceased's family, the participation of the decedent and family in the church congregation, and the time and circumstances of the death. Registered persons without family connections will be given a full burial, even in cases in which neither community members nor the priest actually know them. In such circumstances, community loss and response are minimal: few attend and no meal is served. In a sudden or unexpected death, especially when the victim is young, the disruption becomes more serious, and ritual assemblies to reconstitute the community intensify.

Passages from life to death to resurrection mark the final stage in a social and religious representation of the life cycle. As in other elements of praxis among those who are black and Catholic, the demarcation of this transition combines a seemingly universal and hierarchical religion with innovations and traditions of the community as a whole. The innovations of the community should not simply be regarded as continuities with a black cultural (Protestant) tradition even though they may partake of elements of these traditions, especially in the most general sense of the valuation of family as a cornerstone of community. Funeral meals, for example, are a specific response innovated by the laity within the context of the individual parish; other developments emerge from those informed by attendance at other Protestant or Catholic funerals. Sacraments are explored and expanded by *use* as they deal with profound questions of life and death.

The ritual life cycle that defines a Roman Catholic is an intrinsic part of a universal yet exclusive faith community and a logic of meaning in that universe. Nonetheless, historical circumstances, individual experience, and communal traditions have transformed these key symbols within the social and religious community of those who are black and Catholic in Savannah. From the dramatic disparities of baptism to the local and intimate differences among shared funeral conditions, black Catholics define a distinct world of vision and action. In all this, a sacramental imagination represents and reaffirms as it evokes individual and collective responses.

As this analysis has suggested, sacraments in practice have often been faced by deep social problems in the black community that preclude simple adoption of foreign norms of family and reproduction. These ideals may be too much or, indeed, too little in failing to recognize the tensions of youth or the valuation of the extended family. They may coincide with other blacks and Catholics, as in marriage, or follow different paths that become evident in the events surrounding funerals. Invented traditions have been tested, adapted, and changed. Sacraments thus become concrete statements both of community and of faith, formed in response to contradictions. White Georgian Flannery O'Connor expressed this dichotomy in a letter to a friend: "I think the Church is the only thing that is going to make the terrible world we are coming to endurable; the only thing that makes the Church endurable is that it is somehow the body of Christ." She concluded, "It seems to be a fact that you have to suffer as much from the Church as for it but if you believe in the divinity of Christ, you have to cherish the world at the same time you struggle to endure it" (1979, 90)

As black and Catholic communities have developed over time, changing and questioning, their members have experienced Catholicism as a continuing foundation and as a challenge, as a social experience in the world and an imagination of how the world comes to be. This same dialectic underlies the Eucharist as the heart of black and Catholic faith.

8. The Eucharist: Worship, Belief, and Variation

Tantum ergo Sacramentum
Veneremu cernui et antiquum documentum
Novo cedat ritui Praestet fides supplumentum
Sensuum defectui.
(Come adore this wondrous presence
Bow to Christ the source of Grace. Here is kept the ancient promise
Of God's earthly dwelling place. Sight is blind before God's glory
Faith alone may see his face.)

—Lead Me, Guide Me:
The African American Catholic Hymnal

In the midst of our discussion of relations of black Catholics and Protestants in a time of liturgical changes, a highly educated Saint Mary's parishioner finally brought her own belief into our very social-scientific framework: "Shouting and screaming doesn't provide me peace of God. It does not satisfy my mind. I need to go to mass." When she, along with other Catholics, assemble in their churches for mass, they participate in a relatively worldwide ceremony that now takes many forms and has existed in continuous yet changing practice for centuries. The Second Vatican Council eloquently reaffirmed that:

> The liturgy is the summit toward which the activity of the church is directed; at the same time it is the fountain from which all her power flows. For the goal of apostolic works is that all who are made sons of God by faith and baptism should come together to praise God in the midst of His Church, to take part in her sacrifice, and to eat the Lord's supper. (Constitution on Sacred Liturgy, in Abbott 1966, 142)

For those with whom I have worked in Savannah, as in the formal texts and institutions of the Catholic church, the presentation of Jesus in the Bible, and belief in the physical presence of Christ in the Eucharist are central to the definition of Roman Catholicism. Every Roman Catholic has the formal obligation to attend the mass each Sunday, participating in the visible unity of the church, and to receive communion at least once each year, partaking of the representational meal. In practice, a less frequent reception of the Eucharist within consistent attendance at mass of earlier centuries has been replaced since the Second Vatican Council by much more frequent reception of the Eucharist with decreasing attendance. In a typical weekend in Savannah as well as other areas across the country where I have attended church, nearly all those who attend any Catholic parish receive communion. On the other hand, post-Conciliar Catholics feel less compelled to attend *each* Sunday, even if absences may be commented on by priests and fellow Catholics (McNally 1987). Yet Eucharist remains the most powerful public act of unity of the Catholic church as a "universal" body, as a parish, and as a source of contrasting identity vis-à-vis other Sunday meetings.

Amidst the many social and cultural contradictions traced so far, the Eucharist offers black and Catholic participants a key symbol of belief and unity. At the same time, this sacramental vision distinguishes them from non-Catholics, especially low-church denominations of the South.

Until the reforms of the Second Vatican Council, this ritual manifested a different form that seemed even more enduring and universal to its participants. The priest turned his back to the congregation and spoke Latin, intervening between laity and God. With everyone quietly facing the altar, the focus of the act gazed beyond the community to transcendence in time, space, and power. Uniformity and sacred power were stressed throughout the Catholic world. The deliberations of Vatican II in the 1960s permitted more decentralization, localization, and flexibility in the mass. Biblical readings still are standardized in a yearly calendar, and authorities approve the texts of ritual prayers, but the liturgy of the Eucharist and revitalized liturgy of the word are now said in local vernaculars. Music, settings, and participation follow local norms. The priest faces the people and shares in worship instead of acting as a conduit for it. The laity have gained new roles and participation. Reform has extended to exploration of identities and adaptations drawn from the many groups that constitute the widespread history and experience of Catholicism in the modern world (Dolan 1987; Greeley 1967).

Thus in 1984 the black and Catholic bishops of the United States responded collectively to Pope Paul VI's injunction to the Catholics of Africa to "give your gifts of Blackness to the whole church" (Howze et al. 1984, 3). They echoed the eloquent affirmation of the Second Vatican Council that began this chapter by special reference to Eucharist in the black community:

> In the African-American tradition the communal experience of worship has always had a central position. In our heritage the moment of celebration has always been a time for praise and thanksgiving, and the affirmation of ourselves as God's children. It is a moment of profound expression, not a flight from reality (as some have suggested), but an experience of God's power and love. (Howze et al. 1984, 30)

These bishops, moreover, evoked special traits which to them have defined a black and Catholic spirituality, including a deep love of contemplative and spontaneous prayer (8); a joy of expression (9-10) and a communitarian approach (10). For them, the liturgy unites all into the history of salvation and the historical experience of African Americans, expressing

> the mystery of Christ which transcends all cultures. The way, however, in which this mystery is expressed is mediated by the culture and traditions of the participants. All people should be able to recognize themselves when Christ is presented, and all should be able to experience their own fulfillment when these mysteries are celebrated. Hence, we can legitimately speak of an Afro-American cultural idiom or style in music, in preaching, in bodily expression, in artistic furnishings, and even in tempo. (31)

The complexity of an African-American heritage becomes evident in the practice and interpretation of liturgy in Savannah's black and Catholic parishes. No self-consciously African innovations have been adopted in these parishes, although congregations have adapted practices from Protestant churches and from other Catholic practices. More crucial elements of the liturgy have been defined as everyday behavior by local participants who themselves embody cultural tradition and social processes beyond the strictures of a sacramental church. Who one sits with, how signs of peace are exchanged, which people offer public prayers, or the enthusiasm generated by music, among other details of liturgical practice, constitute significant links among individuals, communities, and history.

Ironically, participants may not perceive their parish difference so much as they believe in their unity with a larger Catholic tradition. The strength of parish commitment reinforces an appearance of universality and immutability in the parish mass to this day that transcends Vatican II reforms. Since people and priests rarely attend other churches, mass as practiced within the parish becomes the norm; only vague evaluations characterize other congregations. Indeed, criticisms by those who visit other parishes usually focus on setting or people more than the liturgy.

Nor are Catholics forced to articulate the theology and beliefs that underlie the Eucharist and its presence within their community. Eucharist is lived in the parish rather than contemplated scientifically. This absence of reflection on that which is everyday and yet transcendent also has an impact on the evaluation of orthodoxy. Ideally, Catholic belief embodies the same unity as liturgy, dogma made concrete in the creed spoken by all in the mass. Authorities in church have demanded correct knowledge, belief, and spiritual state to participate in the ritual. Mass, furthermore, synthesizes Biblical readings, teaching, discussion, and expression of belief. While mass has not encompassed the whole of Catholic teachings, it presents the essence of both ritual and belief for Catholics, black or white. The presumption seems clear, as well, that those who attend share in this knowledge and belief.

Yet belief systems also follow changes in worship. Since the 1960s, the belief once made rigid by rote catechisms has opened to dialogues. Thus, worship and belief in black and Catholic Savannahians come to embody all the variety and challenges of the community as well as all the gifts and questions individuals bring to their parish.

As in previous chapters, however, it would be a mistake to counterpose a monolithic pre-Vatican II Catholicism to a democratic present. Despite the formal and official unity of the mass, parishes long maintained local traditions of feasts and worship, where priests and people introduced flexibility. The southern Catholic church as a whole, as McNally has noted (1987), has been shaped by mission settings, poverty, and anti-Catholicism. Furthermore, laity have faced a tension between accessible devotions and the mystery of the mass, epitomized in the tableau of isolated congregants saying their private rosary during mass in the prereform church or even by a solitary priest saying mass with only an altar server to respond. Vatican II has tended to draw everyone into the *same* practice even as it challenged them to learn and to think more about their individual response to God in worship.

To talk of worship and belief is to talk of the core of Catholic identity. Analysis of this core is fraught with difficulties that must be recognized from the onset. My personal participation and belief always coexisted with the experience and observations I discussed with others. Our common faith and practice established a shared ground of action and experience that proved difficult for me to challenge. Work with students who never before attended a Catholic service has provided other insights as have the comments of my wife, Cindy Wong, and of Jon Anderson and Gwen Neville, with whom I have subsequently worked on general issues of southern and Catholic life. These have interrogated my roles as both informant and analyst and have clarified some of the ambiguities of this arena. (Anderson 1992; McDonogh 1992; Neville 1992; McDonogh and Wong in press).

At the same time, my beliefs are idiosyncratic; thus I appreciate individualism in the rest of the congregation: personal, inchoate, and shifting within public action. Moreover, public action, including reception of communion, entails many personal meanings. On the whole, I have analyzed belief as public action, while pursuing voices and commentaries that continue to show how individuals in these communities understand their lives and worship. But Eucharist is also a mystery of the church (see Kennedy 1988).

This chapter begins with an analysis of the basic history and structure of the mass as a historical phenomenon. While it may be repetitive for some, these details are fundamental to the understanding of history and adaptation in black Catholicism. The chapter then narrows to consideration of the Mass in the black experience, using two areas where historical documentation is adequate to consider long-term conscious adaptation—music and preaching. These themes also enrich the discussion of leadership and adaptation explored in previous chapters. On this basis, I return to black and Catholic liturgy as public celebration in terms of local parish customs in which the Eucharist is a key scenario of community. The chapter closes with comments from subjects who go further in their statement of Eucharist, community, and belief.

THE EUCHARIST AND CATHOLIC TRADITION

Even within the sacramental order, Eucharist holds a special place. Eucharist gives thanks by reenacting the sacrifice of Jesus chartered by culturally valued texts about the Last Supper. It is the sacrament shared most frequently by all Catholics and the most widespread within the church while being a primary continuing area of change. The Liturgy of the Eucharist refers only to part of the action of the Mass as a whole within the classic ritual framework of separation, liminal experience of *communitas,* and reincorporation elaborated by Victor Turner (1967). The Mass begins with the Liturgy of the Word, centered on the Bible and sermon. Both primary foci are framed by rites of separation and penance and by rites of closure. Other facets of the Mass encourage individual prayer, solidarity, offering, and connection with the divine, binding the priest and congregation.

The Passover meal, adapted by Jesus and early Christians from their Jewish tradition, formed the core of the Eucharist in the early church. A Catholic theologian summarizes the interpretation of biblical texts as to the origin and meaning of the Eucharist:

> In the Oriental world of his day, a shared meal was always a sign of peace, trust and communality. Jesus, of course, proclaimed the Kingdom by sharing meals with outcasts, tax-collectors and the like. But this last meal was special. According to the Synoptics it was a ritual Passover meal, a festive farewell meal. Whether it was a Passover meal or not (John says otherwise), it had the same basic structure: the words over the bread, its breaking and sharing; the words over the wine, its breaking and its sharing. But Jesus identified the bread and wine with his own body and blood. And sensing his own impending death he speaks of himself as a sacrifice. . . . All four texts agree that Jesus' death is an atonement and establishes a new Covenant. . . .
>
> With the resurrection the disciples now see the last supper and their own subsequent meals together in a new light. . . . The new fellowship is now characterized by an eschatological joy, a fundamental confidence in the coming of the Kingdom. (Acts of the Apostles 2:46; McBrien 1980, 758-59)

In early centuries, Christians maintained the idea of the meal at which stories were shared and the Passover reenacted (see Feeley-Harnik 1981; Meeks 1983). The establishment of a religious bureaucracy and the formalization of ritual spaces later emphasized a more symbolic, hierarchical enactment. By the Middle Ages, the priest, as celebrant, turned to the altar in the front of the church and reenacted the meal in an almost unheard soliloquy. Renewal of the table as the center of the community was critical to 1960s liturgical reforms.

Prayers have been elaborated and altered over centuries in many different ways, but the same key acts and themes dominate the experience that contemporary Catholics have had of both Tridentine and more recent liturgical forms.[1] The mass begins with a separation from the world outside the liturgy, including prayer and fasting before one arrives at the church. Prior to the 1960s, sacramental cleansing from serious transgressions (penance) and a total fast from midnight were required to receive communion, although not merely to attend mass. These requirements have lessened in recent years, although prayer, occasional fasting, and reflection are found in practice and expected by laws.

On entering the church, congregants genuflect—a brief kneeling facing the place where the sacrament is stored—and sit or kneel to pray. People also mark off this time as separate with special clothes and attitudes, an examination of conscience or a time for reflection. Family unity is also encouraged; families sit together in pews when possible.

The actual inauguration of the liturgy—and the separation of its participants from the secular order—is expressed by sound and movement.

Figure 19. A Pre-Vatican II church interior: the Cathedral of Saint John the Baptist, ca. 1950. Photograph courtesy of the Georgia Historical Society, Cordray-Foltz Collection.

Bells, which may have already announced the onset of the mass to the wider neighborhood, call everyone to stand. Vatican II has encouraged music in order to exhort participation by all assembled. With the entrance song, the priest moves to the altar, often accompanied by altar servers, readers, and a deacon.

When these authorities are assembled around the altar, opening greetings and prayers are initiated. In the past, the priest led the congregation, facing the altar, and the limited responses followed rather than addressed him. The modern opening dialogue joins the priest and the people: "The Lord be with you" (priest) / "And also with you" (others). All mark themselves with the sign of the cross. After this, the priest calls everyone to reflection and repentance, epitomized in the penitential rite (*Confiteor*), which admits sin to God and the community and asks the prayers of the Virgin Mary, angels and saints, and people assembled in the church. Congregants may strike their breasts as a sign of repentance, but this practice has diminished since the eclipse of the Latin liturgy.

A final acclamation, asking God for mercy (*Kyrie*) is followed by opening prayers led by the celebrant. Other rites appear seasonally to augment this period of preparation, such as the inclusion of a blessing with water, recalling baptism. The *Gloria,* an early Christian prayer maintained as part of the church, may also be said by the whole congregation before the opening prayer. (This prayer and the *Alleluia* are suppressed during the penitential seasons of Advent and Lent). After this prayer, everyone sits.

In this liturgy, language has also divided the sacred and the secular. Latin was a mysterious language, especially to early black converts who had no experience with European Catholic traditions. Roman Catholic education until the 1970s included both rudimentary religious theory and Latin, although these classes facilitated only limited participation. A 1911 announcement for Saint Benedict's, for example, noted that "Every member should be provided with a prayer book containing, beside the usual prayers of the mass and of the day, the epistles and gospels of every Sunday and Feast day of the year. . . . Let everyone come in possession of a 'Veil of Heaven' or of a 'Manual of Prayers' which can be purchased at any Catholic book store at a very moderate sum" (*ST* Jan. 23, 1911). The absence of secondary education for blacks, however, appeared to sustain opponents' charges that missionaries offered empty pomp and mystery. Black and white Catholics participated with missal and private devotions within the ambience of the ritual. Today, although English is used, its cadences and vocabulary differentiate it as "religious language."

The first part of the ritualized space and time created by the opening rites is devoted to teaching, reading from sacred texts, and preaching upon them. Prior to Vatican II, readings tended to concentrate on special texts, including nonscriptural writings within the Catholic tradition. Reforms have emphasized the centrality of the Bible to Catholic belief and worship. Today, readings follow a three-year cycle shared with some Protestant denominations, which annually retell the life of Jesus from Advent (preparation) to Christmas (birth), through ministry, and end with Easter (resurrection), and the establishment of the church. The rest of the year is devoted to important lessons; most of the Bible is covered in daily readings through the cycle. Special feasts include veneration of the Virgin Mary, the limited contemporary repertoire of saints—minimally observed in black parishes—and secular events such as Mother's Day, Father's Day, the Fourth of July, and Thanksgiving.

The relation of text and Eucharist remains in flux. Savannah theologians, for example, have encouraged balancing the lectern or pulpit and the altar so that neither is clearly central but both, together, constitute the sacred space. Priests and people generally weigh Eucharist more heavily than the Word. Indeed, priests in black parishes generally descend from the sanctuary to deliver the homily in front of, but amidst, the congregation. This subordination of Bible to Eucharist is more noticeable at daily masses that lack elaborate homilies.

Three selections are read in each Sunday liturgy; two are used during the week. The first reading usually comes from the Old Testament; the congregation or choir responds with a psalm. The second reading draws on New Testament epistles. Both of these are commonly read today by trained lay members of the congregation. After another prayer (*Alleluia*), the ordained priest or deacon reads the Gospel selection. All stand during this reading and are then seated for the sermon, generally some ten to fifteen minutes in length.

After the sermon, all again stand to recite the creed. This text, usually memorized, embodies early decrees of the Christian church and some subsequent modifications. Catholics may use either the Nicene Creed or the shorter Apostle's Creed. Congregants recapitulate Old and New Testament salvation history, the life and nature of Jesus Christ, the nature of the Trinity, and the role of the church and voice their commitment to belief in a collective fashion. The Liturgy of the Word closes with intercessory prayers, where spontaneous petitions augment shared prayers of the diocese. In total, the Liturgy of the Word usually lasts

302

thirty to forty minutes. While shorter in daily liturgy, special feasts also can last longer: the Easter Vigil, with its adult baptisms, and receptions into the church may use ten readings, and lasts for hours.

Music again announces the second major section, the Liturgy of the Eucharist. The movement of "gifts" toward the altar highlights attention toward the sacrifice to take place. In the old Mass, gifts would have been epitomized by the bread and wine alone, while ushers collected money from the congregation, who also responded with offerings of belief. Today parish members often march forward with eucharistic materials as well as monetary collections to be put in the sacred space.

At this point, the ritual intensifies both separation and sanctification, led by the priest. His prayers are joined by the standing congregation. After a second introductory dialogue, the priest begins the Eucharistic prayer, already analyzed in part in previous chapters. After his initial prayer, the people offer an exclamation of praise (the *Sanctus*, Preface Acclamation, or "Holy, Holy, Holy"; in the older Mass, choirs took responsibility for many parts that the congregation now speaks).

The accepted Eucharistic prayers go back to the early centuries of the church (Dix 1945; Jungmann 1959; McBrien 1980). People kneel in silent reverence, broken by their acclamation of faith; bells mark the holiness of these moments for Catholics as faces turn toward the raised bread and wine. The priest prays for the church and the world, ending with the bread and wine held high and a simple acclamation of Trinitarian faith.

At this point, the people rejoin the dialogue of the liturgy, beginning with their assent, "Amen." All then stand, praying "Our Father" together in preparation to receive communion. A call to make peace through word or gesture emphasizes the communal nature of preparation. In Savannah, as in other areas, this has been a contested innovation from Vatican II. Older white informants in particular avoid this action, a reticence that black Catholics may interpret as racist. My experience in white parishes in Savannah and elsewhere in the United States suggests that diffidence is the norm. Black Savannah parishes, by contrast, enthusiastically have adopted it.

After the sign of peace, penitential prayers *(Agnus Dei /* Lamb of God) and kneeling reemphasize preparation. At this point, those who wish to receive communion are prepared to do so. In older days, this entailed moving forward and kneeling at the communion rail of the church, touching the bread only with the tongue. Today, with more frequent communion, people tend to line up and receive communion standing, often taking it in their hands. Breadlike wafers or bread are used, with wine recommended for all in special liturgies. After receiving, communicants return to their pews and kneel in prayer. Catholics perceive this moment as one of intense union with God and community.

After all have received communion, the altar is cleared and the remaining Eucharistic bread removed to the Tabernacle. Priests and people sit; a song or period of reflection follows. Closing is perhaps the most deemphasized aspect of the liturgy. In older days, a second Gospel reading from John marked the ending rite. Now, Mass tends to wind down with prayers, a blessing of the people by the priest, including a marking with the sign of the cross, and a dismissal blessing. General announcements are also thrown in. A closing song and procession, echoing the beginning, signal that people return to the outside world, where families may greet the priest or each other. Some parishes encourage socializing through coffee, others schedule parish activities: both are strong traditions in black churches.

This ritual holds rich meanings for Catholics developed in academic study as well as individual interpretation. Purity and otherworldliness are emphasized by the separation aspects of the ritual, as community is stressed in shared prayers and reliance on others ("I confess to Almighty God and to you my brothers and sisters. . . . I ask Blessed Mary ever Virgin, all the angels and saints and you my brothers and sisters to pray for me to the Lord our God"). Since Vatican II, movement and communication also stress unity, as God and human beings are represented as united in the special presence of Jesus.

Yet this community is not one of equality, despite democratizing reforms. The priest acts as patriarch around the altar-table. This relationship portrays—but obviously as a metaphor—the Catholic mythical relationship of God and humankind. Women and laymen enter the sanctuary space, but their roles remain subordinate. Finally, divisions of insider/outsider and good/bad are rehearsed through the ritual. These are bridged through acceptance into the community (baptism imagery) and forgiveness (penance imagery) which permeate the Mass.

The Mass brings together meaning and knowledge, tradition and experience for Catholics. Just as some recall nostalgically the mystery of the Tridentine liturgy, others find rich meaning in continuing quests. A woman in her twenties explained to me: "I want people to dance, sing, be happy, A few tears. Father Jim takes us further: we laugh. He made me laugh, cry, feel good." This search entails adaptation to the social and symbolic experience of those who constitute the church. While much of everyday life goes unrecorded, the "ordinary" development of universal rituals can be documented through two areas of congregational and priestly history that suggest the complex formation of modern parochial personalities.

MUSIC AND PREACHING

Music has been a realm of continuous interest in the Catholic church for centuries, although centered in ritual elaboration and participation rather than the social constitution of church as community. That is, parishioners were more often sung to, in the past, than asked to contribute in voice. The Second Vatican Council recognized the importance of music to the celebration of the Eucharist in the *Constitution on the Sacred Liturgy*: "Sacred music increases in holiness to the degree that it is intimately linked with liturgical action, winningly expresses prayerfulness, promotes solidarity, and enriches sacred rites with heightened solemnity" (Abbott 1966, 171).

Much Latin liturgical music required a specialized choir that took over almost all responses in the Mass. Vatican II revived music as an intrinsic arena of participation by the entire congregation. The council also encouraged varied congregations to seek their own expression. Black bishops and liturgists have recognized this as an area in which the rich cultural traditions of African Americans have much to contribute. The introduction to a new black Catholic hymnal, now used in all three black Savannah parishes, explains:

> *Lead Me, Guide Me* is born of the needs and aspirations of black Catholics for music that reflects both our African heritage and our Catholic faith. For a long time, but particularly within the last two decades, black Catholics and the pastoral staffs who minister to our people have increasingly seen the need for liturgical and devotional settings and hymnody that lend themselves to the unique and varied styles of song and expression that are characteristic of our people. Similarly, black Catholics, who embody various religious and cultural traditions, wish to share our gifts with the wider ecclesial community and draw from the musical corpus of our own Roman Catholic tradition and that of our Sister churches. (*Lead Me, Guide Me* 1987)

Black congregants have received this musical reform enthusiastically. Music provides a focus for continual workshops as well as a central theme of NOBC conventions. It also shapes the character of each parish and liturgy through lay participation as planners, musicians, and singers.

The scattered evidence for early music in the black parishes points toward a not unsurprising reliance on traditional European Catholic hymnody. Yet Cyprian Davis, in a remarkable document from a Baltimore black Catholic society of 1849, notes that "among the activities, singing was very important. Normally the members were to sing four hymns, but at times they prolonged the meeting by singing more. In fact, the hymns were so important that there was a practice session during the week" (1991, 86-87).

Savannah black and Catholic churches emerged, however, in a weak period for Catholic music, although other religious music flourished in the United States at the time. At the dedication of Saint Benedict's, the *Savannah Tribune* cautiously reviewed Catholic but foreign effects: "The choir under the direction of Prof. W. T. Meir rendered a beautiful mass. At the offertory Cherubine's Ave Maria, a soprano solo was given with fine effect" (Dec. 14, 1889). Most reports only mention the celebrant singing the High Mass or funeral psalms (*ST* Apr. 9, 1910). Black journalists could also seem patronizing; when Bishop Keiley visited Saint Benedict's in 1909, the local black newspaper noted "the St. Benedict's choir distinguished itself; the Latin and English hymns were rendered with delightful charm" (*ST* Oct. 9).

Another black newspaper report underscored the "foreignness" of European Catholic musical traditions to the black community:

> The children of St. Francis Home sang Heckle's beautiful mass and rendered the imposing Liturgical chant with charming sweetness and inspiring devotion. All those present admired the singing and the Bishop most cordially congratulated them after ceremonies. It is certainly a credit for those colored children to sing this difficult church music with such perfection. (*ST* Feb. 6, 1909)

Latin hymns remained standard through the 1960s, when Saint Benedict's maintained both an adult senior choir and a junior choir made up of school children. With reform, Father Clarence Rivers and other black leaders fostered a variety of black musical expression in the Catholic church (Bowman 1987). Parish materials often embody a succession of reforms: Saint Benedict's used a structured folk hymnal, a Baptist hymnal, missalettes, and mimeographs before their 1988 replacement by the new *Lead Me, Guide Me*. In 1982 a woman who had been baptized as a child seventy years before bemoaned the rapid and total musical changes she witnessed:

> Converts at Saint Mary's change things, have new ways. They don't know how to genuflect. They don't know old hymns. They don't got respect. I said when I dies I want to hear them play the *Panus Angelicus*. The choir director said, "What?" I said, "Honey, you better go study an old hymnal." There were too many changes when John opened the window. . . . I ran the choir in the old days, today they just don't know to do it.

Most black and Catholic congregants, however, have been partisans of musical changes. The "new" music, after all, even if denied at Mass, was part of the extended family, schools, and neighborhood, of black history itself (Levine 1977). Even Pie, an older cradle Catholic, admitted, "Black people know gospel songs coming up, not just converts. That's what you learn in school. You sing what everybody else sings." Spirituals and gospel became identified with the culture transmitted within a black collectivity rather than any single denomination. Thus a dissatisfied younger "cradle Catholic," who frequently attends Protestant services, complained that "Catholics need to be more open, more free. We need more of *our* culture into Catholicism, without being ashamed of it. A little more of *our* music; *we* created gospel and added a lot. Even at 11:30, we use the traditional hymnal. People are so cold, so callous. If children are taught to clap, parents are upset. All Baptists have youth choirs; I've seen children blessed in the spirit."

The seven masses each weekend at the predominantly black parishes encompass a variety of musical traditions. Saint Benedict's organized a gospel choir in the 1970s whose adults and children sing at the Saturday 5:30 vigil mass. Sunday morning has a classical hymn mass, with Catholic and Protestant standards, while the last mass relies on a folk group to appeal to youths. Saint Anthony's has used an organist and familiar Catholic hymns for its 8:00 A.M. Sunday mass; a gospel or children's choir sings at the later mass. During my fieldwork, Saint Mary's remained more conservative, the early choir relying on Catholic standards with the 11:30 mass oriented toward spirituals. Choir leaders for the spiritual choir at Saint Mary's and Saint Benedict's gospel pianists and directors have been non-Catholics; parishioners lead, sing, and play in other choirs. This spectrum thus reflects a range of both music and demand within each parish as well as among black Catholics nation-wide. Choirs, priests, and music committees recognize variety in black and Catholic music for different masses; congregants choose according to background and tastes. Apart from gospel choirs, many of the songs, whether Catholic, traditional Christian hymns or folk music, would be heard in other Catholic parishes of Savannah.

As in other Christian churches, music also varies through the year. Advent, Christmas, Lent, and Easter draw especially on medieval and renaissance repertoires as well as modern songs. In Advent, Saint Benedict's gospel choir sings "O Come, O Come Emmanuel," written in the ninth century; the *Pange Lingua* (in English) remains part of Holy Week. Specific songs focus on weekly readings, after discussion among musicians, priest, and planning committees.

By contrast, special celebrations may emphasize black rather than Catholic experience. At the ordination of Robert Chaney, the cathedral resounded with songs by the Saint Benedict choirs, ranging from "I Have Decided to Follow Jesus" and "Wade in the Water" to "This Little Light of Mine." Traditional parts of the Mass used the melodies of "Amazing Grace" (*Agnus Dei*) or "We Shall Overcome" (Profession of Faith). "This Far by Faith" became a meaningful processional at Father Chaney's first mass. At Saint Anthony's seventy-fifth anniversary, spiritual and gospel dominated. Sister Julian Griffin evoked another spiritual, "Tomorrow Comes the Song," for her history of black Catholics in South Georgia (Griffin and Brown 1979). Gospel choirs also employ thematic songs for their annual concerts, such as "Look Where He Brought Me From" in 1988.

Despite reforms, music in black and Catholic churches remains less elaborate than in Protestant services I have observed in the area. This may reflect a larger range and number of masses that divide choirs. It may also reflect limited music education in schools, which constrains Catholic music. Or it may derive from the restraints of middle-class identification among black Catholics. Certainly, no one in the black community takes white Catholic singing as a model (nor do most whites).

Protestant models, however, are not unanimously popular among black Catholics either. An elderly Catholic, born in an old Catholic fam-ily, recalled sneaking into the Sanctified Church of "Daddy" Grace with another friend. She found "sawdust on the ground and benches. Horns blowing. A parade. We laughed: people started falling on the floor. When we giggled one of the men near the door told us to leave. It was like a musical." Others simply reply, "I don't like all that shouting." An equal number praises the singing they hear when attending black Protestant churches for weddings, funerals, or secular events.

Some songs borrowed into the Catholic church also raise theological problems, although these are primarily of irritation to ritual specialists. Gospel songs often preach individual salvation, as opposed to community participation. They also champion salvation by faith alone rather than by Catholic doctrine of faith and works and a personal relation to Jesus rather than a Trinitarian theology. Most congregants, however, are more concerned with the feeling than the words.

The distinctive musical array of those who are black and Catholic thus has come to distinguish them from both Protestants and Catholics precisely as black congregants have been able to take active roles in determining musical styles and values locally and nationally. In the combination of "Immaculate Mary" and "Blessed Assurance," of "Pange Lingua" and "This Far by Faith," musicians, congregation, and priests have defined a liturgical ambiance based on their history and traditions among distinct social and cultural worlds.

While music brings together the worshipping community, sermons establish its order of power through the proclamation of expert knowledge by a consecrated leader. Catholics emphasize preaching much less than southern Evangelicals, although the homily is considered a fundamental part of the liturgy. The Baptist "call to preach" is difficult to accommodate within Catholic hierarchy. Moreover, the training of priests stresses doctrine and counseling over preaching as an art form. Nor have models been handed down in the same way they are entrenched in the black community.

Scattered historical clues suggest a long-term contact between preaching and the needs and values of black missions, although sermons are neither as publicized nor as well recorded as in Protestant denominations. The public relations work of Father Joseph Dahlent in the early twentieth century, however, left an invaluable record of the preaching of the SMA fathers in their first mission churches. Sunday by Sunday he reported the sermon and its interpretation through the local black newspaper. In general, Dahlent described catechistic and doctrinal themes; the SMA pastors evidently saw themselves as presenting the dogma of Catholicism to a learning audience amidst a larger, non-Catholic population. Thus, a typical report from Lent 1909 illustrates the multiple thrust of preaching to the various constituencies from which the missionaries sought to create a community. Dahlent began by situating Lent at Saint Benedict's within the universal Catholic church:

It is a time of prayer and mortification. The law of abstinence and fast-ing is well-known to every Catholic; the rules and regulations will be given next Sunday in the Pastoral Letter of the Bishop of the Diocese. In every Catholic church special services will take place during Lent. The priests of St. Benedict's Church, faithful to their sacred obligation of instructing and exhorting their people, will do their best to render these Lenten services both interesting and edifying. Special sermons will be given on Sundays. Every Wednesday evening special lectures will be given by J. A. Dahlent, and they will be most interesting for Catholics and non-Catholics alike. . . . (*ST* Feb. 20,1909)

This announcement weaves together the contradictions of the black and Catholic community. Saint Benedict's is clearly presented as an active participant in a universal Catholic experience of Lenten preparation. Yet as an instructional church, even those things "well-known to every Catholic" are made explicit. Teachings about basic Catholicism serve both Catholics and non-Catholics: explaining to the outsiders and fortifying those inside who were only beginning to receive continuous parochial care.

After listing hours of masses and devotions, the article enumerates the principle themes of upcoming talks for non-Catholics, which include "Why I am a Catholic," "Divinity of the Bible and Infallibility of the Pope," "Sacra-ments, Penance. Why Catholics Go to Confession," "Blessed Eucharist. Real Presence, Mass, Communion, Veneration of the Saints," "Catholics Do Not Adore Statutes [*sic*]," and "Why I Pray for the Dead." This catalogue in itself is a skeletal catechism of turn-of-the-century Catholicism, much as the SMAs had long taught in their African stations. Elaborations of the titles suggest polemic areas identified in previous chapters: the role of the Bible and the pope, which differentiated Catholicism from most southern religious tradi-tions; the value of confession; the nature of the sacramental presence in Eucharist (repeated four times); and the relation of Catholics to saints: "Catholics Do Not Adore Statues."

Finally, the report returns to Catholic seasonal concerns: "Sunday sermons, morning, 'The Gospel of the Day,' evening 'The great eternal truths. Death, judgment, hell, heaven, eternity.' Preached alternatively by Father Obrecht and Father Dahlent. 'Behold, now is the acceptable time; behold, now is the day of Salvation.' 1 Cor. 6:2" (*ST* Feb. 20, 1909). These are Lenten themes, drawn from the gospel and devotional readings of the church, and were just as present in the 1980s.

More extensive reports on the second topic convey the concerns of the preachers, treated with "simplicity and earnestness, mingled with convincing earnestness." ·

> It was a delicate subject, but Father Dahlent rendered it most interesting to the immense congregation. He showed the love and respect which the Catholic Church has always given to the Bible, how her Monks have translated and copied it in olden times. It is a falsehood to assert that Catholics are not allowed to read the Bible, but the Bible alone, concluded the Rev. Preacher, cannot be the only guide in our belief, an authority and even an infallible authority is necessary to guide men in the sweet consoling road of religious certainty and Christian unity and that infallible authority for us as Catholics is the Roman Pontiff our Holy Father the Pope successor of St. Peter, who died Bishop of Rome the visible head of the Church of Christ. Most interesting was explanation of the Catholic teaching concerning the Pope which for many had been a deep mystery. (*ST* Mar. 6, 1909)

Dahlent's response to questions of the role of the Bible and the pope anticipated the apologetic concerns of the Catholic Laymen's Association of Georgia, which formed to respond to local white prejudices (Cashin 1962). The news report as well as the sermon suggests an appeal to a non-Catholic reader/listener.

Despite attention to the situation of Catholicism in the black community, these sermons manifest little attention to blacks in the Catholic church. A news report on the feast of Saint Benedict the Moor, however, highlighted the role of a black saint and a white hierarchy as preached in 1910:

> St. Benedict is the special Patron of the colored Catholics; he was a Negro himself and also a poor lay brother; he was elected by his fellow monks as Superior of a great Franciscan Convent, where he died in the odor of sanctity. The Catholic church has placed him on the list of her canonized saints, and the Holy Father has appointed him as the Patron Saint of our church. For the first time his feast was celebrated last Sunday with all the splendor of the Catholic ritual. Right Rev. Bishop Keiley sang Pontifical High Mass in the morning, and was assisted by 7 priests and a little army of altar boys; the congregation was very large and followed with rapt attention all the ceremonies of a Pontifical High Mass. The good Bishop also addressed a few touching

and fatherly words to the people and expressed his happiness to be present in St. Benedict's Church on that memorable occasion. In the evening, Father Schadewell, rector of the cathedral, preached a beautiful sermon on the life of St. Benedict the Moor, and applied the practical lessons of that noble life to the conditions of our modern civilization. (*ST* Apr. 9, 1910)[2]

Another *Tribune* note from October 9, 1909, publicized special ecclesiastical recognition of the race of the congregation by the visiting bishop: "At his last interview with the pope at Rome last July, the Holy Father said to Bishop Keiley, 'When you return to Savannah, go to St. Benedict's Church; tell my dear children, the colored people, that the Pope loves them; in my name bless them all.' At the end of the sermon Bishop Keiley gave the Papal Blessing."

Reports from a 1920 Advent revival showed continuity in sermon themes and circumstances. Again, specific invitation was made to Catholics and non-Catholics; a children's mission was also held in the afternoon. The visiting priest, New Orleans Jesuit Father Foulkes preached every night for a week on "The Object of Life; The One Great Evil of Life; The Sentence for a Misspent Life; The Closing Scenes of Life; The Prison House of God; and The Mercy of the Living God." He concluded at the Sunday high mass with "Is One Religion as Good as Another?" (*ST* Dec. 27, 1920). These meetings drew on a long tradition of Catholic revivalism, including integrated meetings in nineteenth-century Savannah where "soldiers and sailors 'who had sailed to every port of the world except into a confessional' joined 'our fellow citizens of the African persuasion' at a Redemptorist revival" (Dolan 1978, 114).

As the parishes solidified, preachers placed a new stress on black self-reliance rather than dependence on whites. The 1940s also saw the first black priest invited for a mission, at Most Pure Heart of Mary. Father Gall, then the pastor, recalled "He was a good speaker, very fluent. Father McNamara from the Cathedral came to listen."[3]

I have derived more thorough analysis of preaching styles in interaction with the parish community from my attendance at masses in each of the predominantly black parishes during fieldwork since 1982. The contrast of regular priests and deacons with visitors and with other parishes facilitates construction of general patterns beyond individual sermons. All the primary preachers I observed have strongly individual—and varied—preaching styles. All are also popular preachers across parish lines and around the state and nation in retreats. In general, their presentation is simple, conversational. Father Smith tended to focus on applying lectionary concerns to the family, the community, and the church, raising questions about reform and commitment. Father Collins raised similar ideas, with a particular emphasis on the call of the gospel for liberation and reform as challenged by the problems of Saint Mary's neighborhood. Father Mayo, at Saint Benedict's, is more exuberant, encouraging interaction and response while linking scripture and situations familiar to the congregation. I have not been able to observe replacements for the first two with the same clarity, although I include some observations nuanced by their preaching as well as that of parish deacons.

Despite this individualism, recurrent themes have permeated years of sermons in all three parishes. One is the relationship of church and neighborhood. This sense of mission is evoked by actions of the parish in the neighborhood, by the problems faced by the city or by the challenges of evangelization and building that should compel each Catholic. This is generally tied to recognition of ongoing programs such as the food bank or Habitat for Humanity. Concerns may go outside the Mass: Stations of the Cross traced local problems in a pilgrimage on the streets and lanes from Sacred Heart to Saint Mary's.

Critique of society provides another major theme. Military spending, crime and drugs, racism, materialism, and other themes mark a reformist stance toward American issues. Some of the most powerful of these sermons have been drawn from the black experience of parish and neighborhood. These may be negative, talking about disruption of families or availability of drugs. Positive preaching recognizes support of the extended family or the leadership of particular members. The black bishops identified this sense of social justice as a cornerstone of a theology for America:

> Our own history has taught us that preaching to the poor and to those who suffer injustice without concern for their plight and the systematic cause of their plight is to trivialize the Gospel and mock the cross. To preach to the powerful without denouncing oppression is to promise Easter without Calvary, forgiveness without conversion, healing without cleansing the wound. (Howze et al. 1984, 33).

Finally, both stylistic and more intrinsically theological values converge in a reliance on personal stories in the homily. These are not artificial stories or anecdotes taken out of context; they involve the priest and people of the parish. Priests draw on the week's experience as they think

313

out sermons, using people who prove identifiable to all members of the church. While they did not feel this was a conscious pattern, priests agreed that this reflected their involvement with the community.

None of the white priests adopted a characteristically black style in preaching; nor did one of the black deacons, who tends to present social gospel parallels to the neighborhood. Another senior black deacon, however, often synthesized Catholic dogmatic explanation and characteristic directions of black Protestant preaching. Yet all are very much a part of their parish. As a priest said, "You have to get to know, to listen to the parish."

This is not always the case; negative reports were given me on other priests who served in the past. These did not stress liturgy or preaching so much as attitude and interaction: "Some priests don't want to study no niggers." This is just as evident when a white priest unaccustomed to the parish, its concerns and people comes in as a replacement. Some, including the bishop, are extremely popular. I have also heard complaints of coldness and boredom, even extended to accusations of covert racism, a normal explanation for awkwardness in interracial settings.

Preaching represents an area of sharp contrast between black and white parishes, even while making allowance for individual variation. Sermons in white parishes in Savannah and the South that I have observed over the years have consistently been more scriptural and doctrinal rather than sociopolitical. They seem removed from everyday experience that permeates sermons in black parishes (see the sermons on marriage in chapter 7). Furthermore, sermons in white parishes are almost invariably impersonal—a trait extended to my experience of other predominantly white parishes outside Savannah. This point was suggested to me by visitors, who found it to be the most striking contrast with white liturgical communities they knew.

Equal contrasts arise when a black preaches to the black and Catholic congregation. I have observed black Protestant ministers leading prayers, revivals, and annual gospel concerts, as well as a few black and Catholic priests who adopt this form. Here different values of preaching and response emerge. The preacher tends toward norms of repetitive and dialogic rhythm that typifies modern black preaching (Davis 1985). The congregation, which may laugh or gently respond "Amen" with their regular priest, shouts, moves, and waves hands. Nonetheless, some Catholics, as noted in the introduction, object to "all that shoutin'." The influence of black evangelical patterns has been striking in opportunities that I have had to see black priests in Savannah or in other Catholic settings such as the NOBC.

314

Preaching complements the liturgical experience both historically and theologically. This analysis, however, has teased apart both historical and experiential components to suggest the growth of black and Catholic traditions, and even more clearly, of the traditions of face-to-face worshipping communities defined by both the parish and the group that regularly attend one or another mass. This tradition and this community are even more evident in the practice of the Eucharist.

LITURGY, PRACTICE, AND VARIATION

Variation in liturgy as public celebration arises from many facets of ambience and action. The settings that I discussed in chapter 4, for example, channel feelings and create atmosphere. Saint Anthony's is light and open while Saint Mary's is darker and narrow. Settings for daily mass differ even more than Sunday liturgies. Saint Mary's celebrated daily mass in the morning in the main church. Seven to ten people are scattered within the church, echoing the structures of Sunday mass. They come together in the central aisle for the sign of peace. Saint Anthony's, by contrast, used the rectory for daily liturgy during Father Smith's tenure. The living room and the dining room table are transformed into an intimate sacred and yet familiar space for those few who attend. The mass was transferred to the church in 1988 under a new priest. Saint Benedict's has a small chapel in the rectory. It replicates the formal structure of the church, on a small scale that also emphasizes family connections among regular congregants.

Variations in practice complement and extend variations in setting. In general, these express many of the same meanings as variations among white parishes, although forms are quite different, making any questions about African-American celebration more difficult to analyze. That is, all variations point to the appropriation of Mass and its meanings for the sustenance of face-to-face communities. My observation of liturgy through the years reveals subtle but meaningful customs that form within the parish and come to characterize the worship of that parish. Most of these traditions grow out of social and cultural characteristics important in the development of other sacraments: an emphasis on family and community, an adaptation to economic and cultural repression, and an awareness of black and Protestant models of religious life. The examination of everyday practice in the predominantly black parishes shows how adaptations take meaning.

The ambience of a face-to-face community takes form even before the mass: each parish emphasizes social contact as people assemble in the church. Greeters or ushers stand at the door, echoing the practice of most Protestant churches. As in white parishes, the priest circulates among those assembled, greeting and exchanging news, while people stop, talk, and embrace their fellow parishioners. Lectors or priests also ask those attending to introduce themselves to strangers. All these parishes recognize visitors by name during concluding announcements; this follows Protestant rather than Catholic models, but it also underscores the intimate image of the parish as family.

As people assemble, seating reveals its significance. In the masses that I know best, everyone has a characteristic seat—not assigned, but held by custom. The geography of seating represents relationships rather than prestige. A lector who participates in the mass joins the procession and sits in the front. The elderly, the infirm, or some especially devout members take front seats. At special events such as First Communion, baptisms, funerals, or recognition of a service group, participants sit in the first rows. Meanwhile, some parish leaders like Pie move to the back at weddings and funerals "to see everyone who comes."

Other seats tend to cluster family and friends. On Saturday evening at Saint Benedict's, Pie sits next to her aunts, for example, while my wife and I will slip into the pew behind along with other members of the household. Other close families occupy the pews in front and behind, while we can expect friends across the aisle. Just as these choices represent unity, however, it also provides a template for expressing disharmony. Shifts in seating may signal quarrels, division, or changing friendships, read by all who attend.[4]

Most Catholic parishes in Savannah begin mass with a procession from the back of the church. At Saint Benedict's, this entrance incorporates the gospel choir each Saturday with a regular prelude, "When I Walk Down Blessed Boulevard." This procession, in its rhythm and music, derives much more from Protestant than Catholic traditions. Acolytes, lectors, and communion ministers bring the congregation into participation around the altar. Altar servers are young males of the parish; to my knowledge, no parish in the city regularly uses females as acolytes. Ironically, this debated innovation in the contemporary church was practiced in Saint Anthony's in the 1930s. Young males had to work in the summer when school was out, leaving the church with a perpetual shortage of altar boys. Girls of the core families were drafted into service. The practice disappeared as the parish stabilized in size.

Much of the variation in the Liturgy of the Word comes from music and preaching. Intercessory prayers, however, illustrate contrasting values of parish life among Savannah Catholics. While all Catholic parishes have such prayers, they are generally presented as a text read by a lector to which the congregation responds. In black parishes, prayers reflect the personal structure of community. Thus prayers from the congregation recognize individual needs, personal losses, and ongoing concerns, bringing them to shared attention. Specific adaptations also reflect ecumenical contact with local Protestants. Saint Anthony's invited males and females to lead prayers for special occasions such as Mother's Day and Father's Day. In 1988 the parish introduced an altar call in which people could come forward to be prayed over by the priest. There was an enthusiastic response at masses that I attended, although Father Smith's departure cut short this practice.

Black parishes also show more personalized traditions within the Eucharist. The offertory, for example, has taken on a form in two parishes that clearly differs from the practice that seems to constitute the standard in many American Catholic parishes. Rather than remaining in the pews as baskets pass, parishioners at both Saint Benedict's and Saint Anthony's file forward to deposit their gifts in baskets before the altar. This custom, which postdates the Second Vatican Council, clearly duplicates the practice of Protestant churches. Once again, it heightens the active physical participation of each member in the liturgy, building the community. As in other Catholic churches, members of the community also bring forward bread and wine. Generally, those selected are families or members who are celebrating some milestone in their lives, such as an anniversary. As a known visitor, I was recruited several times for this task with my students or with Cindy Wong before our wedding.

The form of the Eucharist is standardized, although every priest has a characteristic style in which he celebrates the liturgy. In the earlier missionary days of the SMA fathers, scarce resources nonetheless influenced liturgical practice. Vogel notes that Father Zimmerman at Saint Anthony's

was an intelligent, quite flexible "activist," this priest of Swiss nationality who rooted the insecure African missions very solidly in Ireland. There he had been poor, too, and permitted himself some fancy liturgy. . . . Having in the early days of Georgia no money, a mostly unadorned church, a little flock of poor Negroes from Skidaway Island, no thurible, no "self-lite" coal, no Jerusalem incense, he would at Benediction honor the Lord . . . using a tablespoon and ordinary, self-prepared charcoal and an odiferous pine-resin. (Vogel a, 50)

McNally suggests such adaptations to scant resources were present in other southern missions as well (1987). With the years, all the churches acquired proper accouterments for the liturgy, passing theirs on to poor rural parishes. Yet each parish also has become more individual and expressive.

When Catholics stand to recite the Our Father, for example, congregants in each of the black parishes link hands to form a living representation of unity. At Saint Benedict's gospel mass, people pour out into the aisles to establish a complete circuit around the altar; other parishes adapt to space and attendance. The meaning is powerful for those who attend, as a member of Saint Anthony's observed about their similar practice:

> It's a closeness. Every time we say Our Father's prayer we hold hands. That's something we started about two years ago. I think it has helped people become closer to each other. Right after that, Father has every-one greet each other—shake hands, some people kiss, hug, and I think, all in all, that has made the church closer as a family. I hear more people talking now about the family attitude almost more than anything else. (Rick Brown in Moore 1985, 178)

The historical structure of this innovation reveals much about the nature of parish consciousness. Linked hands were introduced into Saint Benedict's by a white priest, drawing on a coalescence of community and spiritual renewal movements (Charismatic Catholics). It has been steadfast there since the early 1980s. It arrived later in Saint Anthony's, introduced through the choir who had learned about it at Saint Benedict's. It met some initial pastoral resistance and is still rejected by some traditionalists. Yet it also developed a more elaborated form as the Our Father came to be introduced by a preparatory hymn of Protestant origins: "May the words of my mouth and the meditation of my heart be acceptable in Thy sight. Wilt thou teach me how to serve Thee? Wilt thou teach me how to pray?" The custom only came to Saint Mary's in 1987. Again, the priest acted as innovator with more reference to spiri-tual renewal than to other parishes. As of 1988, Saint Mary's remained the only parish in which hands were not linked during daily mass.

This liturgical expression of community did not exist in any white parish Eucharist that I observed in Savannah, although it occurs in spe-cial settings that emphasize religious intensification, such as retreats. Nor were these practices found in Protestant congregations. Thus, what initially appears to be a historic trait of "black Catholicism" is, when disentangled, more clearly visible as a response to parish belief, mediated through leadership and spirituality at the parish level.

The parishes are also set apart from other Catholic congregations by the enthusiasm of the exchange of peace before the Eucharist. In most Catholic parishes in Savannah—and elsewhere in the United States—this ranges from tepid nods and formulae to handshakes or warmer expressions among families and friends. Blacks have acidly characterized such parishes as "having winter all summer." Often, such cool response is interpreted as manifest racism; attending other Savannah parishes as a white, however, I have received much the same reaction.

The sign of peace in the predominantly black parishes is, instead, an eruption of community fellowship. People move up and down the aisles at Saint Benedict's to embrace in a warm extended celebration. Saint Anthony's early morning mass adds waving hands across the church to handshakes and hugs. Saint Mary's tends toward more restraint, but still offers enthusiastic greetings, where priest and people mingle. The universal ritual form is intensified and extended to reaffirm the existence of community. In so doing, it too becomes a tradition of that community.

All three parishes regularly administer communion under both species. That is, communicants partake of both bread and wine. This is not common in other parishes of the city; church practice tends to reserve it for special occasions. One priest, asked about the practice, replied that *any* Eucharist was special; in any case, this is a long-standing practice in every parish. Size may also be a factor; large Catholic parishes are said to face logistical problems that preclude drinking from chalices. Refusal to share the chalice has been mentioned several times to me as an epitome of racism, within a sacramental imagination.

A song or reflection after communion may adapt a gospel selection or traditional hymn; in Saint Benedict's gospel choir mass, the choir's enthusiastic singing takes over the rite of closing, enveloping it within the music. In other cases, closing announcements, as in most parishes, respond to organizational questions. As in preaching, however, stylistic differences between black and white parishes arise in the personalization of this period. Individuals are recognized and applauded, announcements are made, and interaction between priest and congregation encouraged.

Finally, mass closes and the congregation departs; Saint Benedict's has the most distinctive recessional, led by the gospel choir. Yet all the parishes extend onto the steps as groups socialize, exchanging news and affirming community. In fact, people rarely leave before the entire mass is over, a relatively common occurrence I have noted in many white United States parishes.

Many of these elements of practice seem undramatic. Yet small, everyday innovations have a value all their own. In these, identity and belief are exemplified not by an abstraction of "black Catholics" but by the people who meet to constitute community. Here the problems discussed throughout this book can be momentarily laid aside.

BELIEF AND WORSHIP

Ritual, setting, language, music, and preaching focus the community on the Eucharist as a spiritual and physical presence. Posture and attitude reinforce this experience within the liturgy. Participation in the ritual, receiving communion, unites the community in a transcendent enactment. This preparation for receipt of the Eucharist, as noted in the last chapter, insists on an adequate understanding, if in simplified form, of the Eucharist as a central mystery of the Catholic faith. Thus a modern Sunday school teacher at Saint Benedict's explained, "We want them to understand that they're not getting bread and wine but the Body and Blood of Christ. That you're not going to a table for lunch but must be in a certain state and how to prepare . . . to be able to spontaneously confess and reconcile." Those trained in earlier catechisms can recite rote formulas decades later, even after these have been developed by years of belief, sermons, and practice.

With these multiple reinforcements of ideology and belief, it is hardly surprising that most black Catholics with whom I talked expressed a uniform belief in transubstantiation, as they had learned the term in catechism:

Q: What do you believe happens during the Eucharist?
A: The Body and Blood . . . the bread and wine are turned into the Body and Blood of Christ.
Q: Does everyone believe that?
A: That's what we supposed to believe.
Q: Has anyone talked to you about doubting?
A: No. If you think within yourself hard enough you can't help but believe it. [Some] even say at some times you can smell the Blood in the chalice.[5]
Q: Have you ever doubted it?

A: Never. I been taught that all my life. Sometimes, within myself, I've been praying, sitting at mass, and instead of the priest at the altar, I think of Jesus at the altar.

Training, practice, and setting coalesce to reinforce belief. Belief, in turn, reinforces community.

A sense of the Eucharist can represent a sense of difference between Catholics and other religions, as the conversation that introduced this chapter suggests. A professional man in Saint Benedict's treated the whole complex of Catholicism in these terms:

> If you are Catholic, you have something. If you need something, any-
> where, you can go to a priest and half the time you'll get it. And other
> denominations all use some of the same prayers—why do they dislike
> us and yet respect us, too? . . . There's always something about Catho-
> lics, the Mass and all.

Others with whom I talked would refer to their experiences with little analysis: "the sense that something special happens at Mass."

Explanations of the Eucharist also can go far beyond memorized un-derstandings of school catechisms as deepened by years of practice rather than advanced theological study, including those who are skepti-cal. An older and educated woman noted:

> *A:* Well, basically I think . . . we reenact, ah or try to recall to mind
> Christ's death and suffering, you know and so forth and so on. . . .
> Now I'm supposed to say that I believe that the bread actually
> changes into the Body of Christ and the wine actually changes into his
> Blood. Now Father says that sometimes you can actually see it. . . . So,
> a, as a Catholic I suppose I believe in transubstantiation, you know,
> that the actual change takes place, and I actually eat the Body and
> drink the Blood of Christ. That's what I'm supposed to say ain't it?
> *Q:* Well, I'm interested. Do you think most people believe that?
> *A:* No.
> *Q:* What do you think they believe?
> *A:* I think they drinking grape juice, grape wine. . . . I think it the
> same thing they had at the Last Supper. They ate bread and drank
> wine. I think sometimes that's a hard thing to believe and I think it
> depends on the individual. They have to make it up in their own
> mind. To say that you believe in it and to actually believe in it are two
> different things. . . .

Yet this dialogue illustrates the potential and limits of skepticism. The question of belief is treated as one of individual discovery, an attitude that is not classically Catholic, although the speaker later referred to training and values that had shaped her life as a Catholic. She also felt limited in disbelief by participation in the church, summarizing later: "Basically, I believe this and being a Catholic I accept this belief."

A more common representation of the limits of belief lies in the ambivalence of the word *mystery* in Catholicism. In ordinary speech, it is used as something unclear yet special: "As the nuns said, it's a mystery." In theology, it takes on connotations of grandeur and challenge as well as the quest for truth of the sacramental vision. To outsiders, it conjures negative images of Catholic obscurantism, while to insiders, it can become the foundation for mystic contemplation.

The priest of a black parish whom I quoted at length in chapter 5 explained to me how mystery became for him that which challenges, opens up, and teaches in the Eucharist, which he communicated to his parish:

> Is there some easy way to summarize the reality of belief in the Eu-
> charist? . . . I haven't found any. My own response to it is that it con-
> tinues to find new levels of meaning in this or that direction. It's just
> like the whole connection of the reality of bread with the hungry
> world. It's a dimension of solidarity with the hungry, with the poor.
> The connection that's made in the breaking of the bread is one of soli-
> darity.
>
> There are so many implications for one's life attached to this cen-
> tral act. I mean, it's explosive. . . .

The limits of exploration, at least as verbalized, are less than the belief embodied in the entire constitution of the Eucharist, and in the practice and community of the people who embody it. The tension of experience and analysis leads Catholics not to analyze the Eucharist in many cases, whatever their experience. As the priest above concluded about his parishioners, "I don't know if they pick it up in a way that they can summarize it, articulate it, and so forth, but I believe they are caught up in a sense that this is what it's about, that there is some larger dimension in which to be broken in some kind of meaningful way is response to the needs of people." Thus vision and community are reunited in theology as in practice.

The Eucharist, while dominating the sacramental order described in the last chapter, partakes of many of the same defining traits. Thus it absorbs the antagonisms and contradictions of the black and Catholic community to the fullest. When an African American feels uncomfortable approaching the altar at a predominantly white church or a family is divided around the table that will later be the site of a home mass, contradictions have emerged. Ideally, the Eucharist should heal, resolve, transcend these contradictions. Theologian Monika Hellwig follows this train of thought in noting the shift from the theological arguments of catechism to a post-Vatican II reorientation of Eucharist and community:

> That is why the contemporary theologies and the teachings of the Second Vatican Council, especially in the Constitution on the Sacred Liturgy . . . focuses rather on the presence of Jesus to the congregation in the Eucharist rather than on what happens to the bread and wine. It points to the presence of Jesus in the word of Scripture that is read, in the faith of the community that is gathered to participate, and in the action and things used which are the outreach of Jesus himself who initiated this celebration and reaches across the centuries and across space and culture change in this action to touch his followers in the most intimate communion. (1981, 143)

The ideal and the reality of each mass, in tension, constitute a spiritual and concrete community, the parish. Celebration of the Mass is a celebration of community and must embody the contradictions that community faces. The Eucharist is universal, defining to the church, and it imbues belief; yet celebration is divided by macro-categories of race and by micro-social creations as each parish and liturgy establish their own feelings and practices. These customs of the Mass, as undocumented or even unselfconscious traditions, maintain an unspoken but very real power, facing very real contradictions.

The Eucharist, as other sacramental cornerstones of Catholicism, also has an individual element of experience and conscience. The words I have presented in the final pages of this chapter suggest how individuals approach the mystery of faith. Yet, in this sense, belief and practice retain mysteries for ethnography as well.

Conclusion: Contradiction,
Church, and Conscience

In November 1991, I asked those in Savannah what they expected now from my book, and two responses were as telling as anything I had drafted in my original conclusions. Geraldine Abernathy, who has read and commented on chapters, felt that it would

> be enlightening to Catholics in so far as it represents another view of the relationship among Catholics in the Savannah area and the feelings of many toward the role they play in the church. It will give them food for thought and may have a far-reaching impact that will make people think beyond present conditions with a possible eye towards change in the future. You're not gonna revolutionize things, but if it gets one person. . . .

She added, "Whites are going to read it out of curiosity; blacks are going to read it to see what you are saying about them."

Abb's comments grew out of her concerns with the life of the church as well as her experience of the segregated South. Another old friend was more maternal at first, noting that it would show that I had gotten to know and talk to many people. Yet she added a note of regret that surprised me:

> In a way I don't like it, thinking about all that old prejudice. It makes you want to hate them all over again. The Catholic church always told us we were all the same. But some of them didn't believe it.

I asked—only to be corrected—whether a study of the conditions of segregation and racism could not at least open some eyes: "They know they're prejudiced. They don't want to change." These comments can be juxtaposed to that which originally began my conclusions. C. Vann Woodward, a dean among historians of the South, in his review of the *Encyclopedia of the South*. In 1989, he noted that,

> while slavery and segregation, among other things, forced it into distinctive patterns, black culture is very southern and . . . all southern culture is part black. W. E. B. DuBois has an eloquent and often quoted passage about the "two-ness" of being both black and American. An unexplored implication of the work is a third dimension added to the "two-ness"—that of being Southern as well. White southerners also share the "three-ness" by virtue of the biracial component of their culture. Cajuns, Jews, and Creoles have still another, but the southern component bulks large for all. (see Morrison 1991)

His argument could be extended to situate the structures of belief, social interaction, and community that constitute the multiple dimensions of being black, southern, and Catholic. His vision points to the contexts within which this study must be extended and compared. Yet his criticism, in contrast to Savannah voices, points to the incompleteness of an abstraction that escapes both the pain and the joy of black and Catholic life in Savannah, as real experiences, not academic narratives.

This focused examination of Savannah, a single community within southern life, traces a story both personal and idiosyncratic. The haunting multiplicity of roles and categories that have constituted Savannah life, however, are not unique, nor are those circumstances that have shaped black and Catholic life in this and other urban contexts. The dilemmas and resolutions teased out over the past two hundred years can serve to relate Savannah to other urban stories of ideology, differentiation, and power. I personally have situated the city in terms of my experiences elsewhere—in Kentucky, Connecticut, Maryland, and Florida—and have compared it with materials available from these and other places. Even if the tale and its actors have seemed caught up in transcendence, their lives have also taken shape at the intersection of religion and society, in the city and in history. From both these intersections, then, and the lives and voices that have shared knowledge of them, the study must open up to wider implications for understanding religion, the city, and human culture.

SAVANNAH AS CASE STUDY

It is clear from the detailed processes examined in Savannah that the lives and collectivities of those who are black and Catholic have been shaped by a constant dialectic of symbolic representation and political action. I began with the fundamental cultural tension between white and black, inextricably linked in southern history. While whites in the South have repeatedly testified to the fear or pain that their black mirror creates, whites have also been the consistent shadow of black social history. This mutually constitutive relationship has been built on inequality of rights and resources, although it has been challenged by a wide range of resistance. Whites have attempted to impose categories that would substantiate more obvious subordination of blacks and "others" as inferiors, laborers, or disfranchised. Blacks, in different alliances with "others," have resisted categorization while constructing their own identities within white-enforced limits. This fundamental cleavage generates continuing violence and contradiction for both whites and blacks at the heart of southern—and American—life that my ambivalent position in the Savannah community can glimpse, but can also escape.[1] The 1992 riots in Los Angeles, San Francisco, Atlanta, and other cities, moreover, show that multiple conflicts of race and category are not a heritage of the South alone.

The construction of ethnohistorical memory led me to underscore anew the centrality of race over time in examining the black creation of group identity counterpoised to white claims to domination. This general structural tension, in turn, pervaded the initiatives and responses by .which the black and Catholic community emerged. Under slavery, religion was already a significant structure of black adaptation, a strength of the weak that flourished in the fundamental contradictions of southern Christian society. A white Catholic hierarchy, stimulated by Christian charity, national interests, and the desire for growth, created institutions that were perceived as valuable by Savannah blacks. Thereafter, black and white responses entailed the adaptation of both school and worshipping community to groups that could provide home in a foreign land, amidst the contradictions with which they lived. In so doing, blacks have forced an adaptation from the external Catholics who once evangelized them. This suggests the relevance of Protestant sources that treat blacks as a prophetic voice for change to that bureaucracy and group as well (Cone 1969, 1975; West 1982, 1988). At the same time, this experience demands studies of grass-roots black religious thought and ideals of mutually supportive community (Trevor Purcell, personal communication 1992) as a domain for comparative analysis of social and cultural action. This calls for detailed studies of individual congregations as well as settings.

As I turned to the social structure and belief system of the black and Catholic parishes, links between organizational patterns and the actions of individual and familiar agents who unite world view and social life became apparent, though ambiguous. Both formal doctrines and power structures of a white-dominated religious system have been re-formed by their interpretation and context within the black community. The priests and nuns became less white, the laity more powerful—creating in face-to-face exchange a community in which contradictions were mediated. Yet the issues of transgenerational membership and memory also nuance white assimilation and belonging. Again, more comparative data are necessary.

In the adaptation of a Catholic sacramental vision of transcendent truth through concrete signs in the world, a social life cycle based in the varied experience of Savannah blacks who lacked the background of the Old World Catholics was compared with both theology and formal practice. An institutional culture of belief was met by a "mystery of faith" grounded in a sometimes beleaguered community. This experience provided a refraction on Eugene Kennedy's vision of the two (or perhaps more?) cultures of American Catholicism (1988) as well as other Catholic visions of the construction and meaning of church (Dulles 1974, 1988).

In the Eucharist, the center of Catholicism as a world of social interaction and belief, all the ambiguities and pains of black and Catholic life are subsumed in ritual enactments that physically and spiritually unite each parish. Individuals here are united to a vision both private and collective. As an ethnographer and a Catholic, I have found this to be the point at which I am most a part of the community with which I have lived and worked and yet still stand outside of it. Yet through the words of those who participate in the ritual, I have suggested how we may glimpse private meanings as well as collective public worship. And through those who have shared the process of writing with me, I can see the divisions that reemerge on the threshold of the church.

The processual overview that I have provided in each section shows that any religious and personal mediations of social and ideological conflicts have been arrived at only slowly, after struggles and misapprehensions within both black and white communities. These very efforts to resolve problems point to their centrality to black and Catholic life. The disjunctions that I repeatedly have pointed out here—whether within the family and parish, within the church, or grounded in the interaction of universalist ideologies and caste-divided actions—are not mere constructs imposed upon the data to create a narrative. They are also questions that the actors of black and Catholic history have raised and to which they have responded. Actors and their actions substantiate—and challenge—categories, just as cultural values interact with meaningful political and economic action within the city.

BLACK CATHOLICS AS A CRITICAL SPACE

News reports on blacks within the Catholic church that have surfaced throughout the nation in the 1980s and 1990s point to an ever-increasing awareness of the problems and potential that black Catholics are facing. The schism of Father Stallings in Washington in the summer of 1989 tore congregants away from Catholicism into a different and Africanized church. In fact, Stallings attracted a black priest from the Savannah diocese and may have spurred a similar schism in New Orleans. In Detroit in 1989 and Chicago in 1990, church leaders have also made decisions to close down inner-city churches that have become the inheritance of blacks and Hispanics. Ironically, Joseph Cardinal Bernadin of Chicago, himself a southerner by birth, had called upon southern prelates to adapt to the conditions of the southern church, especially the new sunbelt migration that has increased the number of white, often suburban, Catholics in older southern settings like Savannah. Urban migration challenges Catholicism to grow and change while the exodus of whites from older ethnic parishes has not provided money for upkeep or traditional services, much less the ongoing challenge of urban underclasses.

Other debates continue among bishops, clergy, and religious as well as in the ongoing life of Savannah parishes. The questions of individual choice and governance raised by the end of Archbishop Marino's tenure in Atlanta as the first black American archbishop are both local and national in scope. The actions of Clarence Thomas further focused attention on Savannah belief and practice (see Elie 1991). On a more intimate scale, black parishes themselves face the future as a time not of resolved challenges but of contradictions to be met. Each of the parishes has faced serious challenges, especially in their transitions from priest to priest, in the decade I have worked with them. Each has inaugurated new programs, both through the diocesan campaigns to increase solidarity among small groups of parishioners and through specifi c parish and neighborhood efforts. Nonetheless, a wariness lingers among many with whom I have spoken who project the experience of black Catholics in Savannah into the future. As the new pastor of Saint Anthony's, Father John Lyons, wrote on the parish's eightieth anniversary in 1990:

> We know we are a people of a changing Church in a rapidly changing world. Eighty years ago the founders of St. Anthony's had little idea of what the future might hold. . . . As we carry on the Lord's work as we enter the 1990's, we need the same faith in God that has been part of this Church since its beginnings. There is no guarantee of what the next 80 years will hold for us but I find great HOPE as I look around at: the enthusiasm of our young children, in the interest of our young adults, in the commitment of struggling young families, and in the stories of the older folks who help keep the dream alive for the rest of us. (Saint Anthony's Parish 1990, 2)

Such projections should not be taken as a likelihood of problems so much as a possibility made meaningful by the experience of the recent past. Indeed, the patterns of interest and abandonment I have brought to light concerning Catholicism in the black community a century ago amplify the reverberations of historical cycles. Before I began my work these were known only incompletely, if at all, among those who were black and Catholic. Such consciousness may become, then, a weapon against future manifestations of the quiet neglect of the past or even the deafness of planning that hurt as deeply.

Ultimately, the black and Catholic experience may have a prophetic role in understanding the changing nature of the Catholic church as a whole. The Roman Catholic church in the United States in the past three decades has undergone many shifts, making the future unclear to members in such issues as the role of the priesthood, the meaning and necessity of Catholic education, or the continuity of women's religious orders. In these areas the experiences of black Catholics are a microcosm, a history of conscience that takes on meanings as other Catholics are forced to deal with contradictions and choice. Yet there remains a real need for further studies to facilitate an understanding of shared experience and differences within black Catholicism and their relations to pluralist models of religious organization, as compared perhaps with Hispanics, Asians, nineteenth-century immigrants, or groups differentiated by gender, region, or status.

BLACK AND CATHOLIC: THEORETICAL AND PERSONAL CHALLENGES

The processes I have examined are not limited to race, religion, and power in the United States. My ethnohistorical focus suggests a conceptual framework through which to interpret the complexities of the city within the full traditions of anthropological, geographical, and social historical investigation. In all societies in which anthropologists work, categorizations of self and other are fundamental processes of thought. The interaction of different societies and social groups that epitomizes but is not limited to the city brings together multiple categories and systems of categories (see Cohen 1969; 1976; 1980; 1981; Bourdieu 1975; Sahlins 1981; Castells 1983; McDonogh 1986). The human lives of those who classify and are classified create economic structures and political actions that constitute or challenge symbolic dimensions of the city. Contradiction, resistance, and re-creation provide the space, therefore, for insight into the complexities of urban life. Although I have followed these processes within the lives and beliefs of those who are black and Catholic in Savannah, they demand comparative study through richer ethnography on both Catholics and southerners alike (Gallup and Castelli 1987). Ultimately, such urban and cultural processes should be understood through examination of more varied distributions of rights and resources, symbolic maps, and resolutions.

The interlocking elements of urban structuring are vast to describe—as is certainly the case in Savannah, whose white community, professional cultures, neighborhood groups, and generations have only been sketched here. Urban culture and contests for power may nonetheless be examined through identification of primary metaphors and of arenas of contradiction that call into question the systematic process of cultural structuring and thus tease out the relationships between exploitation and the creation of an apparently natural order. My perspective in this work sees the city as both political-economic and cultural product, ambiguous and changing, identified and contested. It allows for individuals to speak and act while it incorporates the ways in which individuals will be categorized in the anonymity of urban life. And it situates the anthropologist as one who must learn to share in this urban culture and yet be distant—and critical—of the conditions that produce and reproduce it. Such a perspective should prove to be a rich paradigm for urban studies, combining culture and political economics in a particularly urban environment, as those in British cultural studies have also suggested in different areas of work.

Yet this paradigm poses its own contradictions. For all my general theoretical concerns, this study has been profoundly concerned with understanding a real and living community of people with whom I have worked over the past decade. It has been my intention to listen and analyze and to incorporate a polyphony of voices as well as a detailed analysis into a text that reflects both the theoretical complexity and the feelings of Savannah life. We may learn from this how we may better understand the symbolic and organizational formation of urban groups while paying heed to the nuances of humanity involved in every choice.

V. S. Naipaul, an acute observer of the modern South, has evoked the centrality of a search for identity that transforms traditional questions of the mind of the South. Talking with a southerner,

> I asked her what way identity was important, and whether there was some practical way in which it helped. She said that, if you moved to a new neighborhood or took a new job, and people were not too friendly, then it could help if you knew who you were; you could last out the hostility. If you didn't know who you were—if (and this was my extension) you were dependent on other people for your idea of your own worth—then you were in trouble.
>
> She was giving the view from below, the view of the poor people she was concerned about. And from what she said I got the impression that these people had raw sensibilities and lived on their nerves. I found that hard to imagine.
>
> (And yet, at another level, and with another, half-buried part of myself, I understood. Perhaps in a society of many groups or races everyone, unless he is absolutely secure, lives with a special kind of stress. Growing up in multi-racial Trinidad as a member of the Indian community, people brought over in the late nineteenth and early twentieth centuries to work the land, I always knew how important it was not to fall into nonentity. . . .) (1989, 33)

Ultimately there are many ways of assembling the elements of this identity among those who are black and Catholic and Savannahian for this analysis. I hope my task will continue to converge with the lives of

331

the parishioners and others in Savannah who will read, interpret, reject, or build upon this work. For this analysis should not give the impression that the processes by which a black and Catholic church identity can take its place within both biracial Savannah and the integrated Catholic world are complete. As the parishioners at Saint Mary's said at their re-dedication, "There is no time to glory in past achievements. . . . For we have miles to go before we sleep." This book discusses the paths in the past and present; in so doing, it may participate in the construction of the future.

The alternative is to reify boundaries, whether of race, caste, class, denomination, or discipline. This alternative was captured by an anonymous poet whom Sandra Smithson quoted at the end of her historical memoir as a black and Catholic nun. Writing about whites in their ghetto—the domain of hegemony—the poet observes: "So locked in, and therefore capable of hearing only their own limited voices, they endanger us all" (Smithson 1984, 59). Such words can penetrate urban categories of race and power, structures that deal with salvation, judgment, forgiveness, and celebration, and not incidentally, explore the task of the anthropologist who tries to stand inside and yet outside such questions.

Notes

INTRODUCTION

1.   The first black priest in the United States, James Healy of Georgia, had been ordained a priest in France and had risen to be bishop of Portland, Maine, before his death in 1900. Two brothers in this Irish-black family also entered the priesthood. The next American black priest, Augustine Tolton, was ordained in Rome in 1886 but died in 1897 (Hemesath 1973). The first black priest consecrated in the United States, Charles Uncles, received holy orders in 1891. Few black priests were ordained in this country until a seminary began to function for blacks in Bay St. Louis, Mississippi, in the 1920s. No other blacks were consecrated as bishops in the United States until 1966.

2.   Ironically, Saint Benedict's, with over 1,500 families, has a larger congregation than the present-day Cathedral parish. Two other, smaller, traditionally black and Catholic parishes also appear throughout this study: Saint Anthony of Padua in West Savannah, with 150 families, and Most Pure Heart of Mary, also on the western side of the city, with a similar membership.

1. THE EVOLUTION OF BLACK RELIGION IN SAVANNAH: CHOICE AND CONSTRAINT

1.   Although I have yet found no relevant information for the antebellum period in Savannah, it would be interesting to pursue Wilson Moses' insights into the meaning of anti-Catholicism as a theme in early black nationalism (1978, 47ff).

2.   They have been replaced, as in the Catholic church, by new recruitment in the twentieth century (Ahrent 1979, 48-49, 65, 81)

3.   The controversy between the First African Baptist Church and its sister church, Bryan Baptist, has continued into the present, with each church claiming to be the original foundation. At the centennial of the foundation, separate and polemical histories were published (Love 1888; Simms 1888). The conflict has eased somewhat after the civil rights period, with both churches recognized as monuments to black history and cooperating in historical commemoration (Luster 1976a, 1976b).

4.   This surrender preserved a large antebellum urban core downtown that now constitutes Savannah's historic and cultural capital.

5.   This was not the same building reopened in 1985; fire destroyed the early cathedral and its records on February 6, 1898, and the present cathedral was dedicated in 1900.

6.   Saint Matthew's, however, according to popular knowledge in the black community, was formed from the synthesis of two prior parishes that had been divided by neighborhood and color.

7.   This curious biblicism evidently refers to the Hebrew captivity in Egypt but seems to confuse it with Rumpelstiltskin.

8.   Thomas had determined through his researches that 1775 was a better founding date, hence this is a 150th anniversary volume. The controversy among Savannah churches, and with other churches such as South Carolina's Silver Bluff Baptist, continues in diminished form to the present. (See Woodson 1945.)

9.   The description continues with more detail of the panoply of the services:

> Between the musical numbers several of the congregation rise and loudly testify to the miracles that Bishop Grace has performed in their behalf. A flourishing sale is conducted in consecrated handkerchiefs and copies of a newspaper published by the cult. These are believed to possess unusual healing powers. . . .
>
> The grand march is spectacular. . . . Occasionally one of the participants stops, and regardless of the hindrance to the rest of the worshippers, jumps up and down wildly, crying out in a shrill, hysterical voice. At length, exhausted, he sinks to the floor and is dragged by friends from under the whirling feet of the others. (Georgia Writers' Project 1940, 46-51)

2. THE DIVIDED CITY: BLACK AND WHITE
AS METAPHORS AND ACTION

1.   The origins of this analysis, while growing from a classic model of structural linguistics, draw together a variety of contemporary approaches to categorization. Models of particular importance include Taylor (1979), Lebow (1976), Goodwin (1989), and the works of Roland Barthes, Abner Cohen, Pierre Bourdieu, and Edward Said.

This study also reflects the strong tradition of southern historians' analysis of and fascination with the mythical foundations of southern life, exemplified in Gaston (1970) and Connelly (1977). McLaurin (1987) is a moving reflection by a historian on his own formation. Classic anthropological analyses such as Dollard (1937), Powdermaker (1939), and especially Doyle (1937), a study that I discovered only late in my work, have also helped me to rethink the South in anthropological terms of caste and class. This approach also must take into account the rich mass media manipulation of categories and images inside and outside the South, as noted in Kirby (1978). Yet my primary source remains the development of these traditions within oral exchange and comment.

Indeed this process could be extended. Robert Murphy, in his sensitive reflections on his identity as a result of quadriplegic paralysis, meditates in a rather similar fashion upon categories and anthropological awareness of them as they relate to selves:

> Many years ago, long before I became disabled, I was talking to a black anthropologist, a friend from our former days as fellow graduate students, and the subject turned to race. In the course of our conversation, my friend said, "I always think of myself as being black, just as you always think of yourself as white." I protested this, saying that even though I did think of myself as white when talking to a black person, my skin color was not in the forefront of my conscious mind at other times. My friend didn't believe me. But I was neither mistaken nor misleading in my observation, for I grew up in and still lived in a white world. Whiteness was taken for granted; it was standard and part of the usual order of things. . . . White is normal; it's what ethnolinguists call an "unmarked category," a word that is dominant within its class and against which other words of that class are contrasted. Why, I would no more have thought of myself as white than I would have thought of myself as walking on two legs.
>
> Before my disability, I was a standard White, Anglo-Saxon, Agnostic Male (WASAM), a member of the dominant part of the society. My roots in tattered-lace-curtain Irish Catholicism made me uneasy in academia, but I never gave much thought to the other components of my identity. My black friend was forced by the reality of white society always to think of himself as black. (1987, 104-5)

2.   Lawrence Friedman has traced the development of these negative associations in the South in his study of racial fantasies in the postbellum South, The White *Savage*. Commenting on the film "Birth of a Nation" whose opening in Savannah was protested by black, but not white, ministers (Dittmer 1977, 186), Friedman notes:

> The movie also reflected the dichotomy in white Southern thought between black savages and white civilization. . . . Most blacks in the film were

clad in filthy rags that covered dirty bodies and some suffered from visible skin blemishes. Clean, cultivated whites would not allow these blacks into their homes. Such a portrayal reinforced the myth of the diseased Negro. . . .
Moreover, the film was set in an urban locale—a moderate size Southern town where whites knew many but not most local blacks. Since an unfamiliar Negro represented a potential threat, the difficulty of applying differential segregation and the need for across-the-board segregation were obvious. . . . (1970, 170; see 119-25 for considerations of the myth of the diseased black)

3. The same reaction occurred in St. Augustine and Sarasota during integration times and has been echoed in South African struggles against apartheid—all indicating the visceral meanings cultural categories come to hold.

4. This is not to say that the situation of Savannah blacks is especially hopeless for the United States or even the South. W. W. Law also has noted that "overall we probably have had for a longer period of time better race relations in this city than almost any Georgia town" (Hepburn 1987, 332).

5. Private here is defined in the way in which it has been used in cultural studies, that is, as meaningful within particular domestic and subcultural realms:

Private forms are not necessarily private in the usual sense of personal or individual, though they may be both. They may also be shared, communal and social in ways that public forms are not. It is their particularity or concreteness that marks them as private. They relate to the characteristic life experiences and historically constructed needs of particular social categories. They do not pretend to define the world for those in other social groups. They are limited, local, modest. They do not aspire to universality. They are also deeply embedded in everyday social intercourse. (R. Johnson 1987, 50)

This seems to characterize black privacy as much as white publicness.

6. As Melton McLaurin reflects on his childhood in North Carolina, "Yet early in life I learned, almost unconsciously, that both races observed the unspoken etiquette of segregation. Blacks who had to enter our house, for whatever reason, came in the back door" (1987, 13). It is a matter of pride to Savannah black domestics not only to enter by the front door but to have a key, indicating trust and belonging to the family.

7. Margaret Mitchell was raised as a Georgia Catholic and was, in fact, more sensitive to the divisions of southern society around religion than was the movie version of *Gone with the Wind,* as her portrayal of the funeral of Gerald O'Hara suggests:

In the absence of a priest Ashley was to conduct the services with the aid of Careen's Book of Devotions, the assistance of the Methodist and Baptist preachers of Jonesboro and Fayetteville having been tactfully refused. Careen,

more devoutly Catholic than her sisters, had been very upset that Scarlett had
neglected to bring a priest from Atlanta with her and had only been a little
eased by the reminder that when the priest came down to marry Will and
Suellen, he could read the services over Gerald. (1936, 489)

Even so, "Ashley knew that half the people present had never heard of
Purgatory and those who had would take it as a personal affront, if he insinuated,
even in prayer, that so fine a man as Mr. O'Hara had not gone straight to Heaven"
(490).

8.   Older blacks with whom I have worked had a richly elaborated system
of neighborhood designations that were familiar only in part to whites of
comparable age. Younger generations tend to coalesce all these neighborhoods
into units manageable in an automotive age—Eastside, Westside, and Southside.

3. CATHOLICS ENTER THE BLACK COMMUNITY:
RACE, SCHOOL, AND MISSIONS

1.   Other laws prevented slaves from setting type (Foster 1831, 319) As
reinforced in 1841, these prevented Catholic or any other schools from even
providing books for blacks, slave or free, since this law enforced penalties:

> if any shop-keeper, store-keeper, or any other person or persons
> whatsoever, shall sell to, give, barter or in any wise furnish or allow to be
> furnished by any person in his, her or their employment any slave, negro or
> free person of color, any printed or written book, pamphlet, or other written or
> printed publication, writing paper, ink or other articles of stationery for his,
> her, or their use without written permission from the owner or guardian
> authorized. (Georgia 1841, 139)

2.   An article in the *Savannah Evening Press,* Mar. 8, 1936, notes this as a
postbellum school.

3.   A lack of Catholic schools for blacks was not only a southern problem,
however. Ochs (1990, 17) discusses a complaint by a New York black Catholic,
Harriet Thompson, that Archbishop Hughes opposed Catholic schools for black
children and would not let them enter existing ones.

4.   Gannon quotes another southern bishop, Patrick Lynch of Richmond, on
the appeal of the liturgy: "The ceremonies of the Church, the Processions, Novenas,
etc. would satisfy the cravings of their still tropical nature for pomp and ceremony
in a way that would draw them away from the cold services of Protestant worship."
(1964, 117). Evidently Lynch identified his competition with the elite Episcopalians
or Congregationalists rather than the Afro-Baptist tradition.

5.   Bishop Patrick Lynch in Charleston, in 1865, had adopted this Orientalizing idea of recreating Paraguay in a project to settle five thousand families on Folley's Island. (McNally 1987, 136).

6.   A stranger educational mission for blacks was that of the Poor Clares who followed the Benedictines to Skidaway Island. In 1887 these nuns opened "Saint Joachim's Abbey of Poor Clares Colletinnes, Skidaway Island, for the Education of Colored Girls." Unfortunately, in their brief career in the diocese, these few nuns proved more controversial than pedagogical, constantly worrying Bishop Becker with their irregular fund-raising and neglect of the rules of their order (Peterman 1982, 194-95). The ephemeral St. Joseph's school appears in Chapter 4.

7.   Although data are unclear and there is no oral history to substantiate either position, it appears possible that Saint Mary's may have built on the foundation of an earlier school, Saint Augustine's. While this is described in some sources as being in Springfield Terrace, in West Savannah, a newspaper ad also listed it as 814 West Thirty-sixth Street, the location of the current school.

8.   The second floor was soon used to hold the convent of the Handmaids of the Most Pure Heart of Mary and the chapel, nucleus of the later parish.

9.   These figures are based on SMA reports to the main office, from which prestige and funding were gained. Hence we tend to view overall trends as more reliable than scattered years. Here, for example, the 1922 figure coincides with diocesan records and may not be the erratic figure that subsequent years represent.

10.   Since the schools have been dismantled, there is no library of primary texts, nor is it clear whether the black schools used the same texts as other Catholic schools in the system. This raises a question concerning the social and cultural content that teachers who came from Ireland and later from the North would bring to their rotations through southern black schools, but neither former students nor retired sisters focused on this disjunction as a problem. One nun who had taught in Savannah in the 1930s recalled that teaching sisters warned newcomers to be careful not to say things that could be interpreted as racial slights. Socialization within the order may have eased the cultural shock or prepared foreign teachers to deal with the social situation in which they encountered themselves. Other nuns, however, recalled outrage at the way blacks were treated, although their training and rule would have precluded social activism.

11.   Although physical punishment was an accepted part of the educational experience sanctified by their religious and moral mission of the school, the pastor, and the parents set limits. In 1947, for example, Father Feeley of Saint Benedict's complained to the vicar-general of the diocese that the school principal "began to fine school children for not attending Mass on Sundays—a step which brought discredit on the Catholic church and St. Benedict's school" (Feeley to Moylan, Aug. 3, 1947, Savannah Diocesan Archives). A reply from the superior general of the Franciscan Sisters, Sister Mary Benignus, to an earlier complaint by Father Feeley had approved the principal's apology "for her unbecoming language and her

disrespectful manner to a priest of God, and that priest the lawfully appointed pastor, who has full permission from Higher Authority to legislate as he judges best for his school as well as his parish" (May 22, 1947, Savannah Diocesan Archives). The authority of teacher to student was constrained by bonds between teaching nuns and priests and thus to their bishops and to God, affirming hierarchies of gender and sanctity.

12. Not all Catholic education was confined to schools. CCD (Confraternity of Christian Doctrine) programs and summer catechetical camps appeared in Savannah in the 1920s (McNally 1987, 169). Such programs appeared at Saint Anthony's and Saint Benedict's by the 1960s. A central Catholic camp on the grounds of the former seminary now handles such activities.

13. Photographs of classroom interaction from the 1962 dedication program show males and females to be strictly divided in the classroom, however.

14. The recent "Heart Renewed" campaign of the diocese (1985-90) includes reading and discussion for adults in black and white parishes.

4. PARISH, NEIGHBORHOOD, AND COMMUNITY

1. The parish has been recognized only slowly as an important unit for historical and sociological study (Fichter 1951 was an important exception). A bias toward hierarchy and generalized portraits in Catholic studies was only controverted by the Notre Dame Parish study of the 1980s (Byers 1985; Dolan 1987; McNally 1987). Such neglect also suggests the ambiguities of the parish within universal Catholicism as an administrative unit that may take on a rich and at times autonomous life, especially in the South's rural mission contexts.

2. This tends to omit blacks who have left the church for one reason or another; such people have been impossible to trace in any systematic fashion, unfortunately, although anecdotal inferences are included where possible. In general, the focus of the study is on community rather than all individual strategies that nevertheless compose it.

3. Later statistics, however, suggest that baptismal records cannot, in the case of black parishes, be taken as an indicator of parish size (see records for the 1930s).

4. A religious history of black Catholics in St. Louis includes a family who left Saint Benedict's to become pillars of the church in that expanding industrial city (Faherty and Oliver 1977).

5. One might have expected Savannah to be a mission territory for the Josephites (Saint Joseph's Society of the Sacred Heart for Foreign Missions), which became an independent community in 1893 with a special interest in black evangelization. One possible explanation is that Joseph Auciaux, a Belgian missionary who became a Josephite in 1904, focused on Bishop Keiley as a racist in his pamphlet "De miserabili conditione catholicorum nigrorum in America"

(Ochs 1990, 138). It is also possible that the Josephites faced too many crises with the resignation and apostasy of their leader, Father Slattery, which made them unable to expand. SMA publications also suggest that Gibbons invited the order to deal with problems of black Americans; he might well have influenced their choice of Savannah.

6.   This east-west split was common among religious groups in the city. Baptists early on were divided between First African Baptist and Bryan Baptist in Yamacraw on the west and Second Baptist on the elitist east side. Among Episcopalians, Saint Stephen's (1855) was on Harris while the splinter Saint Augustine (1872) was on West Broad and Bolton. White Catholics also celebrated rivalries between Yamacraw residents affiliated with Saint Patrick's and the Old Fort clans who attended the cathedral.

7.   My questions are included as well to clarify the way in which the parishioners have experienced the church.

8.   Only direct elicitation gathered other ambient details, on which informants simply do not focus as such, even in the contemporary church:

> *Q: What about* light?
> *A:* It wasn't dark, had plenty of windows. We had electric lights.
> *Q:* And heating?
> *A:* Way back we used to have a coal stove. Then we were given an oil
> stove that kept it very warm.
> *Q:* And in summer?
> *A:* We had windows up, and we thought nothing of it. Mass was only an
> hour, sometimes less, and didn't feel that hot.

9.   Changes in placement of the tabernacle were introduced in 1988-89, part of a controversial interaction between priest and people.

10.   The brother of an Irish priest was married in Saint Anthony's during my work there; this was obviously a rather anomalous relationship, however.

11.   As noted, while the Congregationalist church began as an integrated group, even as the only representative of its denomination, it became all black in normal attendance. Some newer churches, especially outside downtown, are more integrated, as are many political and social "public" events.

5. PRIESTS AND PEOPLE: ORGANIZATION, POWER, AND THE CHURCH

1.   Two black permanent deacons currently serve in the city; they will be dealt with in the context of lay leadership in chapter 6. A Vietnamese priest leads the Vietnamese parish, Saint Peter and Paul.

2.   This epithet was cited as long ago as 1940 in a study of educational

missions of the Sisters of Saint Joseph (Stark 1940, see Quinn 1978) and continues to be part of the folk culture of the convent and rectory. Ochs (1990) points to its more general extension.

3.   The black bishops' 1984 pastoral, however, made an intriguing appeal to Mariolatry by identifying the Virgin Mary as "the Mother of God and the Mother of the African-American community. She is the Poor Woman and the Bearer of the Word . . ." (Howze et al. 1984, 35-36).

4.   This importation, which sustained the church in priests and episcopacy in the nineteenth century, has continued actively in the twentieth, despite the production of native priests. The oldest Irish priest now serving in the diocese arrived in the 1920s. Bishop McDonough also launched a major recruitment campaign in the 1960s. Many of this younger generation, however, were faced with the new questions of the Second Vatican Council and their new lifestyle in the United States and departed the priesthood in the 1970s, contributing to uncertainty and turmoil in some of the predominantly white parishes in which they served. Both Rev. Frank Higgins (at Saint Anthony's and Saint Mary's) and Rev. Liam Collins were recruited in the 1960s from Irish seminaries.

5.   This was also a strong concern among the Josephites, who would not accept black seminarians under thirty (Ochs 1990, 70, 152). Since black sexuality is a culturally based theme of southern racial calumny, evidence is difficult to evaluate. The problems of Archbishop Marino in Atlanta disheartened many in Savannah who had looked to him as a clerical role model, although blacks proved sympathetic critics.

6.   Lay brothers have had minimal participation in this history. A single brother is recalled as the aid to Father Martin at Saint Anthony's in his farming in the 1930s, and an itinerant lay brother has worked with Father Collins at Saint Mary's in the 1980s. Thus, they will not be dealt with here as a significant category.

7.   Ironically, Benedictines forty years before had seen Georgia as a springboard to Africa: "Perhaps after a while we will be able to send Negro missionaries to Liberia and found an abbey for the colored people of Africa" (Moosmuller to Abbot Boniface Wimmer, Sept. 30, 1878; in Oetgen 1969, 174).

6. LAITY, CONTINUITY, AND EMPOWERMENT

1.   A recent symposium in The *Nation* on "Scapegoating the Black Family" assembled black and female leaders who iterated many of these themes and urged solutions based on both political action and black traditions of self-help (Burnham 1989; Clayton 1989; O. Davis 1989; Gresham 1989; Gresham and Wilkerson 1989; Height 1989; M. Waters 1989; Wattleton 1989; Wilkerson and Gresham 1989).

2.   I have consulted with all major parties involved.

7. LIFE CYCLE, FAMILY, AND THE SACRAMENTAL ORDER

1.   McNally (1987) confirms my observation that this obligation is loosely observed in the South. Catholic identity may be based on irregular attendance and lack of affiliation to other churches, although the blacks seem to pay much more attention to who does and does not attend.

2.   The relations of power and godparenthood were insightfully traced by Mintz and Wolf (1950). See Bloch and Guggenheim (1981) for a newer review.

3.   The nature of the training, as administered by nuns and priests, is not especially vivid for adults of the present who received their First Communion decades ago. Most recall learning their catechism, believing in the Body and Blood of Christ and in the forgiveness of sins epitomized in their first confession. Contemporary training uses published materials and lay teachers from the community to prepare children who are generally enrolled in public schools.

4.   Chiniquy's classic anti-Catholic tract *Fifty Years in the Church of Rome* (still available through anti-Catholic publishers whose works are distributed in Savannah) dramatized confession as an area of clerical manipulation and prurient interest:

> For I do not exaggerate when I say that for many noble-hearted, well-educated high-minded women to be forced to unveil their hearts before the eyes of a man, to open to him all the most secret recesses of their souls, all the most sacred mysteries of their single or married life, to allow him to put to her questions which the most depraved woman would never consent to hear from her vilest seducer, is often more horrible than to be tied on burning coals. (1898, 401)

5.   The Lord God said: "It is not good for the man to be alone. I will make a suitable partner for him." So the Lord God formed out of the ground various wild animals and various birds of the air, and he brought them to the man to see what he would call them; whatever the man called each of them would be its name. The man gave names to all the cattle, all the birds of the air, and all wild animals; but none proved to be a suitable partner for the man.

So the Lord God cast a deep sleep on the man, and while he was asleep, he took out one of his ribs and closed up the place with flesh. The Lord God then built up into a woman the rib that he had taken from the man. When he brought her to the man, the man said: "This one, at last, is bone of my bones and flesh of my flesh; This one shall be called 'woman' for out of 'her man' this one has been taken." That is why a man leaves his father and mother and clings to his wife, and the two of them become one body.

6.   Jesus was made for a little while lower than the angels that through God's gracious will he might taste death for the sake of all men. Indeed, it was fitting that, when bringing many sons to glory, God, for whom and through whom all things

exist, should make their leader in the work of salvation perfect through suffering. He who consecrates and those who are consecrated have one and the same Father. Therefore, he is not ashamed to call them brothers (Hebrews 11:9-11).

7.   One woman in the parish suggested that the value placed on children made abortion much less volatile as an issue. Certainly it was a point I rarely have heard discussed either in church or in informal gatherings, but I was unable to pursue the suggestion systematically. My sense is that blacks oppose abortion because they value children even more than because of church dogma. The black bishops observed: "And yet life, especially new life within the mother has always been a value to Africans and African Americans. . . . From our point of view as Catholics and as black people, we see the efforts made 'to provide' low-cost abortions as another form of subjugation. Indeed there are those who would even characterize it as another form of genocide" (Howze et al. 1984, 14-15).

8.   A Catholic analogy exists in calling out the spirit from a deconsecrated church building when moving to a new church. Yet this was not brought up by any Savannah informants.

8. THE EUCHARIST: WORSHIP, BELIEF, AND VARIATION

1.   This coalescence of historical forms does not imply that the transition from a Latin to a gospel mass was easy for Catholics. Many, including most of the black Catholics whom I know, found that reforms opened up new understandings and participation in Catholic worship. Nonetheless, one of my older black Catholic friends, to her death, defended the Pange Lingua and other prayers of her church as "true Catholicism." Another black and Catholic woman of one of the founding families of the black parishes, now in her sixties, responded to queries about the council reforms:

> Some received it pretty good. Half was for and half didn't want. We still have groups that don't. . . . ———— will never cope. Even when we sing the Lord's Prayer, she will not stand up. . . . Maybe some didn't understand. I still hold onto old traditions. When the Blessed Sacrament is exposed just before exposition we strike our breasts. Many people don't. There is no bell ringing. . . . A lot of things are not being done. I still go through my rituals the way I was raised as a child.

Older white Catholics in Savannah often share negative views of the Council reforms, as I have noted (McDonogh 1988b). Converts and young Catholics, black and white, increasingly accept the post-Conciliar Mass as a norm.

2.   In the 1980s churches have taken up black history as part of the liturgical year, choosing one or more Sundays in February to recognize black pioneers in the Catholic church as well as ongoing leaders. These presentations complement the

ethnic consciousness of other parishes, such as Saint Patrick's Day celebrations for local Irish-Americans. Nonetheless, these feasts recognize blacks as an ethnic pillar of the modern Catholic church.

3. While this recollection gives no indication of style or content, the emphasis on fluency is intriguing, given a charge by critics in the diocese that some of the French-born SMA fathers could not be understood by blacks. Most parishioners do not recall any such problem with long-time pastors such as Father Obrecht at Saint Benedict's.

4. *Growing Up Catholic* humorously situates seating divisions in white Catholic churches according to parameters of wealth and piety: "The first few pews are not so much the province of the catatonically devout as one might expect, though entranced communicants may certainly be found there. Rather, they are the preserve of the establishment, the upper crust, the arrives and the arrivistes" (Meara, Stone, Kelly, and Davis 1984, 64). This suggests a more pervasive differentiation between blacks and whites in terms of the bases of recognition of leadership, which I suggested in chapter 6.

5. Two or three people mentioned seeing the Mass more literally as the Last Supper or taking the chalice more completely as Blood, but this does not seem to have any general presence in the parish. It may suggest the presence of traditional Catholic hagiography in the community, tales of saints to whom such miraculous visions were granted.

CONCLUSION: CONTRADICTION, CHURCH, AND CONSCIENCE

1. Emily Martin (1986) has evoked suggestive parallels in her analysis of the construction of the female body by a dominant medical and cultural establishment that never treated its own values as marked.

Bibliography

ARCHIVES

Chatham County Public Library, Gamble Collection and Georgia Collection (Savannah)
Georgia Historical Society (Savannah)
Most Pure Heart of Mary Parish Archives
Sacred Heart Archives
Saint Anthony of Padua Parish Archives
Saint Benedict the Moor Parish Archives
Diocese of Savannah Diocesan Archives (DSDA)
Savannah Diocesan School Board Archives (DS, School Board)
Savannah State Univ., Black History Collection and Civil Rights Scrapbooks
Society of African Missions (SMA) Archives, Tenafly, N.J.
U.S. Works Progress Administration Archives, Manuscript Division, Library of Congress

PERIODICALS

Atlanta Constitution
Bulletin of the Catholic Laymen's Association of Georgia; later, *The Southern Cross* (SC)
L'Echo des Missions Africaines
État de la Société des Missions Africaines de Lyon (État)
The Julian (Savannah Diocese)
The Light (Saint Benedict the Moor Parish, Savannah)
New York Times
Our Negro and Indian Missions

Savannah Evening Press (SEP)
Savannah Herald (SH)
Savannah Morning News (SMN)
Savannah Tribune (ST)
Washington Post

BOOKS AND ARTICLES

Abbott, Walter M., gen. ed. 1966. *The Documents of Vatican II.* New York: Corpus Books.

Ahles, Sister Mary Assumpta. 1977. *In the Shadow of His Wings: A History of the Franciscan Sisters.* St. Paul, Minn.: North Central.

Ahrent, Theodore. 1979. *The Lutherans in Georgia: An Informal History from Spain to the Space Age.* Chicago: Adams.

Anderson, James. 1988. *The Education of Blacks in the South, 1860-1935.* Chapel Hill: Univ. of North Carolina Press.

Anderson, Jon. 1992. "Place and Faith: Catholic Imagination and Inflections and 'Church' in the Contemporary South." Final Research Report, Bible Belt Catholics Project, Catholic Univ.

Andrews, William. 1986a. To *Tell a Free Story: The First Century of Afro- American Autobiography, 1760-1865.* Urbana: Univ. of Illinois Press.

————. 1986b. *Sisters of the Spirit: Three Black Women's Autobiographies of the 19th Century.* Bloomington: Indiana Univ. Press

Ayers, Edward L. 1984. *Vengeance and Justice: Crime and Punishment in the 19th Century American South.* New York: Oxford Univ. Press.

Baer, Hans. 1984. *The Black Spiritual Movement: A Religious Response to Racism.* Knoxville: Univ. of Tennessee Press.

Bailey, Kenneth. 1964. *Southern White Protestantism in the Twentieth Century.* New York: Harper & Row.

Baker, Thomas, and Frank Ferrone. 1987. "The Odd Couple: The Liturgy Committee and the Priest." *New Catholic World.* Mar.-Apr.: 79-83.

Baldwin, Frederick C. 1983 *". . . We Ain't What We Used to Be": Photographs by Frederick C. Baldwin."* Savannah: Telfair Academy of Arts and Sciences.

Baldwin, James. 1953. *Go Tell It on the Mountain.* New York: Signet.

Bane, Martin J., SMA 1959. *Heroes of the Hinterland.* New York: Shamrock Guild.

Banjet, Gerar. 1929. "La legende de l'inférioreté des noirs." *L'Echo des Missions Africaines* 29 (Mar.): 63-64.

Barry, Colman J. 1970. "German Catholics and the Nationality Question." In *Catholicism in the United States,* ed. P. Gleason. New York: Harper & Row.

Barry, James T. 1978. "A Sociology of Belief and Disbelief: Notes toward a Perspective on Religious Faith and Community." In *Toward Vatican III: The*

Work that Needs to Be Done, ed. D. Tracy, H. Kung, and J. Metz. New York: Seabury Press, 249-60.

Barthes, Roland. 1972. *Mythologies.* New York: Hill and Wang.

Bartley, Numan V. 1983. *The Creation of Modern Georgia.* Athens: Univ. of Georgia Press.

———, ed. 1988. *The Evolution of Southern Culture.* Athens: Univ. of Georgia Press.

Barzun, Jacques. 1965. *Race: A Study in Superstition.* New York: Harper & Row.

Baudier, Roger. 1939. *The Catholic Church in Louisiana.* New Orleans: Chancery Office.

Begley, Dennis J. 1965. "In a Southern City of Old-World Charm." *Our Colored Missions.* 4:17-22.

Berzon, Judith R. 1978. *Neither White nor Black: The Mulatto Character in American Fiction.* New York: New York Univ. Press.

Billingsley, Andrew. 1968. *Black Families in White America.* Englewood Cliffs, N.J.: Prentice-Hall.

Blassingame, John W. 1972. *The Slave Community.* New York: Oxford Univ. Press.

———. 1973a. "Before the Ghetto: The Making of the Black Community in Savannah, Georgia, 1885-1890." *Journal of Social History* 6:463-88.

———. 1973b. *Black New Orleans, 1860-1880.* Chicago: Univ. of Chicago Press.

Bloch, Maurice, ed. 1975. *Marxist Analyses and Social Anthropology. ASA Studies* 2. London: Malaby Press.

Bloch, Maurice, and Scott Guggenheim. 1981. "Compadrazgo, Baptism and Second Birth." *Man* 16:376-86.

Borchert, James. 1980. *Alley Life in Washington: Family, Community, Religion and Folklife in the City, 1850-1970.* Urbana: Univ. of Illinois Press.

Bossy, John. 1985. *Christianity in the West, 1400-1700.* New York: Oxford Univ. Press.

Bourdieu, Pierre. 1972. *Outline of a Theory of Practice.* Cambridge: Cambridge Univ. Press.

———. 1979a. *Algeria 1960.* Cambridge: Cambridge Univ. Press.

———. 1979b. *La Distinction: Critique du Jugement Social.* Paris: Minuit.

Bourdieu, Pierre, and Claude Passeron. 1976. *The Inheritors: French Students and Their Relation to Culture.* Chicago: Univ. of Chicago Press.

Bowman, Thea. 1987. "Let the Church Say 'Amen!'" *Extension* 81, no. 9 (Mar.-Apr.): 10-11.

———. 1988. "Black History and Culture." *U.S. Catholic Historian* 7, no. 2 and 3 (Spring/Summer 1988): 307-10.

Brantl, George, ed. 1962. *Catholicism.* New York: George Braziller.

Braxton, Edward K. 1979. "Toward a Black Catholic Theology." In *Black Theology: A Documentary History*, ed. G. S. Wilmore. Maryknoll, N.Y.: Orbis Books, 325-31.

————. 1988. "The National Black Catholic Conference: An Event of the Century." *U.S. Catholic Historian* 7, no. 2 and 3 (Spring/Summer 1988): 301-6.

Breffny, Brian de. N.d. *Unless the Seed Dies: The Life of Elizabeth Hayes (Mother Mary Ignatius O.S.F.), Foundress of the Missionary Franciscan Sisters of the Immaculate Conception*. N.p.

Brown, Gillian. 1984. "Father Michael Smith: From the World of Theory to Real Life Practice." *Southern Cross*, Sept. 6: 9.

Brown, Peter. 1982. *The Cult of the Saints*. Cambridge: Cambridge Univ. Press.

Bryan, T. Conn. 1949. "The Churches in Georgia during the Civil War." *Georgia Historical Quarterly* 33, no. 4: 283-302.

Burnham, Margaret. 1989. "The Great Society Didn't Fail." *The Nation*, July 24-31, 122-26.

Burns, Jeffrey M. 1987. "Building the Best: A History of Catholic Life in the Pacific States." In T*he American Catholic Parish*, ed. Dolan, vol. 2: 7-136.

Byers, David, ed. 1985. *The Parish in Transition: Proceedings of a Conference on the American Catholic Parish*. Washington: U.S. Catholic Conference.

Cahill, Lisa Sowle. 1987. "Divorced from Experience: Rethinking the Theology of Marriage." *Commonweal* Mar. 27, 1987: 171-76.

Calderon, Erma, with Leonard Ray Teel. 1981. *Erma: A Black Woman Remembers 1912-1980*. New York: Random House.

Callahan, Daniel. 1963. *The Mind of the Catholic Layman*. New York: Charles Scribners' Sons.

Campbell, Edward. 1981. *The Celluloid South: Hollywood and the Southern Myth*. Knoxville: Univ. of Tennessee Press.

Carroll, Chas. 1900. *"The Negro a Beast" or "In the Image of God."* St. Louis: American Book and Bible Society.

Carroll, Rebecca E. 1988. "The Black Family." *U.S. Catholic Historian* 7, no. 2 and 3 (Spring/Summer 1988): 311-16.

Cashin, Edward. 1962. "Thomas E. Watson and the Catholic Laymen's Association of Georgia." Ph.D. diss., Fordham Univ.

Casino, Joseph J. 1987. "From Sanctuary to Involvement: A History of the Catholic Parish in the Northeast." In *The American Catholic Parish*, ed. Dolan, vol. 1: 7-116.

Cass, Dann A. 1957. *Negro Freemasonry and Segregation*. Chicago: Ezra Cook.

Castells, Manuel. 1977. *The Urban Question: A Marxist Approach*. Cambridge, Mass.: MIT Press.

————. 1983. *The City and the Grassroots*. Berkeley: Univ. of California Press.

Chalker, Fussell. 1970. "Irish Catholics and the Building of the Ocmulgee and Flint Railroad." *Georgia Historical Quarterly* 54, no. 4:507-16.

Chick, J. T. N.d. *Are Roman Catholics Christians?* Chino, Calif.: Chick Publications.

———. 1981. *Alberto.* Chino, Calif.: Chick Publications

———. 1982. *The Godfathers.* Chino, Calif.: Chick Publications.

———. 1985. *Four Horseman: Alberto Part V.* Chino, Calif.: Chick Publications.

Childress, Alice. 1956. *Like One of the Family: Conversations from a Domestic's Life.* Boston: Beacon Press.

Chiniquy, C. 1886. *Fifty Years in the Church of Rome.* Chicago: A. Craig.

Clarke, Athlone. 1991. "Crossing a Boundary." *Newsweek* 117, no. 19 (May 13, 1991): 9-10.

Clayton, Constance. 1989. "We *Can* Educate All Our Children." *The Nation,* July 24-31, 132-35.

Cohen, Abner. 1969. *Custom and Politics in Urban Africa.* Berkeley: Univ. of California Press.

———. 1974. *Two-Dimensional Man.* Berkeley: Univ. of California Press.

———. 1980. "Drama and Politics in the Development of a London Carnival." *Man* 15 , no. 1:65-87.

———. 1981. *The Politics of Elite Culture.* Berkeley: Univ. of California Press.

Coleman, Father William V. 1967. *The Church in South Georgia.* Savannah: Catholic School System.

Coles, Robert. 1980. *Flannery O'Connor's South.* Baton Rouge: Louisiana State Univ. Press.

Collins, Daniel F. 1971. "Black Conversion to Catholicism: Its Implications for the Negro Church." *Journal for the Scientific Study of Religion 10* (Fall 1971): 208-20.

Cone, James H. 1969. *Black Theology and Black Power.* New York: Seabury.

———. 1975. *God of the Oppressed.* New York: Seabury Press.

Connelly, Thomas L. 1977. *The Marble Man: Robert E. Lee and His Image in American Society.* Baton Rouge: Louisiana State Univ. Press.

Connor Baptist Temple. 1977. Commemorative Pamphlet.

Conzelmann, Hans. 1973. *History of Primitive Christianity.* Nashville, Tenn.: Abingdon.

Copeland, Shawn. 1989. "African American Catholics and Black Theology: An Interpretation." Wilmore, ed., *African American Religious Studies.* 228-49.

Crapanzano, Vincent. 1985. *Waiting: The Whites of South Africa.* New York: Random House.

Crews, Clyde. 1973. *Presence and Possibility: Louisville Catholicism and Its Cathedral: An Historical Sketch of the Louisville Catholic Experience as Seen through the Cathedral of the Assumption.* Louisville: n.p.

———. 1987. *An American Holy Land: The Archdiocese of Louisville.* Wilmington, Del.: Michael Glazier.

349

Cripps, Thomas. 1977. *Slow Fade to Black: The Negro in American Film, 1900-1942.* New York: Oxford Univ. Press.

Crosby, Steve. 1972. "Voyage Back into History." *Savannah Morning News* Feb. 14.

Cuddy, Edward. 1970. "Pro-Germanism and American Catholicism, 1914-1917." In *Catholicism in the United States,* ed. P. Gleason. New York: Harper & Row, 92-100.

Cunningham, Lawrence. 1987. *The Catholic Faith: An Introduction.* Manwah, N.Y.: Paulist Press.

Daniell, Rosemary. 1980. *Fatal Flowers: On Sex, Sin and Suicide in the Deep South.* New York: Holt, Rinehart & Winston.

David, Jay. 1968. *Growing Up Black.* New York: William Morrow and Sons.

Davis, Cyprian. 1988. "The Holy See and American Black Catholics: A Forgotten Chapter in the History of the American Church." *U.S. Catholic Historian* 7, no. 2 and 3 (Spring/Summer 1988): 157-82.

———. 1991. *The History of Black Catholics in the United States.* New York: Crossroad.

Davis, Gerald. 1985. *I Got the Word in Me and I Can Sing It You Know: A Study of the Performed African-American Sermon.* Philadelphia: Univ. of Pennsylvania Press.

Davis, Natalie. 1975. *Society and Culture in Early Modern France.* Stanford, Calif.: Stanford Univ. Press.

Davis, Ossie. 1989. "Challenge for the Year 2000." *The Nation* 249, no. 4 (July 24-31, 1989): 144-48.

Dedication. 1962. Saint Pius X High School. Apr. 1. N.p.

Derrick, Charles. 1961. "A Brief Ascension Church History, Emphasizing Worship and Liturgical Trends." Paper submitted at Lutheran Theological Seminary (now in Georgia Historical Society).

Diggs, Margaret. 1936. *Catholic Negro Education in the U.S.* Washington, D.C.: pub. by author.

Diocese of Savannah-Atlanta. 1939. *Statuta Diocesis Savannensis-Atlatensis Necnon Facultates Sacerdotibus Concessae.* Savannah: Chancery Office.

Diocese of Savannah, Department of Christian Formation. 1978. A *People of Faith.* Savannah: Author.

Dittmer, John. 1977. *Black Georgia in the Progressive Era, 1900-1920.* Urbana: Univ. of Illinois Press.

Dix, Gregory. 1945. *The Shape of the Liturgy.* London: Dacre Press.

Dolan, Jay. 1975. *The Immigrant Church: New York's Irish and German Catholics, 1815-1865.* Baltimore: Johns Hopkins Univ. Press.

———. 1978. *Catholic Revivalism.* Notre Dame, Ind.: Notre Dame Univ. Press

———. 1985. *The American Catholic Experience: A History from Colonial Times to the Present.* Garden City, N.Y.: Doubleday.

————, ed. 1987. *The American Catholic Parish: A History from 1850 to the Present.* 2 vols. Manwah, N.Y.: Paulist Press.

Dollard, John. 1937. *Caste and Class in a Southern Town.* London: Oxford Univ. Press.

Dominguez, Virginia. 1986. *White by Definition: Social Classification in Creole Louisiana.* New York: Rutgers Univ. Press.

Donoghue, Quentin, and Linda Shapiro. 1984. *Bless Me Father, For I Have Sinned: Catholics Speak Out about Confession.* New York: Donald I. Fine.

Doyle, Bertram W. [1937] 1971. *The Etiquette of Race Relations in the South.* New York: Schocken.

Du Bois, W. E. B., ed. 1904. *Some Notes on Negro Crime, Particularly in Georgia.* Atlanta: Atlanta Univ. Press.

————. 1963. *An ABC of Color.* New York: International Publishers.

————. [1903] 1965. *The Souls of the Black Folk.* New York: Avon.

————. [1920] 1969. *Darkwater: Voices from within the Veil.* New York: Schocken.

————. 1973. *The Correspondence of W. E. B. DuBois.* 3 vols. Ed. Herbert Aptheker. Amherst: Univ. of Massachusetts Press.

Dulles, Avery. 1974. *Models of the Church.* Garden City: Doubleday.

————. 1983. *Models of Revelation.* Garden City: Doubleday.

————. 1988. *The Reshaping of Catholicism.* San Francisco: Harper & Row.

Elie, Paul. 1991. "Hangin' With the Romeboys." *New Republic,* May 11, 18-36.

Elliott, Walter. N.d. "The Negro Apostolate in Georgia." SMA Archives.

Ellis, John Tracy. 1969. *American Catholicism.* 2d ed. Chicago: Univ. of Chicago Press.

Ellis, John Tracy, and Robert Trisco. 1982. *A Guide to American Catholic History.* 2d ed. Santa Barbara: ABC-Clio.

England, John. 1849. *The Works of the Right Reverend John England, First Bishop of Charleston.* 5 vols. Rpt. Charleston, S.C.: Arno.

Epstein, Dena J. 1977. *Sinful Tunes and Spirituals: Black Folk Music to the Civil War.* Urbana: Univ. of Illinois Press.

Essed, Philomena. 1990. *Everyday Racism: Reports from Women of Two Cultures.* Claremont, Calif.: Hunter House.

Evans-Pritchard, E. E. 1937. *Witchcraft, Oracles and Magic among the Azande.* Oxford: Clarendon Press.

Faherty, William Barnaby, and Madeline Barni Oliver. 1977. *The Religious Roots of Black Catholics in St. Louis.* St. Louis: St. Louis Univ. Press.

Fallows, James M. 1971. *The Water Lords: Ralph Nader's Study Group Report on Industry and Environmental Crisis in Savannah, Georgia.* New York: Grossman.

Feagin, Joe R. 1968. "Black Catholics in the United States: An Exploratory Analysis." *Sociological Analysis* 29 (Winter 1968): 186-92.

———. 1971. "Black Catholics in the U.S.: An Exploratory Analysis." In *The Black Church in America,* ed. Hart Nelson. New York: Basic Books, 246-54.

Feeley-Harnik, Gillian. 1981. *The Lord's Table: Eucharist and Passover in Early Christianity.* Philadelphia: Univ. of Pennsylvania Press.

Fichter, Joseph. 1951. *Southern Parish.* Vol. 1, *Dynamics of a City Church.* Chicago: Univ. of Chicago Press.

———. 1953. "The Marginal Catholic: An Institutional Approach." *Social Forces* 32 (Dec. 1953): 2.

First African Baptist Church. 1977. "One Hundred Eighty-Ninth Birthday." Pamphlet. Georgia Historical Society, Savannah.

———. N.d. Museum flyer. Savannah. In author's personal collection.

Fitts, Leroy. 1985. A *History of Black Baptists.* Nashville, Tenn.: Broadman Press.

Flannery, Austin, gen. ed. 1982. *Vatican Council II: More Postconciliar Documents.* Grand Rapids, Mich.: Wm. B. Eerdmans.

Flynt, J. Wayne. 1979. *Dixie's Forgotten People: The South's Poor Whites.* Bloomington: Indiana Univ. Press.

Fogarty, William. 1960. *The Days We've Celebrated: St. Patrick's Day in Savannah.* Savannah: Printcraft.

Foley, Rev. Albert S. 1935. The History of the Catholic Church in Georgia. M.A. thesis, Bonaventure College.

———. 1954. *Bishop Healy: Beloved Outcaste.* New York: Farrar, Strauss and Young.

———. 1955. *God's Men of Color: The Colored Catholic Priests of the United States.* New York: Farrar, Strauss.

Foster, Arthur. 1831. *A Digest of the Laws of the State of Georgia.* Philadelphia: Pittsburgh, Hogan and Co.

Fox-Genovese, Elizabeth. 1988. *Within the Plantation Household: Black and White Women of the Old South.* Chapel Hill: Univ. of North Carolina Press.

Franciscan Handmaids of the Most Pure Heart of Mary. N.d. *Who Are These Handmaids?* N.p.

Frazier, E. Franklin. 1963. *The Negro Church in America.* New York: Schocken.

Freydburg, Elizabeth. 1983. *Black Catholics in the United States.* Bloomington, Ind.: Afro-American Arts Institute.

Friedman, Lawrence J. 1970. *The White Savage: Racial Fantasies in the Postbellum South.* Englewood Cliffs, N.J.: Prentice-Hall.

Gadsden, R. W. 1969. "A Brief History of the First Congregational Church, United Church of Christ, Savannah GA, April 1869-April 1969." Mimeo. .Georgia Historical Society

Gallup, George, and Jim Castelli. 1987. *The American Catholic People: Their Beliefs, Practices and Values.* Garden City, N.Y.: Doubleday.

Gannon, Michael V. 1964. *Rebel Bishop: The Life and Era of Augustine Verot.* Milwaukee: Bruce.

————. 1965. *The Cross in the Sand: The Early Catholic Church in Florida, 1513-1870.* Gainesville: Univ. of Florida Press.

Gaston, Paul. 1970. *The New South Creed: A Study in Southern Mythmaking.* New York: Random House.

Geertz, Clifford. 1973. *The Interpretation of Cultures.* New York: Basic Books.

Genovese, Eugene. 1969. *The World the Slaveholders Made: Two Essays in Interpretation.* New York: Random House.

————. 1974. *Roll, Jordan Roll: The World the Slaves Made.* New York: Random House.

Georgia, State of. 1841. *Acts of the General Assembly of the State of Georgia Passed at an Annual Session in November and December 1841.* Milledgeville: Grieve and Orme.

————. 1916. *Acts and Resolutions of the General Assembly of the State of Georgia.* Atlanta: Byrd Printers.

————. 1918. *Acts and Resolutions of the General Assembly of the State of Georgia.* Atlanta: Byrd Printers.

Georgia Writers' Project (WPA). 1940. *Drums and Shadows: Survival Studies among the Georgia Coastal Negroes.* Athens: Univ. of Georgia Press.

Giddens, Anthony. 1984. *The Constitution of Society.* Berkeley: Univ. of California Press.

Giddings, Paula. 1984. *When and Where I Enter: The Impact of Black Women on Race and Sex in America.* New York: William Morrow and Co.

Gillard, Father John Thomas. 1929. *The Catholic Church and the American Negro.* Baltimore: St. Joseph's Society Press.

Ginzburg, Carlo. 1980. *The Cheese and the Worms.* Baltimore: Johns Hopkins Univ. Press.

————. 1983. *The Night Battles: Witchcraft and Agrarian Cults in the Sixteenth and Seventeenth Century.* Baltimore: Johns Hopkins Univ. Press.

Gleason, Philip, ed. 1970. *Catholicism in the United States.* New York: Harper & Row.

Goodwin, Joseph P. 1989. *More Man than You'll Ever Be: Gay Folklore and Acculturation in Middle America.* Bloomington: Indiana Univ. Press.

Gramsci, Antonio. 1971. *Selections from the Prison Notebooks.* New York: International Publishers.

Greeley, Father Andrew. 1967. *The Catholic Experience.* Garden City, N.Y.: Doubleday.

————. 1977. *The American Catholic: A Sociological Portrait* New York: Basic Books.

Green, Nathaniel E. 1972 *The Silent Believers.* Louisville, Ky.: West End Catholic Council.

Gregory, William D. 1988. "Black Catholic Liturgy: What Do You Say It Is?" *U.S. Catholic Historian* 7, no. 2 and 3 (Spring/Summer 1988): 316-21.

Gresham, Jewell Handy. 1989. "The Politics of Family in America." *The Nation* 249, no. 4 (July 24-3l, 1989): ll6-21.

Gresham, Jewell Handy, and Margaret B. Wilkerson. 1989. "The Burden of History." *The Nation* 249, no. 4 (July 24-3l, 1989):115-16.

Griffin, Sister M. Julian. 1983. "The Black Woman as Leader." *Maryknoll* 77, no. 11 (Nov. 1983): 47-49.

Griffin, Sister M. Julian, and Mrs. Gillian Brown. 1979. *Tomorrow Comes the Song: The Story of Catholicism among the Black population of South Georgia, 1850-1978.* Savannah: Diocese of Savannah.

Gudeman, Stephen. 1971. "The Compadrazgo as a Reflection of the Spiritual and Natural Person." *Proceedings of the Royal Anthropological Institute.* 45-71.

Gutman, Herbert. 1976. *The Black Family in Slavery and Freedom, 1750-1925.* New York: Random House.

Hall, Jacquelyn, James Leloudis, Robert Korstad, Mary Murphy, Lu Ann Jones, and Christopher B. Daly. 1987. *Like a Family: The Making of a Southern Cotton Mill World.* Chapel Hill: Univ. of North Carolina Press.

Hamburger, Robert. 1978. *A Stranger in the House.* New York: Macmillan.

Harden, William. 1908. *Recollections of a Long and Satisfactory Life.* Savannah: Georgia Review Publishing Co.

Harris, William H. 1982. *The Harder We Run: Black Workers since the Civil War.* New York: Oxford Univ. Press.

Hauke, Manfred. 1986. *Women in the Priesthood?* San Francisco: Ignatius Press.

Haunton, Richard. 1968. "Savannah in the 1850s." Ph.D. diss., Emory Univ., Atlanta.

Hawkes, Ellen. 1992. "The Anger Sustained Me." *Parade,* May 24, 1992. 12-14.

Height, Dorothy. 1989. "Self-Help—A Black Tradition." *The Nation* 249, no. 4 (July 24-31,): 136-38.

Hebdige, Dick. 1979. *Subculture: The Nature of Style.* London: Methuen.

Hellwig, Monika. 1981. *Understanding Catholicism.* New York: Paulist Press.

Hemenway, Robert E. 1977. *Zora Neale Hurston: A Literary Biography.* Urbana: Univ. of Illinois Press.

Hemesath, Caroline. 1973. *From Slave to Priest: Biography of Rev. Augustine Tolton, First Afro-American Priest in the United States.* Chicago: Franciscan Herald.

———. 1987. *Our Black Shepherds.* Washington, D.C.: Josephite Pastoral Center.

Henri, Florette. 1975. *Black Migration: Movement North 1900-1920.* Garden City, N.Y.: Doubleday.

Hepburn, Lawrence R. 1987. *Contemporary Georgia.* Athens: Carl Vinson Institute of Government, Univ. of Georgia.

Herskovits, Melville. 1958. *The Myth of the Negro Past.* Boston: Beacon.

Hervey, Harry. 1939. *The Damned Don't Cry.* New York: Greystone.

Holt, Grace Sims. 1972. "'Inversion in Black Communication." In *Rappin' and Stylin' Out: Communication in Urban Black America,* ed. T. Kochman. Urbana: Univ. of Illinois Press, 152-59.

hooks, bell. 1990. *Yearning: Race, Gender and Cultural Politics.* Boston: South End Press.

Hoskins, Charles L. 1980. *Black Episcopalians in Georgia.* Savannah: pub. by author.

———. 1983. *Black Episcopalians in Savannah.* Savannah; Saint Matthew's Episcopal Church.

Howze, Bishop Joseph, et al. 1984. *What We Have Seen and Heard: A Pastoral Letter on Evangelization from the Black Bishops of the United States.* Cincinnati: St. Anthony's Messenger.

Hull, Gloria T., Patricia Bell Scott, and Barbara Smith. 1982. *But Some of Us Are Brave.* New York: Feminist Press.

Hunt, Larry L., and Janet G. Hunt. 1975. "A Religious Factor in Secular Achievement among Urban Blacks: The Case of Catholicism." *Social Forces* 55 (June): 595-606.

———. 1976. "Black Catholicism and the Spirit of Weber." *Sociological Quarterly* 17 (Summer): 369-77.

———. 1977. "Religious Affiliation and Militancy among Urban Blacks: Some Catholic/Protestant Comparisons." *Social Science Quarterly* 57 (Mar. 1977): 821-32.

Huntington, Richard, and Peter Metcalf. 1979. *Celebrations of Death: The Anthropology of Mortuary Rituals.* New York: Cambridge Univ. Press.

Hurston, Zora Neale. [1935] 1963. *Mules and Men.* Bloomington: Indiana Univ. Press.

Isasi-Diaz, Ada María, and Yolanda Tarango. 1988. *Hispanic Women: Prophetic Voice in the Church.* San Francisco: Harper & Row.

James, C. L. R. 1963. *The Black Jacobins.* New York: Random House.

Johnson, Daniel M., and Rex R. Campbell. 1981. *Black Migration in America.* Durham: Duke Univ. Press.

Johnson, James W. [1927] 1965. *Autobiography of an Ex-Colored Man.* New York: Hearst Corp.

Johnson, James W., and J. Rosamund Johnson. [1923-24] 1953-54. *The Book of American Negro Spirituals.* New York: Da Capo.

Johnson, Michael P., and James L. Roark. 1984a. *Black Masters: A Free Family of Color in the Old South.* New York: W. W. Norton.

———. 1984b. *No Chariot Let Down: Charleston's Free People of Color on the Eve of the Civil War.* Chapel Hill: Univ. of North Carolina Press.

Johnson, Nessa Theresa Baskerville. 1978. *A Special Pilgrimage: A History of Black Catholics in Richmond.* Richmond, Va.: Diocese of Richmond.

Johnson, Richard. 1987 "What is Cultural Studies, Anyway?" *Social Text* 17 (Fall 1987): 38-80.

Jones, Bessie. 1983. *For the Ancestors: Autobiographical Memories.* Ed. John Stuart. Urbana: Univ. of Illinois Press.

Jones-Jackson, Patricia. 1987. *When Roots Die: Endangered Traditions on the Sea Islands.* Athens: Univ. of Georgia Press.

Joyner, Charles. 1984. *Down by the Riverside: A South Carolina Slave Community.* Urbana: Univ. of Illinois Press.

Jungmann, Josef A. 1959. *The Early Liturgy to the Time of Gregory the Great.* Notre Dame, Ind.: Univ. of Notre Dame Press.

Kauffman, Christopher. 1982. *Faith and Fraternalism: The History of the Knights of Columbus, 1882-1982.* New York: Harper & Row.

Kebede, Asherafi. 1982. R*oots of Black Music.* Englewood Cliffs, N.J.: Prentice-Hall.

Keightley, Georgia Masters. 1988. "Women's Issues Are Laity Issues." *America* 159, no. 4 (Aug. 6-13): 77-83.

Kennedy, Eugene. 1988. *Tomorrow's Catholics, Yesterday's Church.* San Francisco: Harper & Row.

King, Barbara. 1990. "New School to be Established in Savannah." *Southern Cross* Mar. 29, 1-2.

King, Florence. 1975. *Southern Ladies and Gentlemen.* New York: Stein and Day.

———. 1977. *Wasp, Where Is Thy Sting?* New York: Stein and Day.

Kirby, Jack Temple. 1978. *Media-Made Dixie: The South in the American Imagination.* Baton Rouge: Louisiana State Univ Press.

Küng, Hans. 1972. *Why Priests: A Proposal for a New Church Ministry.* Garden City, N.Y.: Doubleday.

———. 1988. *Theology for a Third Millennium.* New York: Doubleday.

Kwatera, Michael. 1982. *The Ministry of Servers.* Collegeville, Minn.: Liturgical Press.

———. 1985. *The Liturgical Ministry of Deacons.* Collegeville, Minn.: Liturgical Press.

Lamanna, Richard A., and Jay. J. Coakley. 1969. "The Catholic Church and the Negro." In *Contemporary Catholicism in the United States,* ed. P. Gleason. Notre Dame, Ind.: Notre Dame Univ. Press, 147-93.

Lancaster, John, and Sharon LaFraniere. 1991. "The Long Climb of Clarence Thomas." *Washington Post National Magazine Weekly,* Sept. 16-22: 6-9.

Lawrence, Alexander A. 1961. *A Present for Mr. Lincoln: The Story of Savannah from Secession to Sherman.* Macon, Ga.: Ardivan Press.

Lead Me, Guide Me: The African American Catholic Hymnal. 1987. Chicago: GIA Publications.

Lebow, Richard. 1976. *White Britain and Black Ireland: The Influence of Stereotypes on Colonial Policy.* Philadelphia: ISHI.

Lester, James A. 1972. *A History of the Georgia Baptist Convention, 1822-1972.* Nashville, Tenn.: Curley.

Levine, Lawrence. 1977. *Black Culture and Black Consciousness: Afro-American Folk Thought from Slavery to Freedom.* New York: Oxford Univ. Press.

Levy, B. J. 1983. *Savannah's Old Jewish Community Cemeteries.* Macon, Ga.: Mercer Univ. Press.

Lincoln, C. Eric, and Lawrence H. Mamiya. 1990. *The Black Church in the African American Experience.* Durham, N.C.: Duke Univ. Press,

Lines, Stiles B. 1960. "Slaves and Churchmen: The Work of the Episcopal Church among Southern Negroes, 1830-1860." Ph.D. diss.

Lissner, Ignatius. N.d. "The Handmaids of the Most Pure Heart of Mary." SMA Archives/Savannah Diocesan Archives. Typescript.

Liu, William T., and Nathaniel Pallone. 1970. *Catholics USA: Perspectives on Social Change.* New York: John Wiley & Sons.

Love, E. K. 1888. *History of the First African Baptist Church from Its Organization January 20 1788 to July 1 1888 Including the Centennial Celebration, Addresses, Sermons, etc.* Savannah: Morning Newsprint.

Lovell, John. 1972. *Black Song: The Forge and the Flame.* New York: Paragon House.

Lucas, Lawrence. [1970] 1989. *Black Priest, White Church: Catholics and Racism.* Trenton, N.J.: Africa World Press.

Luster, Debby. 1974. "Tradition." *Savannah Morning News.* Jan. 14.

————. 1975. "AME Zion Church Stalled by Zoning Board Appeal." *Savannah Evening Press.* Aug. 30.

————. 1976a "Which Church Is Oldest? 'It's a Touchy Little Thing.'" *Savannah Morning News.* Jan. 17.

————. 1976b "Law Tells Church History." *Savannah Morning News.* Feb. 14.

Marks, Carole. 1989. *Farewell—We're Good and Gone: The Great Black Migration.* Bloomington: Indiana Univ. Press.

Martin, Emily. 1986. *The Woman in the Body.* Boston: Beacon.

Martínez-Alier, Verena. 1974. *Marriage, Class and Colour in Nineteenth-Century Cuba: A Study of Racial Attitudes and Sexual Values in a Slave Society.* London: Cambridge Univ. Press.

Marx, Gary. 1967. "Religion: Opiate or Inspiration of Civil Rights Militancy among Negroes?" *American Sociological Review* 32 (Feb.): 64-72.

Mayfield, Chris, ed. 1976-81. *Growing Up Southern.* New York: Random House.

McBrien, Richard. 1980 *Catholicism.* Minneapolis: Winston.

McClaren, Peter. 1986. *Schooling as Ritual Performance: Towards a Political Economy of Education Symbols and Gestures.* London: Routledge and Kegan Paul.

McDonogh, Gary W. 1984. "Past and Present." *Southern Exposure* 12, no. 6 (Nov.-Dec.): 95-96.

————. 1986. *Good Families of Barcelona: A Social History of Power in the Industrial Era.* Princeton, N.J.: Princeton Univ. Press.

————. 1987. "The Geography of Evil: Barcelona's Barrio Chino" *Anthropological Quarterly.* 60, no. 4 (Oct. 1987): 174-84

————. 1988a "Ethnicity, Urbanization and Consciousness in Savannah." In *Shades of the Sunbelt.,* ed. G. Pozzetta and R. Miller. New York: Greenwood Press, 53-73.

————. 1988b. "Black and Catholic in Savannah." In *Land and Sea,* ed. J. Peacock and J. Sabella. Athens: Univ. of Georgia Press, 56-75.

————. 1991. "Structures of Catholic Narrative: An Anthropological Dialogue." Report, Bible Belt Catholics Project, Catholic Univ. of America.

————. 1992. "Catholic Aesthetics in the South: An Anthropological Approximation." Final Research Report, Bible Belt Catholics Project, Catholic Univ.

McDonogh, Gary W, and Gaspar Maza. In press. "Hijo del Barrio, Chaval de la Ciudad." *Revista de Ciencias Sociales.* Barcelona.

McDonogh, Gary W, and Cindy Hing-Yuk Wong. In press. "Religion and Representation in the Filmic South." In *Images of the South,* ed. K. Heider. Athens: Univ. of Georgia Press.

McKenna, Edward. 1983. *The Ministry of Musicians.* Collegeville, Minn.: Liturgical Press.

McLaurin, Melton A. 1987. *Separate Pasts: Growing Up White in the Segregated South.* Athens: Univ. of Georgia Press.

McMillen, Neil R. 1989. *Dark Journey: Black Mississippians in the Age of Jim Crow.* Urbana: Univ. of Illinois Press.

McNally, Michael. 1984. *Catholicism in South Florida, 1868-1968.* Gainesville: Univ. Presses of Florida..

————. 1987. "A Peculiar Institution: A History of the Catholic Parish in the Southeast (1850-1980)." In *The American Catholic Parish,* ed. Dolan, vol. 1: 117-234.

McRobbie, Angela, ed. 1988. *Zoot Suits and Second-Hand Dresses.* London: Unwin Hyman.

Means, Howard. 1986. "God Is Back." *The Washingtonian.* Dec.: 150-69.

Meara, Mary J. F. C., Jeffrey A. J. Stone, Maureen A. T. Kelly, and Richard G. Davis. 1984. *Growing Up Catholic.* Garden City, N.Y.: Doubleday.

Meeks, Wayne. 1983. *The First Urban Christians: The Social World of the Apostle Paul.* New Haven: Yale Univ. Press.

Meier, August, and Elliott Rudwick. 1986. *Black History and the Historical Profession, 1915-1980.* Urbana: Univ. of Illinois Press.

Merkel, R. 1982. "Americans Win City Again." *Savannah Morning News.* July 12.

Miller, Christopher. 1985. *Blank Darkness: Africanist Discourse in French.* Chicago: Univ. of Chicago Press.

Miller, Randall M. 1983a. "A Church in Cultural Captivity: Some Speculations on Catholic Identity in the Old South." In *Catholics in the Old South,* ed. R. Miller and J. Wakelyn. Macon, Ga.: Mercer Univ. Press, 11-52.

———. 1983b. "The Failed Mission: The Catholic Church and Black Catholics in the Old South." In *Catholics in the Old South,* ed. R. Miller and J. Wakelyn. Macon, Ga.: Mercer Univ. Press, 149-70.

Miller, Randall, and Jon L. Wakelyn, eds., 1983. *Catholics in the Old South: Essays on Church and Culture.* Macon, Ga.: Mercer Univ. Press.

Mills, Gary. 1983. "Piety and Prejudice: A Colored Catholic Community in the Old South." In *Catholics in the Old South,* ed. R. Miller and J. Wakelyn. Macon, Ga.: Mercer Univ. Press, 171-94.

Mintz, Sidney, and Richard Price. 1976. *An Anthropological Approach to the Afro-American Past: A Caribbean Perspective.* Philadelphia: ISHI.

Mintz, Sidney, and Eric Wolf. 1950 "An Analysis of Ritual Cogodparenthood (Compadrazgo)." *Southwestern Journal of Anthropology* 6:341-68.

Mitchell, Henry H. 1979. *Black Preaching.* San Francisco: Harper & Row.

Mitchell, J. D. 1920-22. Historical Sketches of the Parish of Saint John the Baptist of Savannah. Various dates, *Bulletin of the Catholic Laymen's Association of Georgia.*

Mitchell, Margaret. 1936. *Gone With the Wind.* New York: Macmillan.

Mohlman, Geoffrey. 1991. "Lincolnville: An Anthropological History of Black St. Augustine." Senior thesis, New College.

Moloney, Francis J. 1990. *A Body Broken for a Broken People.* Melbourne, Australia: Collins Dove.

Moore, Donald S. 1985. "Experience, Dialogue and Process: A Phenomenological Perspective on Subject-Object Interaction in Ethnography." Senior thesis, New College.

Morris, Calvin 1990. *Reverdy Ransom: Black Advocate of the Social Gospel.* Langham, Md.: Univ. Press of America.

Morrison, Toni. 1987. *Beloved.* New York: Alfred A. Knopf.

———. 1992. *Playing in the Dark: Whiteness and the Literary Imagination.* Cambridge: Harvard Univ. Press.

Moses, Wilson J. 1978. *The Golden Age of Black Nationalism, 1850-1925.* Hamden, Conn.: Shoe String Press. Rpt. New York: Oxford Univ. Press, 1988.

Most Pure Heart of Mary Roman Catholic Church. 1978. *Rededication Celebration.* N.p.

Mouffe, Chantal. 1979. "Hegemony and Ideology in Gramsci." In *Gramsci and Marxist Thought,* ed. C. Mouffe. London: Routledge and Kegan Paul, 168-204.

————. 1988. "Hegemony and New Political Subjects: Towards a New Concept of Democracy." In *Marxism and the Interpretation of Culture,* ed. C. Nelson and L. Grossberg. Urbana: Univ. of Illinois Press, 89-102.

Murphy, Robert. 1987. *The Body Silent.* New York: Henry Holt and Co.

Murray, J. Glenn. 1987. "The Liturgy of the Roman Rite and African American Worship." In *Lead Me, Guide Me.*

Myers, Lewis. 1833. "Origins and Progress of Methodism in Savannah." *Methodist Magazine and Quarterly Review* 15: 246-56.

Myrdal, Gunnar. 1944. *An American Dilemma: The Negro Problem and Modern Democracy.* New York: Harper & Row.

Naipaul, V. S. 1989. *A Turn in the South.* New York: Alfred A. Knopf.

Naylor, Gloria. 1988. *Mama Day.* New York: Ticknor and Fields.

Nelson, Dale. 1987. "The Society that Cares: An Anthropological Approach to Organized Ethnicity." Senior thesis, New College.

Neville, Gwen Kennedy. 1992. "Body of Christ/People of God: Metaphors of Church and Community in Central Texas Gatherings." Final Research Report, Bible Belt Catholics Project, Catholic Univ.

New Catechism. 1972. New York: Herder and Herder.

O'Brien, John A. 1939. *The Faith of Millions: The Credentials of the Catholic Religion.* Huntington, Ind.: Our Sunday Visitor.

O'Connell, Jeremiah J. 1879. *Catholicity in the Carolinas and Georgia, 1820-1878.* New York: J. and D. Sadlier.

O'Connor, Flannery. 1979. *The Habit of Being.* Ed. S. Fitzgerald. New York: Farrar, Strauss, Giroux.

O'Hara, Arthur. 1912. *Hibernian Society, Savannah Ga., 1812-1912: The Story of a Century.* Savannah: n.p.

Ochs, Stephen. 1990. *Desegregating the Altar.* Baton Rouge: Louisiana State Univ. Press.

Oetgen, Jerome. 1969. "The Origins of the Benedictine Order in Georgia." *Georgia Historical Quarterly* 53, no. 2 (June): 165-83.

————. 1976a. "Oswald Moosmuller: Monk and Missionary." *American Benedictine Review* 27, no. 1 (Mar.): 1-35.

————. 1976b. *An American Abbot: Boniface Wimmer, O.S.B., 1809-1887.* Latrobe, Pa.: Archabey Press.

Okihiro, Gary Y., ed. 1986. *In Resistance.* Amherst: Univ. of Massachusetts Press.

Osborne, William A. 1967. *The Segregated Covenant: Race Relations and American Catholics.* New York: Herder and Herder.

Our Heritage, Our Future. N.d. The Cathedral of Saint John the Baptist. N.p.

Painter, Nell Irvin. 1984. "Who Speaks for the South?." *Southern Exposure* 12, no. 6 (Nov.-Dec.): 92-93.

——. 1988. "'Social Equality,' Miscegenation, Labor and Power." In *The Evolution of Southern Culture*, ed. N. Bartley. Athens: Univ. of Georgia Press, 47-67.

——. 1991. "A Special Alien Group." In E. Bates, "Of Different Minds." *Southern Exposure* 19 (Spring): 49-50.

Peacock, James, and Ruel Tyson. 1989. *Pilgrims of Paradox: Calvinism and Experience among the Primitive Baptists of the Blue Ridge*. Washington: Smithsonian Institution Press.

Pelikan, Jaroslav. 1959. *The Riddle of Roman Catholicism*. New York: Abingdon Press.

Perdue, Robert. 1973. *The Negro in Savannah, 1865-1900*. New York: Exposition Press.

Peterman, Thomas J. 1982. *The Cutting Edge: The Life of Thomas A. Becker, First Catholic Bishop of Wilmington and Sixth Bishop of Savannah (1831-1899)*. Devon, Pa.: William T. Cooke.

Powdermaker, Hortense. 1939. *After Freedom: A Cultural Study of the Deep South*. New York: Viking.

Powers, Sister Mary Felicitas. 1956. "A History of Catholic Education in Georgia, 1845-1952." M.A. thesis, Catholic Univ.

Powers, Polly. 1982. "80 Years Later, First Black Nun in State Honored." *Savannah News Press*. Nov. 4.

Pozzetta, George, and Randall Miller, eds. 1988. *Shades of the Sunbelt: Essays on Ethnicity, Race, and the Urban South*. New York: Greenwood Press.

Pozzetta, George, and Gary Mormino. 1987. *The Immigrant World of Ybor City*. Urbana: Univ. of Illinois Press.

Price, Richard. 1984. *First-Time: The Historical Vision of an Afro-American People*. Baltimore: Johns Hopkins Univ. Press.

Proctor, H. H., and M. N. Work. 1904. "Atlanta and Savannah" In *Some Notes on Negro Crime*, ed. W. E. B. Du Bois. Atlanta: Atlanta Univ. Press, 49-52.

Quinn, Jane. 1978. *The Story of a Nun: Jeanie Gordon Brown*. St. Augustine, Fla.: Villa Flora.

Raboteau, Albert. 1978. *Slave Religion: The Invisible Institution in the Antebellum South*. London: Oxford Univ. Press.

——. 1988. "Introductory Reflections." *U.S. Catholic Historian* 7, no. 2 and 3 (Spring/Summer 1988): 299-300.

Raines, Howell. 1977. *My Soul Is Rested: Movement Days in the Deep South Remembered*. New York: Putnam Books.

Reed, John S. 1981. "The Same Old Stand?" In *Why the South Will Survive*, by Fifteen Southerners. Athens: Univ. of Georgia Press, 13-34.

Reeves, Frank. 1983. *British Racial Discourse: A Study of British Political Discourse about Race and Race-Related Matters*. Cambridge: Cambridge Univ. Press.

Reid, Richard. 1921-26. *Catholicism in South Georgia.* Articles appearing in the *Bulletin of the Catholic Laymen's Association of Georgia.*

Roggow, Lisa. 1988. "Conjuring Womanhood: Black Woman's Narrative Expression of Self and Community." Senior thesis, New College.

Rosaldo, Renato. 1980. *Ilongot Headhunting, 1883-1974: A Study in Society and History.* Stanford, Calif.: Stanford Univ. Press.

Ruskowski, Leo F. 1940. "French Emigré Priests in the United States." Ph.D. diss., Catholic Univ.

Russell, H. 1981. *Africa's Twelve Apostles.* Boston: Daughters of St. Paul.

Sahlins, Marshall. 1981. *Historical Metaphors and Mythical Realities: Structure in the Early History of the Sandwich Islands.* Ann Arbor: Univ. of Michigan Press.

————. 1985 *Islands of History.* Chicago: Univ. of Chicago Press

Said, Edward. 1978. *Orientalism.* New York: Pantheon.

Saint Anthony's Parish. 1990. *80th Anniversary.* Savannah.

Salley, Columbus, and Ronal Behm. 1988. *What Color Is Your God? Black Consciousness and Christian Faith.* Secaucus, N.J.: Citadel Press.

Scott, Anne Firor. 1970. *The Southern Lady: From Pedestal to Politics, 1830-1930.* Chicago: Univ. of Chicago Press.

Scott, Katherine K. 1976. *The Land of Loving Children: Memories of Four Year's Teaching at Pape School for Girls in Savannah 1916-1918 and 1921-22.* Savannah: n.p.

Scott, Patricia Bell. 1982. "Debunking Sapphire: Toward a Non-Racist and Non-Sexist Social Science." In *But Some of Us Are Brave,* ed. G. Hull, P. Scott, and B. Smith. New York: Feminist Press, 85-92.

Sholes, K. 1900. *An Historical Outline of Savannah.* Savannah: n.p.

Sieg, Chan. 1985. *Eden on the Marsh: An Illustrated History of Savannah.* Northridge, Calif.: Windsor Publications.

Silverstein, Michael. 1985. "Language and the Culture of Gender: At the Intersection of Structure, Usage and Ideology." In *Semiotic Mediation,* ed. E. Mertz and R. Parmentier. New York: Academic Press, 219-59.

Simms, James M. 1888. *The First Baptist Church in North America. Constituted at Savannah, Ga. January 20, A.D. 1788: With Biographical Sketches of the Pastors.* Philadelphia: J. Lippincott Co.

Smalls, K. [1933-34?] *Yearbook of Colored Savannah.* Savannah: Students of the Georgia Industrial College.

Smith, Gregory. 1980. *The Ministry of Ushers.* Collegeville, Minn.: Liturgical Press.

Smith, Lillian. [1949] 1961. *Killers of the Dream.* Expanded ed. W. W. Norton.

Smitherman, Geneva. 1977. *Talkin' and Testifyin': The Language of Black America.* Boston: Houghton-Mifflin Co.

Smithson, Sandra. 1984. *To Be a Bridge: A Commentary on Black/White Catholicism in America.* Nashville, Tenn.: Winston-Derek.

Sobel, Michael. 1979. *Trabellin' On: The Slave Journey to an Afro-Baptist Faith.* Westport, Conn.: Greenwood Press.

Southern, Eileen. 1971. *The Music of Black Americans.* New York: W. W. Norton.

Stack, Carol. 1974. *All Our Kin: Strategies for Survival in a Black Community.* New York: Harper & Row.

Stark, Mary Alberta. 1940. "A Study of Schools Conducted by the Sisters of St. Joseph of the Diocese of St. Augustine, 1866-1940." M.A. thesis, Univ. of Florida.

Steinfels, Peter. 1989. "Bishops Endorse Rite for Parishes without Priests." *New York Times,* Nov. 12.

Stuckey, Sterling. 1987. *Slave Culture: Nationalist Theory and the Foundation of Black America.* New York: Oxford Univ. Press.

Swartz, Sally. 1977. "First African Opens 187 Years of History." *Savannah Morning News.* Apr. 9.

Synan, Vinson. 1971. *The Holiness Pentecostal Movement in the U.S.* Grand Rapids, Mich.: Wm. B. Eerdmans.

Taylor, Julie. 1979. *Eva Perón: The Myths of a Woman.* Chicago: Univ. of Chicago Press.

Taylor, Susie King. 1902. *Reminiscences of My Life in Camp with the 33rd United States Colored Troops, Late 1st South Carolina Volunteers.* Boston: pub. by author.

Teller, W., ed. 1973. "Happiness and Hard Times: Oral Reminiscences of Savannah." Mimeo. Savannah: Armstrong College.

Thomas, Edgar G. 1925. *The First African Baptist Church of North America.* Savannah: pub. by author.

Thompson, E. P. 1963. *The Making of the English Working Class.* New York: Random House.

Trotter, Joe William, ed. 1991. *The Great Migration in Historical Perspective.* Bloomington: Indiana Univ. Press.

Tucker, Susan. 1988. *Telling Memories among Southern Women.* New York: Schocken.

Turner, Henry McNeal. 1971. *Respect Black: The Writings and Speeches of Henry McNeal Turner.* Comp. and ed. E. S. Redkey. New York: Arno Press.

Turner, Victor. 1967. *The Forest of Symbols.* Ithaca, N.Y.: Cornell Univ Press.

United States Catholic Conference. Commission on Marriage and Family Life. 1985. *Families: Black and Catholic, Catholic and Black.* Washington: Author.

Valle, Lincoln. 1924. "The Catholic Church and the Negro." *America:* Jan. 19, 1924.

Vogel, Joseph L. N.d. (a). *Red and White Roses in Black Soil: The African Missions Society in Africa and the U.S. from 1836 to 1940.* n.p.: Printed as manuscript by the SMA fathers.

————. N.d. (b). *Father Ignatius Lissner, SMA (1867-1948): A Biographical Essay.* Printed privately.

Waldron, George. N.d. *The Sad Story of Mary Lilly.* Milan, Ill.: Rail-Splitter Press.

Walkes, Joseph A. 1979. *Black Square and Compass: 200 Years of Prince Hall Freemasonry.* Richmond, Va.: Macoy Publishing and Masonic Supply Co.

Walker, Wyatt Tee. 1979. *"Somebody Calling My Name": Black Sacred Music and Social Change.* Valley Forge, Pa.: Judson Press.

Wallace, James A. 1981. *The Ministry of Lectors.* Collegeville, Minn.: Liturgical Press.

Walton, Anthony. 1989. "Willie Horton and Me." *New York Times Magazine,* Aug. 20, 52, 77.

Waring, C. 1969. "History of the First Congregational Church." Mimeo. Georgia Historical Society.

Washington, Booker T. [1895] 1965. *Up From Slavery.* New York: Avon.

Waters, Ethel. 1951. *His Eye Is on the Sparrow.* Garden City, N.Y.: Doubleday.

————. 1972. To Me It's Wonderful. New York: Harper & Row.

Waters, Maxine. 1989. "Drugs, Democrats and Priorities." *The Nation* 249, no. 4 (July 24-31,1989): 141-44.

Watson, Thomas J. 1917. *Roman Catholics in America Falsifying History and Poisoning the Minds of Schoolchildren.* Thompson, Ga.: Jeffersonian Publishing Co.

Wattleton, Faye. 1989. "The Case for National Action." *The Nation* 249, no. 4 (July 24-3l, 1989): 138-41.

Weaver, Herbert. 1953. "Foreigners in Antebellum Savannah." *Georgia Historical Quarterly* 37, no. 1:1-17.

Wedge, Florence. 1957. *My Brother Benedict: Life of St. Benedict the Moor.* Pulaski, Wis.: Franciscan Publishers.

Weisbrot, Robert. 1983. *Father Divine and the Struggle for Racial Equality.* Urbana: Univ. of Illinois Press.

Wellmeier, Herbert. 1974. *Catholics in Savannah.* Savannah: Diocese of Savannah.

West, Cornel. 1982. *Prophesy Deliverance.* Philadelphia: Westminster.

————. 1988. *Prophetic Fragments.* Grand Rapids, Mich.: Wm. B. Eerdmans

White, Deborah. 1985. *Ain't I a Woman: Female Slaves in the Plantation South.* New York: W. W. Norton.

White, Walter. 1948. *A Man Called White.* New York: Viking Press.

Wilkerson, Margaret B., and Jewell Handy Gresham. 1989. "The Racialization of Poverty." *The Nation* 249, no. 4 (July 24-3l,1989): 126-32.

Williams, Dorothy, and Clarence Williams. 1977. *A History of the First Presbyterian Church of Savannah, Georgia.* Savannah: First Presbyterian Church of Savannah, Georgia.

Williams, Raymond. 1958. *Culture and Society, 1780-1950.* New York: Doubleday.

————. 1973. *The Country and the City.* New York: Oxford Univ. Press.

————. 1983. *Keywords: A Vocabulary of Culture and Society.* New York: Oxford Univ. Press.

Williamson, Joel. 1980. *New People: Black/White Relations in the American South since Emancipation.* New York: Oxford Univ. Press.

———— 1984. *The Crucible of Race: Miscegenation and Mulattoes in the United States.* New York: Free Press.

————. 1986. *A Rage for Order: Black/White Relations in the American South since Emancipation.* New York: Oxford Univ. Press.

————. 1988. "How Black Was Rhett Butler?" In *The Evolution of Southern Culture,* ed. N. Bartley. Athens: Univ. of Georgia Press, 87-107.

Willis, Paul. 1977. *Learning to Labor: How Working Class Kids Get Working Class Jobs.* New York: Columbia Univ. Press.

Wilmore, Gayraud S. 1983. *Black Religion and Black Radicalism.* Maryknoll, N.Y.: Orbis Books.

————, ed. 1989. *African American Religious Studies.* Durham, N.C.: Duke Univ. Press.

Wilson, C. R., and W. Ferris, eds. 1990. *Encyclopedia of Southern Culture.* Chapel Hill: Univ. of North Carolina Press.

Woods, Sister Frances Jerome. 1972. *Marginality and Identity: A Colored Creole Family through Ten Generations.* Baton Rouge: Louisiana State Univ. Press.

Woodson, Carter. 1945. *History of the Black Church.* Washington: Associated.

Woodward, C. Vann. 1960. *The Burden of Southern History.* Baton Rouge: Louisiana State Univ. Press.

————. [1938] 1973. *Tom Watson: Agrarian Rebel.* Savannah: Beehive Press.

————. 1989. "The Narcissistic South" (Review of Wilson and Ferris, eds. *Encyclopedia of Southern Culture*). *New York Times Book Review,* Oct. 26, 13-17.

Work, M. N. 1904. "Crime in Cities." In *Some Notes on Negro Crime,* ed. W. E. B. Du Bois. Atlanta: Atlanta Univ. Press, 18-31

Wright, E. O. 1978. *Class, Crisis and the State.* London: New Left.

Wright, George C. 1985. *Life behind a Veil: Blacks in Louisville, Kentucky, 1865-1930.* Baton Rouge: Louisiana State Univ. Press.

Index

367